POWER AND PLACE

POWER AND PLACE

Canadian Urban Development in the North American Context

edited by
Gilbert A. Stelter
and
Alan F. J. Artibise

University of British Columbia Press
Vancouver
1986

Power and Place: Canadian Urban Development in the North American Context

This book has been published with the help of a grant from the Social Science Federation of Canada, using funds provided by the Social Sciences and Humanities Research Council of Canada.

Canadian Cataloguing in Publication Data

Main entry under title:
Power and place

Based on papers originally presented at the Canadian-American Urban Development Conference held at the University of Guelph in August 1982.
Bibliography: p.
ISBN 0-7748-0236-7

1. Cities and towns – Canada – History – Addresses, essays, lectures. 2. Community power – Canada – History – Addresses, essays, lectures. 3. City planning – Canada – History – Addresses, essays, lectures. 4. Municipal government – Canada – History – Addresses, essays, lectures. I. Stelter, Gilbert A., 1933– II. Artibise, Alan F. J., 1946– III. Canadian-American Urban Development Conference (1982 : University of Guelph)
HT127.P69 1986 307.7'6'0971 C85-091509-0

ISBN 0-7748-0236-7

Printed in Canada

Contents

Preface

The purpose of this collection of essays is to explore the relatively neglected question of power in urban development. Who has it? On whose behalf is it used? To what extent is the nature and shape of an urban place a reflection of the power structure of the larger society? Often these questions are studied in the context of one nation's urban history, but we believe there is a particular value in looking at Canadian development from a larger perspective: in this case, the North American context. Thus, the question: does the border make a difference? Some of the essays in this volume are comparative, others deal primarily with Canada, but in these cases the authors are conscious of the relevant American experience.

The essays have been organized into five sections in order to emphasize different aspects of the relationship of power to place. Section I is an overview which indicates how some of the recent trends in urban history provide a useful set of tools for the study of power and place. Section II concentrates on three levels of the political economy: the national system of cities; the impact of different levels of government on individual city growth; and the local initiatives for growth generated from within communities. Section III examines the forces at work in shaping the physical environment, with essays on planning, land development, the building industry, and internal transportation companies. Section IV examines three aspects of local government: the declining autonomy of municipal government; the move to larger units with metropolitan forms; and the impact of suburbanization on the effectiveness of local government. Section V represents a concluding overview of how the value systems of Canada and the United States affect the character of each country's urban development.

These essays had their origin in the Canadian-American Urban Development Conference held at the University of Guelph in August 1982. We wish to thank the officials at the University of Guelph for their support and also wish to recognize the financial assistance of the Social Sciences and Humanities Research Council of Canada and the Canada Mortgage and Housing Corporation. We are indebted to the members of the conference organizing committee who helped plan the comparative sessions: Blaine Brownell, Michael Conzen, John Ingham, James T. Lemon, Larry McCann, Michael McCarthy, and John Weaver. We also wish to record our sincere appreciation for constant encouragement and advice offered by Dr. Jane Fredeman, the Managing Editor of University of British Columbia Press, and for the fine copy editing work done by Laura Coles.

Gilbert A. Stelter, Guelph
Alan F. J. Artibise, Winnipeg

SECTION 1
GENERAL INTRODUCTION

1

Power and Place in Urban History

Gilbert A. Stelter

The relationship between the complex concept of power and the evolution of urban places was not a central concern of urban historians when urban history developed as a new discipline in the 1960's and early 1970's.[1] Urban history, however, is at a new threshold, with its practitioners often asking a new series of questions.[2] Who has the power? On whose behalf is it used? To what extent are the character and shape of cities a reflection of the power structure of the larger society? Many of those in the United States calling for a more serious analysis of power in urban society argue that Marxist theory represents "the looming frontier."[3] In Britain, much of the current discussion stems from the sociological tradition of Max Weber.[4] It should be possible, however, to explore the implications of power in its various manifestations in the urban context without a doctrinaire commitment to any particular interpretation.[5]

What urban historians will have to take more seriously in the future is the need to clarify the character of the *instruments* and *sources* of power. The theoretical literature usually outlines three *instruments* of power: coercion, whereby submission is won by threat or use of force; compensation, whereby agreement is purchased; and conditioning, which shapes beliefs through persuasion, education, or social commitment to what seems right. Closely related to these instruments of power are three *sources* of power: personality, property, and organization. Personality in the shape of a business or political leader usually depends on an ability to persuade through the instrument of conditioning. The power of property, on the other hand, usually depends on its compensatory, purchasing ability, although in the nineteenth century the prestige of wealth amounted to conditioned power, for it attracted the support of large sectors of society almost automatically. The most significant modern source of power is organization, operating mostly through the instrument of conditioning. If the organization is the state, it also has coercive power and the compensatory instrument because of its vast connection to property.[6]

No general conceptual framework has become widely acceptable in urban history, nor is there much evidence that this would be desirable. What has emerged in the past several years, however, is a series of concepts which are directly relevant to the issue of the relationship between power and place. These include the notion that urban places are subsystems of larger systems; that it is possible to distinguish between urban as product and urban as process; that distinct stages in the evolution of urban environments can be identified; and that what is universal can be isolated from what is uniquely local in urban development. Some of the implications of these current trends for an understanding of the connections between power and place are outlined below.

Urban places as subsystems of larger systems. One sense of how urban history ought to proceed involves a fairly significant redefinition of the urban place as an object of study. This approach suggests reuniting the town or city with its larger social environment. In the past, the study of particular urban places has usually been confined to processes and events within clearly defined political boundaries. Urban biographies, one genre of urban history, tend to divorce the place from its regional context. What is now developing is a stronger realization that the urban is only one dimension of a multi-dimensional society. In other words, towns and cities are subsystems within larger political, economic, and social systems and can only be fully understood from the perspective of those larger systems. A conceptual framework for city-region relationships would include three levels of analysis: at the lowest level, an urban place as a central node of surrounding smaller places and countryside; at a middle level, groups of urban places interacting with each other and with regions such as the American South, the Canadian West, or, as in Oiva Saarinen's chapter in this volume, in a resource-based region such as Northern Ontario; at the highest level are national systems such as the ones described by James Simmons for Canada and the United States.[7]

A positive consequence of a regional framework for urban history is that smaller places such as villages and towns can be seen as an integral part of the complex web of population concentrations within an area or a country. Another is that the elusive term ''urban'' can be more systematically analyzed within such a context. In terms of power relationships, the regional framework offers the possibility of a spatial perspective through the use of concepts such as metropolis-hinterland and core-periphery. Perhaps because the disparity implied by these concepts is more apparent in the Canadian than in the American context, Canadian scholars have made them a more central feature of their work than Americans have.[8]

Distinguishing between urban as product and urban as process. One of the central issues in urban studies concerns the question of just what the role of the urban place is within the larger society. Do towns and cities passively reflect the character of society, or are they creative agencies playing a positive role in economic and social change? The discussion usually focuses on the distinction between urban places as dependent variables—the products of larger social forces—and towns and cities as independent variables, as dynamic agencies which affect life within their boundaries and beyond. The active function of urban places will be designated here by the expression "urban as process."[9] Put most simply, it is necessary to distinguish between those outside factors which affect the nature of communities and those forces which emanate from within the community itself. Sorting out which is which may help the understanding of the complex dynamics between power, people, and place. Ideally, any study of an individual place should deal with both internal and external forces. The mix seems to be different for every place, defying attempts to formulate precise models of development.

Most of the essays in this volume reflect the most popular approach at the present time: that is "urban as product." This includes forces beyond the control of any local community, which affect the location, size, number, function, vitality, and shape of any particular place or group of places. At the level of a national political economy, James Simmons shows how governments can have a major impact on settlement patterns through everything from trade and transportation to immigration policies. As John Mercer and Michael Goldberg argue in the final essay in this volume, a society's political culture may determine the extent to which governments intervene in the economy and society; and this in turn affects the character of urban development. In terms of provincial/state government relationships with urban places, individual communities have become increasingly dependent on the higher levels of jurisdiction. P. J. Smith outlines this clearly in the area of urban planning legislation, as do John Taylor and Philip Wichern for the more general questions of local government. The economic dependency of urban places is argued by Simmons, who stresses urban reliance on the external demand for primary and industrial products as well as the close connection between urban and national or regional economies. Some kinds of communities obviously are dependent places by their very nature, such as the resource-based towns described by Oiva Saarinen, which are the creation of a particular company or outside agency.

To some scholars, urban as product represents the total picture. British sociologists such as R. E. Pahl regard urban places as merely the locus of certain interactions between the actors in the historical process, although "the city as a reflection of a given social and political order will always remain as an object of study."[10] In other words, "'whose city?' becomes the distinctive question."[11] The same conclusions have been reached by the school of "urban Marxists," followers of Henri Lefebre. David Harvey, for example, sees urbanism as "a vantage point from which to capture some salient features in the social processes operating in society as a whole—it becomes, as it were, a mirror in which the other aspects of society can be reflected."[12] It should be pointed out, however, that in the approaches of Pahl, Harvey and others, the concern is no longer basically with urban places in their own right but has shifted to other questions. The urban place has become merely a setting for other explanatory categories such as class and social mobility or capitalism and labour relations. H. J. Dyos's assessment of this approach bears repeating: "What distinguishes the urban historian from the innumerable scholars who may be said to be merely passing through the territory" is the degree to which they were "concerned directly and generically with cities themselves and not with the historical events and tendencies that have been purely incidental to them."[13]

Therefore, it is legitimate to ask if it is valid to treat urban growth and life only as a purely subordinate product of activity generated at regional, national, and international levels. While it is obvious that to some extent cities are made by outside forces, do they not also in some respects make themselves and influence life within and around them? The point to be made is that urban places can be seen in terms of both *product* and *process*. Urban as process can be used to describe local activity—the act of building—and also the way in which the particular character of that local environment affects the behavior and activity within the boundaries of the local container. Urban as process can also be used to understand the influence that an urban place has on the surrounding network of country and smaller places, or even the impact that a system of cities has on a society as a whole.

The connection between the large scale outside forces and prevailing trends, on the one hand, and local initiative, on the other, is neatly summarized in Gertler and Crowley's *Changing Canadian Cities*. In a chapter on "Growth Forces," they write:

> The forces described represent prevailing trends within which cities work out their destiny, but they are not ironclad. Growth is the result not only of these forces but also of the manifold actions of many people—migrant and stayer, entrepreneur and employee, elite and commonfolk. . . . All the ingredients for urban growth may be present but the skill and initiative of the entrepreneur is needed before development can take place.[14]

What this amounts to in terms of urban growth is individuals or groups effectively responding, or failing to respond, to the possibilities emerging from external factors. In this volume, Elizabeth Bloomfield's study of Kitchener-Waterloo gives an example of a community which was able to use its opportunities. It might be argued, of course, that entrepreneurial activity, even when obviously of a collective kind, really represents only class interests and thus should not necessarily be regarded as an urban process.[15] But leadership occurs within the context of the place which provided that leadership with an infrastructure and community base, without which entrepreneurial activity would not be possible or effective. The result, in many places was an "urban ethos," a "booster" mentality, whereby "the activities of various men with disparate interests suddenly begin to coalesce, and the new entity, a city, begins to develop an individuality of its own—to become, in fact, a distinct urban enterprise."[16] As Alan Artibise has pointed out these activities include railway promotion, immigration encouragement, industry attraction, governmental reform, and efforts to achieve status as provincial capital or home to a university; they also included efforts at city incorporation, massive boundary extensions, huge public works projects, deficit financing and land value taxation policies.[17]

Thus, urban as process can be used to describe that element of the city-building act that seems to come from within the community itself. It can also be used to explain the way in which particular urban environments influence social organization and behaviour within the urban container. Using a theatrical metaphor, this involves the city as an actor, not merely as a stage.

> Since the time of Dickens and Baudelaire, the city has been seen at once as social and psychological landscape, both producing and reflecting the modern consciousness. It is an arena of action that in the modernist period often seems to usurp the center stage. In the Dublin of Joyce, the London of Eliot, and the New York of Dos Passos, the city becomes perhaps the most important character of all, determining and imaging every human action.[18]

Some of the best clues to understanding urban as process in this sense derive from Theodore Hershberg's monumental project on Philadelphia. He isolates *work* and *residence* as the basic building blocks of an urban environment and suggests that major changes in these blocks occur when these environments change. Changes in the modes and means of productive activity affect both the setting in which work takes place and the content of that work. For example, during the transition from a mid-nineteenth-century commercial phase to an industrialized, twentieth-century phase, work and residence are separated, tasks become specialized, and work is reorganized hierarchically. According to Hershberg, these "changes gradually affected identity, roles, values and expectations, social networks, class consciousness, and so on through an almost endless list of human experience."[19] The implications of these successive environments for the power arrangements of specific urban places will be discussed more fully in the following analysis of stages in the evolution of Canadian urban environments.

On another scale, urban as process can be applied to what happens when large urban places organize and dominate the life of their immediate hinterland and smaller communities in their region. J. M. S. Careless has used the term "metropolitanism" for the "feudal-like chain of vassalage" between cities in the Canadian urban system, with Winnipeg, for example, tributary to Montreal, but serving as the metropolis of a large region of its own in the Prairie West.[20] In his words, "regions usually center on metropolitan communities, which largely organize them, form their views and deal with outside metropolitan forces on their behalf."[21] Thus the countryside slowly becomes urbanized as the larger cities impose themselves over large territories. Again, it could be argued that this process represents specific entrepreneurs, corporations, or institutions. But the process is more comprehensive than any specific individual, institution, or class and represents what really amounts to the pervasive power of cities over larger segments of society.[22]

Identifying stages in the evolution of urban environments. Students of urban history have long been fascinated by the possibility of defining successive phases in the evolution of urban places from one era to another.[23] Historians in particular are familiar with periodizations, such as the transition from the medieval to the early modern or the changes from a commercially- or agriculturally-oriented society to one based on industry. The following suggestions correspond generally with several well-known formulations of stages of evolution. It should be emphasized that precise dates are not possible, although Canadian development seems to lag about twenty years behind American experience. The succession of environments represents a cumulative process, with each era building on the previous. At least four stages can be described: the colonial entrepôt; the commercial/industrial city of the nineteenth century; the industrial metropolis of the late nineteenth and the first half of the twentieth century; and the decentralized urban field of the present. Each stage has a distinctive function implied in its description. Each can be characterized by a particular metaphor which encapsulates the perceptions generally held about urban places in that era. Each, as well, has a distinctive morphology with its corresponding social landscape. And, important for the purpose of this volume, each stage represents a particular set of power relationships between people, groups, and a place and between places and the larger society.

The earliest Canadian urban places were essentially garrisons established in a hostile and overwhelmingly non-urban context. They were tiny outposts of European imperial or commercial expansion; this central fact determined their function and form. Many of these towns were "planted" in the sense that they were consciously conceived to precede and stimulate more general settlement. In economic terms, these towns were entrepôts, usually acting as collection agencies, shipping staples from their colonies to the metropolitan centre for final processing and in turn distributing the goods from the mother country. While the early towns of the American colonies were dominated by a merchant class which ordered the lives of the communities and their shape and expansion, the function and form of early Canadian places was usually decided upon by imperial officials. Long after American towns were relatively free from imperial control, those in British North America were forced to remain under the antiquated system of government by appointed magistrates. The spatial organization of Canadian towns in this era also reflected the social structure of imperial domination. As was the case in the royally controlled towns of Latin America, the elite of Canadian towns usually lived and concentrated their activities at the centre of town, while the lower classes occupied the periphery or outskirts.[24] The conservative traditions established during this initial phase in Canada were to have a long life in subsequent phases, as is suggested by John Mercer and Michael Goldberg.

During the nineteenth century, the characteristic urban environment was a concentrated settlement based on a combination of trade and industry. Urban North America was still a strange new world, representing only a minority of the total population, but it was generally thought of in positive terms: as a place to make money by selling and developing land, by trade, and by manufacturing. Perhaps the metaphor that best describes it is "marketplace," in contrast to the contemporary perception of British and European cities as "organisms" which were showing signs of disease and hence required some medical attention. An entrepreneurial elite dominated both economic and collective community activity, which was often dedicated to commercial growth through public subsidies for improved infrastructure services and for manufacturing. The source of this elite's power was property and the instrument was compensation, but conditioning was also a potent force, for large segments of society deferred to the supposed wisdom of the propertied classes. In fact, the state itself was essentially an arm of business during this period, as Robert Babcock demonstrates in his essay comparing Saint John, New Brunswick, and Portland, Maine. The application of steam technology to shipping and railroads allowed coastal cities and some interior ports to act as the locus of rapid continental development. In the United States, New York became the central city of a new national system, while in Canada, Montreal played a similar role, later to be challenged by Toronto. As the cities expanded spatially, the direction and extent of development was entirely in the hands of individuals or companies, for local governments had few responsibilities in these areas beyond the provision of services. The social landscape represented a significant separation between work place and residence and sorting out of population by class and ethnicity.[25]

The term "diversified metropolis" best exemplifies the largest places of the period from the late nineteenth century to the end of the Second World War. While this period is usually referred to as the age of the industrial city because manufacturing was regarded as a key factor in urban growth (as transportation had been in the earlier phase), those places which moved beyond an exclusive dependence on industry became the most prominent in the urban hierarchy. The majority of the population now lived in urban places. What has been referred to as the modern consciousness became an urban consciousness, since the urban experience had become so widespread. Functionally, the metropolis extended its economic and cultural dominance far beyond its own boundaries to include entire regions; in the United States, midwestern and western cities achieved regional economic supremacy and something of a parity with New York, whereas in Canada, the national importance of Montreal and Toronto increased, even though major centres in the Maritimes and in the recently developed West held a degree of regional control.

Nineteenth-century notions about the relationship between power and place seemed increasingly inappropriate during the twentieth century because of significant changes in the character of capitalism. Industrial capitalism with its orientation to the family-owned business was strongly identified with a particular town or city, and businessmen successfully convinced the larger community that business-community interests were to be equated. The transition to finance capitalism in the twentieth century with its faceless corporations and career management meant the end of corporate loyalty to any particular location. The result could often be branch closings after corporate takeovers in the trend to consolidation. One of the consequences for local government, as illustrated in the essays by Elizabeth Bloomfield and John Taylor, was less direct business involvement, with local power now more widely dispersed and the total community's real control of its destiny reduced.

The spatial characteristics of the diversified metropolis can best be described as a central city with a suburban ring. An unprecedented spatial expansion was made possible first by the streetcars described by Christopher Armstrong and H. V. Nelles and later by the automobile. While most cities developed a rough core-ring configuration, the product of this rapid growth seemed to many observers to represent a loss of control. Urban society was described as chaotic and a threat to established values and social order. The metaphor "organism" now seemed appropriate, and a reformist impulse took it upon itself to cure this diseased entity by scientific means. Municipal government, for example, took on a greater regulatory function in the areas of health and housing and through planning and regulating suburban expansion. The organizing principle socially was spatial differentiation: intense segregation by class and ethnicity as people were sorted out more than ever before.[26]

A transition to a new phase since the Second World War is more pronounced in the United States than in Canada. The decline of a monocentred metropolis in favour of a polycentric urban field is probably more advanced in the United States; there the old central city cores have been abandoned by the white middle classes to a greater extent than has been the case in Canada, as Mercer and Goldberg demonstrate in their essay. Some of our traditional terms such as "urban" and "city" are in question, for urbanity is no longer the exclusive trait of the city dweller. One observer argues that it is possible to regard "urbanity—the essence of urbanness—not as buildings, not as land use patterns, not as large, dense and heterogeneous population aggregations, but as a quality and diversity of life that is distinct from and in some measure independent of these other characteristics."[27] Yet, how far will this separation of "urban" from "place" actually go? New forms seem to be emerging, based partly on new technologies of information exchange. But the city as a focus of cultural, economic, and transportation relations probably has a future in Canada. One aspect of this is a growing concern to preserve, or in some cases even to create, identifiable symbols of a community in the forms of historic buildings or significant space. And people continue to identify with place in a traditional manner, suggesting a good deal of continuity in how society perceives place even though an increasing proportion of the decision-making authority may be concentrated in bureaucracies at higher and distant levels of government.

Looking for what is universal and what is local about urban places. Sharp divisions have always existed between those historians interested in generalizing and those concerned with the unique and the particular. Ideas about urban places in this respect range from Fernand Braudel's "a town is a town wherever it is," to Asa Briggs's belief that each town is different and has a different story to tell.[28] A fictional account of a conversation about cities between Marco Polo and Kublai Khan brilliantly poses the issue:

> "I have constructed in my mind a model city from which all possible cities can be deduced," Kublai said. "It contains everything corresponding to the norm. Since the cities that exist diverge in varying degrees from the norm, I need only foresee the exceptions to the norm and calculate the most probably combinations". . . .
>
> "I have also thought of a model city from which I deduce all others," Marco answered. "It is a city made only of exceptions, exclusions, incongruities, contradictions."[29]

This basic argument between a nomothetic approach, concerned with the classification of phenomena, and the ideographic, with its emphasis on unique events about which it is difficult to generalize, is founded on philosophical differences which can not be resolved, much like the sterile debates between realists and nominalists in the medieval era. One practical solution is to introduce the comparative method; even those who argue for the case study approach usually accept the validity of generalizations based on the experience of a number of specific cities.[30] When examining the whole issue of power, the most instructive comparisions are those which include urban places in different political contexts. Most of the authors in this volume have addressed themselves to this problem: does the political border between Canada and the United States make a difference? At first glance, comparisons between two such unequal entities might seem unproductive. In this respect, there may be some point to a *National Lampoon* query about how the census in Canada is taken: the answer is, take the American census and divide by ten. Much of the general social science literature about cities is based on the assumption that there is such a thing as a "North American City," with the Canadian portion at most a minor variant, with perhaps a time lag of a generation or so.[31] Compared to the British or European types, this generalization probably has some validity, but are Canadian cities really just northern versions of an American type?

The conclusions reached by the authors in this volume are not totally consistent in this regard, but most find that differing political and cultural values and a differing population mix have resulted in significant, observable distinctions in the way cities are organized. These differences are particularly relevant to the question of how power is distributed in a society and how this relates to power in a particular place. The comparative approach is usually extolled but hardly ever actually attempted; the essays here should be regarded as early ventures in a neglected enterprise, for they point to the possibilities of understanding which elements of the urban phenomenon are universal, or national, and which tend to be particular to a specific place.[32]

The four recent trends in urban history described above are suggestive of several ways in which the relationship of power and place have been or could be explored. One dimension of the connection between power and place involves the community and its setting by elaborating the ties between an urban place and its hinterland or the urban place and other places. Usually defined as "metropolitanism," this approach recognizes the inherent disparity of these relationships, although the dominant element may change considerably over time. Another dimension of the connection between power and place involves the very nature of the urban place itself. In some respects the community is the creation of outside forces and basic structural changes in the economy and society; yet it can also be seen as a dynamic node of power, generating its own growth and form and influencing not only the behaviour of its own population but also that of the society around it. A third dimension of the relationship between power and place is simply the time factor. The instruments and sources of power change dramatically from era to era; for example, the role of the state and organization as well as that of elites can only be precisely determined in a specific historical context. And finally, the relationship between power and place can be explored more thoroughly by a comparative approach which recognizes that what looked like a mountain in a local setting may well turn out to be a molehill in a larger setting.

NOTES

1. For assessments of earlier phases of urban history, see H. J. Dyos, "Agenda for Urban Historians," in Dyos, ed., *The Study of Urban History* (London: Edward Arnold, 1968), pp. 1–60; Michael Frisch, "American Urban History

as an Example of Recent Historiography,'' *History and Theory* 18 (1970): 350–77; Gilbert A. Stelter, ''A Sense of Time and Place: The Historian's Approach to Canada's Urban Past,'' in Stelter and A. F. J. Artibise, eds., *The Canadian City: Essays in Urban History* (Toronto: McClelland and Stewart, 1977), pp. 420–21.

2. Daniel Shaffer, ''A New Threshold for Urban History: Reflections on Canadian-American Urban Development at the Guelph Conference,'' *Planning History Bulletin* 4, no. 3 (1982): 1–10.
3. James Cronin, ''The Problem with Urban History: Reflections on a Recent Meeting,'' *Urbanism Past and Present* 9 (1980): 40–43; Michael Ebner, ''Urban History: Retrospect and Prospect,'' *Journal of American History* (June 1981): 69–84.
4. Philip Abrams, ''Towns and Economic Growth: Some Theories and Problems,'' in Abrams and E. A. Wrigley, eds., *Towns in Societies, Essays in Economic History and Historical Sociology* (Cambridge: Cambridge University Press, 1979), pp. 9–34.
5. The Marxist response is that there is no such thing as neutrality. E. J. Hobsbawm, ''From Social History to the History of Society,'' *Daedalus* 100 (1971): 20–45.
6. One of the clearest recent attempts to categorize the instruments and sources of power in this way is John Kenneth Galbraith, *The Anatomy of Power* (Boston: Houghton Mifflin, 1983); also, Richard Sennett, *Authority* (New York: Alfred E. Kopf, 1980), and Dennis H. Wrong, *Power: Its Forms, Bases and Uses* (New York: Harper Colophon Books, 1980).
7. Some of the general literature for urban systems includes: B. J. L. Berry, ''Cities as Systems within Systems of Cities,'' *Economic Development and Cultural Change* 9 (1961): 573–87; Richard M. Morse, ''The Development of Urban Systems in the Americas in the Nineteenth Century,'' *Journal of Interamerican Studies and Word Affairs* 17 (1975): 4–26; James Simmons, ''The Evolution of the Canadian Urban System,'' in Alan F. J. Artibise and Gilbert A. Stelter, eds., *The Usable Urban Past, Planning and Politics in the Modern Canadian City* (Toronto: Macmillan, 1979): 9–33. The concept of cities and particular regions is best developed by David Goldfield, ''The Urban South: A Regional Framework,'' *American Historical Review* 86 (1981): 1009–34; by J. W. McCarty, ''Australia as a Region of Recent Settlement in the Nineteenth Century,'' *Australian Economic History Review* 13 (1973): 148–67; and by Gilbert Stelter, ''A Regional Framework for Urban History,'' *Urban History Review* 13 (Feburary, 1985): 193–206. Also relevant is Alan F.J. Artibise, ''Exploring the North-American West: A Comparative Urban Perspective,'' *American Review of Canadian Studies*, 14 (1984): pp. 20–44
8. The standard Canadian statement is in J. M. S. Careless, ''Frontierism, Metropolitanism, and Canadian History,'' *Canadian Historical Review* 35 (1954): 1–21. A major Canadian synthesis by geographers is in L. D. McCann, ed., *Heartland and Hinterland, A Geography of Canada* (Scarborough: Prentice-Hall, 1982). For a recent analysis of this approach, see

Donald Davis, "The Metropolitan Thesis and the Writing of Canadian Urban History," *Urban History Review* 14, no. 2 (October 1985).

9. My categorization here represents a considerable development beyond some of my earlier formulations, as in the introduction to Artibise and Stelter, *Canada's Urban Past: A Bibliography to 1980 and Guide to Canadian Urban Studies* (Vancouver: University of British Columbia Press, 1981), pp. xiii–xxxii. Much of the current social science literature remains relatively vague or confused on this question. An example is an article by anthropologist Anton Blok, "South Italian Agro-Towns," *Comparative Studies in Society and History* 11 (1969): 121–135, in which it is stated that the author "shall consider the settlement pattern as the dependent variable and the environment as the independent variable." He then goes on to show, perhaps unwittingly, how the settlement pattern was affected by established norms of behaviour by estate owners and peasants alike.
10. "Concepts in Contexts: Pursuing the Urban of 'Urban' Sociology," in Derek Fraser and Anthony Sutcliffe, eds., *The Pursuit of Urban History* (London: Edward Arnold, 1983), p. 373.
11. Abrams, "Introduction," in Abrams and Wrigley, *Towns in Societies,* p. 5.
12. David Harvey, *Social Justice and the City* (London: Edward Arnold, 1973), p. 16. A similar approach is outlined in Manuel Castells, *The Urban Question: A Marxist Approach* (London: Edward Arnold, 1977).
13. Quoted by David Cannadine, "Urban History in the United Kingdom: The 'Dyos phenomena' and after," in Cannadine and David Reeder, eds., *Exploring the Urban Past: Essays in Urban History by H. J. Dyos* (Cambridge: Cambridge University Press, 1982), p. 208. For a similar assessment as applied to the "urban Marxists," see Francois Bedarida, "The French Approach to Urban History: An Assessment of Recent Methodological Trends," in Fraser and Sutcliffe, *The Pursuit of Urban History,* p. 403.
14. Leonard Gertler and Ronald Crowley, *Changing Canadian Cities: The Next 25 Years* (Toronto: McClelland and Stewart, 1977), p. 152.
15. S. D. Clark, "Canadian Urban Development," *Urban History Review* 1–74 (June 1974): 14–19.
16. A. Theodore Brown, *Frontier Community: Kansas City to 1870* (Columbia: University of Missouri Press, 1963), pp. 88–89. Much of the current discussion about the validity of an "urban variable" has taken place in Great Britain, where the collective growth strategies of urban places so common in North America simply did not exist. When British urban historians look for the "urban variable," they are looking for a larger social dimension, unrelated to any specific place, as in Anthony Sutcliffe's conclusion that the large city played a major role in the evolution of the British interventionist state. "In Search of the Urban Variable: Britain in the Late Nineteenth Century," in Fraser and Sutcliffe, *The Pursuit of Urban History,* pp. 234–63.
17. "Boosterism and the Development of Prairie Cities, 1871–1913," in Alan F. J. Artibise, ed., *Town and City: Aspects of Western Canadian Urban Development* (Regina: Canadian Plains Research Center, 1981), pp. 209–35. See also the review essay by Elizabeth Bloomfield, "Community, Ethos and

Local Initiative in Urban Economic Growth: Review of a Theme in Canadian Urban History,'' in *Urban History Yearbook* (1983), pp. 53–72.

18. William Sharpe and Leonard Wallock, ''From 'Great Town' to 'Nonplace Urban Realm': Reading the Modern City,'' in Sharpe and Wallock, eds., *Visions of the Modern City, Essays in History, Art, and Literature* (New York: Heyman Center for the Humanities, Columbia University, 1983), p. 13.
19. Hershberg, ''The New Urban History: Toward an Interdisciplinary History of the City,'' *Journal of Urban History* 5 (1978): 3–40.
20. Careless, ''Frontierism, Metropolitanism.'' See also his ''Metropolis and Region: The Interplay between City and Region in Canadian History before 1914,'' *Urban History Review* 3–78 (February 1979): 99–118.
21. ''Aspects of Metropolitanism in Atlantic Canada,'' in Mason Wade, ed., *Regionalism in the Canadian Community, 1867–1967* (Toronto: University of Toronto Press, 1969), p. 117.
22. The strongest statement of urban primacy, that by Jane Jacobs, *The Economy of Cities* (New York: Vintage, 1970), has recently been updated by her in ''Cities and the Wealth of Nations, A New Theory of Economic Life,'' *The Atlantic Monthly* (March 1984): 41–66.
23. Among the most useful have been Sam Bass Warner, *The Urban Wilderness: A History of the American City* (New York: Oxford University Press, 1972); David Goldfield and Blaine Brownell, *Urban America: From Downtown to No Town* (Boston: Houghton Mifflin, 1979); and Herschberg, ''The New Urban History.''
24. I have outlined this early phase in ''The Political Economy of Early Canadian Urban Development,'' in G. A. Stelter and Alan F. J. Artibise, eds., *The Canadian City: Essays in Urban and Social History,* 2d ed. (Ottawa: Carleton University Press, 1984), pp. 1–26.
25. Among the most effective descriptions of this phase of urban development in Canada are Peter Goheen, *Victorian Toronto: Pattern and Process of Growth* (Chicago: University of Chicago, 1970) and Michael Katz, *The People of Hamilton, Canada West* (Cambridge, MA: Harvard University Press, 1975).
26. Contemporary ideas about cities during this period have been collected in Paul Rutherford, ed. *Saving the Canadian City: The First Phase, 1890–1920* (Toronto: University of Toronto Press, 1974). The best analysis of the metropolis continues to be Hans Blumenfeld, *The Modern Metropolis: Its Origins, Growth, Characteristics and Planning* (Montreal: Harvest House, 1961). The most comprehensive coverage is available in Anthony Sutcliffe, ed., *Metropolis, 1890–1940* (Chicago: University of Chicago Press, 1984). The best study of a single Canadian city during this period is Alan Artibise, *Winnipeg: A Social History of Urban Growth* (Montreal: McGill-Queen's University Press, 1975). See also, Artibise, ''City–Building in the Canadian West: From Boosterism to Corporatism,'' *Journal of Canadian Studies* 17 (Fall 1982): 35–44.

27. Melvin Webber, quoted by Sharpe and Wallock, "From 'Great Town'," p. 18.
28. Braudel, *Capitalism and Material Life* (London: Weidenfeld and Nicolson, 1973), p. 373; Briggs, "The Study of Cities," *Confluence* 7 (1958): 107–14.
29. Italo Calvino, *Invisible Cities* (London: Picador, 1979), p. 56.
30. See the report by Andreas Weiland of a discussion between the "structuralist" approach of Anthony Sutcliffe and the Italian proponents of building on individual case studies in *Planning History Bulletin* 5, no. 3 (1983): 1–3.
31. An example is Maurice Yeates and Barry Garner, *The North American City*, 3d ed. (New York: Harper and Row, 1980). The authors evidently assume that the study of the past is not one of the serious aspects of knowing a place, for their discussion of overlapping urban-oriented disciplines which inform urban geography does not include a mention of urban history. For a critique of the "North American City" typology, see John Mercer, "On Continentalism, Distinctiveness, and Comparative Urban Geography: Canadian and American Cities," *Canadian Geographer* 23 (1979): 119–39.
32. Comparative history is obviously a difficult task, but some successful examples can be cited in which the Canadian and American experiences are explored in the context of different political and value systems. For differing immigration histories, see Allan Smith, "National Images and National Maintenance: The Ascendancy of the Ethnic Idea in North America," *Canadian Journal of Political Science* 14 (June 1981): 227–57. For architectural trends, see Deryck Holdsworth, "Regional Distinctiveness in an Industrial Age: Some California Influences on British Columbia Housing," *American Review of Canadian Studies* 12 (Summer 1982): 64–81. An attempt by a Canadian art historian to compare Canadian and American painting traditions uses E. N. Gombrich's thesis that developments in a society at large rather than the individual will stimulate new artistic schema: see Ann Davis, *A Distant Harmony: Comparisons in the Painting of Canada and the United States* (Winnipeg: Winnipeg Art Gallery, 1982). Two comparative studies at the regional level are: John P. Radford, "Regional Ideologies and Urban Growth on the Victorian Periphery: Southern Ontario and the U.S. South," *Historical Geography Research Series,* No. 12 (December 1983), pp. 32–57; and Alan F. J. Artibise, "Exploring the North American West: A Comparative Urban Perspective," *American Review of Canadian Studies* 14 (Spring 1984): 20–44. One of the best comparisons between a Canadian and an American city is Norbert MacDonald, "Population Growth and Change in Seattle and Vancouver, 1880–1960," *Pacific Historical Review* 39 (1970): 279–321. Some of the larger issues involved in the comparative urban history are thoughtfully explored by Richard M. Morse, "The Urban Worlds of Latin and Anglo America: Prefatory Thoughts," in Woodrow Borah, Jorge Hardoy, and Gilbert Stelter, eds., *Urbanization in the Americas: The Background in Comparative Perspective* (Ottawa: National Museum of Man, 1980), pp. 1–6.

SECTION II

THE POLITICAL ECONOMY OF URBAN GROWTH

Introduction

The term "political economy" in the section title is used to draw attention to the need to explore the complex relationship between politics and economics in urban growth. The theme here is that the state and political power have a tangible effect on urban growth patterns. This view is not shared by all scholars examining the questions of how and why urban growth takes place. For example, the new social history stemming from the *Annales* school regards political history as largely irrelevant to the changes in the daily lives of ordinary people.[1] Most social science analyses of urban growth still stress market forces or technological innovations as explanations.[2] And even the Marxist interpretation which asserts a causal relationship between politics and economics—between a particular form of government and the dominant mode of production—assumes that the form and function of the state is merely a "derivation" of the capitalist social function.[3]

In outlining the role of the state in the development of the Canadian and American urban systems, James Simmons isolates four elements which could be applied to any system of cities. Perhaps the most basic is that of *bounding,* the setting of national boundaries which determine not only the nature of trade but also investment and immigration flows. In nineteenth-century Canada, federal government policies in these areas tended to accentuate a disparity between core regions and peripheral regions, and hence, between the major cities within these regions. Another element is providing *connections* between cities through building and supporting transportation and communication links. A third is the more recent *homogenizing* action of the state in its efforts to reduce income disparities between cities. Closely related is a fourth element, the attempt to *stabilize* the peaks and valleys of economic cycles.[4]

Have the Canadian and American experiences been similar in this respect? Certainly the general stages of urban growth were comparable, as they were in other countries of recent European settlement such as Australia and New Zealand: the growth of a national economy, the extension of the agricultural frontier, and the process of urbanization all occurred simultaneously.[5] Canadian scholarship usually emphasizes the relatively greater degree of state intervention in the Canadian economy, pointing to the necessity of collective action in occupying an immense land and maintaining a fragile society in the face of American expansionism.[6] But Robert Babcock questions assumptions about national cultural values which assign an interventionist ideology to Canadians and a free enterprise ideology to Americans. As an alternative approach, he suggests a comparative look at governmental structures in his study of public vs. private enterprise in Saint John, New Brunswick, and Portland, Maine. He feels that the higher degree of public expenditure he found in Saint John can be explained by the nature of the Canadian federal system which allowed a focused government action because the city's local representatives were directly involved in the decision-making process at the federal cabinet level. In Portland, on the other hand, public efforts to stimulate economic growth were less concentrated because of a system in which legislative and executive powers were separated.

Local communities in both countries could, of course, make special efforts to harness the impact of higher levels of government. Or they could take direct action themselves by pursuing growth strategies which included canal and railway subsidization, the inducement of industry, and the boosting of a town's reputation. The encouragement of industry through the granting of incentives appears to have been primarily a Canadian municipal acitivity; some American states prohibited the practice. Canadian municipal government was often dominated directly by urban elites or influenced indirectly through boards of trade, as Elizabeth Bloomfield shows. This leadership, however, had to be exercised "with persistence and skill" to ensure that an urban ethos was shared by most groups in the community.[7] The result was that urban places could be "considered not only as local economies, each with a power structure and wealth, but as self-governing political entities with their own initiatives and with relationships to higher levels of government."[8]

Notes

1. A good example is Fernand Braudel, *Structures of Everyday Life: Civilization and Capitalism, 15th to 18th Century* (New York: Harper and Row, 1981). A major example for urban history is Stephan Thernstrom and Richard Sennett, eds., *Nineteenth-Century Cities: Essays in the New Urban History* (New Haven: Yale University Press, 1969).

2. Recent examples are Brian Berry, ''Inner-City Futures: An American Dilemma Revisited,'' in Bruce Stave, ed., *Modern Industrial Cities, History, Policy and Survival* (Beverly Hills: Sage, 1981), pp. 187–220, and Allan Pred, *Urban Growth and City-Systems in the United States, 1840–1860* (Cambridge, MA: Harvard University Press, 1980). One of the best theoretical studies, Brian T. Robson, *Urban Growth: An Approach* (London: Methuen, 1973), concentrates on technical innovations, but the author, in his conclusion, recognizes that ''the scale and nature of power and of the locus of decisions—whether in terms of political power, the activities of manufacturing-corporations, or of other sources—have been sadly neglected by geographers, despite their evident impact upon the more tangible aspects of the economic landscape.'' (p. 228).
3. Gordon Clark and Michael Dear, ''The State in Capitalism and the Capitalist State,'' in Michael Dear and Allen J. Scott, eds., *Urbanization and Urban Planning in Capitalist Society* (London: Methuen, 1981), pp. 45–62.
4. For a general overview of the Canadian urban system, see James Simmons, ''The Evolution of the Canadian Urban System,'' in Alan F. J. Artibise and Gilbert A. Stelter, eds., *The Usable Urban Past, Planning and Politics in the Modern Canadian City* (Toronto: Macmillan, 1979), pp. 9–33. For the United States, see Michael P. Conzen, ''The Maturing Urban System in the United States, 1840–1910,'' *Annals of the American Association of Geographers* 67 (1977): 88–108.
5. Canada tended to lag marginally behind the United States during the nineteenth century in the degree of urbanization. For example, in 1871 the percentage of the total population living in urban places in Canada was 19.6 per cent compared to 25.7 per cent in the United States. The percentage was relatively equal by 1910–11 (45 per cent). However, by a standard of measurement which uses places of 5,000 or more, the Canadian lag was more pronounced. In 1870–71, the Canadian proportion in places of this size was 12.2 per cent, that in the United States, 22.9 per cent. Even by 1950–51, the difference was still 45 per cent to 55 percent. Leo F. Schnore and Gene B. Petersen, ''Urban and Metropolitan Development in the United States and Canada,'' *Annals of the American Academy of Political and Social Sciences* 316 (March 1958): 60–68.
6. Hugh Aitken, ''Government and Business in Canada: An Interpretation,'' *Business History Review* 38 (1964): 4–21; George Grant, *Lament for a Nation* (Toronto: McClelland and Stewart, 1965); Herschel Hardin, *A Nation Unaware: The Canadian Economic Culture* (Vancouver: Douglas, 1974).
7. For general descriptions of this ethos see Blaine Brownell, *The Urban Ethos in the South, 1920–1930* (Baton Rouge: Louisiana University Press, 1975) and Alan F. J. Artibise, ''Boosterism and the Development of Prairie Cities, 1871–1913,'' in Artibise, ed., *Town and City: Aspects of Western Canadian Urban Development* (Regina: Canadian Plains Research Center, 1981), pp. 209–36.
8. The best overview of the local Canadian experience in this regard is

Elizabeth Bloomfield, "Community, Ethos and the Local Initiative in Urban Economic Growth: Review of a Theme in Canadian History," *Urban History Yearbook* (1983), pp. 53–72. For recent case studies, see Leo Johnson, "Ideology and Political Economy in Urban Growth: Guelph, 1827–1927," in Gilbert A. Stelter and Alan F. J. Artibise, eds., *Shaping the Urban Landscape: Aspects of the City-Building Process* (Ottawa: Carleton University Press, 1982), pp. 30–64; Paul-André Linteau, *Maisonneuve, Comment des promoteurs fabriquent une ville* (Montreal: Boreal Express, 1981); and Bloomfield, "Building the City on a Foundation of Factories: The 'Industrial Policy' in Berlin, Ontario, 1870–1914," *Ontario History* 25 (September 1983): 207–43.

2

The Impact of the Public Sector on the Canadian Urban System

James W. Simmons

> The most honoured of the themes of Canadian historiography is surely that the state has played an important role in promoting and shaping Canadian economic development.[1]

The impact of the public sector on urban development is an important theme: each day reveals fresh evidence of the scope of governmental activity in Canada. The great works in Canadian economic history point repeatedly to the interventions by government: the railroads, the tariffs, the subsidies and settlement schemes. What has been lacking, however, is a discussion of the various ways in which the public sector can shape the development of a *spatial* system and, in particular, a system organized around urban nodes: an urban system.

While most students of Canadian urban development are willing to accept the importance of the state, the general literature on urban systems has not explicitly addressed the activities of government, an oversight which reflects perhaps the predominance of American research. The most influential overviews largely ignore the public sector, although a later section in this paper will argue that government has played as significant an urban role in the United States as it has in Canada.[2]

In addressing the role of government, one must link together two bodies of material: discussions of the growth, spatial distribution, and functional specialization of urban places: the urban system; and analysis of the growth and diversification of public sector activities. Urbanization has transformed the Canadian landscape over the last century. More and more people have become more and more intensely concentrated in space. A simple map of Canada can no longer do justice to a geography that includes endless activity and variety within a few kilometres of the centre of Montreal, and then stretches north for thousands of kilometres, virtually empty and unchanging, or in which Toronto and Calgary are far more closely linked than Kingston and Sarnia. Paralleling this urban concentration has been a growth in the significance of the institutional environment, exemplified by the increase in the level and complexity of government activity—measured in employment, expenditures, legislation and regulation—and at all levels in the political hierarchy.

These two trends, urbanization and the growth of public sector activity, can be related in many ways. Both reflect economic growth and technological change, but the intensity of contact in urban life itself leads to conflicts and externalities that invite government intervention. It can also be argued that the particular characteristics of the Canadian urban system—its economic and demographic characteristics—both reflect and encourage certain forms of government action. This paper pursues the latter theme. It develops a logic for certain actions by the state, based on the properties of the urban system; and then outlines a typology for government programmes that affect the system.

THE CANADIAN URBAN SYSTEM[3]

An urban system is a set of cities within a nation together with the linkages that exist among them. In this sense the urban system is much more than a set of dots on the map. It is an ongoing geography of production and reproduction processes, each one absorbing inputs and generating streams of outputs. These processes are linked to each other by varying flows of commodities, money, information, and manpower. The *connections* between places form the essence of the spatial system; an isolated or completely autonomous city is irrelevent to the system.

Relative to other national urban systems, Canada is small and open, closely connected to the world system and highly sensitive to impulses of growth or change from outside. These growth impulses are deflected, absorbed, diffused, or amplified as they pass through the Canadian urban network. The survival of the urban system requires a variety of control mechanisms to steer it and stabilize it in the face of these frequent but erratic exogenous shocks. Many of these mechanisms can be identified. The economy relies on a national financial system and the variety of market feedbacks identified in the economics literature. Reproductive and demographic processes also incorporate control relationships into fertility and migration. More and more, however, the Canadian urban system has turned to government in order to manage the spatial and temporal variations in growth.

The interdependence matrix portrays the transfer of impacts of both exogenous and endogenous impulses from one urban place to another.

Research suggests that the urban system may be described by several interdependence matrices operating simultaneously, each with different patterns of spatial linkages and temporal responses. One such pattern is generated by the production side of the economy; another, by the demographic processes of natural increase and migration. It can be argued that a third set of linkages is generated by the activities of various levels of government as they mediate between the economic and demographic changes.[4]

The Canadian economy is strongly differentiated in space. A closely linked industrial core in Southern Ontario and Quebec largely serves the domestic market, while a diversified primary economy in the rest of the country depends on the strength of world demand for various resource commodities. Urban places on the periphery tend to be highly specialized in the production of a single primary good.

As a result, the space economy is characterized by a high degree of variability over time, especially on the periphery, and a rapid diffusion of growth impulses over space (within a few months), particularly within the core. The economies of smaller places fluctuate with the world demand for their particular commodity, generating growth patterns that are largely independent of one another and of the national business cycle. The cities of the core and the largest cities on the periphery tend to grow in phase with the national economy. Over time, as the economic base of urban regions becomes more and more dependent on single products, the potential for variability in value of production over space and time increases.

Demographic processes such as migration have quite different characteristics in space and time. For instance, the spatial movements of anglophones and francophones are quite different because of the language barrier that divides the industrial core of the country. Although economic theory suggests that migrants flow readily from areas of economic decline to areas of economic growth, the empirical evidence for this relationship is very weak, limited to certain regions at certain times.[5] There may not be adequate migration links between such regions, or economic decline may occur everywhere. Historically, Canada has carried out regional population growth adjustments by means of immigration and emigration rather than by internal migrant flows.

Temporally, it appears that the demographic processes of migration and natural increase are much slower to respond to growth signals than are economic processes. An urban region is capable of a real income growth of 20 per cent in a year. It might take five years to achieve that level of population increase, twenty years to decline by that much. The limited historical evidence suggests that the relative level of interurban migration may have declined over time as the population has aged and the direct response of the demography to economic change has weakened. Fertility, of course, is largely unrelated to economic growth, and at any rate it would require a full generation in order to affect the labour force.

About the third kind of interdependence matrix—the public sector—rather little is known. It encompasses the flow of funds by means of grants and equalization payments among levels of government, taxes and transfers to individuals, direct spatial intervention through government investment and employment, as well as the modification and regulation of interurban linkages of all kinds. The patterns of intervention reflect government's particular responsibility for managing (or compensating for) the imbalances between the economy (jobs, income) and the demography (the labour force) as they change over space and time.

These imbalances may occur in the long run, as reflected by structural unemployment and low incomes; or in the short run, seen as cyclical or even seasonal fluctuations in economic indicators. Both long-run and short-run imbalances may be expressed nationally (in the media, for example) or locally, in the form of regional differences in income levels or unemployment rates. In combination, the long-run/short-run and national/local differences in economic and demographic growth patterns define four kinds of demands on the political system: (1) national economic development, (2) stabilization, (3) regional development, and (4) stabilization. These demands require combinations of programmes to control various aspects of the problem. For instance, variations in wheat yields and prices (relative to a fixed number of farmers) generate political stress that has a particular distribution in space and time. The result may be any one of a variety of government actions—subsidy, crop insurance, or a marketing scheme—but it will be provided in the context of many other government activities, within a federal budget or as part of a comprehensive development strategy. The problem may be attacked by provincial and federal governments as well.

The student of urban systems is interested in both the magnitude of government intervention and the resulting mix of programmes. Does government action initiate growth in new economic sectors or at new locations? Or does it stabilize growth rates over time and space, slowing up the redistribution of economic and demographic activity throughout the urban system that is generated by external events?

THE GROWTH OF GOVERNMENT

Public sector activities have many dimensions and can be measured in a variety of ways. Government investment, employment, and regulatory activity all have different distributions in space and time. Among the many measurement problems are those associated with the activities of crown corporations, or in tracing transfers among levels of governments, or in the notion of tax expenditures (such as tax exemptions). Nonetheless, Figure 1 provides a broad picture of the long-term trend of public sector activity in Canada. A long-run increase in the relative size of direct government expenditures (crown corporations are excluded) is apparent, but it takes place in an erratic fashion. Each world war stimulated an explosion in government activity, followed by a rapid decline to "normal." These wartime experiences are fascinating examples of the full potential of government activity when it is stimulated by external events. The apparent growth in the federal public sector during the Depression largely reflects the relative decline in the private sector. In the post-Second World War period, government expenditures grew regularly but almost entirely

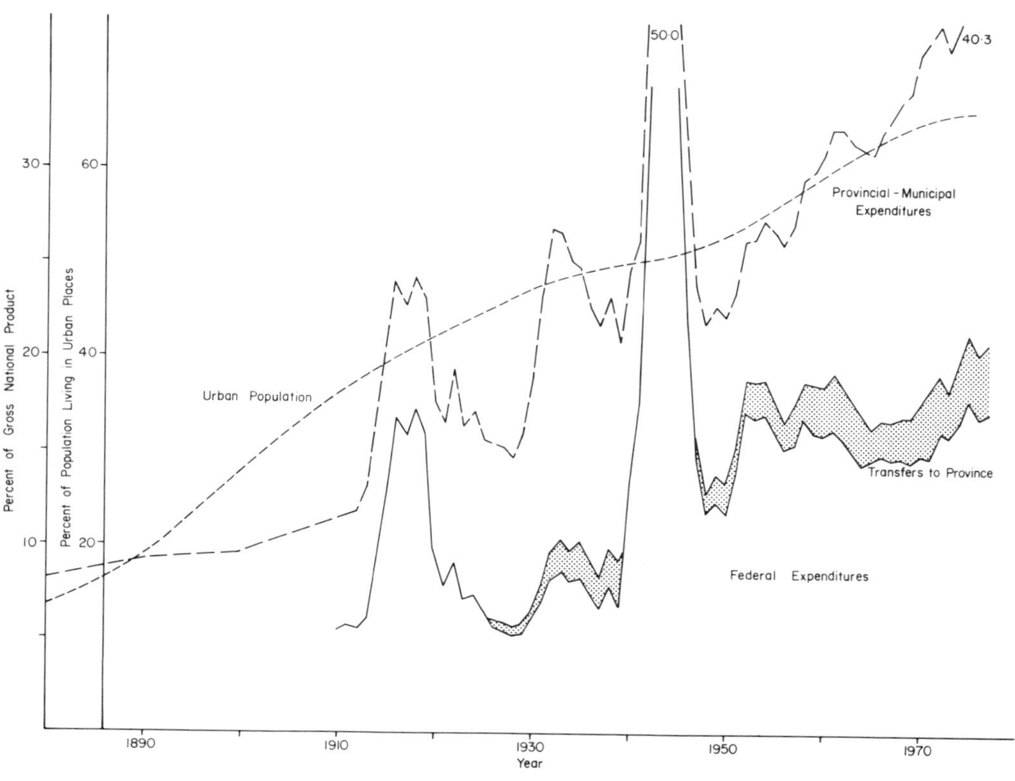

Fig. 1: Public sector activity in Canada.

through the expansion of provincial and municipal services: utilities, education, transportation, and so forth. Bird argues that there is no single explanation for the growth trend.[6] Many different kinds of social, economic, and technological changes on both the supply side (fiscal innovations) and the demand side (expansion of services) have played a part. This paper simply adds the urban system dimension.

TABLE 1

THE EVOLUTION OF THE PUBLIC SECTOR IN CANADA: SELECTED ACTIVITIES
(1949 dollars/capita)

	Expenditures		Public Invest-ment/ Capita[c]	Federal Revenues or Expenditures on:			Employment per 1000 Population[g]		
	Federal Govt.[a]	Other Levels Govt.[b]		Import Duties[d]	Trans-port[e]	Social[f]	Fed.[g]	Prov.[h]	Mun.[i]
1891	$ 24	n.a.	n.a.	$13	$ 8	$ 1	n.a.	n.a.	n.a.
1921	65	19	23	15	22	9	6.9	3.8	10.6
1951	236	100	81	22	15	52	2.6	3.8	15.3
1975	571	771	286	36	43	245	10.0	15.3	11.5

[a] Richard M. Bird, "Government Finance," in *Historical Statistics of Canada* (forthcoming), Item H34.

[b] Bird, *The Growth of Government Spending in Canada,* Table 26: updated from Statistics Canada, "Provincial Economic Accounts," Catalogue 13–213.

[c] Public investments, including public enterprise. M. Urquhart and K. Buckley, eds., *Historical Statistics of Canada* (1965), Item E126, updated by Statistics Canada "Public and Private Investment in Canada," Catalogue 61-205. The 1926 value has been substituted for 1921.

[d] Bird, "Government Finance," Item H9.

[e] Ibid, Item H27, "Transportation and Communications."

[f] Ibid, Items H20 to H26, "Health, Education, Pensions."

[g] Bird, The Growth of Government Spending in Canada, Table 50: supplemented by Statistics Canada, "Federal Government Employment," Catalogue 72-004; "Provincial Government Employment," Catalogue 72-007; "Local Government Employment," Catalogue 72-009.

The data in Table 1, controlled for population growth and inflation, also describe the rising governmental presence, but with some interesting reservations. Although all government expenditures have risen, the provincial and municipal expenditures have increased much more dramatically than those of the federal government. Since the greatest increase has occurred in transfer payments rather than the provision of services, the increase in government employment has been rather slow and somewhat erratic as responsibilities for different services are transferred in and out of the public sector and among the levels of government.

Consistent with the erratic expansion of government over time is the notion that the public sector grows by adding new programmes and activities rather than by increasing the magnitudes of those already in place. Each decade brings new problems and new policy solutions, while, in most cases, maintaining the old. The result is government action that becomes more complex and interdependent, until it has become almost impossible to understand the development of a single programme in isolation from the rest. A port improvement in Saint John must be viewed in the context of other legislation that is part of the same package (such as the annual public works programme within the Atlantic region) or in terms of the continuing commitments made earlier and/or to other locations such as Halifax or Montreal.

It is not easy, then, to make sense of a particular government activity that affects the urban system. The remainder of this paper focuses on the measurable effects of programmes rather than goals, aspirations, or proclamations; it is concerned with broad clusters of activities that seem to redistribute urban growth rather than those schemes that are specifically labelled "regional disparity" and with those activities that affect the development of the urban system as a whole—its size distribution, diversity, rate of growth, and growth variability in time and space—rather than the specific impact on a particular place and time. The public sector affects the urban system in four fundamental ways: bounding, connecting, homogenizing, and stabilizing (Table 2).

BOUNDING

Bounding refers to those government activities that control flows and links across the urban system (national) boundary. For example, the level and variety of foreign trade are determined by negotiated agreements with other countries, by tariffs, and by internal regulations. As a result, a national market is defined, the relative prices of goods are altered, and differential sector growth is initiated within the country. Immigration,

TABLE 2

IMPACTS OF GOVERNMENT ON A NATIONAL URBAN SYSTEM

Intervention	*Effects*
Bounding	
Immigration/emigration Tariffs and other import controls Monetary policy Treaties, trade agreements and international agreements that limit sovereignty War	—determine system openness, hence the variety of internal feedback mechanisms and controls —define market areas —resist, delay, diffuse or distort the impact of external impulses —shape sectoral composition of economy
Connecting	
Transportation investments—mode, location Transport rates, subsidies and regulations Communication and utility systems	—determine the degree and pattern of interdependence within the system hence the openness of urban subsystems —trade determines level of spatial specialization —access/scale economics determine growth by urban size class
Homogenizing	
Government services, spatial transfers (such as equalization payments) Regulatory activities wages, prices quality of environment Degree of subsystem autonomy	—determines the internal variability in economic development, social and political characteristics —provincial autonomy limits spatial specialization and stabilization
Stabilizing	
Income tax Transfer payments Unemployment insurance Marketing boards Equalization payments Government employment	—public sector activity tends to be more stable in space and time than the private sector —negative feedback transfers funds from areas of growth (high income) to areas of decline (low income)

investment, and information flows are also affected by bounding policies and can modify the size and variability of the urban system growth rate, as well as the location of growth.

The small size of the Canadian economy, the sectoral inflexibility of our regional economies, and the propinquity to the United States make bounding a central policy concern for the urban system. Historically, the Canadian border has remained relatively open to economic flows, with imports or exports ranging from 12 to 35 per cent of the gross national product. As a result, most growth or decline is imported as well. In addition to changes in the level of foreign trade, the Canadian urban system has responded to changes in the sectoral mix, reflecting in part the varying permeability of the trade barriers negotiated by government.

The National Policy defined a national market for manufactured goods and led inexorably to the core/periphery spatial structure that is observed in the urban system today, but it also increased the temporal stability of the national economy. By tying a large part of the space-economy to the growth of the demand from the urban system itself, "leakages" were reduced, ensuring that the network of feedbacks beloved by economists—The Invisible Hand, Keynesian, or Monetarists—have some partial applicability. The National Energy Policy attempts to do the same thing today. Without the tariff structure and other boundary controls, the urban system is less sectorally and spatially integrated and is almost immune to policy intervention.

TABLE 3

THE TARIFFS; REGIONAL COSTS AND BENEFITS
(per cent)

Year	Federal Duty (1)	Imputed Subsidy to Domestic Producers (2)	Net (1)–(2)	Regional Impacts Quebec	Ontario	Others
1890	2.98	8.08	5.10	1.1	0.4	–2.1
1910	3.53	5.87	2.34	1.8	1.8	–3.2
1926	3.87	6.43	2.56	2.4	2.6	–4.0
1949	1.79	7.08	5.29	3.6	1.5	–3.9
1969	1.44	5.32	3.88	1.5	0.7	–2.0

Source: Hugh M. Pinchin, *The Regional Impact of the Canadian Tariff,* (Ottawa: Economic Council of Canada, 1979), Tables 1-3 and 1-4. All measures are in terms of per cent of personal income.

Table 3 suggests that the costs of this substantial stabilization effect have been relatively small, particularly when the considerable revenue gains for the federal government are subtracted. (Before the Second World War, import duties accounted for over half the federal government revenue, see Figure 2.) Surprisingly, the regional variations in cost are quite small in

TABLE 4

THE SPATIAL IMPACT OF THE PUBLIC SECTOR
(1976 dollars per capita)

Bounding	Nfld.	PEI	NS	NB	QUE	ONT	MAN	SASK	ALTA	BC	CAN	Inter-Provincial Range
The tariff[a]	$–55	–99	–31	–31	16	26	–36	–48	–33	–39	0	125
Immigration[b]	8.4	15.7	16.4	21.4	17.4	47.5	30.2	11.7	36.8	50.1	33.4	41.7
Financial employment[c]	4.7	7.6	10.6	8.9	14.5	16.3	15.5	10.4	13.8	16.9	16.9	12.2
Connecting												
Provincial transportation expenditure[d]	$193	172	133	183	142	115	84	160	143	141	130	109
Government investment[e]	456	339	342	464	324	269	231	355	441	406	337	233
Transportation investments[f]	435	169	309	560	426	392	698	245	734	618	472	565
Homogenizing												
Equalization payments[g]	$ 382	382	339	308	227	36	183	14	44	18	124	368
Other Federal expenditure[h]	1,163	2,504	2,338	1,948	1,205	1,614	1,465	1,357	1,181	1,360	1,513	1,323
Other Provincial expenditure[i]	1,167	1,184	1,017	1,068	1,361	1,349	1,201	1,440	1,148	1,358	1,342	472

Stabilizing												
Federal Income tax[j]	$ 351	311	426	389	418	724	521	532	729	764	601	453
Provincial income tax[k]	$ 168	136	190	186	478	246	259	219	211	269	302	342
Transfers to individuals[l]	1,271	1,032	910	1,004	954	754	744	804	706	987	847	565

[a] Estimated costs and benefits per resident of Canadian tariffs on manufactured goods in 1974 as estimated by the Province of Ontario, quoted in Canada, Minister of Finance, ''Press Release on Provincial Economic Accounts by the Hon. Donald MacDonald,'' Ottawa, 6 June 1977.

[b] Immigrants from abroad per 1000 Population, 1971–76, Statistics Canada, *Census of Canada,* 1976.

[c] Numbers per 1000 Population employed in finance, Statistics Canada, *Census of Canada,* 1976.

[d] Provincial government expenditures only: Statistics Canada, ''Provincial Government Finance,'' Catalog 68-207, Table 1. Federal expenditures amount to $120 per capita. Ibid., ''Federal Government Finance,'' Catalog 68-211, Table 2, but the location of expenditure is not given. Data for fiscal year ending 31 March 1977.

[e] Capital investment by governments and institutions, including construction, machinery and repairs in 1976: Statistics Canada, ''Private and Public Investment in Canada,'' Catalog 61-205, Tables 9–19.

[f] Capital investment in Transport and Utilities, Public and Private. Ibid.

[g] Statistics Canada, ''Provincial Economic Accounts,'' Catalog 13-201, Table 9, item 4. Includes other minor transfers as well.

[h,i] Ibid., Table 3, items 76 and 77 (excluding 4, above).

[j,k] Revenue Canada, *Taxation Statistics,* 1976.

[l] Statistics Canada, ''Provincial Economic Accounts,'' Catalog 13-213, Table 8, item 25.

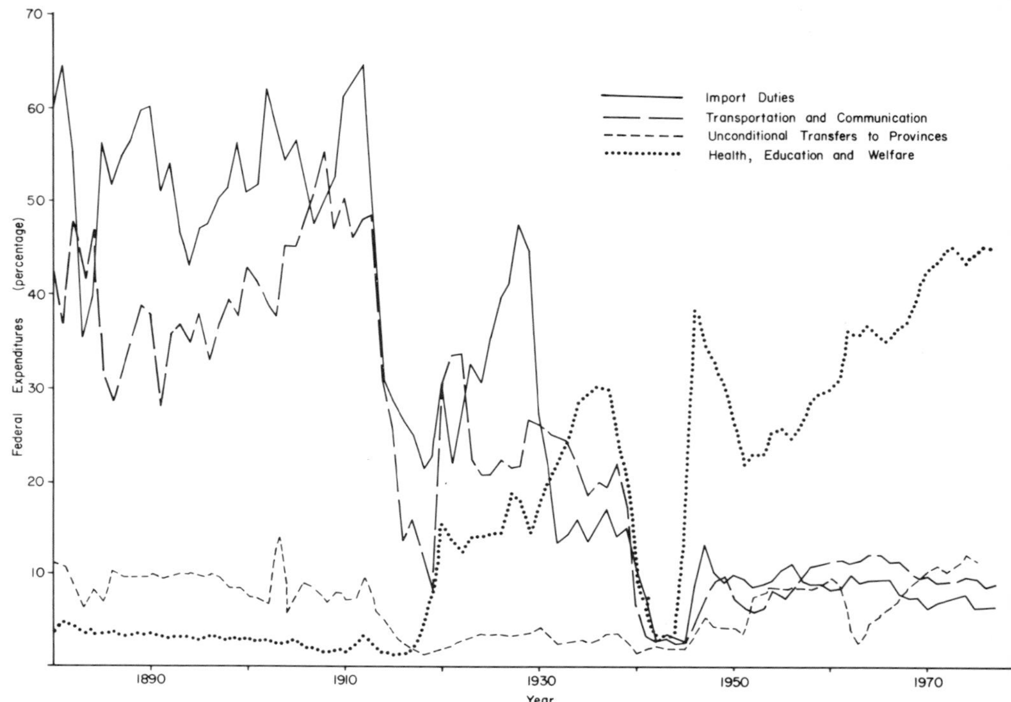

Fig. 2: Federal expenditures.

comparison to other governmental activities, amounting to an interprovincial range of only $125 (Table 4).

Nonetheless, the core of the urban system—the Quebec-Windsor manufacturing corridor—is clearly the beneficiary of the tariff in a redistributive sense. The two great metropolitan centres at the top of the urban hierarchy are particularly blessed—not only by the tariff on manufactured goods, but also by the complex of corporate, financial and communications regulations that require national financial institutions, information networks and head office activity, while permitting the spatial concentration of such activities within the urban system. The national banks, their location and the fluidity of capital movement that they represent, are clearly an outcome of public policy. The international corporate and financial linkages are channelled through the two largest centres. Without the national boundary, Toronto becomes indistinguishable from Buffalo or Cleveland or Milwaukee. The boundary effect need not always be positive: one can argue that the province of Quebec, by systematically restricting the interprovincial role of Montreal, has shaped that city's relative decline in the last decade.

By and large, the desire for the rapid development of the urban system, either nationally or regionally, leads to the opening of the system boundaries in various ways. A concern for temporal stability argues for more closure. An open primary economy such as Canada's generates high levels of variability in economic growth over space and time. Demographic, or financial, systems cannot respond as rapidly and may require immigration, or foreign investment, to provide the necessary population, or capital, redistribution. Immigrants are attracted directly to the region of economic growth, with fewer problems with distance and language barriers than native Canadians. The growth of the West in either the first wave (1896–1914) or the more recent surge (since 1973) could not be accomplished by internal migration alone, nor could the rapid decline of the Maritimes in the 1920's.

Canada's ability to control her boundaries has declined over time. Internal policies about tariffs or controls on investment are restricted by international agreement and economic reprisal.[7] Capital and information flow rapidly and easily from one nation to another. Emigration opportunities decline; traditional sources for immigration dry up.

As a result, Canada has moved towards a combination of boundary conditions that seem to be fraught with future difficulties for the urban system. A series of trade negotiations have lowered the tariff walls, while immigration restrictions have reduced the level of population mobility. As a result, the spatial variability of economic growth increases while the spatial variability of demographic growth declines. Will the process of internal migration be rapid enough to avoid severe regional surpluses and deficiencies in manpower? Can the language barrier be penetrated, or must there be separate economic development policies for francophones and anglophones? Will government have to play an even greater role in redistributing economic activity?

CONNECTING

Students of urban systems have paid more attention to the linkages within the system than to external relationships between the system and the rest of the world. The matrix of internal connections, such as transportation and communications, determines the relative accessibility of an urban centre to the rest of the system, hence the choice of its sources of input or destinations of output. Improvements in accessibility across the urban system as a whole lead to increased internal integration and trade, and the possibility of greater economic specialization, hence increased efficiency. In the process they also lead to increased urban concentrations, as McIntosh points out.[8]

Improved transportation systems leading to increased trade between two urban regions are not necessarily equally advantageous to both participants. A smaller centre may lose a localized trade monopoly while gaining access to a national market (which it may or may not be able to penetrate). Local economic stabilization is increased to the degree that the city can now serve a larger and therefore more regular and predictable market. Stabilization is decreased in the sense that the city may produce within only one or two industrial sectors instead of a variety. The smaller centre has substituted the uncertainty of a particular product market (such as automobiles) for the uncertainty of a particular regional market (such as southwestern Ontario). If increased internal trade and the specialization of local economies are the means of increasing overall national income, then government programmes to ensure regional stabilization may be a necessary cost in order to enable certain localities to specialize in highly cyclical industries.

Table 1 and Figure 2 indicate that the development and support of transportation and communication networks has been a significant government activity in Canada from the beginning. Transportation expenditures were the largest item in the federal budget up until the First World War; their apparent decline since that time simply reflects the expansion of the public sector into other spheres of activities as well as the transfer of many transportation/utility activities into crown corporations: the C.N.R., Air Canada, the C.B.C., provincial utilities, and most recently, the Post Office. As Buckley and Fowke have pointed out, the National Policy involved the integration and economic specialization of the urban system as well as tariffs and industrialization.[9]

The pervasive presence of government in the planning and financing of new transportation and communication linkages (Table 5) suggests that political systems may have a strong interest in the level of interdependence itself, as theories of political integration argue. Greater economic interaction and improved labour mobility tend to increase the allegiance to the national government and to weaken regional identity. Governments are particularly active in extending such networks from the core region into areas of low density and high isolation where the marginal returns, in an economic sense, may be very low, but the political returns may be considerable. In these areas, governments sell the illusion of regional development, coupled with the reality of outmigration. The overall result may be significant overinvestment in transportation infrastructure, as Buckley suggests. Canada, of course, has two levels of government competing for

TABLE 5

INVESTMENTS IN CONNECTING ACTIVITIES, 1976
(in millions)

Transportation		Utilities		Communications	
Air	$ 292 million	Grain Elev.	74 million	Broadcast	164 million
Rail	1,461	Electricity	4,622	Telephone	2,496
Water	196	Gas	229		
Road	415	Other	55	Total	2,685 (14.4 per cent)
Transit	401				
Pipelines	375	Total	4,996 (29.6 per cent)		
Total	3,162 (17.0 per cent)				

Institutions		Government Departments	
Church	62 million	Federal	1,265 million
University	244	Provincial	2,413
Schools	806	Municipal	2,329
Hospitals	526		
Other	103	Total	6,007 (32.3 per cent)
Total	1,741 (9.4 per cent)		

Source: Statistics Canada, "Private and Public Investment in Canada," Catalog 61-201, Tables 4 and 6. Both private and public investments are included.

citizens' allegiance, and both of them make substantial investments in transportation and utility systems.

Figure 3 presents an overview of public investment in Canada and its variation over time. First, note that capital expenditures are a relatively large and stable component of the economy, averaging about 20 per cent of the gross national product, except during the Depression and the Second World War. In the last thirty years, even the cyclical swings in investment have been relatively gentle. Second, the public sector—including crown corporations—presently accounts for one-third of this activity, a proportion that has increased slowly over time. To some extent public sector investment is countercyclical, increasing in proportion as the overall level of investment declines.

The map of new capital stock, particularly that invested in networks of connections, shapes the future geography of the urban system. Each year

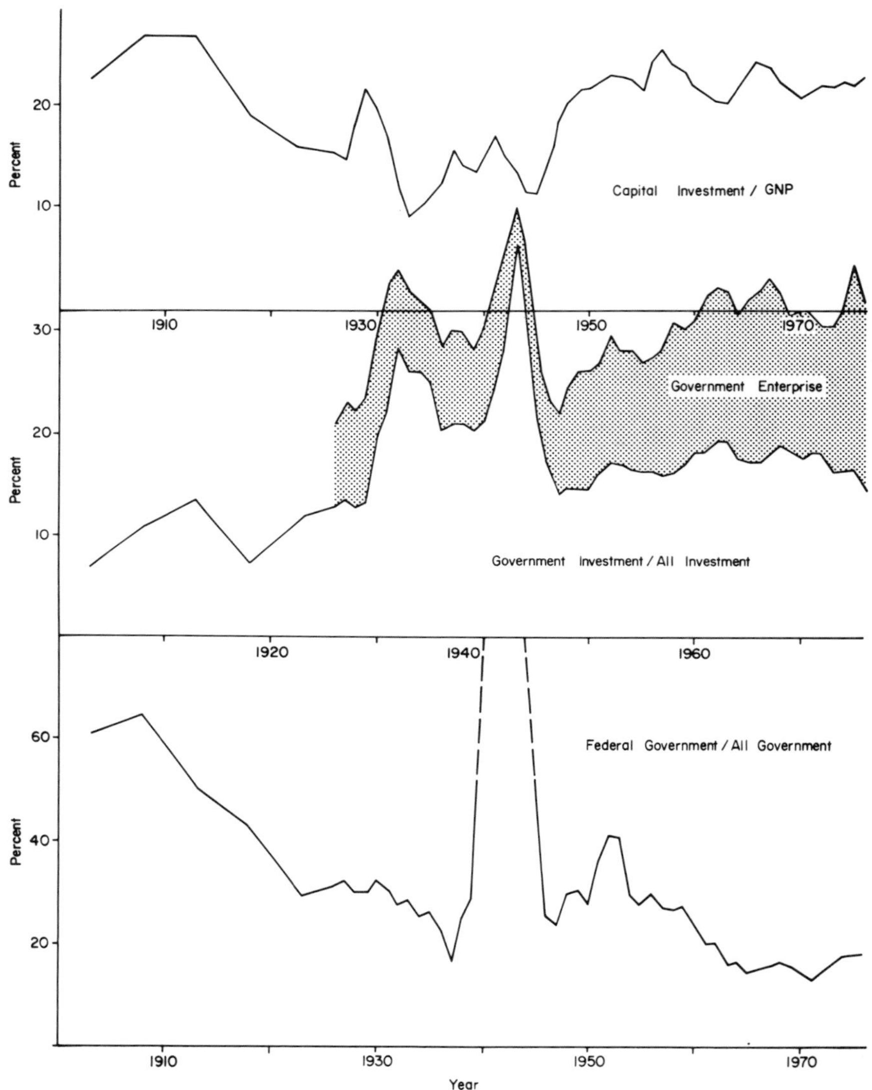

Fig. 3: Public investment in Canada.

an amount equal to 5 to 7 per cent of the existing (gross) capital stock in the country is added (or replaced). If the map of new investment resembles the map of existing capital stock, the system is maintaining itself. If the map of new investment is significantly different, the urban system is changing or evolving. The public sector component includes almost all the investment in transportation, communication and utility systems. Is it changing? Does it lead or lag the private sector? Does it generate growth in the short run (two years) or in the long run (ten years)? In a spatial sense, little is known at present.

The decline of the federal role in public investment in general and in transportation in particular was especially rapid in the first quarter of this century.[10] The significance for the urban system is revealed in Table 6, which shows that the higher the level of government (the larger the spatial jurisdiction), the greater the spatial variation that is possible. The federal government invests less than other governments, but the impact is more variable over space. For example, the ratio of the range in per capita provincial investments by the federal government to the national value was 1.64 in 1976, whereas the ratio for combined provincial and municipal investments was only 0.72. At the same time, significant provincial policy variations are evident in the table. Buckley states that between 1900 and 1930 the province of Ontario invested three to four times as much as the larger province of Quebec.

Historically, the geography of public investment has wavered between two goals. There are powerful internal political pressures to keep the urban system as it is: to reinforce the existing economic roles, patterns of access, and regional advantages of today's urban centres. The best examples here are the efforts to balance the growth of competing places: the relationships among the ports of Halifax, Saint John, and Montreal,[11] the level of federal government presence in Toronto and Montreal, or the allocation of provincial institutions to Regina and Saskatoon, Calgary and Edmonton.

But on occasion, external growth pressures are too large to be managed or diverted, and public initiatives must be taken to alter the urban system: actions that Aitken has described as "defensive expansionism."[12] New linkages are forged in the interdependence matrix, and new nodes emerge to challenge the older centres in order that the urban system as a whole may survive. In Canada, these external pressures come largely from the overwhelming presence of the United States, but war has also made a significant impact.

HOMOGENIZING

Homogenization refers to those government actions that impose a common way of life on all components of the spatial system. This includes programmes that provide certain services (the post office, the police) in all locations, grants to lower-tier governments and transfers to individuals that

TABLE 6

INVESTMENT IN INFRASTRUCTURE
(1976 dollars/capita)

A. Gross Capital Formation by Government Departments

1926[a]	Nfld.	PEI	NS	NB	QUE	ONT	MAN	SASK	ALTA	BC	CAN	range/ mean
Federal	–	9	10	12	4	30	4	7	11	29	16	1.81
Provincial	–	7	16	24	13	21	6	12	18	41	17	2.05
Municipal	–	–	–	–	–	–	–	–	–	–	33	–
Total		7	26	36	17	51	10	19	29	70	66	1.91
1948[a]												
Federal	27	57	59	44	10	20	38	12	51	53	28	1.68
Provincial	{38	55	64	75	44	35	43	40	61	96	54	{1.19
Municipal		2	23	10	12	32	38	39	52	42	30	
Total	65	114	144	139	66	87	119	91	164	191	112	1.13
1976[b]												
Federal	54	34	101	30	42	37	54	112	71	48	50	1.64
Provincial*	235	144	121	227	95	80	80	162	158	125	110	{
Municipal	49	17	69	97	125	104	109	27	152	143	116	0.72
Total**	348	195	291	355	262	222	243	401	381	315	227	0.74

B.[c] Total Public Investment (Capital and Repairs)

	731	356	614	877	659	537	901	962	792	742	667	0.91

C.[d] Public and Private Investment by Sector

Transport/ Utilities	434	169	309	560	426	283	699	462	732	618	472	1.19
Institutions	129	84	104	120	80	49	68	89	80	111	76	1.05
Govt. Dept.**	328	254	239	344	219	238	238	329	360	296	261	0.54
Total	891	508	641	1024	749	552	1023	847	1171	1024	809	0.87

* includes hospitals

** roughly equivalent measure: different sources

[a] Canada, Department of Trade and Commerce, *Private and Public Investment in Canada, 1926–1951*. Tables 89, 97 and 115.

[b] Statistics Canada, ''*Provincial Economic Accounts,*'' Catalog 13-213, Table 3, items 94–98.

[c] Statistics Canada, ''Private and Public Investment in Canada,'' Catalog 61-201, Table 7, item D.

[d] Ibid, Tables 11 to 19.

subsidize living standards in low-income areas, as well as regulatory provisions that require uniform levels of wages, environmental controls, housing or business procedures. While these effects may appear to fly in the face of the economic specialization engendered by increased integration, the local economic base directly affects fewer and fewer workers each year. The emphasis in the modern urban system is on a common pattern of working conditions, take-home pay, and lifestyle in all sectors and at all locations. The goal is to reduce the political stress of regional inequality. Homogenization policies are part of the price paid for such urban system development initiatives as tariff modifications or infrastructure investments.

This role of government is comparatively recent, as Figure 3 suggests. Although modest federal-provincial grants have existed since the very first decade of Confederation, it is within the last quarter-century that equalization payments and provincial grants to municipalities—direct spatial transfers from the well-to-do to the impoverished—began to expand rapidly (perhaps not independently of the intensification of communications linkages).[13] The formal commitments to equalization of the provincial tax base followed the Rowell-Sirois studies of 1937–40, but full implementation did not take place until the mid-1950's. In recent years, the continuing negotiations about these transfers between federal governments and provinces have become critical to the development path of the urban system, with substantial proportions of federal income involved (see Table 4). The negotiated transfers from the federal government to the provinces have become side-payments that can overcome jurisdictional conflicts (as in the energy domain) or offset development strategies that concentrate growth at a limited number of locations (as with megaprojects). The Atlantic provinces have become highly dependent on federal largesse, as Table 7 indicates, but smaller centres throughout the urban system benefit substantially as well. The combined effects of taxes, transfer, and public services reduce interurban income disparities by about one-quarter.

Efforts by the federal government either to generate new regional growth initiatives or to compensate areas of decline run directly into the powers and activities of provincial jurisdictions that attempt to enforce their own standards. Provincial governments argue that public activities tailored to suit a particular region can avoid substantial political externalities (that is, the costs of providing residents wtih more or less public goods than they really wish to have, given the price they have to pay in taxes). Over time, many of these jurisdictional conflicts have been resolved in favour of the national government, reflecting the increased spatial externalities created by growing economic and demographic interdependence. Nonetheless, one of the notable features of Figure 1 is the increasing role of subnational

TABLE 7

DIRECT REDISTRIBUTION BY THE PUBLIC SECTOR, 1976
(Dollars Per Capital)

1. *Income tax, Federal and Provincial*

	Vancouver	Winnipeg	Toronto	Montreal	Halifax	Total
Order 4,5	$ 1152	949	1132	1038	775	1054
3	961	822	908	621	572	817
2	939	492	765	427	538	744
1	882	684	664	367	453	655
Total	1034	842	875	897	567	798

2. *Transfer Payments*

	Vancouver	Winnipeg	Toronto	Montreal	Halifax	Total
Order 4,5	242	143	221	205	221	292
3	289	149	255	299	338	254
2	227	214	297	273	345	280
1	274	186	315	337	719	298
Total	249	163	250	246	427	215

3. *Wages of Government Employees*

	Vancouver	Winnipeg	Toronto	Montreal	Halifax	Total
Order 4,5	826	906	667	972	1062	753
3	1473	826	550	1312	665	671
2	740	720	641	764	681	705
1	730	767	550	487	937	607
Total	864	849	628	894	654	755

4. *Net Benefits** (Items 2 + 3 – 1)

	Vancouver	Winnipeg	Toronto	Montreal	Halifax	Total
Order 4,5	–81	101	–189	142	508	–61
3	801	153	–100	122	403	111
2	24	341	172	230	486	242
1	121	270	201	230	786	244
Total	81	169	–98	170	447	99

* The net benefits are positive because of the partial nature of the revenues and expenditures recorded here.

Source: James W. Simmons, "The Impact of Government on the Canadian Urban System: Income Taxes, Transfer Payments and Employment" *Research Paper No. 126.* These values are computed for urban-centred regions, grouped by size (orders 4,5 are the largest) and by region, as defined by the principle regional centres. Vancouver includes B.C. and the Yukon. Winnipeg is the prairies plus N.W.T.; Toronto is Ontario except for the Ottawa Valley and the Lakehead. Montreal is Quebec plus the Ottawa Valley and francophone New Brunswick.

governments during the postwar era. As a result, the spatial redistribution of a growing share of taxes, of government services, and of infrastructure investment takes place among intraprovincial locations. Considering the range of alternative locations in terms of any economic measure of disparity that exists within provinces such as New Brunswick or Alberta makes evident the problem implied by this trend. The poor provinces have no rich urban areas, the rich provinces have no poor ones, and only the federal government can transfer funds across the border. The provincial boundaries have become profound geographical factors in their own right, owing to the ability of the provinces such as Alberta and Saskatchewan to redistribute income and economic growth within their own boundaries but not across them.

Gillespie showed that provincial and, especially, municipal governments tend to be much less progressive in terms of income redistribution than the federal government.[14] As the role of these levels of government increases, the ability of the urban system to manage variations in growth and economic development declines. In theory, the appropriate spatial scale for redistribution (and stabilization) activities should reflect the spatial scale of variation in growth rates. If the predominant variation is interregional (East versus West), the federal government should respond; but if growth and income variations reflect the urban size hierarchy—or at least rural/urban differences—the problem should come under provincial jurisdiction. One can argue that the increased economic productivity that led to the surge of urbanization in the post-Second World War era required the rapid growth in compensatory services to rural areas that Crowley has identified.[15]

STABILIZING

The notion of economic stabilization at a regional level has received little attention in the literature, but it provides an important justification for overall increases in public sector activity, particularly as high levels of international trade and sectoral specialization place local economies at the mercy of uncertain world markets. The argument goes as follows: public sector employment and transfers to individuals (or to municipal jurisdictions in order to subsidize public services) provide a stable local economic base that is largely independent of variations in the local value of production. For instance, the performance of the auto industry is highly cyclical, affecting the level of income in specialized production centres, whereas government pension payments are as regular as clockwork. Both production workers and pensioners place money in the hands of local services and thereby support the local economy. The one source is highly irregular; the other is very predictable. Public expenditures are more closely related to *demographic* change than to *economic* change.

If transfer payments and public employment tend to level out the uncertainties in the local economy, income taxes and unemployment benefits are even more corrective. They draw extra sums out of the local economy in times of prosperity and insert subsidies when times are tough. Such schemes work well on the Canadian periphery where the space-economy is strongly differentiated, with regions following cyclical patterns that are largely independent of one another. The places that boom subsidize those that bust at any particular time.

What is remarkable in recent times is the magnitude of the various government expenditures that stabilize local economies. The growth in government activity revealed in Figure 1 has brought about a situation in which the equivalent of 40 per cent of the gross national product reflects the temporal and spatial rhythms of the public sector. This activity is either countercyclical or at least neutral. Figure 2 shows the degree to which this growth in expenditure has occurred in social welfare payments that are oriented to demographic characteristics rather than economic growth or growth potential. The result is both a net redistribution towards slow-growth, low income areas and a levelling out of the peaks and valleys of the economic cycles that characterize those urban places that produce a single product for an uncertain external market.

The impact of these stabilizing activities is shown for Saskatchewan in Figure 4. Government expenditures are shown beneath the axis; private sector activities, above it. The economic base in this case—net farm income—is extremely erratic over time, though part of it is absorbed by income tax variations. Government activity, in contrast, is highly stable and maintains a reasonably regular provincial economy.

Again, the stabilizing role of government is relatively recent and is almost a by-product of other public sector activities. The necessity arises from the concentration of economic activity in primary commodities and in urban areas that are vulnerable to cyclical fluctuations. Government programmes have replaced the mixed (or subsistence) family farm as a cushion in hard times. The explosion of stabilizing programmes in the postwar period coincided with the final severance of most Canadians from their rural base.

The stabilization activities of government take place over time as well as space, and, as Davis shows, redistribution mechanisms can be financed as readily from debt as from taxation.[16] In this way, regional stabilization policies become linked to the stabilization of the national economy using debt ratios, interest levels, exchange rates and so forth, especially as

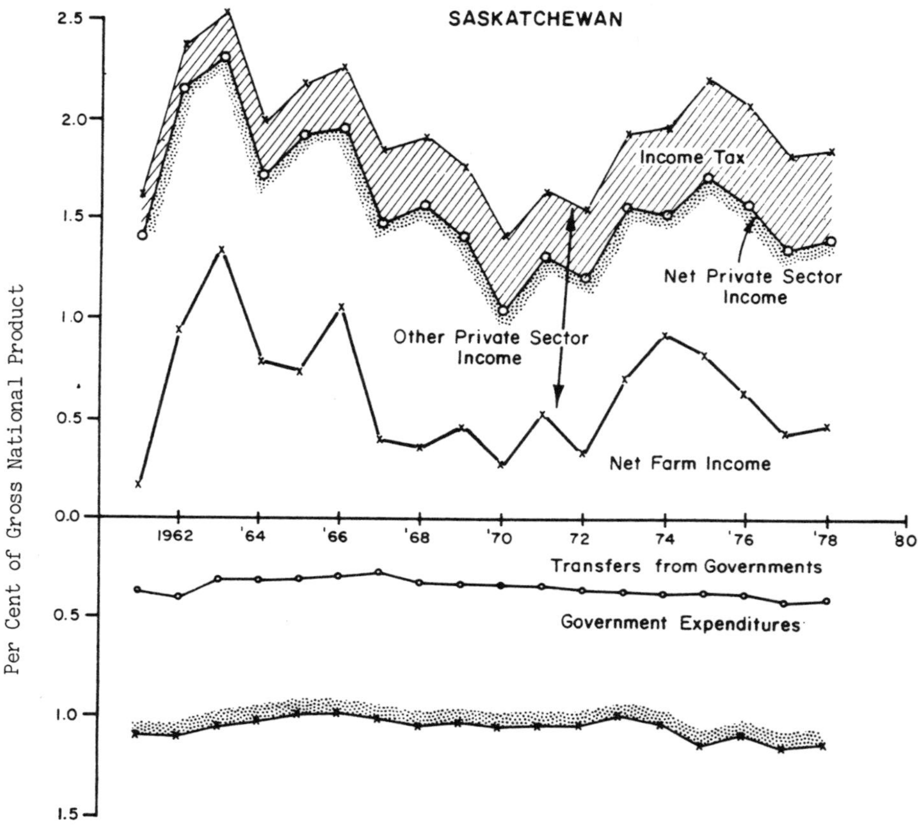

Fig. 4: Public- and private-sector activity in Saskatchewan.

redistribution programmes have come to dominate public sector expenditures. It is worth noting, though, that current public indebtedness (expressed as per cent of the gross national prouduct) is unlikely to approach the level of the railway era or of the Second World War.

CONCLUSIONS

The various activities of the public sector are enormously important for the urban system. The spatial variation across the system is both the rationale for government action and the effect of that intervention. In

Canada, these public sector activities are both large and diverse, penetrating almost every aspect of the urban system. One cannot really understand the evolution of either the urban system or the public sector without understanding the other.

To summarize the arguments:

1. Urban systems process streams of inputs varying over space and time. Economic and demographic processes differ considerably in their patterns of response.
2. While many different mechanisms mediate between the imbalances between economic and demographic change (such as famine, migration, loans or welfare payments), the public sector has played an increasing role over the last century.
3. In this sense the public sector intervenes between the external economic impulses that affect the urban system and the impacts of these impulses on particular urban nodes.
4. Those external impulses that are perceived to be of short duration and/or of local impact are resisted or dispersed gradually over space and time. Those of great magnitude or lasting impact may generate system-changing development initiatives by the public sector.
5. As particular places within the urban system have become more specialized, more interdependent, and more vulnerable to external shocks, the public sector has responded by adding new programmes to cope with the variations in growth across the urban system and over time.
6. The bounding activities of the public sector control the nature and magnitude of external impulses permitted into the urban system. In the past, Canada has chosen to restrict certain kinds of economic shocks by means of tariffs while encouraging internal demographic adjustments by means of immigration and emigration.
7. Tariffs define a national market, which in turn requires a national network of transportation, utilities, and communications linkages. These activities are often spatially conservative, maintaining the structure of the existing system but occasionally respond directly to the external impulses.
8. The specialization in economic base that results from the activities of bounding and connecting may lead to unacceptable variations in growth, income or lifestyle. Homogenizing activities impose a common social environment across the system, using grants, transfers, public services, and regulation.
9. The provinces present an increasing barrier to homogeneity as their

role relative to the federal government increases. The level of services (or taxes) available at an urban centre is a function of the set of other urban places with which it is grouped by means of a provincial boundary.

10. Over time, the overall impact of the public sector has become more spatially conservative as homogenization and stabilization activities have grown more rapidly than development expenditures.
11. The stabilization (gross) activities of government are much more significant to the urban system than the spatial redistribution (net). The enormous financial resources of governments and the spatial and temporal inertia of their activities, as well as explicit negative feedbacks slow down the effects of rapid economic change.
12. The different aspects of government intervention into the urban system are closely intermeshed, but it is of interest to try and understand how programmes lean to development and then shift to stabilization: to pursue issues of national growth and then to address the difficulties of disparities and localized uncertainty. A model of the political process should reflect the priorities and coalitions of spatial interest groups.
13. The model should also focus on the way groups of programmes are packaged into complexes of costs and benefits that simultaneously satisfy many different demands.
14. Without venturing too far into the counterfactual, one can argue that the actions of government have a) increased the urban/rural ratio, b) accelerated the growth of the largest cities, c) maintained a balance between competing regional centres, d) strengthened east-west linkages, e) increased the specialization of the economic base of cities, f) generated the industrial corridor, g) reduced interurban income disparities, and h) reduced the variance in urban growth rates in time and space.

The notion of a spatial system, with each place dependent on the others, coupled with the knowledge that every governmental action modifies the spatial system in some fashion, opens the door to an enormous variety of nation-building policies and processes carried out in the public sector. The urban system is not only man-made; it is collectively shaped. In this sense one of the most important attributes of an urban place is the set of collectivities, state, nation, or empire, to which it belongs. Perhaps nowhere is this better demonstrated than in Newfoundland. A recent study documents the enormous impact of Confederation, of provincial investment decisions, of international fishing agreements, of unemployment benefits and alternative petroleum development schemes.[17] The rest of the country differs only in degree.

A UNITED STATES COMPARISON

Without a public sector, the Canadian urban system would be fundamentally different.[18] Can the same be said for the United States? The lack of literature directly addressing the topic suggests not, but a brief exploration reveals similar patterns of public sector intervention. In fact, the papers by Mercer and Goldberg and by Babcock in this volume argue that government in the United States, although it works in different ways, is equally important for urban development. The magnitude of intervention is similar, but there are some significant differences in jurisdictional responsibilities and in conventions about the public and private spheres. The following discussion applies the typology used above.

Perhaps the major differences in the two urban systems is the lesser importance of *bounding* in the United States. The size and self-sufficiency of the American economy (until the events of OPEC and the Japanese invasion of the last decade) have generated conventional economic feedbacks in the urban system. The importance of the public sector has been more apparent in immigration policies: first the open door, then the closed, and more recently illegal entrants from Latin countries, with each stage having major implications for regional growth.

Goodrich has thoroughly documented the major *connecting* role of government in the canal/railroad era, a story that could be brought up to date using the Interstate system, the railway reorganization, and airline regulation/deregulation.[19] The spatial significance arises from the shift from predominantly state and local investments in the antebellum stage towards an increasing federal role. Clark has traced a similar evolution from local to national markets through the courts, as state restrictions on commerce were systematically broken down.[20] The greater degree of closure in the U.S. economy increased the need for internal interdependence in trade.

Homogenization occurs by means of transportation and communication facilities, the national market and national media; but also by direct government intervention. Since the Second World War, a very powerful relationship has existed between the net federal transfers to a state and the rate of that state's economic growth.[21] Federal money flows South and West, bringing about a rapid convergence in per capita income across the country. The U.S. differs from Canada in that the federal government negotiates directly with cities and regions within states, and such programmes have been part of both "the New Deal" and the "Great Society." In part, the long-term convergence of regional disparities in the U.S. can be thought of as a recovery from a major trauma to the American urban system—the Civil War—that combined accelerated industrial growth in the North with widespread economic dislocation in the South.

A nation that produces for its own market is less troubled with regional stabilization. Instead, the problem is seen in terms of variations in the amplitude of the same business cycle. Yet in the primary producing areas of the U.S., pressures for marketing controls, subsidies and stockpiles are as strong as they are in Canada.

The public sector is important in both urban systems, but similar problems lead to different solutions. What is missing from both is a logic of when and where and why, and in what form governmental intervention will occur in a spatial system.

NOTES

1. W. L. Easterbrook and M. H. Watkins, ''Introduction,'' in *Approaches to Canadian Economic History,* (Toronto: McClelland and Stewart, 1967), p. xiv.
2. For example, John Borchert, ''American Metropolitan Evolution,'' *Geographical Review,* 57 (July 1967): 301–32; David Ward, *Cities and Immigrants: The Geography of Change in Nineteenth Century America* (New York: Oxford University Press, 1971); Allen R. Pred, *City Systems in Developed Economies* (New York: John Wiley and Sons, 1977); and Michael P. Conzen, ''The American Urban System in the Nineteenth Century,'' in D. T. Herbert and R. J. Johnson, eds., *Geography and the Urban Environment,* vol. 4 (London: John Wiley and Sons, 1981), pp. 295–347.
3. A brief description of the Canadian urban system is provided in James W. Simmons, ''The Evolution of the Canadian Urban System,'' in A. F. J. Artibise and G. A. Stelter, eds. *The Usable Urban Past,* (Toronto: Macmillan, 1979), pp. 9–33.
4. These matrices are described in a series of more technical papers: James W. Simmons and Patrick Flanagan, ''The Movement of Growth Impulses through the Canadian Urban System,'' *Research Paper No. 120* (Toronto: University of Toronto, 1981); James W. Simmons, ''Changing Migration Patterns in Canada: 1966–1976 to 1971–1976,'' *Canadian Journal of Regional Science* 3 (August 1980): 139–62; and James W. Simmons, ''The Impact of Government in the Canadian Urban System: Income Taxes, Transfer Payments and Employment,'' *Research Paper No. 126* (Toronto: University of Toronto, 1981).
5. See M. G. Termote and R. Frechette, ''La renversement recent des courants migratoires entre les provinces Canadiennes: essai d'interpretation,'' *Canadian Journal of Regional Science* 3 (Autumn 1980): 117–38; and Stanley Winer and Denis Gauthier, *Internal Migration and Fiscal Structure* (Ottawa: Economic Council of Canada, 1982).

6. Richard M. Bird, *The Growth of Government Spending in Canada,* (Toronto: The Canadian Tax Foundation, 1970).
7. Stephen Clarkson has recently documented some of these constraints: *Canada and the Reagan Challenge,* (Ottawa: Canadian Institute for Public Policy, 1981).
8. W. A. McIntosh, *The Economic Background of Dominion-Provincial Relations,* (Toronto: McClelland and Stewart, 1939).
9. See Kenneth Buckley, *Capital Formation in Canada, 1896–1930,* (Toronto: McClelland and Stewart, 1955); and Vernon C. Fowke, *The National Policy and the Wheat Economy* (Toronto: University of Toronto Press, 1957). Michael Bliss disputes whether these simultaneous activities were undertaken consciously, but not the results. ''The Evolution of Industrial Policies in Canada: An Historical Survey,'' *Discussion Paper No. 218* (Ottawa: Economic Council of Canada, 1982).
10. Buckley, *Capital Formation in Canada,* and Canada, Department of Trade and Commerce, *Public and Private Investment in Canada, 1926–1951* (Ottawa, 1951).
11. See, for example, Charles N. Forward, ''The Development of Canada's Five Leading Ports,'' *Urban History Review* 10 (February 1982): 25–46.
12. A truly Canadian approach to the challenge of the frontier: Hugh G. J. Aitken, *The State and Economic Growth,* (New York: Social Science Research Council, 1959).
13. The roots, magnitude and function of these transfers are discussed in D. P. L. Auld and F. C. Miller, *Principles of Public Finance: A Canadian Text* (Toronto: Methuen, 1977); and Robert J. Bennett, *The Geography of Public Finance* (London: Methuen, 1980).
14. G. Irwin Gillespie, *The Redistribution of Income in Canada* (Toronto: Gage, 1980).
15. Ronald J. Crowley, ''Provincial-Municipal Grants: Estimates of Intercounty Income Redistribution through Ontario's Grant Programme in 1961,'' *Canadian Journal of Economics* 4 (February 1971): 61–77.
16. J. Tait Davis, ''Government-Directed Money Flows and the Discordance between Production and Consumption in Provincial Economies,'' *Canadian Geographer* 26 (Spring 1982): 1–20.
17. Economic Council of Canada, *Newfoundland: From Dependency to Self-Reliance* (Ottawa: 1980).
18. The one dissent to this view is that of Bliss, ''Evolution of Industrial Policies,'' but his point is closer to the one that is developed below: that the role of the state in Canada's economic history, while important, was not necessarily greater than that of the other countries. See also his ''Rich by Nature, Poor by Policy: The State and Economic Life in Canada,'' in R. W. Canty and W. P. Ward, eds. *Entering the Eighties: Canada in Crisis* (Toronto: University of Toronto Press, 1980).
19. Goodrich suggests that about 70 and 30 per cent of antebellum canal and

railway investments, respectively, came from the public purse: *Government Promotion of American Canals and Railroads, 1800–1890* (New York: Columbia University Press, 1960). See also Carter Goodrich, ed., *Canals and American Economic Development* (New York: Columbia University Press, 1961). For a more recent view, see Lloyd I. Mercer, *Railroads and Land Grants Policy: A Study in Government Intervention* (New York: Academic Press, 1982).

20. Gordon L. Clark, "Law, State and the Spatial Integration of the United States," *Environment and Planning, A* 13 (1981): 1197–232.
21. A recent study does an impressive job of assembling historical materials on the convergence of economic development in the U.S. and on the role of federal expenditures in this process: The Advisory Commission on Intergovernmental Relations, *Regional Growth: Historic Perspectives,* Part I, and *Regional Growth: Flows of Federal Funds* Part II (Washington: Government Printing Office, 1980).
22. Wilbur Thompson describes the U.S. problem: *A Preface to Urban Economics* (Baltimore: Johns Hopkins Press, 1965).

3

Private vs. Public Enterprise: A Comparison of Two Atlantic Seaboard Cities, 1850–1925

Robert H. Babcock

A generation ago, when the American historical experience was widely believed to offer lessons for newly emerging Third World nations, economic historians began to analyze the role of public enterprise in America's economic development. They challenged directly the notion that private enterprise had been solely responsible for America's prosperity, arguing instead that federal, state, and local governments had adopted deliberate policies to promote economic growth in the decades before the Civil War. Public enterprise (a varying mixture of public capital, strategic planning, or management) commanded widespread support, meshed with popular democratic principles in nineteenth century America and was justified by its contribution to the welfare of the community rather than for making a profit. An unrestrained booster mentality, historians found, prompted Americans to open their public coffers to promoters who promised instant prosperity when their development schemes were completed. States and cities built bridges, canals, turnpikes, and railways, loaned money, educated workers, and enacted laws to spur economic development. These government-assisted projects probably accelerated the urbanization process by helping cities to extend and consolidate control over their hinterland regions. But urban historians have only recently begun to explore the direct effects of public policies on American cities.[1]

By contrast, the role of the public sector in Canada, as James Simmons has noted elsewhere in this volume, continues to receive heavy emphasis in analyses of economic development. The debate among economic historians has centred upon the origins of Canadian public enterprise and its impact upon the country's development. Hugh Aitken argued some years ago that government involvement resulted from the greater vulnerability of Canada's staples economy; it was "designed to forestall, counteract, or restrain the northward extension of American economic and political influence.''[2] Ottawa assumed responsibility for strategies of economic development and provided the capital and sometimes the management, while local businessmen devised the tactics to implement government plans. Kenneth McRae agreed with Aitken that state activity in Canada ''has always been decided upon pragmatic . . . grounds,'' but others have stressed ideological determinants. S. M. Lipset implied that a conservative political culture derived from Canada's Loyalist heritage sanctioned the growth of a positive state, and Gad Horowitz and George Grant have agreed that this ''Tory touch'' was a key reason for government intervention into the Canadian economy.[3] Herschel Hardin has attempted to fuse these two approaches by inflating both the ''Tory touch'' and Aitken's ''defensive expansion'' into a fullblown Canadian public enterprise ''culture'' which he believes is the most important part of the contemporary Canadian national identity, if only Canadians would acknowledge it.

> General Motors and Coca-Cola and the other great ''private'' corporations symbolize the American way of life. The great public enterprises in transportation and communication symbolize the independent, creative Canadian spirit.[4]

Others have debated the relative costs and benefits of government intervention in the Canadian economy. Hardin has found predictable support from nationalists on the left who ardently defended the Trudeau government's takeover of a portion of the Canadian oil industry.[5] On the other side, Michael Bliss concluded recently that Canadians have become addicted to government intervention not because of any proven benefits, but as a result of an evolving nationalist ideology which serves to justify intervention by the state.[6]

A new series of books on the state and economic life in Canada reflects the greater interest in these questions north of the 49th parallel.[7] Reviewing the first three volumes of this series, Douglas McCalla questions the assumption that the Canadian state played an unusually extensive role in the economic development of Canada, noting that few if any empirical or comparative studies ever have been undertaken. If the staples economy was more vulnerable, he says, then ''the precise nature and degree of that extra vulnerability over the normal uncertainties of economic life'' have rarely been delineated. McCalla also cautions against the tendency to impose a rationality and consistency in decision-making where it never existed. To him these books suggest that Canadian public enterprise policy was ''determined by economic life far more than the reverse.''[8]

Following McCalla's suggestion, this essay compares the origins and impact of public enterprise on port development in a Canadian and an

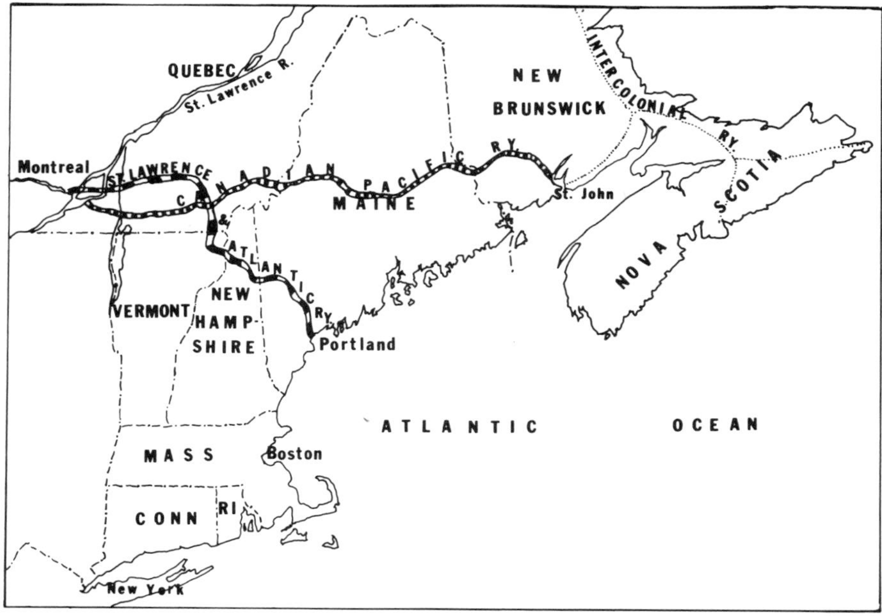

Fig. 1: Eastern Canada and New England.

American city. Both Saint John, New Brunswick, and Portland, Maine were close to trans–Atlantic shipping lanes; both developed rail connections into the North American interior; and the two cities became rivals for Canada's winter port trade during those months when the St. Lawrence River was frozen. Portland was closer to Montreal by land, but Saint John was nearer by sea to Liverpool. Contributions from private and public sources obtained by merchant and civic elites pursuing their economic development strategies are compared and their effects evaluated. In order to assess the impact of differing institutional contexts, the political processes through which public aid was garnered will also be compared. If the "Tory touch" is a key to understanding Canada's public enterprise "culture," it ought to surface in the preeminently Loyalist city of Saint John.

The evidence presented here shows that both cities relied upon a mixture of public and private enterprise to develop their ocean terminals. Although the Canadians invested greater amounts of public capital in Saint John's port facilities than various American governments spent on Portland's waterfront (about $16.5 million compared to about $5.1 million, exclusive of shipping subsidies), this difference is better explained through an examination of the local economic and political contexts rather than by attributing public involvement to amorphous cultural determinants. A series of decisions originating among local elites shaped both the patterns of public spending and the outcome of the two cities' rivalry for Canada's winter port trade. Consequently, it seems reductionist to argue that these two portions of Canada and the United States, at least, were irrevocably divided by "cultures" of private and public enterprise.

Both private and public enterprise contributed to making Portland the winter port of Canada in the middle of the nineteenth century. An American law in 1845 permitted foreign goods to move in bond through the U.S., allowing Portland to take advantage of its geographical proximity to Montreal. Under the leadership of a dynamic Maine lawyer and promoter, John A. Poor, Portland and Montreal interests completed a railway between the two cities in 1853, which was promptly leased to the Grand Trunk Railway of Canada. The connection would make Portland "the easiest, cheapest, and most expeditious outlet," Poor anticipated, "for the trade that accumulated at Chicago seeking the European market."[9] While New York City's canal and railways already had garnered the largest share of that business, Poor clearly expected the Chicago-to-Portland trackage of the Grand Trunk to dislodge New York as a favoured route into the interior. In December of 1853, the English steamer *Sarah Sands* arrived in Portland harbour to inaugurate a regular weekly service to Liverpool that was subsidized by an annual grant of 50,000 from the Province of Canada. Poor redesigned Portland's waterfront, focusing the attention of local elites for the first time on their harbour as the key to their prosperity. Later, the city spent $60,000 to construct two large piers for Britain's monster steamer, the *Great Eastern,* with the Grand Trunk adding another $25,000. The Army Corps of Engineers began to dredge Portland harbour and sped construction of a breakwater. After the Civil War, city fathers put up over $3 million in public funds to build additional railways to the "golden" West.[10] In all of these endeavours, Poor, his colleagues, and successors blended private with public capital to underwrite Portland's development as a major North American port.

Nevertheless, the volume of trade passing through Portland did not always live up to expectations. Severe competition with New York City and Boston, coupled with a chronic imbalance between imports and exports at Portland, forced the Grand Trunk to slash its rates in the late 1860's. An improvement in the volume of trade in the early 1880's was followed by a sharp decline toward the end of the century. For example, in 1886–87 nearly forty steamers called at the Maine city, but only sixteen ships were booked for the 1896–97 winter season. The downturn resulted from depression conditions and from Portland's inadequate terminal; the grain

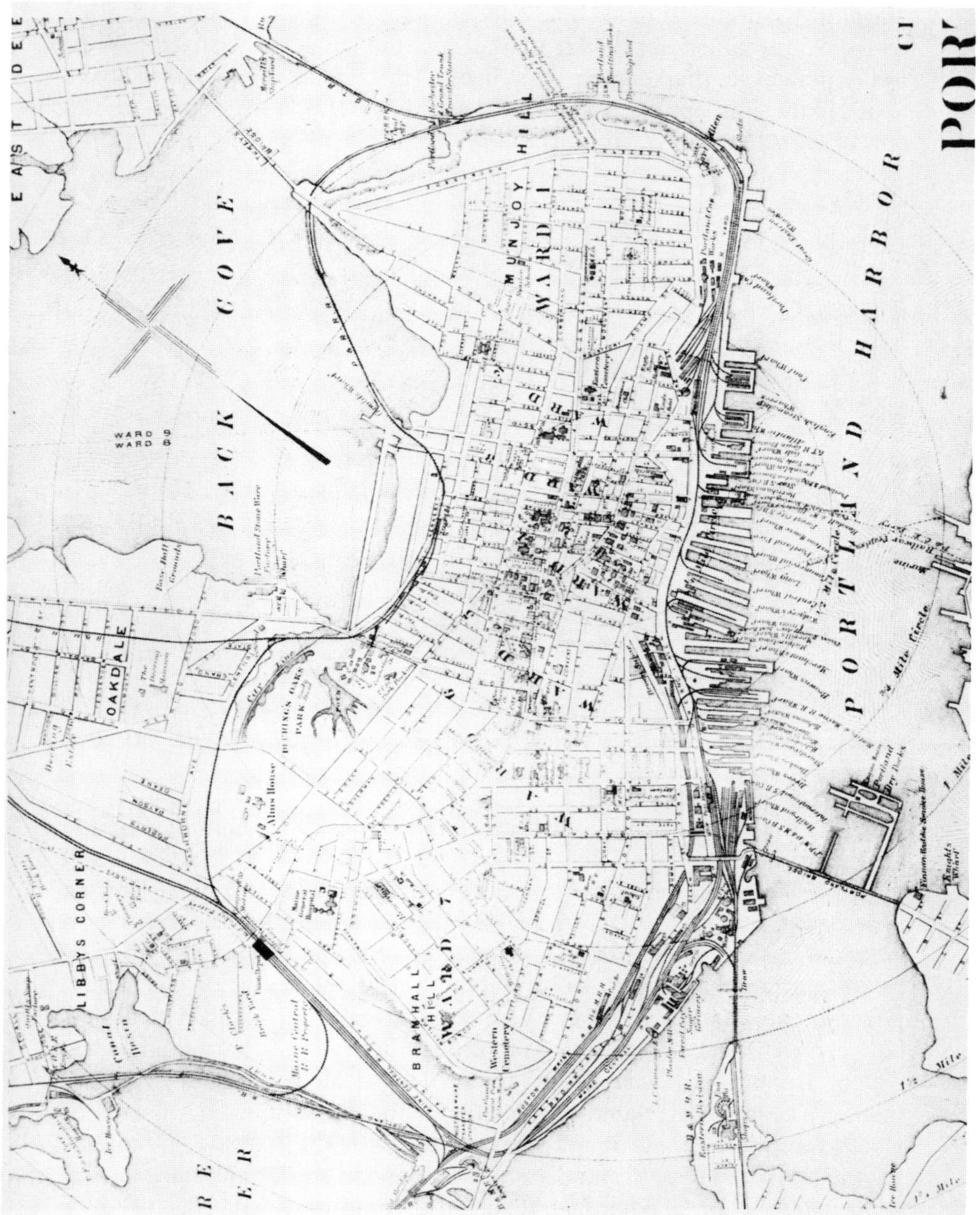

*Fig. 2: Map of Portland, Maine, 1901 (*source: Stuart's Atlas of the State of Maine, *1901).*

elevator, for instance, could load only one ship per week. The slow decline of the South American timber market and the sudden decision by West Indies planters to market their sugar in cloth bags rather than wooden boxes added to the port's problems. Portland merchants appointed a committee to confer with the Grand Trunk Railway.[11]

Fig. 3: Grain elevator of the Grand Trunk Railway Company, Portland (source: *Maine Historical Society*).

Revealing a perceptible shift from earlier tactics, the committee did not take the problem to city or state officials, perhaps because Portland was still paying interest and principal on nearly a million dollars in bonds for the now bankrupt western railways.[12] While recognizing the need for port enlargement and modernization, Portland's elites had apparently decided by the turn of the century to rely upon the private sector or the federal government. The U.S. government spent over a half a million dollars between 1870 and 1896 (Table 1) to dredge Portland Harbor and adjacent waters. But the entire waterfront remained in private hands, and no federal money was made available to upgrade Portland's antiquated wharves or warehouses. The Grand Trunk spent a mere $40,000 in 1886 to rebuild its wharf, and the Maine Central Railroad financed hardly any harbour improvements at all.[13] What had begun in the mid-nineteenth century as a mixed undertaking had become an almost exclusively private responsibility.

TABLE 1

UNITED STATES FEDERAL GOVERNMENT EXPENDITURES FOR PORTLAND HARBOR, 1836–1917

Year	Purpose	Amount
1836	breakwater	$ 10,000.
1837	breakwater	25,000.
1838	breakwater	26,366.
1866	dredging, breakwater	105,111.05
1870	improving harbor	10,000.
1871	improving harbor	40,000.
1872	improving Portland harbor, Back Bay	45,000.
1873	improving harbor	50,000.
1874	improving harbor	20,000.
1875	improving harbor	20,000.
1881	improving harbor	20,000.
1882	improving harbor	35,000.
1884	improving harbor	30,000.
1886	improving harbor	30,000.
	Back Cove	26,250.
1888	improving harbor	40,000.
	Back Cove	25,000.
1890	improving harbor	40,000.
	Back Cove	25,000.
1892	improving harbor	30,000.
	Back Cove	20,000.
1894	Back Cove	20,000.
1896	improving harbor & Back Cove	20,000.
1897	improving harbor & Back Cove	350,000.
1898	improving harbor & Back Cove	200,000.
1901	improving harbor & Back Cove	21,000.
1905	Fore River & Back Cove	100,000.
1906	Fore River & Back Cove	80,000.
1907	Fore River & Back Cove	59,000.
1912	anchorage basin and Back Cove	100,000.
1913	anchorage basin and Back Cove	150,000.
1914	anchorage basin and Back Cove	105,000.
1915	anchorage basin and Back Cove	105,000.
1917	improving harbor	300,000.
	Total	$2,282,727.05

Source: Table E-1, Maine State Harbor Commission, *Report Upon the Advisability of Building a Public Pier at Portland* (Augusta, 1919), p. 76.

Merchant and civic elites had adopted an economic development strategy based upon the city's proximity to Montreal and on its potential as an ocean terminal for British North America during the winter months. During the initial start-up phase in the 1850's and 1860's, Poor and his colleagues had organized a mixture of private and public capital to construct railways and create port facilities. Long after his death, John Poor's vision still captured the imagination of city elites. But after the economic downturn of the 1870's and for the remainder of the nineteenth century, business and political leaders placed almost complete reliance upon the Grand Trunk Railway to modernize the port.[14] While Washington continued to dredge Portland Harbor, there was no additional aid from the city, state, or federal government for wharves, sheds, additional grain elevators, or a drydock, despite recognition in some quarters that the port was inadequate in all of these areas.

John Poor's dreams spread beyond his native state of Maine and into the Maritime provinces of British North America. Maritimers also hoped to provide a shorter, speedier, and less hazardous route from North America to Europe than Boston, New York City, or even Portland could offer to prospective shippers or travellers.[15] In the 1880's, Saint John and Halifax competed with each other and with Portland to become the eastern terminus of the new Canadian Pacific Railway. Public officials and private businessmen in Saint John joined together to make the New Brunswick port the ocean terminal of Canada's great new transcontinental railway. C.P.R. officials reluctantly agreed to use Saint John rather than an American port because they desperately needed the federal subsidy of $186,000 a year (for twenty years); at the end of the 1880's a 482-mile "short line" was built from Montreal across northern Maine to the New Brunswick port (Table 2). The arrival of C.P.R. trains in Saint John completed the first stage of that

TABLE 2

RAILWAY MILEAGES TO NORTH ATLANTIC PORTS

Route	Mileage
Montreal–Portland via Grand Trunk Railway	282.7 miles
Montreal–Saint John via Intercolonial Railway	740.6 "
Montreal–Saint John via Short Line (C.P.R.)	481.7 "
Montreal–Boston	354.9 "
Montreal–New York City	384.0 "

Source: M. E. Angus, "The Politics of the 'Short Line,' " Master's thesis, University of New Brunswick, 1958, appendix.

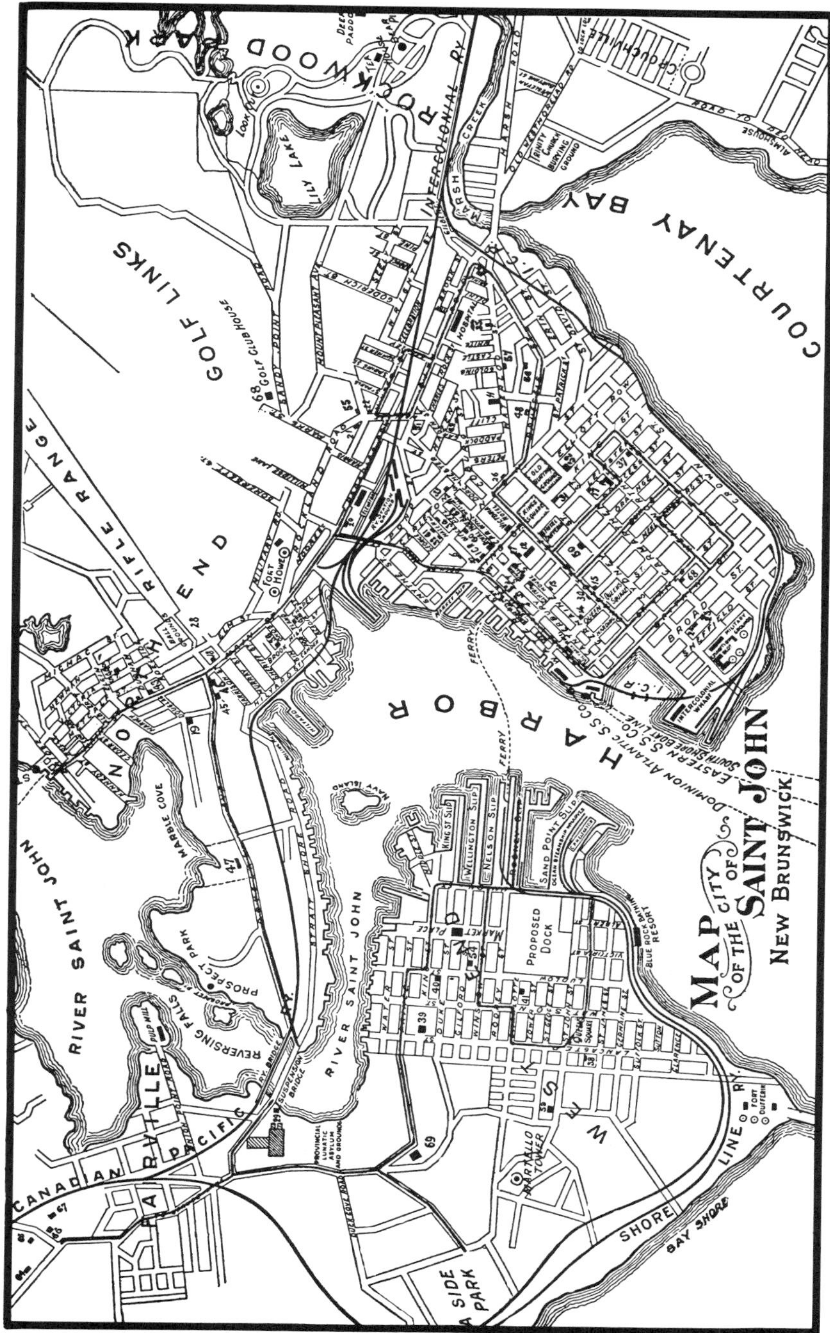

Fig. 4: Saint John, New Brunswick.

city's campaign to displace Portland as Canada's winter port.[16]

The second stage began when local officials invested public funds in waterfront development, aided by a provision in Saint John's royal charter granting ownership and control of the harbour to the city.[17] In 1890, Saint John bought a short railway for $40,000 on the west side of the St. John River and leased it to the C.P.R., which in turn built a wharf and two sheds at nearby Sand Point. In the following months, the city contributed another $40,000 toward the erection of a grain elevator and spent $169,000 on two wharves. By 1904, Saint John had invested approximately $900,000 in dredging, wharves, warehouses, and related facilities. City elites recognized that the success of these efforts ultimately depended upon the availability of annual government subsidies to persuade the steamship lines to call at the less lucrative Maritimes ports rather than at Boston or New York City. Only Ottawa or London possessed the resources for this level of public enterprise.[18]

During the last two decades of the nineteenth century, discussion arose in both Canada and in England about the merits of a subsidized "Fast Atlantic" steamship service (F.A.S.) between Britain and its senior dominion. At a time when imperialists were calling for the economic and strategic integration of the empire through the creation of "All-Red" routes and

Fig. 5: Harbour of Saint John circa *1900* (source: *New Brunswick Museum).*

tariff preferences, the F.A.S. proposal attracted considerable attention on both sides of the Atlantic.[19] Saint John merchants and civic elites were quick to take up these suggestions, and two of the city board of trade's officers, George Robertson and W. Frank Hatheway, pursued them with considerable energy and ingenuity. Along with the C.P.R., they justified the requisite Canadian subsidies and public investments by arguing that it would be a"national undertaking" to create a Maritimes port for winter trade. When the initial contract for a Fast Atlantic Service fell through, Hatheway persuaded the Beaver Line, a small steamship company that had participated in the Portland service, to make Ottawa a reduced request. A $25,000 yearly subsidy was agreed upon, and regular trips between Liverpool and Saint John began during the winter of 1895–96. Although it was not a twenty-knot service, it was enough to generate more optimism in Saint John than had been felt for years. A nearby coal mine began selling a "Winter Port" brand of coal, and Saint John's hockey club renamed itself "The Winter Ports."[20]

At about the time that the "Winter Ports" began to look upon Halifax as the team to beat, Saint John civic leaders fought attempts by the railways to take advantage of the growing rivalry between Halifax and Saint John. On several occasions around the turn of the century, the C.P.R. threatened to withdraw its business from Saint John, accusing steamship lines of "utterly disregarding" C.P.R. interests in favour of the Intercolonial or Grand Trunk lines. At the same time, it tried to cut into Intercolonial business in the Maritimes and schemed to obtain its own outlet at Halifax. City leaders complained to Ottawa, and the C.P.R.'s manoeuvres were effectively blocked by Andrew Blair, the New Brunswick politician who served as Laurier's first minister of railways. Blair used his authority over the Intercolonial to garner some of the C.P.R.'s grain trade until Sir Thomas Shaughnessy finally relented in 1901 and agreed to promote the C.P.R.'s New Brunswick outlet more vigorously. By then, Shaughnessy had become accustomed to working through Saint John elites to persuade Ottawa to spend more public funds on the port, while the local leaders relied upon their elected representatives in parliament to help keep the C.P.R. committed to their town. In this endeavour they received crucial assistance not only from Blair but from a succession of Grit and Tory cabinet members who regularly advocated Saint John's winter port development strategy in federal cabinet meetings. As a result, the goals of both the C.P.R. and local politicians were generally harmonized and achieved.[21]

By the turn of the century, the ports of Saint John and Halifax were regularly receiving various kinds of public assistance. The steamship subsidies begun on a temporary basis in the 1890's acquired an air of permanence. Ottawa underwrote the mail boats to Liverpool, which had been transferred to Saint John from Portland in 1897, as well as a passenger and freight service to Glasgow, Dublin, Belfast, and London. Shipping agents regularly importuned Saint John merchants to request additional aid from Ottawa. The board of trade adopted a plan of harbour improvements, and local members of parliament and New Brunswick's cabinet minister began to note how the government's largesse would benefit the party in power. As might be expected, rivalry between Saint John and Halifax occasionally moved beyond the hockey rinks and burst into angry disputes within the cabinet itself between ministers from the two competing Maritimes ports.[22]

Neither traditional nor legal obstacles seemed to prevent the Canadian government from deciding to spend money on wharves, warehouses, and grain elevators when the occasion warranted. Indeed, the government had already erected Long Wharf and provided port-related accessories as part of its operation of "The Peoples' Railway" (the Intercolonial).[23] Consequently, after 1895, delegations from the Saint John Board of Trade

Fig. 6: Wharf construction, Saint John Harbour, circa *1900* (source: *New Brunswick Museum).*

regularly petitioned Ottawa for aid. Although the Laurier regime decided to build two powerful dredges, the St. John River continued to deposit so much silt in harbour channels in the interim that shipping companies threatened to withdraw regular service to the city Saint John merchants increased the pressure on Blair, who contracted for two smaller dredges after local Grits had warned Laurier personally about the dire political consequences if he failed to act. It was clear that Laurier's decision to develop the port of Saint John had depended upon prior local initiatives regarding harbour improvements. After the turn of the century, the growth in size and tonnage of steamers required additional work.[24] The federal government, which had spent only $47,500 on dredging at Saint John between 1890 and 1900, poured $1.4 million into these efforts over the next decade. During this later period, city and federal governments also began to construct wharves and sheds on the west side. In 1908, the city erected a sixth wharf; two years later Ottawa extended it and added a seventh. In all Ottawa poured nearly $2.7 million into wharves, warehouses, breakwaters, dredging, and immigration buildings in Saint John between 1890 and 1910. By comparison, the city spent about $1 million, and the

Fig. 7: Grain elevator, Saint John, New Brunswick, circa *1900* (source: *New Brunswick Museum).*

Canadian Pacific Railway invested an estimated $1.5 million. Public and private enterprise had joined together in pragmatic fashion to advance the development of Saint John's ocean terminal by pooling resources to accomplish the improvements. Fueled by the wheat boom, the volume of trade passing through the city spiralled.[25]

Despite the growing volume of trade, the continuing export of some Canadian goods through American ports aroused hostility in Quebec as well as in Saint John, and the Laurier administration appointed a royal commission to study the problem. After extensive hearings, the commission reinforced Saint John's position that it had undertaken a national task by urging the creation of fourteen "national ports" to be operated through local boards of commissioners.[26] Although the government did not carry out this recommendation to nationalize harbours, it informally recognized Saint John's increasing importance by spending more money and starting new projects. During the next decade, it authorized a fivefold increase in public spending for dredging, grain conveyors, breakwaters, and other improvements, nearly half ($5.2 million) devoted to a new project on the east side at Courtenay Bay. This scheme had been advocated for some time in cabinet by Saint John's William Pugsley, who was serving as Laurier's minister of public works. The planned dredging, breakwater, wharves, and drydock were also linked to Laurier's naval policy, for it was anticipated that naval vessels would be constructed at the place which had been one of Canada's premier shipbuilding centres in the nineteenth century. But the Laurier government fell from power, and the new administration of Robert Borden had campaigned on a very different naval strategy. Nevertheless, largely through the efforts of Borden's new minister of marine, the New Brunswicker J. D. Hazen, the Borden government accepted the Courtenay Bay scheme because the Grand Trunk Pacific still planned to use it as a port. Work began during the summer of 1912.[27]

Despite Ottawa's backing, the Courtenay Bay project was soon mired in difficulty. The outbreak of war dried up the company's London-based working capital, and by 1916 less than half the dredging had been completed, the breakwater was unfinished, the drydock had only been roughed out, and no wharves had been constructed. Ottawa finally cancelled the Courtenay Bay contract in 1916 and suspended work for the duration of the war.[28]

Meanwhile, the west (C.P.R. and Intercolonial) side of the harbour had not been neglected between 1910 and 1920. Ottawa replaced an Intercolonial grain elevator destroyed by fire, and it reluctantly agreed to build the conveyors for a new one-million bushel C.P.R.-financed grain elevator. Federal authorities, now publicly acknowledging the "national character" of the port of Saint John, authorized expenditures for more wharves and dredging. During the war years, they cautioned the citizenry not to demand additional public enterprise, but by then there seemed to be plenty of war-related business. Several new port-related private industries were launched or enlarged during the war. Despite the scarcity of shipping, the port was usually congested during the winter months, although summer trade remained dull.[29]

The armistice had not yet been signed when Saint John leaders demanded that Ottawa finish the Courtenay Bay project and undertake new port expansion. But the political situation had changed by 1917, casting a shadow over Saint John's ability — and Ottawa's determination — to pursue a national port strategy. With the appointment of Hazen to a judgeship, the city was left with no cabinet representation for the first time since 1896. Saint John's board of trade interviewed the only remaining New Brunswick minister while the war was in progress, but Frank Carvell of rural Carleton County was more concerned with port security than with its expansion. After the armistice, Carvell did authorize the completion of existing projects, and a new federal contract was awarded to the Saint John Shipbuilding and Drydock Company for $4.6 million to complete the Courtenay Bay dredging, breakwater, and drydock, but not the wharves, since a railhead was no longer contemplated on that side of the city. Instead of handling general cargo, Courtenay Bay became a petroleum terminal.[30]

Although Carvell urged Saint John elites to press for nationalization of the harbour, the board of trade and many citizens were reluctant to permit Ottawa to gain control of their greatest asset until federal politicians had made an unequivocal pledge to promote its use. Saint John citizens were acutely aware that Ottawa had taken over the bankrupt Grand Trunk Railway in 1919 and now controlled that concern's wharves, sheds, and grain elevators at the rival Portland, Maine, terminal. Furthermore, the same Tory government had increased freight rates on the Intercolonial by over 100 per cent between 1916 and 1920, raising fears throughout the Maritimes concerning Ottawa's long-range intentions for the region. Uncertainty over the federal government's economic policies, coupled with a severe depression between 1921 and 1923, elevated port development into a major political issue in a series of federal constituency elections in Saint John. Both Portland and Saint John interests dispatched spokesmen to the Canadian prairies to drum up business. Only when the citizens of Saint John were satisfied that Ottawa would not build up its holdings on the Portland waterfront did they permit the nationalization of their port.[31]

As Table 3 indicates, public enterprise had played an increasingly important role in the development of the port of Saint John. The strategy for designating national ports in Canada and for using public funds to construct terminals and subsidize steamship connections had originated pri-

TABLE 3

CANADIAN FEDERAL GOVERNMENT EXPENDITURES ON SAINT JOHN HARBOR, 1867–1927

Buildings	1867–90	1890–1900	1900–10	1910–20	1920–27
Quarantine	$ 7,935	29,112	151,127	122,468	190,258
Immigration	–	–	43,664	8,110	8,554
Detention Hospital	–	–	–	21,265	–
Marine Hospital	50,781	831	–	–	–
Cattle Quarantine	259	–	6,637	1,125	–
Construction					
Partridge Island	1,492	725	13,749	39,805	22,771
Negro Pt. breakwater	426,191	61,227	177,848	120,910	25,694
Long Wharf	–	550,347	–	–	–
Beacon Bar Development	–	–	–	2,239,230	–
West Side wharves, sheds	–	–	245,775	–	732,305
Grain Galleries	–	–	–	164,847	–
Dredging					
Main Channel	–	768	95,533	507,003	–
Beacon Bar Development	–	–	265,004	3,123,789	–
Main Harbour	58,548	46,739	1,040,733	190,990	163,155
Courtenay Bay Development					
Dredging	–	–	–	2,444,477	–
Dredging & Breakwater	–	–	–	1,181,588	4,431,239
Breakwater	–	–	–	1,617,605	–
Subsidy	–	–	–	–	1,437,921
Totals	545,206	689,749	2,040,070	11,783,212	7,011,897

Source: Supplementary Brief, Submission of the Saint John Board of Trade to Royal Commission on Dominion-Provincial Relations (1938), appendix.

marily among local elites rather than in Ottawa, as Aitken asserted. Of course, it was linked to Ottawa's railway construction projects, but federal aid depended upon prior evidence of local public effort and upon substantial commitments from private enterprise, in this case the Canadian Pacific Railway. After the city had invested nearly a million dollars, Ottawa spent money on a wide variety of port-related projects, including dredging the harbour, subsidizing steamer services, and constructing wharves, grain elevators, and grain conveyors. The great bulk of the actual work was done by private companies under government contract. Private and public enterprise had achieved considerable integration because federal cabinet ministers from the city had played a crucial role in aggregating the city's desires with those of the C.P.R. and the federal government. Port development increasingly dominated local politics in Saint John, and by the end of the 1920's it was clear that Ottawa had made a long-range commitment to keep a busy and up-to-date Saint John harbour serving as a major Canadian winter port.[32]

Fig. 8: Waterfront, Portland, Maine, circa *1900* (source: *Maine Historical Society).*

With the return of prosperity in the late 1890's, Portland business and civic elites renewed their attention to Maine's ties with Canada. They still believed, with John A. Poor, that Canada was an inseparable part of

Portland's hinterland. To many Portlanders, the Canadian wheat boom which began in the late nineteenth century proved the wisdom of Poor's scheme. Freight sheds now seemed ready to burst with merchandise, railway cars clogged Grand Trunk sidings, and timekeepers rushed around the wharves night and day, trying to keep track of crews of longshoremen. A record fifty-four steamers departed from Portland in 1897. Under the aggressive leadership of Charles M. Hays, the Grand Trunk's new American-born manager, the railway began a major new investment of over $2 million in its Portland facilities. Two huge new grain elevators with a combined capacity exceeding two million bushels of wheat soon dominated the Maine city's skyline, enabling three ships to be loaded simultaneously. Merchants believed that Portland would grow in size and importance "as a direct result" of the Grand Trunk's private enterprise.[33]

If good times obscured any need for public investment in Portland's waterfront, bad times provoked worry and an occasional reassessment. During the 1899–1900 winter season, six steamship lines dispatched a record total of ninety-three steamers from Portland to Liverpool, London, Glasgow, Bristol, Antwerp, and Hamburg. Collectively these ships spent an average of $1.5 million a year in Portland for labour and stores. The dollar value of Portland's exports rose from $28.6 million in 1899 to $47.5 million in 1901, but port business occasionally could and did take a turn for the worse. Grain shipments dropped over 50 per cent in 1901–2, and exports fell sharply during the business recession of 1907–9. A few residents concluded that Portland ought to take charge of its waterfront. The board of trade's *Journal* warned that "powerful influences" were working to divert Portland's trade "to other ports showing greater local interest." The board appointed a special committee to formulate a plan for the harbour in order to get Congress's attention. But most city leaders remained content to let the Grant Trunk make the chief effort and shoulder most of the expenses; no plan was forthcoming, and no city-owned wharves or warehouses were built. City officials had shown more interest in the 1850's in accommodating the *Great Eastern* than in servicing the ships which regularly called by 1900.[34]

Consequently, Portland businessmen and civic leaders sought public assistance from Congress rather than from City Hall. In 1896, the federal government authorized the expenditure of nearly a million dollars to excavate the harbour to a depth of thirty feet at low tide. By 1902 nearly four million cubic yards had been removed by the contractors, enabling the largest steamships to use Portland harbour and smaller vessels to dock at Back Bay (see Table 1). The Maine congressional delegation also obtained several navigational aids for the harbour approaches. Working through the National Rivers and Harbors Congress, a lobbying agency, board of trade officials persuaded the government to station a ship nearby to destroy derelict vessels. Although they failed to persuade the navy to establish a base or construct a drydock at Portland, they pressed successfully for greater fortification of the harbour. Within four years, well over a million dollars was spent by the war department to construct or improve Portland's coast defence fortifications against a possible attack by British forces intent upon using the Grand Trunk. The thousand-odd artillerymen seconded to these installations aided the local economy; their batteries provided Portlanders with one of the most heavily fortified harbours in the nation. These new forts, along with a new lightship, a new revenue cutter, and a new immigration quarantine station, also testified to the political clout of Maine congressmen as well as to current military strategy. Nevertheless, these piecemeal gifts failed to match the coordinated programme of port expansion and development which had been launched by entrepreneurs and politicians in Saint John. At this time, a few Portland merchants publicly noted the absence of large, modern, fireproof wharves in the city's harbour, but the majority of business and civic leaders had abandoned Poor's vision and instead had adopted a new development strategy based on mercantile and manufacturing activities.[35]

In the latter part of the nineteenth century, steamers plying the waters between Boston, New York City, and Portland began to deposit thousands of visitors in hotels and cottages on the shores of Casco Bay. By the turn of the century, this stream had grown into a torrent of 200,000 tourists who spent somewhere between $10 million and $50 million in Maine. Portland officials began to look at their city with a tourist's eye, and in 1903 the board's *Journal* published its first full page advertisement "selling" Portland. Three years later, merchants created a new standing committee on advertising and raised $3,000 to market the city's virtues as a tourist centre. In subsequent years, thousands of booklets promoted the city's hotel, dining, and recreational facilities, and also assured timid strangers that Portland was an "orderly city" with "no objectionable element": that is, no "lawless" immigrant class.[36]

Whether or not a result of the board of trade's advertising, the number of tourists arriving in Portland seemed to increase yearly. New hotels sprang up; summer playhouses, motion-picture theatres, and bowling halls appeared. Even the annual manoeuvres at Fort Williams were now billed as a tourist attraction. The new emphasis on tourism could also be seen in the city's harbour. Graceful yachts, their sails billowing in the harbour breezes, dominated the waterfront during the summer months. Warships from both the British and American fleets paid occasional summer courtesy calls to Portland, fascinating both the natives and the tourists alike. In 1905, in response to these guests, the city finally set aside a small piece of waterfront property to construct a landing for both military and civilian sailors. Both the motive and the amount ($258.70) of Portland's sole local initiative in the harbour sharply contrasted with the extraordinary local expenditures for wharves and sheds in Saint John, which by 1918 totalled $1,235,000 and included fourteen municipally owned wharves.[37]

Why did tourism rather than the winter port trade capture the imagination of Portland's civic and business leaders? Tourist dollars seemed to be more evenly distributed throughout the business community. It was well nigh impossible, merchants declared, "to name a branch of trade that has not been directly or indirectly benefited by our ever-increasing summer tourist business," which was believed to be worth a million dollars a year to Portland. While this amounted to just two-thirds of the estimated annual winter port earnings, tourism was believed to have a more positive effect on property values.[38] Moreover, it was easy for civic leaders to quantify the beneficial effects of this wonderful new 'industry," and consequently they were able to generate public support for it. Tourists beating a path to board of trade rooms were avidly counted year after year. Passengers on the city's trolleys and ferryboats were similarly enumerated. Hotel managers and retailers frequently reported "remarkable" increases in business. "We reap a benefit from these visitors," they concluded, adding, "they gain in health and we in wealth." Thus Portlanders enthusiastically endorsed efforts to promote tourism while leaving the winter port business in the care of Grand Trunk Railway officials.[39]

The tourist industry also prompted Portland businessmen to cultivate their northern New England market rather than the more elusive Canadian hinterland. As chambermaids and waitresses from Kittery to Bar Harbor began to adopt the styles of Maine's more affluent summer guests, merchants experienced a greater demand for fashionable and expensive goods. Setting out to win business that had formerly gone to Boston or even to New York City, they decided to promote Portland as a retail distribution centre. Boston might have larger stores, they boasted, but not better ones. They journeyed beyond the state's borders to nearby New Hampshire and Vermont and laid plans for a national tour. In 1915, the merchants reorganized into a chamber of commerce and broadened their journal to reflect the commercial interests of the whole state. Through all of these efforts, Portland businessmen expected to make their city the crown jewel for a surrounding coronet of northern New England municipalities.[40]

In many ways, tourism and rural business trips shared an obvious common denominator; they produced the same wonderful jingle of cash register bells. By luring rural New Englanders to Portland during the "off-season," canny Portland merchants had found a way to extend their tourist business beyond the dreaded Labour Day exodus. From their viewpoint, funds spent on new street lighting, a new city hall and auditorium, and on a new exposition building — rather than on wharves and warehouses — made Portland "a city of progressiveness and refinement." Later, manufacturing joined tourism, retailing, and the convention business as the major elements in Portland's new development strategy. Clearly, the harbour and winter port trade had lost favour, and the city's waterfront was no longer deemed vital to Portland's future as it had been from the 1850's to the turn of the century. Instead Portland had become the "Metropolis of Maine," "Queen City of the East," "Gateway to the summer playground of America," and the centre of commercial enterprise in northern New England.[41]

Some people fretted over the consequences of this reordering of priorities. By the century's second decade the harbour was so badly crowded that ships were often forced to anchor in the channel. Although the Grand Trunk rebuilt its Galt Wharf, dredging failed to keep pace with the ever larger steamships which sometimes could not take on a full cargo. The board of trade invited a congressional committee to inspect Portland's waterfront. The congressmen were amazed to find no publicly owned piers. They told merchants that the city should build municipal docks "at any cost" if they wanted their harbour to remain competitive with other ports. They implied that city-owned docks would provide the "strongest argument" for additional federal aid.[42] A few Portlanders agreed: "The city has given more attention to our inspected ash-carts than it has to the harbor." In November of 1914, the board of trade appointed a special committee to petition the city to prepare a public dock area, and called attention to the miles of underdeveloped shoreline along the eastern promenade and in South Portland.[43]

City fathers moved instead to regulate the harbour, for an entirely different reason. Visiting tourists, irate over thefts from their yachts and fuming at residents who regularly dumped their garbage into the harbour, made their grievances known to local officials. The city bought a power boat and assigned three men to guard the yachts day and night. The patrols ended on Labour Day. "This harbor is deserving of better treatment," a few merchants complained. Others agreed, but there were not enough dissident voices to force civic action. No municipal docks or warehouses were built on Portland's commercial waterfront. Many citizens seemed more interested in the efforts of Robert E. Peary, the Arctic explorer, to persuade the navy to build an air base on an island in Casco Bay.[44]

In 1917, the U.S. Congress belatedly tackled Portland's problem. Just a few weeks after President Woodrow Wilson had asked Congress to declare war against Germany, a Maine senator attached a Portland harbour-dredging authorization to an emergency war measure. It passed, to be sure, but unlike previous bills, it demanded prior assurance from local officials that "adequate berthing space" would be provided for deep-draft vessels.

In other words, the Congress would no longer require the engineers to dig harbours deeper and deeper while local authorities neglected to build wharves. As a result, city elites appealed to the state legislature for assistance, and a commission was appointed to investigate their request.[45]

In 1919, the commission filed a report endorsing the need for publicly owned piers. But first the commissioners chronicled the extent to which Portland's waterfront had deteriorated. Most of the forty-six privately owned wharves had been erected on pilings. Few of these old docks were found to be adequate, "and the buildings on many of them seem to be relics of by-gone days." Only the Grand Trunk maintained four modern piers, and even these were "not the latest" in design. Elsewhere, the commissioners reported, most of the successful seaports were publicly owned or controlled, "but neither the State of Maine nor the City of Portland has expended one cent to improve the port facilities of Portland harbor."[46] Meanwhile Portland's rivals — including, of course, Saint John — had already spent millions on harbour improvements. These arguments persuaded both the legislature and the voters of Maine to float a $2 million bond issue for the construction of a dock adjacent to the Grand Trunk wharves. In 1922, the new $1,665,000 Maine State Pier opened for business. The city (which had purchased the site for the pier) and the state had taken the first tardy step toward the modernization of Portland's waterfront.

But this particular public enterprise was "too little and too late." The Canadian federal government had already virtually adopted the national port strategy which Saint John elites had been promoting since the turn of the century. Despite the new Maine pier, shipments through Portland gradually declined, and in 1925 the Ottawa government tried to sell its facilities in Portland to Maine. Both the steady deterioration of these installations and the lack of business at the Maine State Pier revealed the extent to which Saint John had won control over Canada's winter port trade.[47]

It seems clear that both public and private enterprise played a substantial part in the development of the ports of Saint John and Portland. In both cities, public enterprise was designed to create long-term improvements rather than short-term profits. In both cities, local businessmen assumed important roles in garnering public capital through their respective boards of trade. Most of the public enterprise projects in Portland and Saint John were performed by private contractors; private businessmen, whether railway magnates, steamship managers, or forwarding agents, were expected to make use of the facilities created by tax dollars. But there were some significant differences as well. Ottawa's need to create a terminal for the government-owned Intercolonial Railway resulted in construction of wharves, warehouses, and a grain elevator in Saint John through public enterprise at a time when Portlanders were placing increased reliance upon the privately owned railways for their own port development. Thus, more public capital and technical assistance were available for a wider range of improvements and at a later date than was true for Portland.[48] The greater commitment by Saint John elites to port development through public enterprise is understandable, given the narrower range of alternatives available to them at the turn of the century and the fact that most of the waterfront had remained in the public domain. Possessing a less populous commercial hinterland (Table 4), which the New Brunswick city was forced to share with Halifax, and unlikely to attract Portland's volume of tourists and shoppers, Saint John merchants campaigned instead to make

TABLE 4

A COMPARISON OF THE POPULATIONS OF PORTLAND AND SAINT JOHN AND THEIR HINTERLANDS, 1880–1920

	1880–81	1890–91	1900–1	1910–11	1920–21
PORTLAND	33,810	36,425	50,145	58,571	69,272
SAINT JOHN	41,353	39,179	40,711	42,511	47,166
CUMBERLAND COUNTY	75,723	90,949	100,689	112,014	124,376
SAINT JOHN COUNTY	52,966	49,574	51,759	53,572	60,486
Proportion of City Population in County: per cent					
PORTLAND	44.6	40.0	49.8	52.3	55.7
SAINT JOHN	78.1	79.0	78.7	79.4	78.0
MAINE	648,936	661,086	694,466	742,371	768,014
NEW BRUNSWICK	321,233	321,263	331,120	351,889	387,876
Proportion of City Population in state/ province: per cent					
PORTLAND	5.2	5.5	7.2	7.9	9.0
SAINT JOHN	12.9	12.9	12.3	12.1	12.2

Source: U.S. and Canadian Census data.

their harbour one of Canada's national ports, despite the market forces operating in Portland's favour.

Census data suggests that Saint John's strategy for economic development was successful in the long run. Portland initially doubled its population as advancing industrialism consolidated the manufacture and distribution of goods for northern New England. In contrast, Saint John had already achieved urban dominance over a much less populous hinterland. It did not grow much larger between 1880 and 1920 and actually lost people during the latter part of the nineteenth century. But economic data (Table 5) do not follow these demographic curves. Whereas in 1880 Portland had invested twice as much capital in manufactures and produced goods of more than twice the value of Saint John businesses, that situation had

TABLE 5

A COMPARISON OF CAPITAL INVESTED, VALUE OF PRODUCTS, NUMBER OF ESTABLISHMENTS, AND PEOPLE EMPLOYED IN PORTLAND AND SAINT JOHN, 1880–1919

	1880–81	1890–91	1900–1	1910–11	1919
Capital Invested:					
PORTLAND	$4,243,225	6,887,557	6,991,251	9,597,000	22,194,281
SAINT JOHN	$2,143,064	4,838,766	5,252,797	9,242,338	26,129,347
Value of Products:					
PORTLAND	$9,832,931	11,371,487	11,440,201	11,950,000	29,168,000
SAINT JOHN	$4,336,733	8,131,790	6,712,769	10,081,667	40,253,494
Number of Establishments:					
PORTLAND	302	662	639	271*	308*
SAINT JOHN	204	773	187*	177*	307*
Number of Employees:					
PORTLAND	7,129	5,338	5,699	5,891	6,710
SAINT JOHN	2,690	5,888	4,688	5,270	5,855

* five or more employees

Source: U.S. and Canadian Census data.

changed radically by the end of the First World War. By then Saint John's capital investments had surpassed Portland's, and it was producing goods that were more valuable. It is likely that Saint John elites had overcome the handicap of a weaker hinterland by capturing a significant share of Canada's winter port trade. Port-related industries such as shipbuilding, marine engineering, provisioning, and sugar-refining probably account for most of the spread effects revealed in these figures.

The greater impact of public enterprise on the New Brunswick port can be linked not only to the larger overall investment of public dollars, but also to the superior integration of public and private enterprise activity. Local elites, C.P.R. executives, and Ottawa ministers were in constant communication. In Canada, the cabinet system of government blended and focused these private and public initiatives under the guidance and impetus of Saint John's cabinet-level advocates, Andrew Blair, William Pugsley, and Douglas Hazen. But in the United States, the separation of legislative and executive powers resulted in a diffuse and uncoordinated series of public expenditures by the federal government in Portland. A fort here and a lightship there, despite all the dredging by the Army Corps of Engineers, did not serve to create a modern ocean terminal.

Why did Canadians rely more heavily upon public enterprise? The evidence presented here supports Aitken's argument that they turned to the public sector to "forestall, counteract [and] restrain" American control over Canada's winter port trade. As already shown, the contest between the two cities was more crucial to Saint John, because that city commanded fewer options than Portland, and in this respect at least, it was more vulnerable to the fluctuations of the staples economy. Portland elites abandoned Poor's winter port strategy and began to promote tourism, retailing, and manufacturing, leaving port development to the Grand Trunk Railway. Because they viewed Canadians as cousins rather than foreigners, the Americans failed to understand the political implications of the international boundary for government-assisted development. Saint John elites, lacking alternatives, pursued a strategy of building up their port as a national endeavour. Before the First World War, British imperial sentiment defined Saint John's national vision; after the war, the city's strategy reflected a more pronounced anti-Portland bias. By that time, Portlanders had finally begun to modernize their terminal, but it was too late to retain the winter port trade; by then the Canadian government had virtually committed itself to Saint John's strategy. Thus the particular mix of public and private enterprise in North American economic development must be assessed in the context of time and place, as McCalla suggests, rather than explained only by reference to *a priori* cultural values. The role of both private and public capital in the struggle between Portland and Saint

John for Canada's winter port trade casts doubt upon Hardin's rather facile assertion that the 49th parallel separates a private from a public enterprise "culture."

NOTES

1. On the contributions of public enterprise to economic development in the United States, see Carter Goodrich, *Government Promotion of American Canals and Railroads, 1800–1890* (New York, 1960); Louis Hartz, *Economic Policy and Democratic Thought: Pennsylvania, 1776–1860* (Cambridge, MA, 1948); Oscar and Mary F. Handlin, *Commonwealth: A Study of the Role of Government in the American Economy: Massachusetts, 1774–1861* (New York, 1947); Milton S. Heath, *Constructive Liberalism: The Role of the State in Economic Development in Georgia to 1860* (Cambridge, MA, 1954); James N. Primm, *Economic Policy in the Development of a Western State: Missouri, 1820–1860* (Cambridge, MA, 1954). Goodrich provides an excellent overview in his edited volume, *The Government and the Economy, 1783–1861* (Indianapolis, 1967). On the public sector in recent urban history see Deborah S. Gardner, "American Urban History: Power, Society, and Artifact," *Trends in History* 2 (Fall 1981): 52.
2. "Defensive Expansion: The State and Economic Growth in Canada," in Hugh Aitken, ed., *The State and Economic Growth* (New York, 1959), pp. 79–114. See also his "Government and Business in Canada: An Interpretation," *Business History Review* 38 (1964): 4–21.
3. S. M. Lipset, *The First New Nation: The United States in Historical and Comparative Perspective* (New York, 1963), pp. 86–87, 251–56; George Grant, *Lament for a Nation* (Toronto, 1965), p. 14; Gad Horowitz, *Canadian Labour in Politics* (Toronto, 1968), chapter 1; Kenneth McRae, "The Structure of Canadian History," in L. Hartz, ed., *The Founding of New Societies* (New York, 1964), p. 270n.
4. *A Nation Unaware: The Canadian Economic Culture* (Vancouver, 1974), p. 92.
5. Mel Watkins, "In Defence of the National Energy Program," *Canadian Forum* 61 (June–July 1981): 7.
6. "'Rich by Nature, Poor by Policy': The State and Economic Life in Canada," in R. K. Carty and W. P. Ward, eds., *Entering the Eighties: Canada in Crisis* (Toronto, 1980), pp. 78–90.
7. The series is edited by Mel Watkins and published by the University of Toronto Press.
8. Douglas McCalla, "Review Article: The State and Economic Life," *Journal of Canadian Studies* 16 (Fall–Winter 1981): 212–15.
9. Poor, "The Commercial Importance of Portland," in *Poor's Miscellanies*, vol. 2, 25, Maine Historical Society, Portland. His efforts are described in detail in Laura E. Poor, *The First International Railway: Life and Writings of*

John Alfred Poor (New York, 1892). See also Robert H. Babcock, 'Economic Development in Portland (Me.) and Saint John (N.B.) During the Age of Iron and Steam, 1850–1914,'' *The American Review of Canadian Studies* 9 (Spring 1979): 3–37.

10. Goodrich considered Portland's efforts ''exceptional'' for their boldness: *The Government and the Economy, 1783–1861,* pp. 133–34, 248–50.
11. *History of the Work of the Board of Trade of Portland, Maine* (Portland, 1887), pp. 11–19; A. W. Currie, *The Grand Trunk Railway of Canada* (Toronto, 1957), pp. 4–6, 61–62, 100, 126; *Industrial Journal* [Bangor], 25 December 1885, 15 January 1886, 25 February, 25 March, 6 May, 18 November 1887, 29 April 1887: ''More ships would have been sent to Portland . . . had the terminal facilities been greater''; *Board of Trade Journal* [Portland] 1 (July 1888): 91, (January 1889): 285, 7 (February 1895): 298–99, 9 (November 1896): 198, Bangor Public Library.
12. City of Portland, *Annual Reports,* 1906, Fogler Library, University of Maine, Orono.
13. ''Record of Harbor Work Done Here Since 1836,'' *Board of Trade Journal* 15 (September 1902): 142; *Industrial Journal,* 29 October 1886. Merchants had hoped that leasing one of the city's bankrupt railways to the Maine Central would fill the wants of western shippers, create another terminal, and ''bring great Ocean Steamers to our docks year round'': *Board of Trade Journal* 1 (July 1888): 91.
14. The decline of Portland's post-Civil War public enterprise efforts followed a pattern sketched by Goodrich for America as a whole and undermines a recent description of federal aid as ''common'' throughout late nineteenth century North America: see Elizabeth McGahan, *The Port of Saint John,* vol. 1 (Saint John 1982): 14.
15. In the summer of 1850, Poor had convened an ''international railway convention'' in Portland which had attracted delegates from throughout New England and the Maritime provinces. For a description see Babcock, 'Economic Development,'' 7–9; for its impact on one area of the Atlantic provinces see J. Hiller, ''The Railways and Local Politics in Newfoundland, 1870–1901,'' in J. Hiller and P. Neary, eds., *Newfoundland in the Nineteenth and Twentieth Centuries* (Toronto, 1980), p. 124.
16. Murray E. Angus, ''The Politics of the 'Short Line','' Master's thesis, University of New Brunswick, 1958; McGahan, *The Port of Saint John,* pp. 107–14.
17. 45 *Victoria* chap. 51; McGahan, *The Port of Saint John,* p. 219: public ownership was deemed to prevent any future disruption of ferry services linking the two halves of the city.
18. John A. Bowes, ''The City's Finances,'' *New Brunswick Magazine* 4 (September 1904): 32–42 and (October 1904): 76–92; F. W. Wallace with Ian Sclanders, *The Romance of a Great Port: The Story of Saint John, New Brunswick* (St. John, 1935), pp. 36–46; McGahan, *The Port of Saint John,* pp. 133–34.

19. Edward F. Bush, "The Canadian 'Fast Line' on the North Atlantic 1886–1915," Master's thesis, Carleton University, 1969, chapters 3–4.
20. J. W. Daniel to Laurier, 26 July 1900, Laurier Papers, Public Archives of Canada [hereafter PAC]; Board of Trade Minutes [Saint John], 22, 28 March, 2, 3, 25 April, 23 May, 5, 7, June, 3 July 1894, 29 October 1895, 10 February 1896, 24 October, 1, 23 November 1898, 2 May 1899, 6 October, 1 August, 26 July 1902, New Brunswick Museum, Saint John [hereafter NBM]; Shaughnessy to S. Fleming, 11 January 1900, Shaughnessy to R. Cartwright, 4 April 1900, Shaughnessy to G. B. Williamson, 9 November 1901, *CP Letterbooks* PAC; G. Carr, "Some Aspects of Sporting Affairs in Saint John in the 1890s," unpublished paper, University of Maine, Orono, 1979, p. 24; McGahan, *The Port of Saint John,* pp. 166–73, 200. Although McGahan claims that the Saint John "business and civic elite had played a role which was in itself insufficient to garner the presence of the . . . Beaver Line," both her evidence and mine contradict this assertion (p. 140).
21. This rivalry is detailed not only in the Saint John Board of Trade Minutes but also in two additional sources overlooked by McGahan: the *CP Letterbooks* , and evidence in sixteenth Parliament of Canada, *Sessional Papers,* no. 174 (1930). The 1901 agreement, far from being a "benchmark" in Saint John's port development (McGahan, *The Port of Saint John,* p. 158), was merely the opening salvo in a continual struggle that culminated in 1913 when Borden reversed previous policy and permitted the Canadian Pacific to use Intercolonial tracks into Halifax. The effects of the shift in trade were obscured, however, by the wartime boom.
22. Board of Trade Minutes, 3, 27 April, 29 June 1900, 28 June, 15 October, 5, 15 November, 1901, 10, 15 January, 19 February, 1, 11 March, 6, 13, 30 May, 12 June 1902, 28 December 1904, 10 January 1905, 23 May, 12, 19 June 1894, 5 February, 5 March, 15 May 1895, 19 April 1905; Pugsley to Laurier, 29 August 1907, *Laurier Papers*.
23. Section 91 of the British North America Act vested Ottawa with control over beacons, buoys, lighthouses, navigation, and shipping; Section 145 contained a promise by the new federal government to build the Intercolonial Railway "with all practicable speed."
24. Board of Trade Minutes, 18 December 1895, 4 July 1899, 2 October 1900, 9 January, 4, 5, 25 February, 12 March, 2 April, 4, 28 June, 28 October 1901, 3, 27 February, 6, 21 March, 30 October 1903, 5 January, 2 December 1904, 26 January 1905, 19 April 1905, 17 May 1906, 3 January 1908; Special Committee of Board of Trade to Laurier, 4 January 1904, H. Wanhoper to Laurier, 6 January 1904, Laurier to H. Emmerson, 18 January 1904, telegram: J. J. Tucker to Laurier, 11, 27 January 1904, Laurier to Tucker, 18 January 1904, H. Emmerson to Laurier, 1 February 1904, T. McAvity to Laurier, 30 January 1904, Emmerson to Laurier, 5 February 1904, telegram: Board of Trade to Laurier, 6 February 1904, H. H. McLean to Laurier, 8 February 1904, Emmerson to Laurier, 8 February 1904, Laurier to Tucker, 21 December 1904, Hugh A. Allan to Laurier, 4 October 1906, Laurier to Allan, 5 October

1906, Allan to Laurier, 6 October 1906, Allan to Laurier, 13 October 1906, W. Downie to J. B. M. Baxter, 19 July 1907, *Laurier Papers*. See also W. Frank Hatheway, *Injustice to New Brunswick: A Few Facts for Thoughtful, Impartial Liberal Liberals* (St. John, n.d. [1908?]).

25. For Ottawa's expenditures see Table 3; on city spending see F. W. Wallace, *The Romance of a Great Port,* p. 36.

26. Board of Trade Minutes, 19, 26 May, 3, 28 August, 11 November 1903, 30 March 1905; Parliament of Canada, Report of the Royal Commission on Transportation, *Sessional Papers,* 1906, No. 19a; McGahan, *The Port of Saint John,* p. 161.

27. Ernest R. Haynes, "The Development of Courtenay Bay, Saint John, New Brunswick, 1908–1918," Master's thesis, University of New Brunswick, 1969; Cabinet papers, 28 October 1909, for letter from Board of Trade to Hazen of 9 September 1909, Public Archives of New Brunswick [hereafter PANB]; Board of Trade Minutes, 3 September, 21 October 1909. Ottawa provided federal subsidies for drydock construction in 9–10 *Edward VII,* chapter 17.

28. Haynes, "Development of Courtney Bay," 33–78; *Labour Gazette* 12 (May 1912): 1036, 13 (May 1913): 1177, 14 (September 1913): 239, 14 (October 1913): 395, 15 (June 1915): 1369, 14 (November 1913): 526; Board of Trade Minutes, 2 January 1914, 4 January 1915, 8 December 1916, 9 January 1917, 28, 31 March, 7 February 1916; Hazen to J. A. Likely, president, Board of Trade, 17 January 1916, Hazen Papers, Harriet Irving Library, University of New Brunswick.

29. Wallace, *The Romance of a Great Port,* p. 49; *Labour Gazette* 13 (October 1912): 313, 15 (January 1915): 768; Hazen to Rogers, 5–6 August 1913, Shaughnessy to J. D. Reid, 7 August 1913, H. & A. Allan to Borden, 9 August 1913, R. Reford to Borden, 13 August 1913, *Borden Papers,* PAC; Board of Trade Minutes, 5 April, 8 May, 30 July, 27 August 1915, 27, 31 July 1916, 13 December 1918.

30. Board of Trade Minutes, 27 December 1917, 26 February, 17 October 1919, 13 December 1918, 1 November 1920, 24 November 1921, 6 January 1922; Courtenay Bay Development at Saint John, memo on Courtenay Bay Development, January 1923, letter H. W. Thornton to minister of railways, 25 February 1925, C.N.R. President's Files, PAC; Allan M. Trueman, "New Brunswick and the 1921 Federal Election," Master's thesis, University of New Brunswick, 1975, chapters 1, 2.

31. Trueman, "New Brunswick and the 1921 Federal Election," chapter 3; Board of Trade Minutes, 17, 31 October 1919 (where Meighen assured Saint John businessmen that their city and Halifax would be "infinitely better off" with the Grand Trunk in government hands); Ministry of Marine, St. John Harbour Commission, Transfer of Harbour to Federal Government, 1919–26, PAC; McGahan, *The Port of Saint John,* pp. 220–35.

32. By 1926, grain exports from Portland were 25 per cent of their 1919 levels, "due partly to more extensive use of Saint John and Halifax": U.S. War

Department, Corps of Engineers, *The Port of Portland, Me.* (Washington, 1928), p. 89.

33. *Board of Trade Journal* 10 (April 1898): 358, 12 (May 1899): 12, 13 (October 1900): 172, 15 (December 1902): 235, 18 (November 1905): 345–46, 18 (January 1906): 498, 21 (January 1909): 425–26, 22 (January 1910): 427, 23 (October 1910): 289, 23 (November 1910): 383, 23 (April 1911): 659, 9 (March 1897): 326, 10 (May 1897): 6, 10 (February 1898): 294, 298, 12 (May 1899): 9, 12 (February 1900): 294, 13 (November 1900): 207; Mayor's Address, 1901, p. 35, *Portland Municipal Reports,* Fogler Library, University of Maine, Orono.

34. *Board of Trade Journal* 12 (June 1899): 40, 13 (February 1901): 303, 10 (September 1897): 138, 15 (November 1902): 204, 16 (July 1903): 70, 17 (February 1905): 484, 19 (January 1907): 443–46, 10 (December 1897): 230 (quotation), 23 (October 1919): 313. In "The Method of Friendly Approach: Portland, Maine, as Canada's Winter Port," Master's thesis, University of New Brunswick, 1976, Allan Jeffrey Wright concludes that Portlanders had adopted a "wait-and-see" attitude, but board of trade records make it clear that they had opted instead for other paths to growth.

35. *Board of Trade Journal* 10 (January 1898): 270, 273, 10 (April 1898): 359, 12 (February 1900): 305, 16 (February 1904): 375, 13 (February 1901): 220, 26 (June 1913): 681, 15 (December 1902): 236, 15 (April 1903): 362, 366, 18 (August 1905): 239, 20 (June 1907): 105, 20 (November 1907): 316–17; War Department, *Report of the Chief of Engineers, 1899–1903,* Part 1, 687–703, 734–68, 699–713; 622–38; Rowena A. Reed, "The Endicott Board—Vision and Reality," *Journal of the Council of Abandoned Military Posts* 11 (Summer 1979): 6–9 [I am indebted to Prof. Joel Eastman of the University of Southern Maine for the last two references.]

36. *Board of Trade Journal* 10 (April 1898): 365, 12 (December 1899): 234, 12 (September 1899): 136, 15 (June 1902): 38, 18 (January 1906): 504, 24 (June 1911): 55, 12 (March 1900): 328, 13 (June 1900): 38, 15 (July 1902): 76, 15 (March 1903): 338, 16 (May 1903): 19, 19 (January 1907): 476–77, 20 (May 1907): *passim,* 20 (June 1907): 68, 20 (August 1907): 197.

37. *Board of Trade Journal* 13 (August 1900): 201, 16 (August 1903): 105–6, 16 (October 1903): 166, 18 (July 1905): 183, 15 (May 1902): 13, 15, 18 (August 1905): 239, 22 (February 1910): 460, 22 (March 1910): 511, 25 (October 1912): 321, 26 (October 1913): 842, 18 (July 1905): 119, 21 (June 1908): 63; City of Portland, *Annual Reports,* 1906, p. 62; Maine, State Harbor Commission, *Report Upon the Advisability of Building a Public Pier at Portland* (Augusta, 1919), p. 102.

38. *Board of Trade Journal* 21 (September 1908): 241–42, 21 (October 1908): 282.

39. *Board of Trade Journal* 22 (August 1909): 157, 23 (April 1911): 655, 24 (May 1911): 4: Tourist letters of inquiry rose from 1,600 in 1906 to more than 9,000 by 1913; 26 (July 1913): 669 (quotation).

40. *Industrial Journal,* 26 August 1887; *Board of Trade Journal* 23 (January 1911): 481, 23 (February 1911): 519, 24 (December 1911): 406, 24 (January

1912): 553, 25 (June 1912): 71–72, 26 (January 1914): 403–4; *Chamber of Commerce Journal* 28 (May 1915): 19, 21, 29 (November–December 1916): 204.

41. *Board of Trade Journal* 25 (January 1913): 427, 25 (December 1912): 384, 26 (December 1913): 905, 16 (July 1903): 72, 19 (January 1907): 479, 20 (January 1908): 427, 21 (April 1909): 545, 23 (May 1910): 31, 24 (May 1911): 39, 24 (January 1912): 460, 26 (October 1913): 822; *Chamber of Commerce Journal* 28 (July 1915): 96, 28 (May 1915): 19, 29 (July 1916): 93–95, 29 (March 1917): 301, 28 (May 1915): 4.
42. *Board of Trade Journal* 23 (January 1911): 476, 24 (September 1911): 251, 27 (January 1915): 331, 26 (October 1913): 821, 26 (November 1913): 864–65, 26 (June 1913): 624; *Portland Municipal Reports,* 1911, p. 223.
43. *Board of Trade Journal* 26 (January 1914): 411 (quotation), 27 (January 1915): 335; *Chamber of Commerce Journal* 28 (July 1915): 101.
44. *Board of Trade Journal* 25 (January 1915): 137 (quotation); *Chamber of Commerce Journal* 28 (October 1915): 263.
45. *Chamber of Commerce Journal* 29 (June 1916): 56, 30 (May 1917): 375; U.S. Board of Engineers for Rivers and Harbors, *The Ports of Portland and Searsport, Maine, and Portsmouth, N.H.* (Washington, 1954), p. 2; Frederic H. Fay, "New State Pier at Portland, Maine," in Directors of the Port of Portland, *Port of Portland* (1923), pp. 45–46.
46. Maine State Harbor Commission, *Report Upon the Advisability of Building a Public Pier at Portland* (Augusta, 1919), pp. 8, 29, 6–7, 10, 44, 102.
47. U.S. War Department, Corps of Engineers, *The Port of Portland, Maine* (Washington, 1928), pp. 89–90. Both Wright and E. R. Forbes, *The Maritime Rights Movement, 1919–1927* (Montreal, 1979), pp. 112–14, overstate the role of the Duncan Commission on the winter port issue. As Wright admits, political pressure from Saint John and Halifax had already resulted in a diversion of exports from Portland by 1924.
48. Given the work of Goodrich et al. cited in note 1, it could be argued that public enterprise in Canada reflected only a later experience of industrialization for Canada than for the United States.

4

Community Leadership and Decision-Making: Entrepreneurial Elites in Two Ontario Towns, 1870–1930

Elizabeth Bloomfield

Questions of community power, leadership and decision-making—"who governs, where and when," and "who gets what, why and how"—have long fascinated social and political scientists and have been addressed by urban historians.[1] How did leaders emerge in New World frontier communities, removed from the power of hereditary rulers? How unequal was the distribution of power and influence, and how was this related to wealth and social status? Could the founding leaders maintain their power as the community grew in size or changed in functions or social structure? Did leadership structures develop in different ways, depending on the community's size, rate of growth, age, economic base and region?

In his thorough survey of American scholarly research in this field, David Hammack found six contradictory interpretations among historical works on community power. Three of these support the stratificationist position, that wealth has been the basis of power and that elites have always dominated communities; they diverge over whether an exclusive, well-to-do elite has continuously maintained power, whether an original patrician elite kept control by absorbing capitalist newcomers, or whether the new capitalists displaced the old patricians.[2] The other three interpretations lean to the pluralist position that power is exercised as a bargaining process among competing elites who must secure an "underlying consensus" in the community, and therefore, that power is less strongly related to wealth, economic position, or social prestige than to the participants' persistence and skill. The pluralists differ on whether power has always been dispersed or whether this dispersal has declined or increased over time.[3]

Hammack considered that "conflicts between these various interpretations of the history of power in American communities stem mainly from the historians' choices of approach and subject matter," each historian tending "to ascribe a significant measure of power to the individual or group he has studied most closely."[4] The various interpretations might be reconciled with one another by the hypothesis that "power has become increasingly dispersed as American communities have become larger, as their economies have become more specialized and more dependent on expertise and coordination and as their populations have become more diverse."[5] Hammack concluded that the most useful method of study, which would apply to all communities in all periods, regions and cultures, would be the "careful examination of a series of concrete decisions," as proposed by Robert Dahl and others. This approach would permit direct observation of the exercise of power.[6]

Studies of community leaders and decision-making in Canada have been less quantitative, less systematic, and less theoretical than those in the United States. Few have been comparative in approach or findings. Of Canadian urban history, even more than of American, it can be said that "none of the leading propositions about the history of power can be evaluated against a set of studies which clearly, consistently and comparatively describe the distribution of power in any group of communities since the eighteenth century, let alone in a representative group over the entire period."[7]

However, a good deal of evidence of the power of elites in Canadian urban development has appeared in the past fifteen years.[8] In his presidential address to the Canadian Historical Association in 1968, J. M. S. Careless appealed for more serious historical inquiry into the roles of urban elites and decision-making groups of merchants, financiers and entrepreneurs. Careless himself pioneered research on several Canadian cities as well as considering groups of cities comparatively.[9] Various important studies of individual cities have stressed the crucial power and influence of business leaders, especially at an early, formative stage of development. For the period to 1860, these include Tulchinsky on Montreal, Sutherland on Halifax, Acheson on Saint John, and Katz on Hamilton.[10] For the years between 1860 and 1914 (and later), there have been studies by Artibise on Winnipeg, McDonald on Vancouver, Voisey on Calgary, Linteau on the Montreal suburb-town of Maisonneuve, McCann on the metal towns of Pictou County, and Frank on the Cape Breton coal towns.[11]

Canadian urban elites have been discussed in terms of their occupations, wealth, and business interests, their participation in municipal politics and voluntary associations, their representativeness of the ethnic or religious groups in the community, as well as their attitudes to economic development and degree of identification with the local community.[12] The urban elite has usually been associated with wealth and business achievement, rather than with upper-class birth or inherited advantages.[13] In Hamilton of the 1850's, Katz found an "overlapping elite" of entrepreneurs, interconnected by ties of kinship, marriage, church and business, who controlled "economic, political and associational life."[14] After analyzing all municipal officeholders by their property status and business interests, Artibise found Winnipeg to be dominated by a commercial elite of the richer businessmen: merchants, real estate agents, financiers, contractors, and manufacturers. Overwhelmingly Anglo-Saxon and Protestant, Winnipeg's elite shared a "growth ethic" and were able to use the powers of municipal government to promote the city and their own interests.[15]

Longitudinal and comparative studies of community leadership and decision-making have been rare, though they offer valuable suggestions for further research. Bourassa's analysis of municipal office holders in Montreal between 1840 and 1960 (modelled on Dahl's study of New Haven in *Who Governs?*) found significant change through three main phases from a homogeneous "financial aristocracy" to a pluralist pattern in which political organization and personal popularity became the most valuable attributes.[16] R. A. J. McDonald has most usefully distinguished between the top business elite and the smaller businessmen of Vancouver as to their involvement in municipal politics betwen 1886 and 1914. After a brief initial period, the elite left direct participation to the middle-level occupational groups, though they still tried to exert indirect influence on the decision-making process.[17]

Acheson's study of the Canadian business elite from 1880 to 1910, though not primarily concerned with leaders in individual urban centres, has illuminated important differences between major Canadian regions, notably the persistence of groups of community entrepreneurs and of "local autonomy" in the urban centres of the Lake Peninsula of western Ontario longer than elsewhere in Canada.[18] Otherwise, comparative studies have mainly concerned Western Canada. In his essay on the four western cities of Winnipeg, Edmonton, Calgary and Vancouver, Careless described the similar institutional patterns developed by the urban elites to promote their shared interest in growth, especially their use of strong boards of trade.[19] Artibise has shown that the other large Prairie cities resembled Winnipeg in the dominance of business elites, who maintained their boosterist attitudes and growth policies with remarkable continuity from the 1870's to the 1940's.[20] In his reinterpretation of the "urban reform" movement in the period from 1890 to 1920, Weaver has argued that the business elites in many cities took leading roles in campaigns to reform city government for motives and towards ends which were entirely consistent with their earlier growth strategies.[21]

This paper reports a systematic effort to measure community leadership and decision–making in two Ontario towns over a period of sixty years, from 1870 to 1930. Small, contiguous towns about 65 miles west of Toronto, Berlin and Waterloo, grew rapidly from the 1870's, mainly by industrialization. The main centre of German language and culture, Berlin (renamed Kitchener in 1916) developed at a faster rate, so that by 1930 it contained about four-fifths of the combined Twin-Cities population of nearly 40,000 (Table 1).

TABLE 1

POPULATION GROWTH, 1871–1931

	Berlin/Kitchener	Waterloo
1871	2,743	1,594
1881	4,054	2,066
1891	7,425	2,941
1901	9,747	3,537
1911	15,196	4,359
1921	21,763	5,883
1931	30,793	8,095

Source: Census of Canada

The small size of the two communities permitted a detailed analysis of wealth, business success, occupation, municipal office-holding, participation in the boards of trade and other voluntary associations, ethnocultural background and church affiliation. The interrelationships among these various factors were considered in order to determine significant changes during the sixty-year period. Only a summary of the main generalizations is presented here.[22] Against this background of the structure of community leadership, two phases of decision-making, of different types, are examined briefly. It should be noted that leadership and elite status are measured purely in relation to each community. The term ''elite'' should not be confused with its denotation in some studies of a national business elite.

MEASURING COMMUNITY LEADERSHIP

The community leaders of Berlin and Waterloo were defined by their economic, political and associational roles, and the extent to which individuals combined two or more of these roles. Those who achieved wealth or business success exercised economic power in the community by their ability to provide employment and their influence on the supply of urban land or rental property. Those who played a significant part in municipal politics had to make decisions about urban services which affected the progress and welfare of the whole community, while the few who represented the towns in provincial or federal politics had to lobby for local community interests. Associational leaders were prominent in various local groups such as churches, clubs, labour and business organizations. All these types of leaders were mentioned frequently in the local newspapers, and most were cited as models to be imitated or deferred to.

Economic leadership was measured as wealth and business success above the community mean, using assessment records and, especially, the R. G. Dun estimates of "pecuniary strength" of local businesses.[23] Both these data sources emphasize real property and successful enterprise in commerce and industry and do not measure wealth in the form of outside investments or the salaried incomes of executives and managers. Persons identified by this method for each decade between 1870 and 1930 in both towns were designated with an "E" in tables and diagrams.

Political leadership was considered as service on the municipal council, longer than the mean for each decade. Mayoral service was given extra weighting; each year as a mayor counted as an additional year on the council. Those who served longer than the mean were designated with a capital "P." Councillors who served shorter periods on municipal council, but who may have combined this minor political role with leadership in other aspects of community life, were designated with a lower-case "p." Service on the local municipal councils was the primary criterion for political leadership. But those who represented the district in provincial legislature or federal parliament or served on the various local boards or commissions from the 1890's tended to be veterans of the municipal councils.

Associational leadership might have been defined in terms of prominence in a wide variety of voluntary social, cultural, and philanthropic associations. Leadership of the local boards of trade was chosen as the main criterion in this study, partly because of the power of these groups in both communities and also because of their continuous existence throughout most of the period. The Berlin Board of Trade was chartered in 1886; the Waterloo board in 1890. Board of trade members who served on the governing council for longer than average terms, including those who held office as president, vice-president, secretary, or treasurer, were defined as associational leaders. They are indicated by an "A," while those with a smaller role on the board of trade council, but who may have combined this with other forms of community leadership, are described by a lower-case "a."[24]

Community leaders were thus identified in each of the three roles—economic (E), municipal politics (P), and associational represented by the boards of trade (A)—using wealth or participation greater than the mean as the differentiating factor. Persons who combined two or more leadership roles were also distinguished, in the following combinations:

EPA	Leader in all roles: economic, political, associational.
EPa	Economic and political leader; some Board of Trade service.
EpA	Economic and associational leader; some municipal service.
EP	Economic and political leader.
EA	Economic and associational leader.
PA	Municipal and associational leader; wealth below the mean.
Epa	Economic leader; some municipal and associational service.
Ep	Economic leader; some political service.
Ea	Economic leader; some associational service.
Pa	Municipal leader; some associational service.
Ap	Associational leader; some political service.
E	Economic leader only.
P	Political leader only.
A	Associational leader only.

Community leaders who combined a major role with at least one other major or minor leadership role are described as "dominant."

Diagrams were designed to illustrate the extent to which community leadership roles were combined, their form inspired by the concept of overlapping elites. Three circles, made proportional to the number of leaders in each field, were arranged to intersect according to the degree of role combination. The shaded circles represent groups of leaders, defined according to the criteria for economic (E), political (P) or associational (A) roles. Thus, the extent of overlap and combination of roles is represented graphically. With a truly coincident elite, all the circles would be superimposed on one another; with entirely separate leadership roles in each field of activity the circles would not overlap at all. To the basic diagrams were added the unshaded circles (or modified shapes) with broken lines to indicate minor leadership roles in the board of trade (a) or municipal council (p). The numbers of persons identified in each leadership role or combination of roles are stated. The diagrammatic representation permits visual comparison of the leadership structures in the two towns in each decade between 1870 and 1930 (Figures 1 and 2).

SIGNIFICANCE OF FOUNDING ELITES

Berlin and Waterloo had developed as informal hamlets within the German Company Tract (later Waterloo Township) which was settled by Pennsylvania German Mennonites at the beginning of the nineteenth cen-

FIGURE 1

BERLIN/KITCHENER: LEADERSHIP STRUCTURES

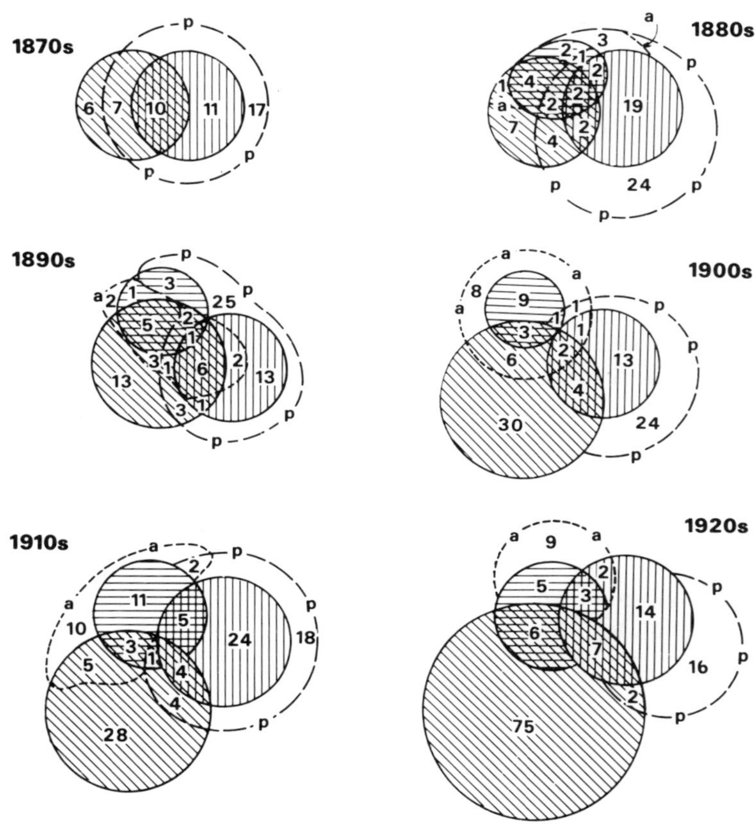

Leadership Types

- E Economic leader only
- EA Economic and associational leader
- A Associational leader only
- PA Municipal and associational leader
- P Political leader only
- EP Economic and political leader
- EPA Leader in all roles—economic, political, associational

Major roles also combined with minor ones — as in EPa, EpA, Epa, Ep, Ea, Pa, Ap types.

FIGURE 2

WATERLOO: LEADERSHIP STRUCTURES

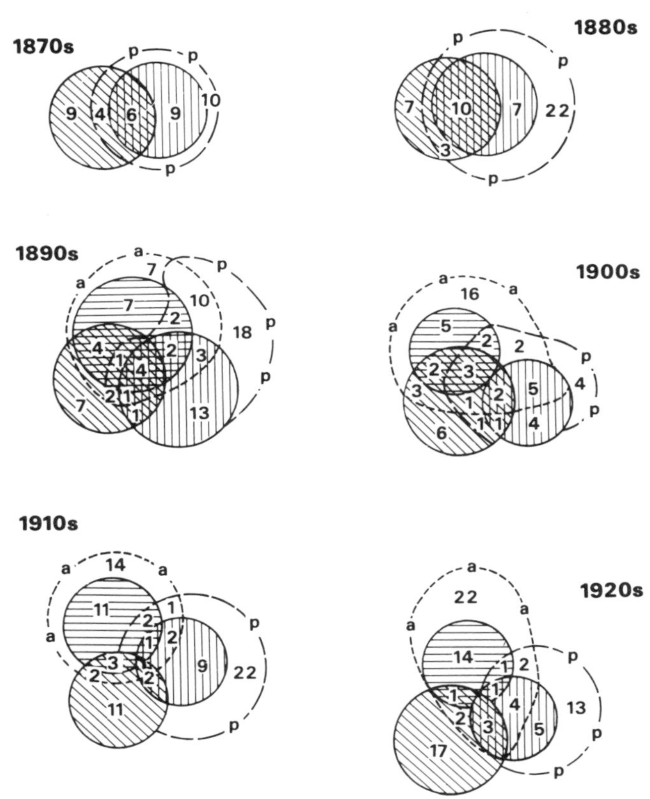

Leadership Types

▧	E	Economic leader only
▧	EA	Economic and associational leader
▤	A	Associational leader only
▦	PA	Municipal and associational leader
▥	P	Political leader only
▧	EP	Economic and political leader
▩	EPA	Leader in all roles—economic, political,associational

Major roles also combined with minor ones – as in EPa, EpA, Epa, Ep, Ea, Pa, Ap types.

tury. As a centre of German language and culture, the area became known as a desirable destination for refugees from the southwestern German states in the 1830's and 1840's. These European Germans tended to settle in Berlin because of the more permissive attitude of the Mennonite landowners there. Favoured by better water-power resources, Waterloo developed into a small industrial village by the 1850's. Berlin's central position in the township enabled it to become the main market centre and, more significantly, the county seat of the new County of Waterloo from 1852. Berlin also found itself on the main line of the Grand Trunk Railway in 1856, which stimulated the village economy and led to a boom in land speculation. Railway construction and the new judicial-administrative functions also brought new ethnic and occupational groups: lawyers, surveyors, and doctors from other parts of Ontario, American and British railway contractors, Irish and other labourers. From the 1850's to the 1870's, Berlin expanded its central service functions, but also developed several small manufacturing enterprises. Waterloo grew more slowly but, with the founding of two insurance companies in the 1860's, acquired a new and lasting function which also attracted residents of English and Scots extraction.

The community leaders of Berlin and Waterloo in the 1870's may be considered as founding elites, their composition and main characteristics reflecting the towns' past development and contemporary functions. Remarkably varied in ethnic background, skills, and occupations, they shared the advantages of a head start, of having arrived in the early stages of urban development, especially if they brought capital.[25] In Berlin, the dominant EP group, which combined above-average wealth with longer-than-average service on the town council (see Figure 1), included three Lutheran merchants, five manufacturers (two Mennonite, two British, and one German), a German-born newspaper publisher, and a Mennonite speculative landowner who had previously been a manufacturer. Three were Lutherans, one a Catholic, one each Methodist and Congregational, while there were two each of the distinctive local Evangelical and Swedenborgian churches which would continue to be overrepresented among the community leaders of both towns. Leaders of EP type are distinguishable from the E type, who had above-average wealth but no municipal service, by their active entrepreneurial activities and stronger local identification. Most of E leaders in the 1870's were non-Germans who were not active in business and who had significant connections outside the local community.[26] Four were of British origin, having come to Berlin in the railway-courthouse boom, one as a railway contractor, one as a merchant, and two as professional men. One E-type leader had started as a Mennonite farmer but had also organized lumber-cutting contracts, subdivided land and constructed dwellings, and financed new industries, notably Berlin's largest button factory; by the 1870's he was devoting himself to organizing the settlement of Russian Mennonites in southern Manitoba.[27] Berlin's other leadership groups, while quite varied in occupations, ethnic and church backgrounds, were less heterogeneous than the dominant EP group. The Ep group was overwhelmingly German by background and less varied in occupations than the EP group; slight majorities of the P and p groups were also German and Lutheran.

In the smaller Waterloo community, half the leaders were of German origin, compared with 63 per cent in Berlin. Leaders of Mennonite origin were more significant, especially those with above average wealth, though most no longer belonged to the Mennonite church. Leaders of British or American background were also more important in Waterloo and were more active politically than in Berlin. EP leaders included, for example, Waterloo's wealthiest citizen, an American merchant-distiller who had made money out of a railway construction contract in the 1850's, as well as another considerable landowner of British origin. Merchants, large and small, were more strongly represented among Waterloo's leaders, as manufacturers were among Berlin's, while the link between the insurance business and several of Waterloo's leaders of all types was already evident.

Space does not permit a description of the leadership structure in all six decades. Instead, certain aspects are traced through the whole period, to detect significant changes and to relate the patterns and processes found in Berlin/Kitchener and Waterloo to those in other towns and cities. Community leaders continued to be drawn from varied ethnocultural backgrounds, the Mennonite proportion declining and the British rising. Leaders of European German origin formed a majority among all leaders, larger in Berlin/Kitchener; their significance was even larger among leaders with multiple and overlapping roles in both towns. Lutherans and, especially, Catholics, the largest church groups in both communities, were increasingly underrepresented among the leaders, notably those with multiple roles, while some minority churches were disproportionately significant. Active entrepreneurs continued to have more dominant leadership roles. Manufacturers became even more important as leaders after the 1870's; they were especially prominent in Berlin/Kitchener, and were even more strongly represented among the dominant leaders than among the total group of leaders.

The various elements of change and continuity over the sixty years are organized in terms of the relationship between wealth and political power, the composition of the municipal councils and the role of the boards of trade, and the transition from elitism to pluralism.

ASSOCIATION BETWEEN WEALTH AND POWER

The leadership roles of the wealthy elites changed as urban economies became more complex and diversified. Those with above-average wealth continued to have highly important economic roles; wealth became more rather than less concentrated over the sixty-year period.[28] The wealthy and successful tended to combine other business interests with their principal occupation. This was true particularly of the dominant leaders. Over one-third of the eighty-seven men in Berlin/Kitchener who combined wealth with other leadership roles (Types EPA, EpA, EPa, EP, EA, Epa, Ea, Ep) had other local business interests. These might include ownership of development land or rental property or shares in manufacturing enterprise, urban utility, or newspaper publishing company. Over one-quarter of Waterloo's economic leaders had such interests, notably in the nine insurance or savings companies established there between 1863 and 1923.

Business leaders became less directly involved in municipal politics during this period. This is clear, both in terms of the proportion of those with above-average wealth who were active in local politics and in terms of the proportion of municipal councillors who were wealthy. It happened both in Berlin/Kitchener, where the urban economy expanded significantly during the six decades, and in Waterloo, where the numbers of business leaders remained much the same (Table 2).

TABLE 2

PROPORTION OF WEALTHY ACTIVE ON MUNICIPAL COUNCILS

	Berlin/Kitchener	Waterloo
	per cent	
1870's	74	53
1880's	45	65
1890's	40	35
1900's	15	42
1910's	20	11
1920's	10	13

However, wealth and business success remained important qualifications for dominant leadership status in municipal politics, especially for election as mayor or to the various boards and commissions established from the 1890's and also for councillors serving longer than average periods. Although wealth and business success were not indispensable to service on the municipal council, members of the elite were certainly helped by widespread deference to entrepreneurial success expressed in such maxims as "a man with little at stake cannot be expected to have as genuine an interest in the town as a large taxpayer and employer."[29]

Did the business leaders turn to the boards of trade as associations through which they could promote their shared interests and exert influence less directly on the town councils? The evidence in Berlin and Waterloo shows that those with above-average wealth did identify strongly, at first, with the local boards of trade. In Berlin, virtually all those with above-average wealth were among the sixty-three charter members of the Berlin Board of Trade in 1886; nine of the business elite served on its council during the rest of the 1880's. A similar pattern may be noted in Waterloo, following the establishment of a board of trade there in 1890. However, after the first two decades, the wealthy ceased to be much more active on the board of trade councils than they were on the municipal councils. Almost all would remain ordinary members of the boards and, in times of crisis, when business interests seemed threatened, would rally in support. But leadership of the boards of trade was left increasingly to smaller businessmen, salaried executives and bank and insurance company managers and clerks—notably in Berlin/Kitchener between 1900 and 1920 and in Waterloo from 1910. By the 1920's, both the membership and influence of the boards had declined, one factor being the formation of other civic and social groups at this time.

Businessmen—whether wealthy or not—continued to be the dominant community leaders. When defined to include merchants, manufacturers, builders and those engaged in finance, real estate, and business services like transportation and newspaper publishing, businessmen made up 76 per cent of all Berlin's community leaders and over 80 per cent of Waterloo's. Businessmen had an even stronger hold on the dominant leadership roles: 85 per cent in Berlin/Kitchener and 88 per cent in Waterloo. In all decades, businessmen filled most seats on both municipal councils, though the proportions declined steadily (Table 3).

TABLE 3

PROPORTION OF MUNICIPAL COUNCILLORS WHO WERE BUSINESSMEN

	Berlin/Kitchener	Waterloo
	per cent	
1870's	89	86
1880's	78	82
1890's	78	87
1900's	81	96
1910's	64	60
1920's	60	60

More finely classified, the occupations of the community leaders may be seen to reflect the economic base of the two towns. Manufacturers predominated in both, especially in Berlin/Kitchener, and were even more strongly represented among the dominant leaders. In Berlin, manufacturers constituted 37 per cent of all leaders but over 51 per cent of those with multiple and overlapping roles. In Waterloo, the corresponding figures were 29 and 39 per cent. The prominence of manufacturers matched the heavy dependence of both towns on industry. Throughout the period studied, well over one-fifth, and at times over one-third, of the urban population was employed in factories, ranking both towns among the ten most industrialized centres in Ontario. The significance of manufacturers as community leaders may be contrasted with their smaller role in other Canadian cities and towns.[30] In Waterloo, the local specialization in insurance was reflected in the fact that 15 per cent of all leaders were engaged in financial occupations, but these men had a smaller and less dominant role in the town council.

Professional men—lawyers, doctors and dentists—were more prominent as community leaders in Berlin/Kitchener than in Waterloo, matching its role as county seat with administrative and judicial functions. They were most active on the municipal council between 1885 and 1919, and occupied nearly one-quarter of council seats between 1910 and 1914. Professional men were quite often elected mayor of Berlin, out of deference to their education and social standing.

The numbers of workingmen in both councils rose dramatically from pre-1900 averages of 3.7 per cent in Berlin and 1.6 per cent in Waterloo to between one-quarter and one-third of all seats in the 1920's.[31] Professionals, financiers and workingmen tended to have single leadership roles more commonly than manufacturers or merchants and to serve for shorter periods. After 1900, small but significant numbers of men without advantages of wealth or business success won dominant political leadership roles by persistence and political skill, some being elected mayor or member of the provincial legislature.

TRANSITION FROM ELITISM TO PLURALISM

To what extent could the leadership structure of Berlin/Kitchener or Waterloo be described as an "overlapping elite"? What proportion of leaders had multiple or overlapping roles, or areas of activity—the measure declared by Presthus to be the best comparable index of elitism?[32] From Figures 1 and 2, it is clear that most community leaders did not combine major roles in economic, political and associational activity. Just over half the leaders identified had multiple or overlapping roles, when considered for the whole period, the proportion slightly higher in Waterloo than in Berlin.

The index of elitism declined during the sixty years, resembling the classic transition from "elitism" to "pluralism" found in New Haven by Dahl.[33] In Berlin, community leadership roles overlapped more closely in the 1870's, 1880's and 1890's, while from 1900 there seems to have been a steady loosening of the leadership structure. Waterloo leaders combined roles most closely from the 1880's to about 1910 and then remained slightly more overlapped than Kitchener between 1910 and 1930, though with a similar tendency toward a looser structure (Table 4).

TABLE 4

INDEX OF ELITISM (PROPORTION OF ALL LEADERS WITH MULTIPLE OR OVERLAPPING ROLES)

	Berlin/Kitchener	Waterloo
	per cent	
1870's	50	36
1880's	39	48
1890's	50	43
1900's	25	57
1910's	26	28
1920's	17	25
1870–1930	50.5	55

What kinds of men combined leadership roles? Only very few were leaders in all three roles—economic, political, and associational—and mainly between 1870 and 1900 rather than later. These leaders of the EPA type did combine roles to a remarkable degree. Most ranked among the top property-owners in the assessment records and had ramifying business interests in addition to their main occupations. Most served as mayors of their communities and on the various ad hoc boards and commissions, and several were active in provincial or federal politics and in other associations besides the boards of trade. It is significant that EPA leaders had their greatest influence before 1914 and that most were chiefly active before 1900. It was easier to combine varied business interests with political and social leadership while the towns were quite small and all forms of organization were simpler. Several were helped by the initial advantage of a family owning land or other property built up in the very early stages of settlement and town development. Others obtained capital or influence through marriage, kinship or church connections.

Nearly as active and varied in their leadership roles were those classified as EPa and EpA, who differed from the EPA group only in degree. Most of the leaders of these types in Berlin/Kitchener and half in Waterloo were active in the second half of the study period and therefore lacked the advantages of the previous generation. Some of these were late arrivals or those who worked their way up from employee status to own their own businesses. With more complex business organization and more available candidates for public or associational office, it was less common for individuals to combine leadership in several fields. In some families, there was a tendency to division of labour; one member might serve on the city or town council, another on the board of trade while both worked in the family business.

Leaders who combined above-average service in both municipal council and the board of trade (PA type) may have lacked the property or business stake in the community of the EPA, or EpA or EPa types of leader, but some played highly important roles in community affairs, notably between 1910 and 1930. Some were self-employed businessmen on a small scale, others were executives in the insurance companies; there were also newspapermen. Several in Kitchener were professional men, or even workingmen. Though lacking substantial property, this group had a considerable influence on community life. Three of the six political-associational leaders in Berlin/Kitchener became mayors and two of the six in Waterloo; and most of them gave considerable service on the various boards and commissions, as well as in voluntary associations. The number of such leaders, together with those of Pa and Ap types, illustrates the opportunities for men to gain power without wealth but with persistence, personal popularity or political organization. However, few used their power in opposition to the business elite; most were enthusiastic boosters and effective promoters of urban growth policies.

Close examination of the characteristics and interrelationships of community leaders shows that, despite the trend to a pluralist structure, individual leaders continued to be linked in ways not evident in the diagrams. Dominant leaders tended to remain leaders for more than a single decade, some for four or even more. A fair proportion were also interconnected, closely as sons, brothers, or nephews of other dominants or less directly through marriage or church affiliation. Two of these factors are summarized in the following table. Church connections are reflected in the disproportionate representation of some minority churches among the dominant leadership groups, notably the distinctive Evangelical and Swedenborgian churches. Such interconnections reinforced the continuity and cohesion of the elite group (Table 5).

TABLE 5

CONTINUITY AND KINSHIP AMONG DOMINANT LEADERS

Berlin/Kitchener	Total number of dominant leaders	Number already dominant in previous decade	Number related to other dominants as son, brother, or nephew (same surname)
1870's	17	–	–
1880's	18	2	4
1890's	27	11	7
1900's	17	8	1
1910's	22	7	2
1920's	20	4	8
Waterloo			
1870's	10	–	–
1880's	13	6	1
1890's	16	5	2
1900's	20	9	2
1910's	12	4	3
1920's	12	5	–

Three generations of the Breithaupt family of Berlin may serve to illustrate most of the generalizations about dominant community leaders. The founder of the family was Louis Breithaupt, born in the German state of Hessen in 1827, who migrated to Buffalo and established a tannery with his father. Through Evangelical Association church contacts, he married Catherine Hailer of Berlin and, in 1857, set up a branch tannery in the village, transferring his whole business there from Buffalo when the American Civil War began in 1861. With all the advantages of a head start, he was able to buy a good deal of real estate, both in the commercial core and on the periphery, thus creating a valuable long-term investment for his family. Though Louis Breithaupt died prematurely in 1880, the tannery flourished under the management of two of his sons. It was incorporated as a joint stock company in 1890 (with branch tanneries in Penetanguishene, Listowel, Hastings and Campbellford). The Breithaupt Company and Estate remained the largest property owner in Berlin until about 1914. Breithaupts helped to organize and came to control the Berlin Gas Company, the Berlin and Waterloo Street Railway and the Berlin and Bridgeport Street Railway. Breithaupt capital was also used to start new industrial enterprises, making such products as furniture, rubber goods, ladies whitewear and leather trunks and bags, often in association with other businessmen belonging to the Zion Evangelical Church.

The first Louis Breithaupt is classified as an EP leader, with service as town councillor and mayor. Two of his sons were EPA leaders, one as EPa, and two as Ea, one grandson was an EPa and another EA, during the period to 1930. Four Breithaupts were elected mayor, and various members of the family were long-serving chairmen or members of various ad hoc boards and commissions. The second Louis Breithaupt represented the district in the Ontario legislature, the third was a federal member of parliament. Two Breithaupts were charter members of the Berlin Board of Trade; they and others served on the council. Between them, members of the family were active in most community associations. The father-in-law of two Breithaupt brothers was another EPA leader; and through other marriages and church connections the Breithaupts were linked with a good many community leaders in Berlin/Kitchener, and some in Waterloo.

TWO "CONCRETE DECISIONS"

How did community leaders exercise their decision-making power? This important question cannot be fully answered here, but a comparison of two policy issues of different types and at different times can illustrate the main dynamics as well as the transition from an elitist to a more pluralist leadership structure.

First, the active encouragement of new manufacturing industry by the municipal councils comprised a series of decisions between 1870 and 1914 in Berlin, between 1900 and 1914 in Waterloo.[34] Specific decisions were made on direct inducements such as bonuses, loans or tax exemptions to individual enterprises, well over 100 in Berlin and 25 in Waterloo. Further decisions on the improvement of urban services were consistently made in the interests of industrialists. The priorities and interests of the entrepreneurial elite clearly had great influence on the municipal council, board of trade and daily newspaper. However, success was not automatic; both sorts of measures required the consent of most local ratepayers; so the leaders had to seek an "underlying consensus." They appealed to local loyalties and especially to the notion that industry was the engine of general urban growth: that all sections of the community would benefit from new industries and should gladly make small sacrifices to help manufacturers become established. The board of trade also undertook to "organize the voters" at the annual municipal elections or in votes on specific money by-laws.[35] It could count on the deference of most workingmen to a successful self-made entrepreneur and, in Berlin especially, could quote earlier successes of the "industrial policy." In Berlin, the procedures were compared by one long-term newspaper editor to clockwork: "The city was like a watch; wheels within wheels. The factories were the great wheel, industry the mainspring; the Council the balance wheel, and the Board of Trade the hair-spring."[36] Community leaders, who could disagree violently on politics and personalities, proved remarkably cohesive in support of growth strategies. It is noteworthy that the decades of greatest activity—the 1880's and 1890's in Berlin and 1900–10 in Waterloo—were those of more multiple and overlapping leadership roles and higher "indices of elitism" (see Figures 1 and 2).

In contrast, the local city planning movement from 1912 to the mid-1920's was not helped by either a cohesive leadership structure or a consensus based on the interdependent interests of entrepreneur and community.[37] At first, the new awareness of the environmental problems of urban growth, associated with Berlin's cityhood celebrations in 1912/13, did attract considerable, if superficial, interest. The early planning movement was helped by some overlap, during 1912, of community leaders between the Berlin City Council and the board of trade. But this was not characteristic of Berlin's leadership structure after 1900, as it steadily loosened into a more pluralist pattern. While dominant leaders of the entrepreneurial elite had solidly supported the growth strategies and had actively compaigned for their success, they did not show the same close or sustained interest in planning. Leaders of the Berlin Civic Association were mainly middle-level businessmen and professionals, only one in six having above-average wealth or business success. Despite their attempts to appeal to local boosterist feelings and to use other tactics, they failed to persuade either the leading entrepreneurs or the workingmen to support their cause. This policy issue may be described as a non-decision: the municipal council evading any action because of the hostility or indifference of most business leaders. In the 1920's, the community finally did accept a master plan and zoning by-law, but only for a weakened concept of planning which did not threaten the rights of property-owners.

In conclusion, how may we answer, for Berlin/Kitchener and Waterloo, the questions posed at the beginning of this paper? Which of the six interpretations of community power structure best fits these two towns? No one interpretation, stratificationist or pluralist, is appropriate by itself. A founding elite, entrepreneurial rather than patrician, did combine above average wealth with dominance in direct political and associational roles, to 1900 in Berlin, 1910 in Waterloo. But the small core group with multiple and overlapping roles was always open to newcomers who qualified by entrepreneurial effort or identification with entrepreneurial interests. While measurement of leadership roles shows a classic transition from elitism to pluralism over the sixty years, the founding elite was able to maintain strong indirect influence on the community through kinship, marriage and church connections, as well as through board of trade and newspaper policies. On the other hand, analysis of the industrial policy decisions suggests that, even in the nineteenth century, power had to be exercised with persistence and skill, as a "bargaining process" to secure an "underlying consensus." This proved easier with the promotion of industry, when the benefits of growth to all interests could be readily accepted, than with any attempt to apply planning principles to the problems of growth.

NOTES

1. The basic questions have been posed in, for example, H. D. Lasswell, *Politics: Who Gets What, When, How* (Cleveland: World Publishing, 1958), and D. M. Smith, "Who Gets What, Where and How . . . ," *Geography* 59, no. 4 (1974): 289–97. For bibliographies of the estimated two thousand community power studies in the United States, see: Michael Aitken and Paul E. Mott, *The Structure of Community Power* (New York: Random House, 1970); Carl Beck and J. Thomas McKechnie, *Political Elites: A Selected Computerized Bibliography* (Cambridge, MA: M.I.T. Press, 1968); Terry N. Clark, "Power and Community Structure: Who Governs, Where and When, " *The Sociological Quarterly* 3 (Summer 1967): 291–316; Claire W. Gilbert "Community Power and Decision-Making: A Quantitative Examination of Previous Research," in Terry N. Clark, ed., *Community Structure and Decision-Making: Comparative Analysis* (San Francisco: Chandler Publishing, 1972) pp. 139–56; Willis D. Hawley and James H. Svara, *The Study of Community Power: A Bibliographic Review* (Santa Barbara: American Bibliographic Center-Clio Press, 1972); Irving P. Leif and Terry N. Clark, "Community Power and Decision-Making. Trend Report and Bibliography," *Current Sociology* 20, no. 2 (1972); Glenn D. Norval, John P. Alston and David Weiner, *Social Stratification: A Research Bibliography* (Berkeley: The Glendessary Press, 1970); Roland J. Pellegrin, "Selected Bibliography on Community Power Structure," *Social Science Quarterly* 48 (December 1967): 451–56.

   The contributions by American urban historians to this field have been reviewed in David C. Hammack, "Problems in the Historical Study of Power in the Cities and Towns of the United States, 1800–1960," *American Historical Review* 83, no. 2 (1978): pp. 323–49, and more briefly in Kathleen Neils Conzen, "Community Studies, Urban History and Local History" in M. Kammen, ed., *The Past Before Us: Contemporary Historical Writing in the United States* (Ithaca: Cornell University Press, 1980) pp. 284–87, and

Deborah S. Gardner "American Urban History: Power, Society and Artifact," *Trends in History* 2, no. 1 (Fall 1981): 59–61.
2. Hammack, "Historical Study of Power," pp. 329–33.
3. Ibid., 333–38.
4. Ibid., 339.
5. Ibid., 341.
6. Ibid., 341–48.
7. Ibid., 324.
8. J. M. S. Careless, "Somewhat Narrow Horizons," *Canadian Historical Association, Historical Papers* (1968), pp. 1–10.
9. See, for example, J. M. S. Careless, "The Development of the Winnipeg Business Community, 1870–1890," *Transactions of the Royal Society of Canada*, 4, no. 8 (1970): 239–54; Careless, "The Business Community in the Early Development of Victoria, B.C.," in D. S. Macmillan, ed., *Canadian Business History: Selected Studies 1497–1971* (Toronto, 1972), pp. 104–23.
10. G. J. J. Tulchinsky, *The River Barons: Montreal Businessmen and the Growth of Industry and Transportation, 1837–1853* (Toronto, 1977), D. A. Sutherland, "The Merchants of Halifax, 1815–1830: A Commercial Class in Search of Metropolitan Status," (Ph.D. Thesis, University of Toronto, 1975); M. B. Katz, *The People of Hamilton, Canada West: Family and Class in a Mid-nineteenth-century City* (Cambridge, 1975) pp. 176–208; T. W. Acheson, "The Great Merchant and Economic Development in Saint John, 1820–1850," *Acadiensis* 8 (Spring 1979): 3–28.
11. A. F. J. Artibise, *Winnipeg: A Social History of Urban Growth, 1874–1914* (Montreal, 1975); P. Voisey, "In Search of Wealth and Status: An Economic and Social Study of Entrepreneurs in Early Calgary," in A. W. Rasporich and H. Klassen, eds., *Frontier Calgary, 1875–1914* (Calgary, 1975) pp. 221–41: R. A. J. McDonald, "Business Leaders in Early Vancouver, 1860–1914," (Ph.D. thesis, University of British Columbia, 1977) and "The Business Elite and Municipal Politics in Vancouver," *Urban History Review* 11, no. 3 (February 1983): 1–14. P.-A. Linteau, *Maisonneuve. Comment les promoteurs fabriquent une ville* (Montreal, 1981); L. D. McCann, "The Mercantile-industrial Transition in the Metal Towns of Pictou County, 1857–1931," *Acadiensis* 10, no. 2 (Spring 1981): 26–64; David Frank, "Company Town/Labour Town: Local Government in the Cape Breton Coal Towns, 1917–1926," *Histoire sociale* 14 (mai 1981): 177–96.
12. Few of the studies here have used systematic or statistical methods of analysis in their discussion of local elites, but the work of Robert on the socially prominent "notables" of Montreal should be mentioned: J.-C. Robert, "Les notables de Montreal au XIXe siècle," *Histoire sociale* 15 (1975): 54–76.
13. However, a few essays on the early years of some Ontario cities have shown the importance, albeit short-lived, of a "patrician elite." See, for example, Michael S. Cross, "The Age of Gentility: The Formation of an Aristocracy in the Ottawa Valley," *Canadian Historical Association, Historical Papers* (1967), pp. 105–17; R. J. Burns, "God's Chosen People: The Origins of

Toronto Society, 1793–1818,'' *Canadian Historical Association, Historical Papers*, (1973), pp. 213–28.

14. Katz, *The People of Hamilton*, pp. 177–86.
15. Artibise, *Winnipeg*, pp. 23–42.
16. Guy Bourassa, ''The Political Elite of Montreal: From Aristrocracy to Democracy.'' In L. D. Feldman and M. D. Goldrick, eds., *Politics and Government of Urban Canada: Selected Readings* (Toronto: Methuen, 1969), pp. 124–34.
17. R. A. J. McDonald, ''The Business Elite and Municipal Politics.''
18. T. W. Acheson, ''The Social Origins of Canadian Industrialism: A Study in the Structure of Entrepreneurship,'' (Ph.D. Diss., University of Toronto, 1971). See especially pp. 191, 235, 254–55, 260.
19. J. M. S. Careless, ''Aspects of Urban Life in the West,'' in G. A. Stelter and A. F. J. Artibise, eds., *The Canadian City: Essays in Urban History* (Toronto: McClelland and Stewart, 1977), pp. 125–41. For a more detailed discussion of the role of boards of trade in Canadian urban centres, see E. Bloomfield, ''Boards of Trade and Canadian Urban Development,'' *Urban History Review* (October 1983).
20. A. F. J. Artibise, ''In Pursuit of Growth: Municipal Boosterism and Urban Development in the Canadian Prairie West, 1871–1913,'' in G. Stelter and A. Artibise, eds., *Shaping the Urban Landscape: Aspects of the Canadian City-Building Process* (Ottawa: Carleton University Press, 1982), pp. 116–47; and ''Continuity and Change: Elites and Prairie Urban Development, 1914–1950,'' in A. Artibise and G. Stelter, eds., *The Usable Urban Past: Planning and Politics in the Modern Canadian City* (Toronto: Macmillan, 1979), pp. 130–54. For a more general review of the role of urban elites in promoting the growth of their cities, see also Elizabeth Bloomfield, ''Community, Ethos and Local Initiative in Urban Economic Growth: Review of Theme in Canadian Urban History,'' *Urban History Yearbook* (1983).
21. John C. Weaver, ''Elitism and the Corporate Ideal: Businessmen and Boosters in Canadian Civic Reform, 1890–1920,'' in A. R. McCormack and Ian MacPherson, eds., *Cities in the West* (Ottawa: National Museum of Man, 1975) pp. 48–73. See also: J. C. Weaver, ''Tomorrow's Metropolis Revisited: A Critical Assessment of Urban Reform in Canada,'' in Stelter and Artibise, *The Canadian City*, pp. 394–418: J. C. Weaver, *Shaping the Canadian City: Essays on Urban Politics and Policy, 1890–1920* (Toronto: Institute of Public Administration, 1977).
22. The rest of the paper summarizes research reported more fully in Elizabeth Bloomfield, ''City-Building Processes in Berlin/Kitchener and Waterloo, 1870–1930,'' (Ph.D. Diss. University of Guelph, 1981). Sources included municipal records, assessment rolls, directories, manuscript censuses for 1871 and 1881, newspapers, obituaries and short biographies in the Waterloo Historical Society's annual volumes, Dun and Bradstreet reference handbooks and the earlier R. G. Dun manuscript credit ledgers. Biographies of some Berlin/Kitchener and Waterloo leaders were included in J. F. Middleton and F. Landon, *The Province of Ontario—A History* (1927) and A. Fraser, *History of Ontario* (1907).

23. Assessment records could not be used as the primary source as they have not survived in Berlin/Kitchener except for 1897 (in partial, printed form) and 1923. The records for these years were used for Berlin and Waterloo, with 1878 also for Waterloo, in order to corroborate the Dun credit ratings. The Dun ratings for persons and firms in Berlin/Kitchener and Waterloo were analyzed for 1875, 1885, 1895, 1905, 1915 and 1925 to represent each decade from the 1870's to the 1920's. Those with above-average "pecuniary strength" were identified, and this information was correlated with other evidence of community leadership.
24. The technique of measuring community leadership described here might be modified in various ways, depending on available source materials and the purposes of the study. More than one category of wealth might be used; political leadership might be based on service on boards and commissions as well as the municipal councils; and participation in a variety of associations instead of or as well as the boards of trade might be used as the criterion for associational leadership.
25. The advantage of a head start for the founding leaders has been noted in R. S. Alcorn, "Leadership and Stability in Mid-Nineteenth Century America: A Case Study of an Illinois Town," *Journal of American History*, 61 (December 1974): 685–702.
26. For explanation of the distinction between "local" "and cosmopolitan" community leaders, see R. K. Merton, "Patterns of Influence: Local and Cosmopolitan Influentials," in *Social Theory and Social Structure* (Glencoe, 1949), pp. 387–420.
27. "Biography of Jacob Y. Shantz by his son Menno B. Shantz," unpublished typescript, n.d. c. 1931 (Kitchener Public Library); "J. Y. Shantz" *Waterloo Historical Society Annual Report* 12 (1924) 85–100.
28. Increasing concentration of wealth (measured as real property) is suggested by analysis of the assessment rolls for Waterloo in 1878 and 1897, and for Berlin/Kitchener in 1897 and 1923. In 1878, Waterloo's top 4.1 per cent of ratepayers owned 35.2 of the total assessed value; the same proportion owned 45.5 per cent in 1897. In 1897, the top 2.1 per cent of Berlin's ratepayers owned 25.4 per cent of total assessed value; the same proportion owned 39 per cent in 1923.
29. *Berlin News Record*, 31 December 1896.
30. In Winnipeg, Artibise found that only 10 per cent of the city councillors were manufacturers, while real estate agents and financiers comprised one-third to one-half. (Artibise, *Winnipeg,* pp. 24–27). The smaller importance of manufacturers in Hamilton is more surprising, for that city was strongly industrialized. But between 1895 and 1910, while Hamilton had a definite policy of industrial promotion, only one-fifth to one-quarter of its municipal councillors were manufacturers compared with well over one-third in Berlin and Waterloo. Diana J. Middleton and David F. Walker, "Manufacturers and Industrial Development Policy in Hamilton, Ontario, 1890–1910," *Urban History Review* 8, no. 3 (February 1980): 23–29.
31. For a detailed study of workingmen's participation in the municipal govern-

ment in a different type of town, see Frank, "Company Town/Labour Town." Frank notes that, at first, workingmen would not vote for a candidate of their own class; this was evident, also, in Berlin for the first few years after the Trades and Labor Council was formed in 1900.

32. R. Presthus, *Men at the Top: A Study in Community Power*, (New York, 1964) pp. 94–97. This concept is discussed also by W. Glazer, "Participation and Power: Voluntary Associations and the Functional Organization of Cincinnati in 1840," *Historical Methods Newsletter* 5, no. 4 (September 1972): 151–68.
33. Dahl, *Who Governs*? It is possible also to relate the numbers of leaders to the size of the community population. A simple index may be obtained by calculating the percentage of leaders in each decade of the approximate average number of heads of households or male ratepayers. For Berlin, the percentages were 6 per cent in the 1870's, 4.4 per cent in the 1880's, 3.4 per cent in the 1890's, 2.9 per cent in the 1900's, 2.3 per cent in the 1910's and 2.0 per cent in the 1920's. In the smaller town of Waterloo, the percentage was 10 per cent in the 1870's, declining to about 4 per cent in the 1920's.
34. The industrial policies of Berlin and Waterloo are discussed more fully in Bloomfield, "City-Building Processes in Berlin/Kitchener and Waterloo," pp. 183–331.
35. Municipal bonusing powers in Ontario are summarized in E. Bloomfield, "Municipal Bonusing of Industry: The Legislative Framework in Ontario to 1930," *Urban History Review* 9, no. 3 (February 1981): 59–76.
36. W. V. Uttley, *History of Kitchener* (Waterloo: The Chronicle Press, 1937), p. 408.
37. For a more detailed study of the planning movement, see E. Bloomfield "Reshaping the Urban Landscape? Town Planning Efforts in Kitchener-Waterloo, 1912–1926," in G. A. Stelter and A. F. J. Artibise, eds., *Shaping the Urban Landscape: Aspects of the Canadian City-Building Process*, (Ottawa: Carleton University Press, 1982), pp. 256–303.

SECTION III

SHAPING THE URBAN ENTITY

Introduction

The complex factors involved in shaping the urban environment include vast changes in technology, national and international styles in architecture and planning, economic cycles, and decision-making at various levels of government, as well as thousands of private decisions by groups and individuals. To further complicate the process of city building, the way in which these factors act and interact changes considerably from one historical period to another and varies from community to community within the same time period.[1] Nevertheless, it is possible to isolate some of the major features of this process, such as land development and building, internal transportation, planning and architecture, and relate them to a central theme of this volume: who made the decisions and for whom were they made?

During the nineteenth century, the city-building process was largely a private matter and began with subdivision by an urban commercial and economic elite which had acquired much of the land surrounding towns and cities.[2] Subdivision usually meant surveying a simple grid and duly registering it with the proper authorities.[3] The sale of these lots often took place by public auction; as subdivision usually took place far ahead of real building needs, sales could be very slow indeed, and subdividers were as likely to lose as to make money.[4] Actual development (the construction of buildings) could take a long time, with the result that nineteenth century urban expansion tended to be uncoordinated, unregulated, and decentralized.[5] Those involved in the city-building process did not necessarily specialize in only one aspect of it, as is illustrated by Susan Buggey's case study of a nineteenth-century Halifax entrepreneur, John D. Nash. Although not one of the city's top elite, Nash was a land speculator, entrepreneurial builder, an auctioneer for property sales, while also serving as alderman with membership on several municipal committees dealing with development. In Edmonton, the frontier business community led the way in development, as is shown by John Gilpin. Through close connections with the civic administration, landowners could count on a vast expansion of public services, including street railroads, to the newly subdivided suburban fringe.

In most other cities, however, the issue of street railroad expansion to the suburbs was a major bone of contention between municipal councils and street railroad magnates. Christopher Armstrong and H. V. Nelles describe the conflicting claims for authority between companies, who were interested only in high ridership and short routes, and councils (in Montreal, Toronto, and Vancouver), who thought they could decide routes, standards of service, and extensions. In Toronto, the company's policies actually forced the city to remain a fairly compact entity making possible the later public transportation success. Intransigence on the part of some companies, especially in Toronto, made it almost inevitable that the system would become publicly owned when the franchises expired.[6]

A transition from a totally unregulated building process in the nineteenth century to one in which provincial and municipal governments occasionally intervened took place during a period of reform early in the twentieth century. In two decades when Canadians developed a heightened consciousness of the city, planning became professionalized, with some high profile planners like Thomas Adams and Horace Seymour as central figures, and the provinces introduced the legislative basis for planning.[7] The philosophy and practice of Canadian urban planning was a mixture of the British and American traditions and the particular political situation of individual provinces, as P. J. Smith shows. A key feature of Alberta's legislation, for example, was the adoption of the American model's chief instruments of control, the comprehensive plan and zoning, with the province retaining the ultimate power with respect to the form and procedures of planning. The general trends in the sources of planning authority are particularly apparent in resource town building, as Oiva Saarinen demonstrates in his detailed look at Northern Ontario towns. Companies planned their own "single-sector" towns before 1920, but with the Ontario government's involvement in the planning of Kapuskasing in the early 1920's, the intervention of government became more common and by the 1950's had become the norm.[8]

This does not mean that the public was directing urban development in post-1945 Canada. In her essay on Milton Park, a neighbourhood near the central business district of Montreal, Phyllis Lambert forcefully argues that an alliance of a big developer and municipal council effectively threatened the rights of the residents of a local community. Associates of William Zeckendorff, the New York entrepreneur who developed Place Ville Marie as a major commercial project, attempted to reconstruct Milton Park as a high density residential development. Architecturally, his project was conceived in the spirit of Le Corbusier's "Unité d'Habitation" at Marseilles, implying a vast concentration of financial resources and political cooperation. Determined residents were able to stop the project eventually, with cooperatives now attempting to introduce new principles of property rights. Lambert's research indicates not only the close connection between municipal authorities and large-scale developers which characterized the 1960's, but also points to the negative impact, in human terms, that architects like Le Corbusier have had on the urban fabric. As Lambert suggests, those interested in the urban past will have to look more seriously at the way in which technocratic conceptions have affected the evolution of Canadian cities.[9]

NOTES

1. The standard theoretical statement is still Roy Lubove, "The Urbanization Process: An Approach to Historical Research," in A. B. Callow, ed., *American Urban History* (New York: Oxford University Press, 1969), pp. 642–54. The application to American history is perhaps most effectively handled in Sam B. Warner, *The Urban Wilderness: A History of the American City* (New York: Harper and Row, 1972). A Canadian example is Gilbert A. Stelter, "The City-Building Process in Canada," in Stelter and A. F. J. Artibise, eds., *Shaping the Urban Landscape: Aspects of the Canadian City-Building Process* (Ottawa: Carleton University Press, 1982), pp. 1–29.
2. The best overview of the development literature is Michael J. Doucet, "Urban Land Development in Nineteenth-Century North America: Themes in the Literature," *Journal of Urban History*, 8 (May 1982): 299–342. The most important studies of suburban development are still Sam Warner, *Streetcar Suburbs: The Process of Growth in Boston, 1870–1900* (Cambridge, MA.: Harvard University Press, 1962); and H. J. Dyos, *Victorian Suburbs: A Study of the Growth of Camberwell* (Leicester: Leicester University Press, 1961).
3. The technical and legal aspects are described in detail in Michael J. Doucet, "Building the Victorian City: The Process of Land Development in Hamilton, Ontario," Ph.D. Diss. (Toronto: University of Toronto, 1977).
4. For an analysis of the land market and its financial rewards or failures, see Homer Hoyt, *One Hundred Years of Land Values in Chicago* (Chicago: University of Chicago Press, 1933) and Michael J. Doucet, "Speculation and the Physical Expansion of Mid-Nineteenth Century Hamilton," in Stelter and Artibise, *Shaping the Urban Landscape*, pp. 173–99.
5. Isobel Ganton, "The Subdivision Process in Toronto, 1851–1883," in Stelter and Artibise, *Shaping the Urban Landscape*, pp. 200–31; Michael P. Conzen, "The Morphology of Nineteenth-Century Cities in the United States," in Woodrow Borah, Jorge Hardoy and Gilbert Stelter, eds., *Urbanization in the Americas: The Background in Comparative Perspective* (Ottawa: National Museum of Man, 1980) pp. 119–42; Eric Lampard, "City Making and Mending in the United States: On Capitalizing a Social Environment," in ibid., 105–18.

6. Donald Davis, "Mass Transit and Private Ownership: An Alternative Perspective on the Case of Toronto," *Urban History Review*, 3–78 (February 1979): 60–98; Michael Doucet, "Politics, Space, and Trolleys: Mass Transit in Early Twentieth-Century Toronto," in Stelter and Artibise, *Shaping the Urban Landscape*, pp. 356–81; J. E. Rea, "How Winnipeg Was Nearly Won," in A. R. McCormack and Ian MacPherson, eds., *Cities in the West* (Ottawa: National Museum of Man, 1975), pp. 74–87.
7. The general literature on the international development of urban planning is extensive and sophisticated. An excellent overview with particular emphasis on the growing place of government intervention is Anthony Sutcliffe, *Towards the Planned City: Germany, Britain, the United States and France, 1780–1914* (Oxford: Basil Blackwell, 1981). For the planning of the world's largest cities, see Anthony Sutcliffe, ed., *Metropolis, 1890–1940* (Chicago: University of Chicago Press, 1984). A Marxist overview is Michael Dear and Allen J. Scott, eds., *Urbanization and Urban Planning in Capitalist Society* (London: Methuen, 1981). For the ideas of Canadian planners, see Paul Rutherford, ed., *Saving the Canadian City: The First Phase, 1890–1920: An Anthology of Articles on Urban Reform* (Toronto: University of Toronto Press, 1974). A number of recent studies of Canadian planning are in Alan F. J. Artibise and Gilbert Stelter, eds., *The Usable Urban Past: Planning and Politics in the Modern Canadian City* (Toronto: Macmillan, 1979). The best known planner in Canadian history is described in Michael Simpson, "Thomas Adams in Canada, 1914–1930," *Urban History Review* 11 (October 1982): 1–16. The federal agency which first brought Adams to Canada is the subject of Artibise and Stelter, "The Canadian Commission of Conservation in Historical Perspective," in Roger Kain, ed., *Planning for Conservation: An International Perspective* (London: Mansell, 1981), pp. 17–36.
8. Historically-oriented materials on general trends in resource town building are still relatively few. Exceptions are L. D. McCann, "The Changing Internal Structure of Canadian Resource Towns," *Plan Canada* 18 (March 1978): 46–59; Oiva Saarinen, "The Influence of Thomas Adams and the British New Towns Movement in the Planning of Canadian Resource Towns," in Artibise and Stelter, *The Usable Urban Past,* pp. 268–92; Stelter and Artibise, "Canadian Resource Towns in Historical Perspective," in Stelter and Artibise, *Shaping the Urban Landscape*, pp. 413–34.
9. For a similar interpretation see James Lorimer, *The Developers* (Toronto: Lorimer, 1978).

5

American Influences and Local Needs: Adaptations to the Alberta Planning System in 1928–1929

Peter J. Smith

"In Canada," wrote Horace Seymour in 1939, "we have been influenced in our Town Planning from two important sources, and naturally so, these being England and our neighbouring country, the United States."[1] This was a frank, if realistic, admission, and it gains all the more weight from having been written by one of the most prominent of Canada's first generation of practising planners. It continues to be a valid generalization today, although the strength of the influences has diminished as planning has matured in Canada. In the formative years, however, British and American ideas dominated Canadian planning, and they tended to be received as massive injections of comparatively undiluted concepts and practices.[2] The ability of host communities to assimilate borrowed ideas, and the implications for the development of planning systems distinctively adapted to local needs and conditions, provide this essay with its underlying theme.

The notion of distinctiveness is one that has not been given sufficient attention in Canada. Yet, quite apart from the possibility that Canadian planners might be innovative (and they have been), the very act of blending British and American ideas and adapting them to local circumstances must produce something unique. Whether that also means there is a distinctively *Canadian* approach to planning is arguable, given the fragmentation of authority amongst the separate provincial governments. But, since their formal origins in the years before the First World War, planning institutions in Canada have never been purely British or purely American. Rather, they have evolved through an increasingly complex process of cumulative adaptation. Always under the stimulus of a perceived local need for a more effective form of control, some elements are dropped from the planning system while new ones are grafted on. Today, the new elements are likely to be locally devised modifications of established instruments and procedures, but in the founding stages of planning system development they were normally borrowed. Sometimes the borrowing was direct from American or British sources; at other times, the borrowed elements had themselves been filtered through some earlier Canadian adaptations. They might then be modified yet again in the new situation. Thus, there is a high potential for variation among the provinces.

A fairly obvious research approach can be built around this construction. To understand why planning in Canada has assumed its present forms, it is necessary to set the individual planning systems in their evolutionary contexts, province by province. This is much more than a matter of determining what changes were made when. It requires a detailed understanding of the exigencies of time and place, ideological as well as practical, and their implications for the assessments that were made of planning needs and opportunities, including all that was thought to be known about comparable experiences elsewhere.

In total, this would be a huge undertaking, but much can be learned, to begin with, from an analysis of certain key pieces of planning legislation. The Alberta statutes of 1928 and 1929 fall into this category for two reasons: they were the first examples, in Canada, of a deliberate reorganization of a planning system and an equally deliberate reorientation from a British model to an American one; and they were considered, in their own time, to have set new standards of planning legislation for all the Canadian provinces.[3]

There is a more general sense, as well, in which it is logical to begin this line of research with an analysis of legislative changes. In the words of two of the earliest scholars of American planning, Theodora Kimball Hubbard and Henry Vincent Hubbard: "Sound legislation is an essential implement for any widespread social movement which is to be permanently useful."[4] To a quite remarkable degree, the development of planning practice has depended upon the availability of enabling legislation in the United States no less than in Canada or the United Kingdom. And although good legislation, on its own, is no guarantee of effective planning, it is certainly regarded as a necessary precondition.

FOUNDING PRINCIPLES: THE 1913 ACT

If the Alberta statutes of 1928 and 1929 are to be interpreted as a case of cumulative adaptation, it is necessary to establish the bases on which the adaptations were made. These are to be found in Alberta's original planning legislation, the Town Planning Act of 1913, which was itself closely modelled on one section of the British Housing and Town Planning Act of 1909. The section was not borrowed directly, though. New Brunswick adopted a slightly modified version of the British statute in 1912, and it was this that was copied, with some further small modifications, by Alberta. From the outset, then, Alberta's planning system incorporated a mix of direct and indirect borrowing and local innovation.[5]

The principal feature common to all three statutes was their reliance on a single method of control known as the "town planning scheme." In North American terms, this was a combination of subdivision, zoning and public facilities plans; it was designed to permit a direct, detailed control over the land development process. Schemes were restricted to undeveloped land, normally in fairly small tracts, and then only with the assent of the owners, whose cooperation was to be sought at all times. Landowners might even seek to have schemes prepared, but a scheme always had to be adopted by a local authority to have legal force. It was also envisaged that the initiative for preparing schemes would normally come from the local authorities. In short, the legislation was jointly founded on the principles of local responsibility and limited interference with the rights of private property.

At the same time, in all three cases, considerable supervisory powers were reserved to the central governments, and it was here that the Canadian statutes diverged from the British model and from each other. The borrowed instruments of town planning had to fit with established administrative systems and attitudes. Thus, distinctively Canadian approaches emerged. The chief source of difference was the fact that the British legislation came at a comparatively advanced stage in a long evolutionary process for which there was no parallel in the Canadian provinces. This leads to two important points. The first is that public administration was far more highly developed in the United Kingdom; in particular, the responsibility for enforcing all environmental health legislation was firmly in the hands of the Local Government Board, which was the logical body to administer the town planning act as well. The two provinces had nothing remotely comparable, although Alberta had at least set up its Department of Municipal Affairs in 1912. The second point arises from the highly charged political milieu in which the British legislation was forged and the threat that it was thought to pose to the traditional rights of private property.[6] The result was a curiously ambivalent statute. While British cities were given the right to a powerful new tool, which they could use or not, essentially at their own discretion, they were also constrained in various ways to ensure that they would not abuse their trust. In effect, the chief role for central authority in the planning system was to guard against local *ir*responsibility, whether of negligence, at the one extreme, or of misguided zeal, at the other. In the former case, the Local Government Board could intervene to require that a town planning scheme be prepared; in the latter, which troubled parliament far more, an elaborate approval procedure was constructed for the protection of private interests in property.[7]

These nuances were lost in their Canadian translation. Although the clauses for the protection of property rights were repeated, the statutory procedures of town planning were simplified in ways that threw British caution to the winds. Three successive barriers were built into the British process, but in the New Brunswick act they were collapsed into one, and the responsibility for reviewing and sanctioning town planning schemes, which in Britain was shared by the Local Government Board and parliament, was placed solely on the lieutenant-governor in council.[8] In Alberta, the process of executive delegation was carried a step further, to the newly-created minister of municipal affairs.[9] Cabinet's only task in the Alberta system was to adopt town planning regulations, a concern that persists to this day. The principle of ministerial sanction has also persisted, though in much-modified form.

Since neither New Brunswick nor Alberta put its planning system to any test, it is impossible to know what practical effect the procedural changes would have had. One point is clear, however; without the technical skills of an experienced administration, the potential for effective central direction was substantially reduced. This had to put more responsibility on the local authorities, who, of course, were no better equipped for the technical work of planning than their senior governments. But that, at least, was a familiar problem in North America, and it had already produced a formula solution: the planning commission. In its original development, the commission concept married the civic reform ideals of progressivism with the City Beautiful movement, and it found quick acceptance in Canada on both counts.[10] In 1911, for example, city planning commissions were created in Winnipeg and Calgary, and the Calgary commission was an influential advocate for an Alberta planning statute.[11] Commissions were seen as a way of capitalizing upon the energy, civic pride, and expert knowledge of business and professional leaders who would not normally be drawn into civic politics. Indeed, so great was the faith in the integrity and efficiency of the commission form of government that local authorities in New Brunswick and Alberta were given the option, under the planning statutes, of appointing commissions with full power to prepare and implement town planning schemes. In the North American situation, it was a logical adaption of a planning system lifted from an altogether different administrative context.

THE PRACTICAL AND IDEOLOGICAL CONTEXT OF REFORM

As a development control measure, the Alberta Town Planning Act of

1913 was outdated as soon as it was passed. The great western real estate boom, which had provided the economic incentive for town planning schemes, was already collapsing, and with it went any opportunity to make use of the act. So extravagant was the supply of subdivided land around Alberta cities that it was not until the new boom conditions of the 1950's that planned developments of the kind envisaged in 1913 at last became feasible.[12] In the meantime, however, the Alberta planning system had been required to adapt to the very different environment of the 1920's. This it did in three ways: by replacing or revising those parts of the planning system that were no longer thought to be effective; by filling critical gaps in the original system; and by adopting innovative responses to new concerns (or to renewed expressions of old concerns).

The initial impetus came from the civic administrations, especially the city of Edmonton, which began to be troubled by its limited control over private development. The 1920's brought a fresh spurt of growth to Alberta's cities, and construction of all kinds increased substantially. Some regulatory powers were available in the local building codes, and these had even begun to evolve towards a primitive form of zoning, with a patchwork of density regulations and partial land-use segregation.[13] But, in Edmonton at least, a more comprehensive approach was thought to be needed, if private development were to be regulated in the public interest. As early as 1926, then, the civic administration began to look to American planning theory and its chief instruments, the comprehensive plan and zoning, for a more appropriate basis of control.[14]

Throughout 1927, one of Edmonton's city commissioners was in correspondence with prominent Canadian planners, most notably Horace Seymour, who was then working on the comprehensive plan of Vancouver under the direction of Harland Bartholomew. Seymour's influence was extremely important, because no Canadian planner was more familiar with the requirements of American theory or more experienced in its application.[15] In association with Thomas Adams, as consultants to the cities of Kitchener and Waterloo between 1922 and 1924, Seymour had actually participated in the first American-style comprehensive planning exercise in Canada. He had also learned that Canadian cities faced a jurisdictional barrier that American cities did not, in the sense that there was no Canadian equivalent of the constitutional police power from which American zoning ordinances derived their legitimacy. Since Canadian municipal governments had no constitutional rights of their own, the zoning power could be granted only by provincial statute.[16]

The implication for Edmonton was obvious. If American techniques of development control, meaning zoning above all, were to be available to Alberta cities, the existing statute had to be rewritten. And the model that was turned to was British Columbia, which in 1925, after years of criticism for its tardiness, had finally adopted a statute incorporating the major elements of contemporary American planning theory. In particular, as Seymour later observed, British Columbia's act was the first in Canada to grant municipal governments the right to zoning and the first to describe, in considerable detail, the matters that could be regulated under a zoning by-law.[17] To Edmonton's civic officials, the Alberta act of 1913 suffered badly in comparison. It was said to be "not . . . nearly so useful" as the British Columbia statute, which was thought to be "a more practical type of legislation." Late in 1927, therefore, the city of Edmonton began to lobby the provincial government to replace the original statute with "a new Act framed to meet modern requirements."[18]

For its part, the provincial government was entirely sympathetic to this approach. Several officials in the Department of Municipal Affairs, including the minister, were actively interested in the reform of the planning system and were soliciting advice for themselves.[19] In fact, a great deal of information was collected from many sources, but one point in particular made a critical impression. This was the argument, which planners like Thomas Adams and Alfred Buckley had been making for years, that the chief weakness of planning administration across Canada occurred at the provincial level, in the failure to organize some systematic means of providing professional assistance to municipal governments. Among all the provinces, only Saskatchewan had a provincial planning officer, and the British Columbia government had expressly refused to provide for such a position in its otherwise highly regarded statute of 1925. To another prominent Canadian planner, Nolan Cauchon, it seemed clear that "our failure to advance town planning . . . is largely due to the indisposition of provincial governments to appoint competent staff to make the acts intelligible and acceptable to our people."[20]

By the winter of 1927–28, the force of this general line of criticism had come to be accepted by the Alberta government, for three reasons. The first was the all-too-evident failure of the 1913 act, which had been attributed, at least in part, to the lack of a provincial planning agency.[21] In view of the changed circumstances after 1913, the claim was not well founded, but the fact that it was made at all is the important point. Next, it became obvious that the reconstruction of the municipal planning system, as advocated by the city of Edmonton, was a radical undertaking. The government therefore decided that the legislation should be revised in two stages, and one of the purposes of the first stage, in the words of the premier, was to create a position for "a skilled town-planning engineer" whose immediate responsibility would be to draft a completely new statute.[22] The post was filled, late in 1928, by Horace Seymour.[23]

As well as addressing these administrative concerns, the idea of a central planning body gained favour in Alberta because it allowed the government to respond to special demands from its political constituency. The government of the day, the United Farmers of Alberta, had won office in 1921 as a local expression of the agrarian unrest then stirring so powerfully throughout western Canada. Six years later, the passion for reform had cooled considerably, but the government's attitude towards planning was nonetheless influenced by three key elements of U.F.A. political belief. The first was its strong rural orientation. The second and third, in Macpherson's terms, were the core ideas of U.F.A. political theory: the "concept of democracy as a non-exploitive social order and [the] concept of democratic government as a scheme of popular control of elected representatives."[24] And underlying both ideas was a deeply held faith in the cooperative principle, for it was only through cooperation that "the natural harmony of group interests" could be expected to express itself.[25] The U.F.A.'s particular conception of grassroots democracy also demanded an organized system of strong local communities, willing and able to manage their own affairs responsibly and cooperatively.

In practice, the U.F.A. government was unable to live up to the requirements of its theory, but the idea of responsible local government was always important. Between 1927 and 1929, for example, the legislation respecting municipal corporations was extensively revised, and it was no coincidence that the planning legislation was being revised at the same time.[26] It was all part of a general concern that the local governments should be provided with whatever statutory instruments were needed to ensure effective community control, including control over the physical environment. The quality of rural and small-town life was especially important in the U.F.A.'s view of its mandate. Yet these were precisely the communities that were least likely to have access to the technical skills that would allow them to make effective use of modern planning instruments. A central planning agency, designed to help the local communities help themselves, in a cooperative atmosphere, was the obvious solution.

The U.F.A. government was also highly sensitive to issues raised by the grassroots organizations which represented the principle of popular control in action. In 1927, two of these organizations voiced concern about physical planning matters. The first was the Edmonton Local Council of Women, which petitioned the city council to appoint a broadly based planning commission, essentially to provide advice on civic beautification.[27] The second, the United Farm Women of Alberta, addressed itself directly to the provincial government, this time in the cause of rural beautification: specifically, to protest the uncontrolled spread of billboards and gasoline stations along Alberta's highways. As it happened, this plea could not have been more timely. Premier Brownlee had, that summer, visited England, with results that are best recalled in his own words:

> The countryside of England is beautiful. It thrilled me. And one gospel I am going to preach from now on, in season and out of season, is to beautify Canada. We stand in Alberta today with the greatest heritage of natural beauty in the world, a potential source of wealth which, in the years to come, will yield a greater wealth than we are today obtaining from the flood of grain that is pouring into our granaries. Beautify our towns. Beautify our highways. Inspire our people with a sense of beauty in their surroundings that they may leave a more splendid heritage to coming generations.[28]

In this mission, too, there would be a role for a central planning body.

THE TOWN PLANNING AND PRESERVATION OF NATURAL BEAUTY ACT, 1928

The first step towards a reformed planning system was completed in the spring of 1928 with the passage of the Town Planning and Preservation of Natural Beauty Act, a short and deceptively simple statute which began to move Canadian planning in important new directions. Its central purpose was to establish, under the name of the Town and Rural Planning Advisory Board, the kind of provincial agency that Canadian planners had sought for so long.

In its composition and functions, the board combined elements of the planning commission concept with the British Local Government Board. Like the former, it was a means of bringing informed and even expert advice to bear on planning matters, in a forum that was also intended to foster popular interest in planning and to carry it forward as a cooperative enterprise. These aims were reflected in the original membership. The chairman was C. Lionel Gibbs, an Edmonton architect and erstwhile alderman who had become one of the leading advocates of planning in the provincial legislature. Premier Brownlee and the minister of municipal affairs represented the government; the members at large were an engineer, a farmer, and a businessman (an explicit attempt to draw several economic group interests together, in accordance with U.F.A. theory); and there were representatives from two influential women's organizations, the United Farm Women of Alberta and the Women's Institute.[29] Finally, the act provided that one member of the board should be paid a salary, thus opening the way to Seymour's appointment as Alberta's first director of town and rural planning.

In its advisory capacity, the board was required to do five things: "to cooperate with any local authority" desiring assistance in the preparation and implementation of a town planning scheme; to compile information on town planning schemes; to advise the minister of public works about subdivision regulations; "to assist and advise any rural authority in devising ways and means of preserving the natural beauty of the locality" and ensure that new buildings and structures (such as billboards) would not mar the landscape; and "to promote in any community a pride in the amenities of its neighbourhood." In addition, like the Local Government Board, the Town and Rural Planning Advisory Board had a variety of executive and regulatory powers, particularly with respect to the control of development along the frontages of designated provincial highways. It could even order the demolition of buildings erected without permission in the highway zones, and was empowered to buy or expropriate land for provincial park purposes and for the preservation of natural beauty or historic sites. These were extraordinary powers to have delegated to a board of this kind, even allowing for the fact that they were under cabinet supervision. In effect, the planning board had been given some of the characteristics of an administrative tribunal. And the fact that the provincial planning director was also a full statutory member of such a board did much to enhance the authority of the central planning establishment. The real impact of these developments was not to be felt until the 1950's, when the board's quasijudicial role was strengthened considerably, but they were a crucial step in the evolution of a distinctive Alberta approach to planning system organization.

There was a more obvious respect in which the Town and Rural Planning Advisory Board was an innovative concept — indeed, in which the 1928 Act was in the forefront of international planning thought. This was the bracketing of town planning with rural planning, a theme that Thomas Adams had pursued repeatedly during his years with the Commission of Conservation.[30] It was also basic to the garden city concept, of course, and to Patrick Geddes's theory of regional town planning, then at its peak of influence in Great Britain and the United States.[31] Whether these ideas carried much weight in Alberta is open to question, but the 1928 act proved to be remarkably in tune with the times. To Alfred Buckley, for example, it was a manifestation of "the inescapable thought-drift to regional planning" that must occur whenever the problems of urban development were faced responsibly.[32] It also anticipated an important trend in planning legislation, as became clear in 1931 when the British parliament began to debate its new Town and Country Planning Bill.[33]

In another respect, too, the 1928 act was in the vanguard of contemporary planning thought. In Seymour's opinion, the establishment of a provincial board satisfied some of the objects of what had come to be known in

American theory as "state planning."[34] The concept gained little favour with state legislators in the 1920's, but various techniques were being employed to encourage cities to plan for themselves, and at least two states, Pennsylvania and Massachusetts, had set up central agencies for this purpose.[35] In most cases, however, state governments were deterred from a more active role by the home rule movement, which one of the earliest authorities on American planning law described as being "especially applicable to city planning."[36] Ironically, then, it was much simpler for Alberta to adopt the principles of "state" planning than it would have been for most state governments.

THE TOWN PLANNING ACT, 1929

With the passage of the 1928 act, Alberta was in the anomalous situation of having two planning statutes, since the 1913 act had been neither repealed nor amended.[37] Seymour's first task, therefore, was to draft a bill by which the existing legislation would be consolidated and revised. His general mandate was to combine the innovative features of the 1928 act (which was incorporated, virtually intact, in the new statute) with his own interpretation of American theory and practice, suitably adapted to local circumstances. The result was the Town Planning Act, 1929, the longest and most complex piece of planning legislation then available anywhere in Canada. It was also the most thorough illustration, to that time, of the process of cumulative adaptation and, in its new provisions, the most complete expression of American planning techniques in Canadian law. The British Columbia act was the immediate model, particularly with respect to zoning, but the Alberta act was far from a direct copy.[38] Even the borrowed clauses were likely to be revised, sometimes with critical changes of meaning, and features unique to Alberta were threaded throughout.

As a legal draftsman, Seymour had to accommodate a mix of ideological prescriptions drawn, on the one hand, from prevailing social and political attitudes and, on the other, from his own vision of scientific town planning and the "city efficient." Fortunately, these prescriptions had much in common. The ideals of cooperation and community responsibility, for example, were as firmly entrenched in international planning thought as they were in U.F.A. political theory, thus creating an environment in which "advanced" planning ideas could be accepted without hesitation. The most notable instance was the power granted to adjoining municipalities, rural as well as urban, to enter into voluntary coalitions through the organization of regional planning commissions. There had been some precedent for this in the 1913 act, and in the British act of 1909, but the term "regional planning" appears for the first time in 1929 and was an obvious adaptation to one of the strongest trends in planning thought in the 1920's.[39] Simultaneously, the idea of autonomous communities cooperating for their mutual benefit was in full accord with the U.F.A. conception of responsible local government.

Yet, just as Seymour's mentor, Thomas Adams, never really reconciled his social ideal of cooperative individualism with the technical requirements of planning as an applied science,[40] so Seymour was not particularly adept at marrying his professional expectations with the U.F.A. brand of populism. "The keynote of the Town Planning Act," he wrote, "is co-operation and yet under certain conditions the Government can exercise compulsory powers."[41] For the most part, those powers were vested in the Town and Rural Planning Advisory Board and had been inherited from the 1928 act, but there can be no question that Seymour himself approved. Like Adams, Seymour was squarely in the utilitarian tradition of planning. His conception of the public interest demanded that some ultimate authority, acting on the advice of disinterested experts who truly understood the "facts" of the situation, should always be able to step in and prevent individuals or communities from behaving foolishly or selfishly. And if Seymour looked to contemporary American practice for the instruments of effective community control, he also continued to look to British precedents to set an appropriate role for central authority in the reformed planning system.

In pragmatic terms, the principal purpose of the 1929 act was to ensure that municipal governments were provided with the means to be able to plan for themselves responsibly and efficiently. The central element of the community planning system, following American theory, was the comprehensive plan, or the "official town plan" as it was styled in the Alberta and British Columbia statutes. It was also established that the official plan could comprise many separate plans and "schemes," all of which could be adopted and enforced independently of one another. There could be plans for parts of the municipal territory and for specific public improvements, along with city-wide measures such as a zoning by-law or a street widening by-law and, in the Alberta act (where these matters were itemized in greater detail), programmes for capital works and the phasing of development. These last ideas seem to have come directly from the Vancouver plan, which Seymour regularly referred to as his practical model.[42]

For all the emphasis on the comprehensive plan, however, it was zoning that formed the heart of the development control system. And although it was commonly said that zoning was only one part of a comprehensive plan, it was also the standard legal device for regulating the use of land and buildings and so had its own highly specialized purposes and information needs.[43] In the planning theory of the 1920's, zoning was not thought of as serving the ends of the comprehensive plan, which is the way their relationship is normally conceived today.[44] Rather, the plan served the ends of zoning, by giving it "scientific" legitimacy. "The very purposes of zoning," according to the Hubbards, "imply the necessity for comprehensive planning, since if the rights of one individual are to be limited, this limitation must be imposed for the *general* community benefit."[45] Unless the zoning plan was set in the context of the total package of studies and proposals that made up the comprehensive plan, they continued, quoting Bartholomew, it "becomes largely an instrument of expediency, subject to constant and often whimsical change." Unhappily, the Alberta Planning Act did nothing to remove that risk. As in the British Columbia act, the comprehensive planning power and the zoning power stand separate and apparently unconnected, with a predictable result: many Alberta municipalities adopted zoning by-laws in the 1930's, and some claimed they were taking the first step towards a comprehensive plan, but none ever arrived at that destination.[46]

As well as failing to establish any clear legal relationship between the comprehensive plan and the zoning by-law, the 1929 act was silent on the means by which regulations should be prepared. For his part, again following the example of the Vancouver plan, Seymour expected all planning measures to be based on scientific surveys and analyses.[47] But for purposes of the statute, it was more important to lay down the procedures by which plans would be given legal force. "Functional planning," wrote Seymour, "implies an intelligent control on municipal development — in fact, a way of municipal living, of cooperation between individual and community, of doing things under legislative authority and democratic forms of procedure."[48] In practice, however, in the 1929 act, the notion of planning as a democratic process did not translate well, probably because U.F.A. political theory and American planning theory were equally vague about its requirements.

Building on the initiative of the 1913 act, the responsibility for preparing and implementing all facets of a comprehensive plan was vested chiefly in town planning commissions. By 1929, the commission approach had won general acceptance in the United States; in Alberta it held the additional attraction of appearing to embody the principle of cooperative planning by responsible communities. In reality, however, American commissions fell far short of that ideal and in their origins were frankly elitist. Their role was one of providing leadership in the community planning system, and their relationship with the general public was governed by the desire (which in some cases was a legal necessity) to win popular approval for their plans.[49] To Seymour, this was a mark of democratic planning in action, but to critics like Robert Walker it was quite the opposite. It could lead, he feared, to self-serving and propagandistic commissions which would be more likely to thwart the constitutional instruments of democratic government than to sustain them.[50]

There is no evidence that Alberta's planning commissions succumbed to this danger, but neither is there evidence that they were particularly effective agents of popular control. In Edmonton at least, the commission functioned in a technical plan-making and administrative capacity, as the 1929 act gave it the authority to do. This outcome also suited Seymour's own conception of the planning process, his frequent appeals to democracy and cooperation notwithstanding. "A planning commission," he had written in 1927, "is useless unless its members are either qualified themselves to prepare a plan and get the law behind it or are wise enough to appoint qualified planners who know not only how to make a plan but also how to get it into operation."[51] The technical requirements of scientific town planning could tolerate no less. The 1929 act therefore granted town planning commissions the power to hire technical staff, and both Edmonton and Calgary did so immediately.

In Seymour's own theoretical descriptions of the commission concept, it is a technical, policy-making role that is particularly emphasized. Following the general run of American practice, he saw the planning commission as a coordinating body, the one public agency charged with the responsibility of taking a comprehensive overview of urban development needs and interests. "To be successful," he continued,

> a planning commission must, first of all, be a fact finding body and should have the facts relating to civic development obtained and brought out in graphical studies by competent technicians so they may be easily understood by the public as well as by civic officials. It should assimilate and correlate the facts so found and have plans prepared under technical guidance relating to both present and future development.[52]

These plans, in turn, would be the commission's means of conveying advice to the city council, where the ultimate decision-making authority rested. Under the 1929 act, for example, official town plans, schemes and regulations (including zoning) had to be adopted by by-law before they could take legal effect. The by-laws then had to be approved by the minister of municipal affairs, for the same reason as in 1913: to provide a check against local irresponsibility by ensuring that the by-laws lived up to professional standards, as determined by Horace Seymour.[53] Also as in 1913, the minister was authorized to order municipal governments to adopt planning by-laws if he thought them to be warranted in the public interest, a power that no minister saw fit to exercise under either statute.

By these means, the municipal planning system was placed under a degree of central control, but only with respect to the forms and procedures of planning. The policy substance of the plans remained a matter for local determination. Seymour also believed that all members of a community should be given an opportunity to express their views about the community's needs and future before any by-law was adopted. His concern, however, was more for the technical qualities of the planning policies and their acceptability than for the principles of participation and popular control. In his own words, "The public should be consulted as the plan is being prepared and their opinion woven into it."[54] But the "consulting" was to be done by the planning commission as part of its fact-finding mandate, and it was expected to lead to a clear community consensus upon which the planners could act. Today, such ideas look innocent beyond all imagining, and even in 1929 they were given a most limited interpretation in the statute. Their nearest approximation, in fact, appeared in a requirement that all planning by-laws be well advertised in advance, to give time for objections to be heard. This followed the lead of the U.S. standard planning act, although the Alberta act seems to have been one of the first (and certainly the first in Canada) to have made public hearings a formal condition of the process for adopting a comprehensive plan. In general, the public hearing was thought to be most applicable to zoning by-laws or ordinances, and then, of course, it was designed to protect individual interests in real property.[55]

The concern that the rights of private property should be adequately represented in the planning system was expressed in another way as well. In common with American practice, a right of appeal was granted in zoning cases, although the chosen procedure was distinctly un–American. In the first instance, appeals were to be directed to the planning commissions (in effect, empowering them to hear appeals against their own decisions); and in the second and final instance they were to go to the Town and Rural Planning Advisory Board, a point that generated the only serious opposition to the 1929 act. The argument, simply, was that property owners were being denied their right to a fair hearing in a proper court. The members of the board were described as experts in their own fields, but "like most experts," it was said, they "had only one viewpoint."[56] To this it was responded, by Premier Brownlee and Chairman Gibbs, that the courts were in no better position to judge zoning matters, technically and impartially, than were the admitted experts. On the contrary, in keeping with the tenets of scientific town planning, they saw zoning as essentially a technical issue and were quite willing to trust to the judgment of putative experts. The

Town and Rural Planning Advisory Board had taken a large step in its evolution as a quasijudicial tribunal.

Yet the situation was not without irony. In the first place, the arguments in the legislature seemed to ignore the board's popular base and the breadth of interests represented by its members, of whom only Seymour could be regarded as an expert on zoning. In the second place, the emphasis on expert judgment was in danger of undercutting a fundamental principle that had been made explicit in the British Columbia act. There, zoning appeals were to be judged by local boards which were instructed to "make such relaxations as special cases call for, and endeavour to see that substantial justice is done and that the interests of any individual are not unduly or unnecessarily sacrificed for the benefit of the community."[57] That principle had been implicit in the Alberta Act of 1913, as well, and it pointed to the desirability of local community control. In 1931, therefore, the Alberta Planning Act was amended to permit any municipality that had implemented zoning to appoint its own appeal board. And whatever the arguments for and against this approach, it sat more happily with both U.F.A. political philosophy and American planning theory. Although, as Bassett argued, the principle of due process and the broadness of the police power made it essential for there to be a right of ultimate appeal to the courts under the American system, technical boards of appeal or adjustment were considered equally necessary as the first line of defence against arbitrary or unfair ordinances.[58]

The constitutional differences between Canada and the United States, particularly with reference to the police power, also had some bearing on the one substantive issue that the 1929 act attempted to address. This was the issue of beauty, which had been so important a factor in the pressure to reform the Alberta legislation. Unhappily, in contemporary American theory the concept of beauty was under double jeopardy, suffering from "the bugbear of the City Beautiful" on the one hand and, on the other, from the unwillingness of the courts to accept it as a legitimate aspect of the police power.[59] Yet, no matter how strong the orientation to the "city efficient," the belief in civic beauty and natural beauty as proper ends for planning was still most powerful. The intellectual problem for planners therefore became one of rationalizing the criteria of beauty into those of efficiency. The Hubbards, for example, argued that the "fundamental beauty" with which planners should be concerned was to be found in the "pervading orderliness" of the well-planned city, with its "convenient and effective organic structure."[60] Seymour advanced similar views. "Beauty can only grow out of utility," he wrote; it "must be founded on order."[61] And although it did not necessarily follow that an efficiently arranged city would also be a beautiful one, this line of argument removed much of the case for attempting to treat beauty as a statutory concern in its own right. Seymour might claim that "architectural control, a consideration of the amenities, the preservation of natural beauty—all these are included in the scope of the Alberta Town Planning Act."[62] But in reality they appeared chiefly in the sections carried forward from 1928. The only innovation in 1929 came under the zoning power, where authority was granted to regulate "the architectural design, character and appearance" of buildings. Still, few if any American cities would have dared claim a similar right.

TOWARDS A DISTINCTIVE ALBERTA PLANNING SYSTEM

Three motives inspired the changes to Alberta's planning legislation in 1928 and 1929: to create a central planning agency and so correct what was generally regarded as the chief oversight of the 1913 act; to establish public responsibility for environmental protection and beautification, in both rural and urban areas; and to obtain the benefit of contemporary American planning practice, particularly with respect to zoning. All three motives were related to a desire for a more effective system of environmental control and reflected the conversion of local needs and concerns into real political pressure. But while there was much about Alberta's political environment in the 1920's that made it uniquely responsive to planning system reform, a complete break with the past was neither desired nor intended. Both in spirit (in the importance attached to the principles of local responsibility and limited interference with the rights of private property), and to a lesser extent in substance (in the use of ministerial sanctions and planning commissions), there was a considerable degree of continuity between the statutes of 1913 and 1929. In this sense, the adaptations were truly cumulative.

At the same time, in the details of its form and procedures, the 1929 act was radically different from its predecessor. In small part, this was because of some uniquely Albertan features, notably the quasijudicial role of the Town and Rural Planning Advisory Board and its executive powers over development in rural areas. But the distinctiveness of the new statute rested less in the originality of its planning ideas than in its blend of concepts and practices drawn from many different sources. In one way or another, the 1929 act attempted to accommodate all the important ideas of the day and to fit them into an appropriate administrative framework. In some respects, indeed, the Alberta statute was in the very forefront of planning thought: in the moves towards rural, regional and "state" planning, in the explicit adoption of a conservation ethic, and in the desire to provide the planning system with a popular base. Certainly, it went well beyond the standard range of American statutes or its immediate model, the British Columbia act of 1925, in giving expression to theoretical concepts that had gained little, if any, legislative acceptability elsewhere. Equally, however, in its conception of the municipal planning system, it went well beyond the British statute of the day, the Housing and Town Planning Act, 1919, which was still fixed upon the town planning scheme as the only instrument available to local governments. And although there was much that was common to planning thought on both sides of the Atlantic in the 1920's, the detailed practices of planning were very different. By accepting the entire package of techniques that made up the American comprehensive plan and marrying it to administrative procedures that still owed much to British conventions, it was inevitable that a different kind of planning system would be forged.

Even in Canada, the Alberta Town Planning Act, 1929 was unique. The British Columbia Act, for all that it had helped set the stage for Alberta's reforms, simply accepted the American approach to municipal planning, unadulterated by British practices or by larger concerns. Saskatchewan was then the only province with legislation to rival Alberta's in scope, and it, too, had been revised in 1928, but only by the addition of a section on zoning. The other elements of American comprehensive planning theory were ignored. Yet no other province in Canada had as much at that time. Manitoba was still operating under a statute modelled upon the British act of 1909, Quebec had no legislation at all, and Ontario's, in Seymour's view, was "very inadequate."[63] In fact, at the time of his death in 1940, Seymour was reported to be lobbying the Ontario government to adopt a consolidated planning statute "to facilitate Town Planning as an economic measure and in particular to provide for a Provincial Planning Board to encourage Town Planning throughout the Province."[64] His experience in Alberta had reinforced his conviction that most municipal governments, if left to their own devices, could not be expected to carry out effective functional planning. He was also distressed that planning progress in Canada appeared to be lagging far behind the United States, where, as early as 1934, some seven hundred towns and cities had organized planning agencies, while more than twelve hundred were zoned and at least two hundred had general or comprehensive plans.[65] Whenever he was given the opportunity, therefore, Seymour urged other provincial governments to remodel their planning legislation on the Alberta example. His greatest success came in New Brunswick in 1936, in a statute that was a polished version of the Alberta act with one important addition: the responsibilities of the provincial planning board were expanded to include the preparation of an "official provincial plan." It was quite a breakthrough for Seymour to have achieved, but it was effectively stillborn, and no other Canadian province moved so far along the path to ''state'' planning. In 1939, for example, when Nova Scotia revised its statute under Seymour's guidance, the 1929 act was again the model, but the idea of a central planning agency was completely rejected.

Within Alberta, however, Seymour's legislation can be described, in a critical sense, as a success. The physical achievements may not have been great, except for the complete disappearance of highway billboards, but the combination of a highly-regarded statute and Horace Seymour's energy stood Alberta in good stead twenty years later.[66] In the postwar boom period, no province in Canada was able to adapt its planning services more quickly or more forcefully to the new circumstances; in Alberta the bases of a workable organization were already in place, not just in the statute but in reality. The agencies of planning administration functioned at a low level between the mid-1930's and the mid-1940's, but at least they functioned.[67] They also helped to nurture a receptive attitude towards planning and with that, in one of Seymour's favourite catch-phrases, a determination not to repeat the mistakes of the past.[68]

From the standpoint of the historical interpreter, that may be the most important point of all. If the Alberta experience can be taken as a reliable guide, the process of cumulative adaptation by which planning legislation evolves is a conscious, deliberate, learning process. The quality of the learning is no doubt open to question, since it must always be conditioned by the available experience and by prevailing attitudes and beliefs. It is also extremely difficult to give adequate expression to abstract ideas in the language of statute law, but the Alberta acts of 1928 and 1929 make it clear that the process of legislative revision was treated with the utmost seriousness, even at this comparatively early stage in Canadian planning history.

NOTES

1. ''Memorandum to accompany a draft of the Nova Scotia Town Planning Act, 1939,'' (Horace L. Seymour Papers [hereafter Seymour Papers] Public Archives of Canada. As of August 1981, when they were consulted for this essay, these papers had not been sorted or classified.)
2. The results have never been as bizarre as those experienced recently by one British planning consultant in Tanzania (the basic similarities in cultural context among the three countries have ensured that), but there are issues of common concern whenever social institutions such as planning are translated from their original settings. Patrick McAuslan, *The Ideologies of Planning Law* (Oxford: Pergamon, 1980), pp. xi–xii. In his role as legal advisor on the design of a new capital city, McAuslan ''was struck by the extreme oddity of having to draft regulations under the authority of an English colonial ordi-

nance, promulgated in 1956 and based on English models from the 30's, to implement a Master Plan drawn up by Canadian planning consultants and geared, for all its language, to create a North American city beautiful in the heart of the independent socialist self-help society of Tanzania in the 1970s." See, also, A. D. King, "Exporting planning: the colonial and neo-colonial experience," in Gordon Cherry, ed., *Shaping an Urban World* (London: Mansell, 1980), pp. 203–26.

3. "The New Alberta Town Planning Act," *Journal of the Town Planning Institute* 7 (1928): 63–64; "The New Alberta Town Planning Bill," *Journal of the Town Planning Institute* 8 (1929): 40–41; and "Alberta Town Planning Board—First Annual Report," *Journal of the Town Planning Institute* 9 (1930): 52.
4. In the preface to Edward M. Bassett, Frank B. Williams, Alfred Bettman and Robert Whitten, *Model Laws for Planning Cities, Counties and States* (Cambridge, MA: Harvard University Press, 1935), p. v.
5. For more detailed interpretations of the 1913 act, see David G. Bettison, John K. Kenward and Larrie Taylor, *Urban Affairs in Alberta* (Edmonton: University of Alberta Press, 1975), pp. 18–25, and P. J. Smith, "The Principle of Utility and the Origins of Planning Legislation in Alberta, 1912–1975" in Alan F. J. Artibise and Gilbert A. Stelter, eds., *The Usable Urban Past: Planning and Politics in the Modern Canadian City* (Toronto: Macmillan 1979), pp. 196–213.
6. John Minett, "The Housing, Town Planning, etc. Act, 1909," *The Planner* 60 (1974): 676–80.
7. These interlocking themes of central vs. local authority and collective control vs. individual freedom were to bedevil the environmental health legislation of the Victorian and Edwardian periods. For a recent case study, see P. J. Smith, "The Legislated Control of River Pollution in Victorian Scotland," *Scottish Geographical Magazine* 98 (1982): 66–76.
8. The Local Government Board had first to authorize the preparation of a town planning scheme and then to approve the completed scheme before it could be laid before parliament, which had a final right of veto.
9. This Alberta variation may reflect a strikingly different attitude towards local government. In New Brunswick, local autonomy has been described as seriously eroded by 1900, and the provincial government was in direct control of many matters affecting the municipalities: Ralph R. Krueger, "The Provincial-Municipal Government Revolution in New Brunswick," *Canadian Public Administration* 13 (1970): 58–59. The government of Alberta, on the other hand, was actively encouraging the development of responsible municipal government in the years before the First World War: Eric J. Hanson, *Local Government in Alberta* (Toronto: McClelland and Stewart, 1956), pp. 20–33.
10. Mel Scott, *American City Planning Since 1890* (Berkeley: University of California Press, 1969), pp. 47–109.
11. Alan F. J. Artibise, *Winnipeg: A Social History of Urban Growth, 1874–1914* (Montreal: McGill-Queen's University Press, 1975), pp. 267–80, and J.

David Hulchanski, *The Origins of Urban Land Use Planning in Alberta, 1900–1945* (Toronto: University of Toronto, 1981), pp. 17–20.

12. For a case study see P. J. Smith and D. G. Harasym, "Planning for Retail Services in New Residential Areas Since 1944," in Brenton M. Barr, ed., *Calgary: Metropolitan Structure and Influence* (Victoria: University of Victoria, 1975), pp. 157–91.
13. E. H. Dale, "The Role of Successive Town and City Councils in the Evolution of Edmonton, Alberta, 1892 to 1966," (Ph.D. Diss., University of Alberta, 1969), pp. 210–11. See also, Hulchanski, *The Origins of Urban Land Use Planning*, p. 5.
14. City council was made aware of the limitations of the Town Planning Act, 1913 in a letter written by the city solicitor on 10 May, 1926.
15. For brief reviews of Seymour's career see Hulchanski, *The Origins of Urban Land Use Planning* pp. 57–59, and Shirley Spragge, "Biographical note: Horace Seymour," *Plan Canada* 15 (1975): 45–46. See also, "Mr. Horace L. Seymour goes to Alberta," *Journal of the Town Planning Institute* 7 (1928): 156–57.
16. Elizabeth Bloomfield, "Town Planning Efforts in Kitchener-Waterloo, 1912–1925," *Urban History Review* 9, No.1 (1980): 30–36.
17. "Comments prepared by George S. Mooney and Horace L. Seymour on the Model Zoning By-law, October 1939," Seymour Papers.
18. From a letter from one of Edmonton's commissioners to Alfred Buckley, editor of the *Journal of the Town Planning Institute*, 2 December 1927, and a Commissioners' report to City Council, 6 January, 1928.
19. Based on a variety of sources including correspondence in the Edmonton City Archives, sundry references in the *Journal of the Town Planning Institute*, and a speech of Premier Brownlee's, as reported in the *Edmonton Bulletin*, 10 March, 1928.
20. Nolan Cauchon, "The Legislative Aspects of Town Planning in Canada," *Journal of the Town Planning Institute*, 7 (1928): 4–5. The same point was made many times in the journal in the late 1920's and early 1930's.
21. *Journal of the Town Planning Institute*, 5, no.6 (1926): 28, and 6, no.6 (1927): 201.
22. *Edmonton Bulletin*, 10 March, 1928.
23. From correspondence in the Edmonton City Archives it is known that Seymour expressed interest in the position as early as 28 June, 1928, no doubt because of the imminent completion of the Vancouver contract. He was then advised to contact Premier Brownlee directly, as he "will be likely to dominate the situation." And although Seymour's appointment did not become official until January 1929 (*The Alberta Gazette* 25 (1929): 43), he was certainly at work the previous November. On 1 December, 1928, in a letter to one of Edmonton's commisioners, he made reference to the new town planning bill he was drafting.
24. C. B. Macpherson, *Democracy in Alberta: The Theory and Practice of a*

Quasi-Party System (Toronto: The University of Toronto Press, 1953), p. 54.
25. Ibid., 47.
26. Bettison, Kenward and Taylor, *Urban Affairs in Alberta*, p. 47.
27. A copy of the petition can be seen in Edmonton City Archives, File: Town Planning 1927–1931. Its success is made clear from a letter of 2 August 1927, in the same file: "The City Council have recently appointed a Committee consisting of Messrs. Aldermen Gibbs (Chairman), Keillor, Fairmile, Hazlett and Dineen to act as a special Town Planning Committee along with representatives from the various public organizations in the city who may be interested in city development with a view to their acting in an advisory capacity to the City Council relative to the important subject of Town Planning." See also the lengthy report on the "renaissance" of town planning in Alberta in *Journal of the Town Planning Institute* 6 (1927): 200–206.
28. *Journal of the Town Planning Institute* 6 (1927): pp. 192–93.
29. Horace L. Seymour, "The Province as a Planning Unit," *Journal of the Town Planning Institute* 8 (1929): 62.
30. See, for example, Canada, Commission of Conservation, *Report of the Eighth Annual Meeting* (Montreal: Federated Press, 1917), pp. 93–95.
31. In Scotland, through the leadership of Geddes's son-in-law, Frank C. Mears (F. C. Mears, "Regional Survey and Civic Development," *Quarterly Illustrated of the Incorporation of Architects in Scotland*, 13 [1925]: 25–26); in England, most notably in the work of Patrick Abercrombie (Gerald Dix, "Patrick Abercrombie," in Gordon Cherry, ed., *Pioneers in British Planning* [London: Architectural Press, 1981], pp. 106–11); and, in the United States, under the general influence of the Regional Planning Association of America (Roy Lubove, *Community Planning in the 1920's: The Contribution of the Regional Planning Association of America* [Pittsburgh: University of Pittsuburgh Press, 1963]).
32. *Journal of the Town Planning Institute* 7 (1928): p. 73.
33. Horace Seymour was at pains to draw out parallels between the British bill of 1931 and the Alberta acts of 1928 and 1929: "Technical Observations on Town Planning Progress in Alberta," appendix to a paper read at the conference of the Pacific Northwest Association of Planning Commissions, Vancouver, 11–12 September 1931, Seymour Papers.
34. "Memorandum on a Draft Town Planning Act for Nova Scotia, 1939," ibid.
35. Theodora Kimball Hubbard and Henry Vincent Hubbard, *Our Cities Today and Tomorrow: A Survey of Planning and Zoning Progress in the United States* (Cambridge, MA: Harvard University Press, 1929), pp. 65–76.
36. Frank Backus Williams, *The Law of City Planning and Zoning* (New York: Macmillan, 1922), p. 545.
37. Initially, before Premier Brownlee's intentions were understood, the 1928 act was greeted with expressions of bewilderment and disappointment, but the tone of the reviews soon changed: see, for example, *Journal of the Town Planning Institute* 7 (1928): 41–42, 63–64.

38. According to Seymour, the 1929 act "was copied in part from the British Columbia Act and is very similar in regard to zoning," but he also claimed to have tried "to combine the good features of all Acts": "Memorandum on a Draft Town Planning Act for Nova Scotia, 1939," and "Comments Prepared by George S. Mooney and Horace L. Seymour on the Model Zoning By-law October 1939," Seymour Papers.
39. Chapters or sections on regional planning were regularly featured in the texts and surveys of the day. See Hubbard and Hubbard, *Our Cities Today and Tomorrow*, pp. 46–64; Harlean James, *Land Planning in the United States for the City, State and Nation* (New York: Macmillan, 1926), pp. 249–72; Thomas Adams, *Recent Advances in Town Planning* (London: J. and A. Churchill, 1932), pp. 113–37; and the several volumes of the *Regional Plan of New York and its Environs*.
40. See Thomas Adams, *Rural Planning and Development* (Ottawa: Commission of Conservation, 1917), and Michael Simpson, "Thomas Adams in Canada, 1914–1930," *Urban History Review* 11 (1982): 1–16.
41. "Synopsis of suggested paper: Town Planning in the province of Alberta—a forward movement," n.d., Seymour Papers.
42. "A plan for the City of Vancouver", manuscript of a speech presented in Edmonton, 22 November, 1929, ibid. See, also, Vancouver Town Planning Commission, *A Plan for the City of Vancouver, British Columbia, including Point Grey and South Vancouver and a General Plan of the Region* (1929), pp. 264–69.
43. See, for example, James, *Land Planning in the United States*, pp. 231–48, a chapter entitled "Zoning and its relation to comprehensive planning."
44. "Zoning is probably the single most commonly used legal device available for implementing the land-use plan of a community": Robert M. Leary, "Zoning," in William I. Goodman and Eric C. Freund, *Principles and Practice of Urban Planning* (Washington, DC: International City Managers' Association, 1968), p. 403.
45. Hubbard and Hubbard, *Our Cities Today and Tomorrow*, p. 165.
46. For a critical interpretation of the consequences for Edmonton, see Edmund H. Dale, "Decision-Making at Edmonton, Alberta 1913–1945: Town Planning Without a Plan," *Plan Canada* 11 (1971): 134–47.
47. "The British Columbia Town Planning Act of 1925 shows the influence of practice in the United States, particularly in regard to zoning. This legislation and the technique established in making surveys and collecting data for the preparation of a zoning by-law as part of a comprehensive plan have established leadership in both modern town planning and zoning in Canada. The complete report on the Plan of Vancouver is recommended as a text on these subjects": "Comments Prepared by George S. Mooney and Horace L. Seymour on the Model Zoning By-law, October 1939," Seymour Papers. See, also, "Planning against loss," an address to the Calgary Knights of the Round Table, 28 April, 1931, and "The scientific aspects of town planning,"

an address to the Science Association, University of Alberta, 20 October, 1932.

48. Horace L. Seymour, "Town Planning Reduces City's Taxes," *The Canadian Engineer* (25 April, 1939): 4.
49. For contemporary discussions of the commission concept see Hubbard and Hubbard, *Our Cities Today and Tomorrow*, pp. 31–45; James, *Land Planning in the United States*, pp. 273–82; and Williams, *The Law of City Planning and Zoning*, pp. 553–68.
50. Robert A. Walker, *The Planning Function in Urban Government* (Chicago: University of Chicago Press, 1941), pp. 133–65.
51. From a speech reported in *Journal of the Town Planning Institute* 6 (1927): p. 56.
52. "The function of a town planning commission", n.d., Seymour Papers.
53. One of Seymour's first tasks, after the 1929 act became law, was to draft a model zoning by-law for Alberta municipalities. He also intended to prepare a model planning by-law, to guide municipal governments through the adoption of their "official town plans," but there is no evidence that this was ever done. "Model zoning by-law," 30 August, 1930, Seymour Papers.
54. Seymour, "Town Planning Reduces City's Taxes," p. 5.
55. Williams *The Law of City Planning and Zoning*, pp. 293–304, and Hubbard and Hubbard, *Our Cities Today and Tomorrow*, p. 86.
56. This debate began in February 1929 and was renewed in March 1930, during second reading of a bill to amend the 1929 act: "Alberta Scrapbook Hansard," Provincial Archives of Alberta (PAA).
57. Much the same wording was followed in Section 36(3) of the Alberta act, but there the criteria of judgement were directed at the provincial board rather than local boards. There was also a strange alteration which quite undermined the sense of the original clause. The word "relaxations" in the British Columbia act became "regulations" in the Alberta act, a change that looks suspiciously like an error in transcription.
58. Edward M. Bassett, "Zoning in Practice," in *Planning Problems of Town, City and Region*, (New York: Proceedings of the International City and Regional Planning Conference, 1925), pp. 423–30.
59. Williams, *The Law of City Planning and Zoning*, pp. 381–442, a section entitled "Planning for the promotion of beauty."
60. Hubbard and Hubbard, *Our Cities Today and Tomorrow*, p. 263.
61. "Technical observations on town planning progress in Alberta," and "Planning Against Loss," Seymour Papers.
63. "Memorandum to accompany a draft of the Nova Scotia Town Planning Act, 1939," Seymour Papers.
64. Ottawa *Evening Citizen*, 22 April, 1940.
65. "Memorandum to accompany a draft of the Nova Scotia Town Planning Act, 1939," Seymour Papers.
66. Seymour's last annual report, to 31 December, 1931, gives a good account of

accomplishments to that time.

67. Seymour's office was a victim of the Depression. It narrowly avoided a crippling budget cut in 1931 (*Edmonton Bulletin*, 7 March 1931 and *Calgary Albertan*, 31 March, 1931) and was closed a year later. The board continued to operate, however, and A. P. C. Belyea was appointed as the second director a few years later: Letter from Belyea to *The Ottawa Journal*, 12 March, 1945, PAA. The Edmonton and Calgary town planning commissions also continued to function until city planning departments were organized in 1949 and 1950, respectively.
68. Smith and Harasym, "Planning for retail services," pp. 159–60.

6

Land Tenure and Concepts of Architecture and the City: Milton-Park in Montreal

Phyllis Lambert

This paper is a case study of Milton-Park, a neighbourhood in Montreal, now actually in transition; an area of two, three and four storey residential buildings, as well as churches and neighbourhood shops that were to be demolished in order to construct high density, multi-use buildings, a form of megastructure that became the ideal of architects immediately following the Second World War. Forms of land tenure and municipal legislation, road buildings and zoning, have much to do with the story. So do attitudes—changing attitudes—about what a city ought to be.

Milton-Park, the neighbourhood under discussion, is a sub-neighbourhood in an historical sense. Physically, it is an area of roughly twenty-five acres composed of six blocks, which takes its name from two streets that cross at right angles just east of McGill University, just north of the Sherbrooke Plateau. It is on the northeast edge of the major business district of Montreal. The name today is highly charged, signifying in the last fourteen years a struggle for a sense of community. Milton-Park has become the first large-scale cooperative housing renovation in Canada. Planning began in 1979, construction was to be completed by the end of 1983.

Two thousand residents are forming some twenty not-for-profit housing cooperatives and organizations to purchase and renovate six hundred residential and twenty-five commercial units within this six-block area in downtown Montreal. The goals of the project are: 1) to provide good housing in the downtown area for people with low incomes; 2) to renovate existing housing stock without incurring gentrification;[1] 3) to make it possible for families and seniors to live in the downtown area; and, 4) to reinforce neighbourhood structures in the city. Inherent in these goals is the concept of the acquired rights of those who live in the neighbourhood and who must be able to remain there after purchase and renovation, and the

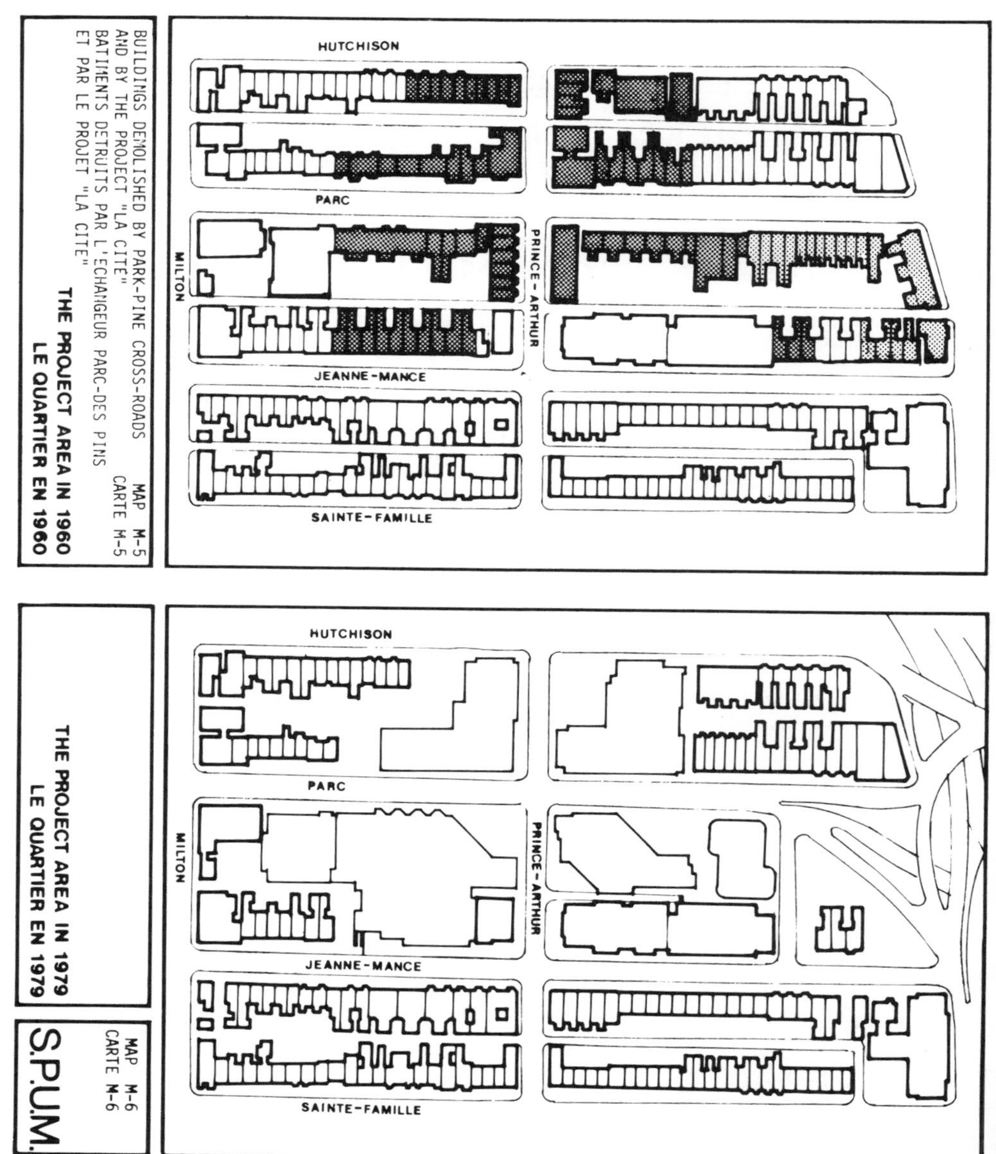

Fig. 1: Milton Park: Project area 1960 and 1979 (source: *S.P.U.M.*).

necessity of providing non-profit low-income housing in the centre city.

The history of the initial land tenure, and its effect on the maturing of the area in the nineteenth century must be examined before the political realities and goals of the project can be discussed. The history of human intervention in the area goes back to the seventeenth century, when the concession of thirty arpents (just over twenty-five acres) was made between 1662 and 1666 by Paul Chomedey de Maisonneuve and subsequently by the Sulpiciens to the notary, Bénigne Basset.[2] This strip of land, two arpents wide by fifteen arpents long (roughly four hundred feet wide by 3/5 of a mile in length) was the beginning of a second "rang," a linear extension of the earlier and original concessions made by Chomedey. This second "rang" or row of subdivided land lay mostly above the steep incline of the Sherbrooke Plateau.

In 1730, Benoit and Gabriel Basset, the sons of Bénigne, donated the land to the Religieuses Hospitalières de St–Joseph de l'Hôtel-Dieu established on rue St-Paul in the city, now old Montreal. The Basset land became known as the "Terre de la Providence." The nuns earned income from it, selling fire wood,[3] and, in 1745 at least, exploiting a quarry on the land and running lime kilns.[4] Between 1771 and 1791, we know that the land was leased as pasturage for horses and cattle.[5] In 1783, the nuns sold part of the land above and below Sherbrooke Street to Jacob Jordan and in 1791 gave him a thirty-year emphyteutic lease to another part of the land.[6] In 1806, Jordan erected a villa on this land. This was the first stone building in the area and first of the villas to be built by prosperous British merchants along the edge of the Sherbrooke Plateau.

The stone villas erected by British merchants on large properties are descendants of the pride of British architecture, country seats built by country gentlemen in England, Scotland and Ireland. In Montreal, they were modified by the quality of the native stone, by the climate, and by 150 years of a French colonial building tradition. For example, the house built by Jacob Hall, a hatter, on the Sherbrooke Plateau in 1816,[7] a villa with cut stone front and wings, is in contrast to the compact house of roughly coarsed and roughly dressed stone with high projecting gable walls built in the Old City thirty years earlier by Pierre Foretier.[8] Foretier was a fur trader; he also had a general store in this house, but his principal activity was real estate, and he became the major land developer in Montreal in the eighteenth century. He was primarily active in the St-Laurent suburb, in which lay the land of the Hôtel-Dieu.[9] Thomas Torrance also built a very sophisticated British mansion on the Sherbrooke Plateau in 1816. In 1832, ownership was transferred to John Molson of the great brewing family of Montreal.[10] However, a photograph in the Notman archives taken one hundred years later points to the changes that occurred in the area: by 1930 the house was used for offices of the United Automobile Services and had an adjacent gas station.[11] In 1935 it was destroyed by fire.

The increase in the number and density of buildings in the area in the second quarter of the nineteenth century can be seen by comparing John Adam's map of 1825 and James Cane's map of 1846.[12] Between these years, new houses were built to the west and east of the open land held by the Hôtel-Dieu. These were now mansions on large lots rather than villas on large estates. Further east, row houses were constructed near St-Denis Street, and the first institution in the area made its appearance in 1846 when the Bon–Pasteur monastery was begun. The Bon–Pasteur, which was added to over the nineteenth century[13] and the Meredith/Notman mansion of 1844, both stand today as evidence of the beginnings of the urban rather than the suburban development along the Sherbrooke Plateau.

The process of urbanization on this section of the Sherbrooke Plateau was deeply affected by the legal structures involved in the transmission of property: the seigneurial system and the British courts. Through the *Coutume de Paris*, the seigneurial system regulated the way in which inherited property was transmitted. The British government allowed the system to exist along with the British system of courts until 1854, when the seigneurial regime was finally abolished. However, the courts' unfamiliarity with the intricacies of the seigneurial system created great difficulties in the first generations of British rule. Thus the Fief Closse, the strip of land two arpents wide, running along the east side of St-Laurent mostly above Sherbrooke Street was blocked from development for close to thirty years, from the time of death of the owner who held title to the land, Pierre Foretier, until litigation over the tangled succession of his estate was settled in 1842.[14]

Once the Foretier estate was settled, major land transaction and building activity in the Fief Closse and on the adjacent Fief Lagauchetière began almost immediately, as is evident on Cane's map of 1846. The land transactions were undertaken by an association of Dr. Pierre Beaubien, Joseph Bourret and Louis-Hyprolite Lafontaine, who followed Pierre Foretier as the next major land developer in the Faubourg St-Laurent.[15] As did Foretier, they sold title to the land but were not involved in building. They were an illustrious group and represented a new level of sophistication in land development in Montreal. Beaubien studied medicine in Paris and returned to Montreal to practice in 1820. He also served on city council in 1843 when Bourret, a lawyer, was mayor. Both men were also directors of the Banque d'Epargne and members of the Sociéte St–Jean–Baptiste. In the Lafontaine-Baldwin government of the Canadian Assembly from 1848–51, Beaubien served as a representative from the county of Chambly, and Bourret became a member of the cabinet as commissioner of public works. When Lafontaine retired from the assembly, Bourret and Beaubien left with him. The close connection between land speculation and political office was endemic to urban expansion in Montreal.[16]

Transactions of scale in the area would not be undertaken again for another 120 years. This would be in Milton-Park, but it would involve not urban expansion, but intensification of land use, replacing existing low-rise by high-rise buildings. It would involve a more sophisticated level of organization: involving specialized land developers who were also builders and intended to rent the buildings they constructed, while maintaining the ownership of land and buildings. Financing for Milton-Park was provided by American and Canadian banks. The illustrious Ford Foundation of New York, and a crown corporation, the Canada Mortgage and Housing Corporation, participated as equity partners and mortgage guarantors.

The area now known as Milton-Park was first built up from 1860 to 1910. The boom of the 1860's set in motion development of the Hôtel-Dieu property on the Sherbrooke Plateau. The Religieuses hospitalières de St–Joseph de l'Hôtel-Dieu had been established in the old city since 1645. By the late 1850's, however, increased activity in the port of Montreal and the beginning of industrialized workshops in the Old City made the area unsuitable for such institutions as the Hôtel-Dieu, in part because of the noise and fumes, in part because there was no room for expansion of the facilities needed to serve the rapidly increasing population. In addition, the centre of population had moved well beyond the Old City. Thus the Bishop of Montreal, Monseigneur Bourget, instigated the move of the Hôtel-Dieu from the land it had first been built on in 1645, to its still open land above the Sherbrooke Plateau, the "Terre de la Providence" which had become known as "Mont Sainte-Famille." The first wing of the new buildings was completed in 1860. The nuns subdivided the property south of the hospital in 1864; in 1867, they formally donated the land for Ste-Famille Street to the city.[17]

The action of the nuns activated the two adjacent major landowners, the heirs of the large estates of the Platt and Lunn families, who had been established here since the beginning of the nineteenth century. The Platts conceded the land for Jeanne-Mance Street to the city in 1866 and in 1873 conceded the land for Park Avenue. Park Avenue was an extension of the old prestigious Bleury Street. Its change of name above Sherbrooke Street celebrated the creation of Mount Royal Park by the Corporation the city of Montreal in 1871, designed by Frederick Law Olmstead. Unlike the Hôtel-Dieu, the Platt and Lunn families did not actively sell their land. As late as 1890, both families still owned most of the lots north of Milton Street on both Jeanne-Mance Street and Park Avenue.[18] The Hôtel-Dieu needed the revenue from property sales in order to finance its continuing

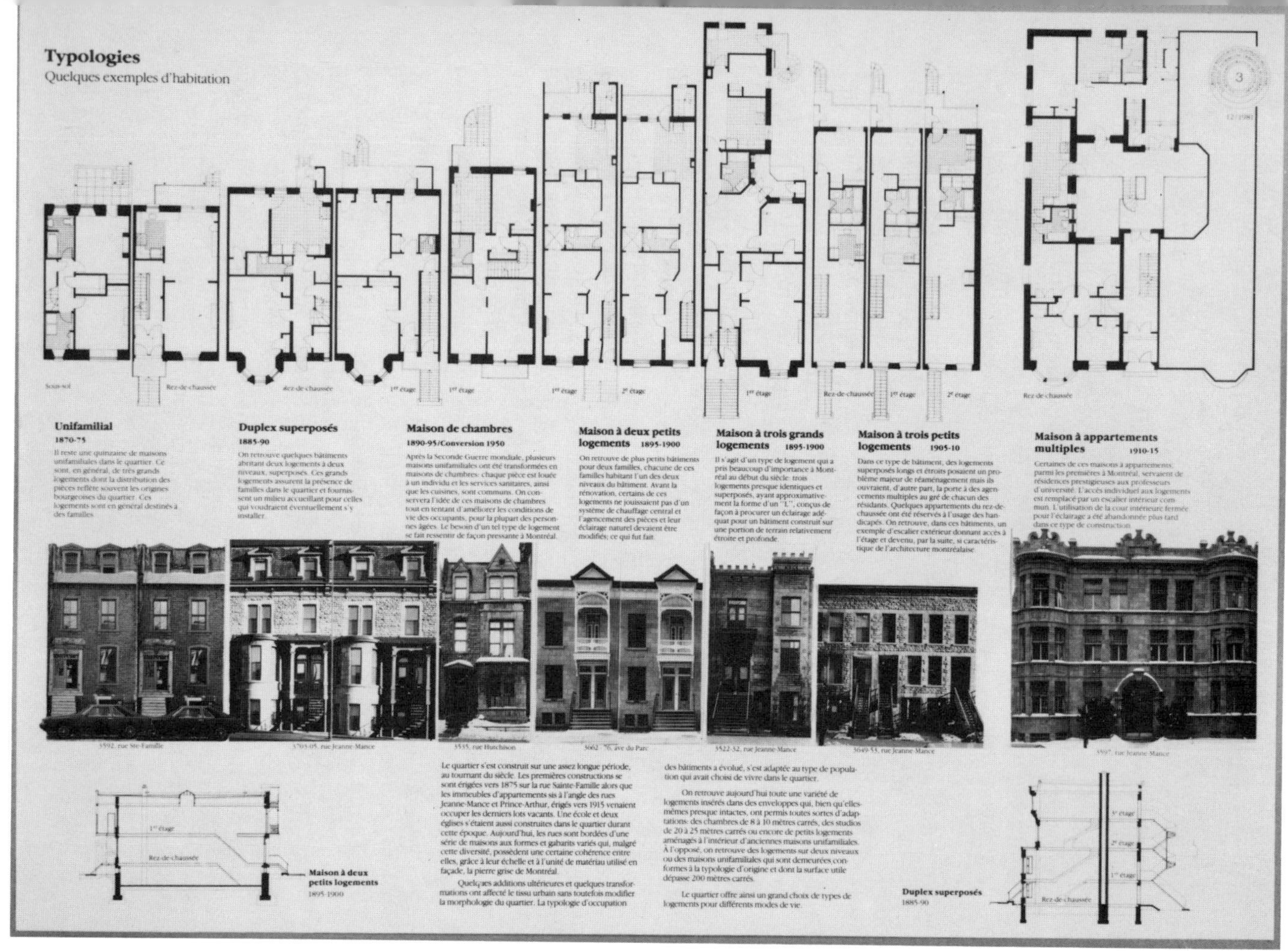

Fig. 2: Milton-Park: Residential Building Typologies.

building programme. Perhaps the Lunn and Platt families did not need the revenue. By 1890, however, the population pressure for housing forced development to take place.

As in all new areas above Sherbrooke Street, single family homes were developed first. By 1874, they lined the west side of Ste-Famille Street. Duplexes and triplexes then succeeded single family dwellings and became the standard residential building type in Montreal in the next decades. However, in 1890, there was still undeveloped land along the east side of Ste-Famille Street near the Hôtel-Dieu and along Jeanne-Mance Street. If we look at Goad's Atlas of 1890 showing land divisions, the reason is clear: the undeveloped lots were large lots, "mansion type lots" laid out by the nuns. When subdivided in the 1860's, the strategy had been one of an earlier period of development, and these lots, too large for row housing, remained empty until a new building type developed in Montreal in the first decade of the twentieth century: the apartment house. Institutional buildings were also built on such large lots; for example, the Presbyterian Church and School on Jeanne-Mance Street were erected on the former Platt family land in 1906.

The street car running northward from the business centre in the Old City permitted the development of this now essentially residential area. It ran along Bleury and its extension, Park Avenue. The neighbourhood had the advantage of being adjacent to Mount Royal Park and McGill University; churches, schools and a shopping area along Park Avenue made it self-contained. Who were the residents? The tax rolls of Montreal provide population characteristics. The residents of Milton-Park from 1890 through 1915 maintained the same occupation: 35 per cent of the heads of families were in business; 20 per cent were clerical, 15 per cent professionals. There was no substantial difference in represented occupations on any street in particular. The only slight economic differentiation within the neighbourhood was that people working in clerical occupations tended to live in three family buildings rather than single family houses.

Between 1900 and 1915, despite newly-built, higher-density housing, apartment buildings and multi-family row houses, there was still no dramatic change in the types of occupations found in the neighbourhood. Apartment buildings appealed to people in different conditions: substantial numbers of unmarried or widowed women were attracted to apartment living as were some professionals and businessmen. At least 48 per cent of all buildings in the area were owner occupied. The predominant language group was English, although there was a 10 per cent increase of French-speaking residents between 1890-1915.

Gradually the location lost its solidly middle-class population. By the end of the Second World War, it had become an area of low-income residents, and since that time the percentage of elderly has risen steadily from 14 per cent in 1976 to about 20 per cent in 1982.[19] Today almost 70 per cent of the elderly are on fixed income resulting from their pensions. The wage earners of 73 per cent of all household units in Milton-Park earn less than $15,000 per year, 84 per cent of all households earn less than $20,000. The mother tongue of 35 per cent of the residents was French in 1976, which was low compared to 65 per cent for the city at large. For 39 per cent of residents, the mother tonge was English, compared to 16 per cent for the city. In 1876, all property was in the hands of speculators, today it is being transferred 100 per cent to nonprofit resident owners.

Major changes in Milton-Park were generated by the municipal government after the Second World War. The mood was for road building, creating urban interchanges and urban highways. This, of course, occurred in many cities. In Montreal, the intersection at Park and Pine Avenues was chosen as an appropriate place for a grade separation interchange. Funds were appropriated for a preliminary study in 1956.[20] Park was a busy street; it had been enlarged above Pine Avenue in 1931 to facilitate traffic flow.[21] But it was not until 1959 that the newspapers reported that a city study declared this intersection to be the busiest in the city.[22] There is a high probability that location of the interchange at Pine and Park Avenues was attractive to the city because Park Avenue north of Pine Avenue bisected park land; the city could use its own land for the acres required for radial interchange, rather than incur the expense and time required to buy up private property. However, one block of twenty-five three-storey houses was acquired and demolished.[23] No objection to the transformation of part of the park land into a roadway was published.[24] Nevertheless, construction of the interchange began in 1959 and was completed in 1961.[25] It is ironic, and symptomatic of the problems of planning, that the present chairman of the executive committee of the city recently stated that he would not have permitted the construction of the interchange had he been responsible.

For entrepreneurs with a sharp eye and familiarity with post-Second World War urban planning concepts which linked traffic interchange modes with high-density residential and commercial buildings, the Milton-Park area was an ideal place for real estate speculation. The new large scale real estate development was introduced to Montreal by the Svengali of the new real estate wheeler-dealers, the New Yorker, William Zeckendorf.[26] On an emphyteutic lease from the Canadian National Railways (C.N.R.) he undertook building Place Ville Marie over the railroad tracks in the very centre of the downtown core of Montreal. Filling in this gap in the urban fabric was positive, as was construction of the Queen Elizabeth Hotel, also built on open C.N.R. land and connected to Place

Ville Marie through an underground shopping plaza. They represented large development almost without demolition. However, the development intent—the creation of enormous highrise buildings or groups of highrise buildings—set a future image of development in Montreal, inevitably causing the demolition of large areas in the downtown core. Thus, demolition was required for construction of the Bank of Commerce, CIL House and Place Bonaventure which followed Place Ville Marie. Place Ville Marie not only set the conditions for redevelopment in the commercial core, it did so also for a basically residential area: Milton-Park. Skills developed in the construction of Place Ville Marie and Place Bonaventure—skills related to construction techniques and management, financing, real estate negotiations, collaboration of the private developer and government, and in the then "avant garde" concept of architecture and planning—were applied to Milton-Park.

Some of the actors in Place Ville Marie and Place Bonaventure became key actors in Milton-Park. These were the project managers who initially worked for Zeckendorf's real estate firm, Webb Knapp, Canada, and the project manager for the Foundation Company, responsible for construction of Place Ville Marie. They were later brought together with the developers of Milton-Park, Concordia Estates, by Ray Affleck of the firm of architects named ARCOP.[27] Affleck was the partner in charge of Place Ville Marie and Place Bonaventure, and later briefly of Milton-Park. The development firms of Concordia Estates was composed of three McGill University graduates involved in residential development in Montreal, until they became the successful bidders for the construction of Place Bonaventure. Concordia Estates was to be the developer of Milton-Park.

There is also a strong architectural connection between Place Ville Marie, Milton-Park and the "International Style." The intellectual concepts leading to high-density, multi-functional highrise buildings was transposed into reality in Montreal for Place Ville Marie by Zeckendorf's architectural team, headed up by I. M. Pei, a former student of Walter Gropius at Harvard. Gropius was the founder of the Bauhaus, a school of architecture established in Germany in the 1920's. It was the centre of the new theories of architecture and urban planning, variously called "Functionalist Architecture," "International Style," and "Modern Architecture." An important characteristic of this school was a deliberate rejection of history, the history of architecture, the history of cities. The International Style was the ideal of all architectural students after the Second World War, but its concepts were certainly reinforced for the young McGill University trained team named ARCOP who worked side by side with members of Pei's group on Place Ville Marie. With Concordia Estates, ARCOP architects created the basic architectural scheme for

Milton-Park. It was called Cité Concordia, a city within the city. The firm eventually broke up over Milton-Park. His consciousness raised by Milton-Park people, Ray Affleck, partner in charge for ARCOP, objected to the scheme: to tear down a whole neighbourhood. At his insistance, ARCOP resigned as architects of Milton-Park. Other members of the firm did not agree, and left ARCOP in order to take over the commission. Affleck's resignation was a brave gesture; it is a rare occurance for architects to put principles before profit, and in addition, La Cité was in the forefront of architectural thinking of the time, promising fame and glory to its designers.

If Walter Gropius may be seen as the godfather of Place Ville Marie, Milton-Park is the descendant of another leading architect of the International Style, Charles Jeanneret, known as Le Corbusier. Born in Switzerland but working in Paris, Le Corbusier planned on a vast scale and publicized his ideas in a series of books that were on the desks of every architectural student in Europe and North America by the 1950's. In *The Developers*, James Lorimer discusses the influence of Le Corbusier on the influential planner and chief advisor to the Canada Mortgage and Housing Corporation (C.M.H.C.), Humphrey Carver. Lorimer quotes the following passage from Carver's *Cities in the Suburbs* (1962):

> (Le Corbusier) dealt like a giant with the landscape of sky and sun and rolling hills. The family is not to be enclosed by small hedges and picket fences; it is to be lifted up and shown the horizon from the upper floors of the great city habitation. The whole building is itself lifted from the ground on stilts so that the landscape goes rolling on right through and underneath.[28]

Carver is almost ecstatic:

> The impact of Le Corbusier upon the minds of his architectural contemporaries in the 1920's was not just that of an invigorating fresh wind on a sultry afternoon. It was a sensation: like the arrival of the first sputnik in the fifties. Suddenly an entirely new dimension of imagination was opened up. Until this moment the whole vocabulary and art of architecture and city planning had been an extension of the past.[29]

It should be noted that C.M.H.C. later insured 1,350 residential units in the three residential towers of La Cité constructed from 1973 to 1975 in Milton-Park.

Le Corbusier's "Unité d'Habitation" at Marseilles became the ideal for building in the "sky and sun and rolling hills" of the suburbs and influenced much building on the outskirts of London, Chicago, and Toronto, for example, in the 1950's and 1960's. But Le Corbusier also applied the concept of "Unité d'Habitation" to the city. In his *Plan Voisin* of 1925, Le Corbusier projected a whole new structure on Paris.[30] His drawings showed tall large cruciform buildings replacing blocks of traditional low-rise buildings, small narrow streets replaced by vast roadways densely covered with automobiles. The plan implied that hundreds of individual lots, and the buildings on them, must first be purchased then demolished in order to erect the new buildings. As in the Paris schemes of Baron Haussmann a century earlier, such a plan required vast allocation and concentration of financial resources, the dislocation of thousands of people, and the collaboration and collusion of the municipal authorities in doing so. It also created centralized control of large areas of the city. In our society, this meant giving control and advantage to large profit-making corporations. The relationship of architecture to land tenure in the 1920's has been little discussed by architectural and urban historians, yet it is in this respect that the International Style has had it profound effects on cities, particularly after the Second World War.

As stated earlier, in Montreal the implications of these theories had a happier effect in the case of Place Ville Marie and the Queen Elizabeth Hotel, both built on empty land crossed by railroad tracks. La Cité in Milton-Park was typical of post-Second World War development in North America and in Europe; people were forced to leave their low-rise residential buildings, which then were demolished to be replaced by high-rise residential or more often, commercial buildings. The La Cité project is the direct heir of Le Corbusier's cataclysmic proposals, with their implied and real effects on tenure and on the lives and freedom of thousands of people.

In the late 1950's and 1960's, Concordia Estates covertly purchased over three hundred lots and the buildings on them in six contiguous blocks, all of which became the property of one land owner. Some five thousand residents lived in the six blocks. Cité Concordia was to replace them and their homes by an office building, a hotel and heliport, apartments, shopping, entertainment, sports and other recreational facilities, and underground parking. In 1962, a school and medical centre were also included despite the fact that these facilities already existed in the area. Thus a traditional self-contained low-rise community was to be replaced by another with a much higher population density, designed as a superblock excluding through traffic on the surface streets, routing it underground. This incredibly ambitious project was to cost $250 million.[31]

The first submission made by Concordia Estates in 1962 proposed that in order to create the superblock, the city declare an urban renewal area, expropriate the land and sell it to the developer at cost. Members of the recently formed City Planning Department objected to public expropriation because they did not feel that this was a valid case for urban renewal. The development team solicited letters supporting the concept of redevelopment from the internationally acclaimed architects Alvar Aalto and Mies van der Rohe. Despite their endorsement, the city turned down the plan for expropriation. The project would be a private venture with room for city cooperation in such things as widening the streets, cession of lanes and other city-owned land.[32] The City Planning Department considered "some planning better than none." The chairman of the City Planning Department stated:

> Most of our economy is based on the private sector and therefore the city will not stop Concordia which can help the general economy and alleviate, to a certain extent, unemployment problems . . . one advantage of the project is that it will add to the city's total housing stock . . . the private sector will not build just anywhere, for example, on land that just happens to be vacant unless it is very well located. The private sector will only build in attractive areas with amenities; the Milton-Park area is an obviously good location.[33]

The idea of the super block was dropped, but five years later,in the wake of post Expo '67 confidence, the project was restructured with a new architectural team. The original investor, Great West Life of Winnipeg, found a partner who could come in with new financing: the Ford Foundation of New York. The policy of the Ford Foundation was to couple its investment portfolio, which required a high return on investment, with programmes for social improvement. Advanced thinkers were beginning to consider that bringing back residents to the downtown was an antidote to urban sprawl. Suburbia, applauded two decades earlier, was now to be despised. There was some good reasoning behind these attitudes, but they were not thought through and tended towards fadism. It is astounding and appalling that the Ford Foundation could consider that wiping out whole areas of the city and removing the residents en masse, replacing them by a totally different population, was social improvement. But this pattern was repeated in all North American cities at this time.

By 1968, 85 per cent of the land in the six blocks had been assembled by Concordia Estates. The first citizens committee in Milton-Park was also formed the same year. In March 1969, the Milton-Park Street Committee began publication of a community newsletter, *Bulldozer*. Its slogan was "citizen power will stop Concordia." The committee held weekly meetings. In 1970, FRAP, a municipal political party, was formed around the issue of "uprooting the poor." There were sit-ins, demonstrations, marches on city hall, court cases, hunger strikes and arrests. The Montreal *Gazette* later reported that in May 1972, "thirty helmeted riot police quashed a protest by residents who had formed a human chain to forestall the wreckers ball." Fifty-five people were involved. They were charged with disturbing the peace and were subsequently acquitted.

In May 1979, just after the first stage of the Cité Concordia was completed, a story on the first page of the business section of the Montreal *Gazette* reported:

> With the Save Milton-Park campaign and its hunger strikes, demonstrations and resulting arrests forgotten, Concordia Estates washed its hands of the controversial development by selling its interest to YUL Associates, a private group of Chicago businessmen. It seemed Concordia, soured by the La Cité experience, had also washed its hands of Montreal and Canada with the bulk of its major projects shifting to the U.S.

This story was basically concerned with the move of developers to the United States and was not quite accurate. What Concordia Estates did do was bring in YUL to help finance the deficit and capital cost problems, and in fact, Concordia and YUL both are still financially involved.

Clearly, Cité Concordia was not a financial success. The city downzoned it back to an area of three- and four-storey buildings. The residents continued their fight for a decent neighbourhood. Because of the Park Pine interchange and a change to one way streets, heavy traffic now flowed down Jeanne-Mance Street, formerly a quiet, local road. In 1977, the Jeanne-Mance Sainte-Famille Street Committees came to Héritage Montréal requesting help to gain control of their housing through the formation of not-for-profit housing cooperatives.[34] Héritage Montréal is a private foundation formed to help fund citizens' groups fight the destruction of the city by removal of its older buildings and to help to strengthen the neighbourhood structure. After various attempts at working through the private sector, Héritage Montréal went to the president of C.M.H.C. and also brought the case to members of parliament. In addition, the federal elections were close and the incumbent Liberal party did not want to hear from two thousand irate citizens. On 16 May 1979, six days before the federal election, the affiliate of Héritage Montréal, La Société du Patrimoine Urbain de Montréal signed an agreement with the federal government. The government purchased the properties for 5.5 million dollars. Renovation costs were to be 7.5 million dollars, with mortgages available to cooperatives at 2 per cent interest. La Société would manage the properties and would form not-for-profit housing cooperatives which would purchase and renovate their buildings. There were to be twenty to thirty cooperatives of twenty to thirty units each. The residents of Milton-Park and Héritage Montréal had a common objective: that no resident would be forced to leave the neighbourhood because he or she could not pay the rent after the houses were purchased and renovated.

La Société du Patrimoine Urbain de Montréal later became La Société d'Amélioration de Milton-Parc and developed a staff which consisted eventually of nine architects, six animators, an executive director and a four-person administrative staff. All work went forward in collaboration with the residents, including the *Action Plan* and its many technical studies.[35] There were, of course, many difficulties, but today the cooperatives have renovated three-quarters of the units (four hundred units). The project will be completed in 1983.

The understanding of the principles of this urban intervention has matured and clarified. The principle of acquired rights and accessible rents distinguishes Milton-Park housing from traditional market housing. New property rights have been established; they are collective rights rather than the traditional forms of single ownership. This form of property rights is assured by the formation of not-for-profit housing cooperatives, where each member is a tenant owner and all decisions are made by consensus. The principles also state that housing is not a commodity and that everyone has the right to safe and secure housing.

These principles are being translated into contracts to transfer the property. These cover conditions of protection against high-rises buildings, insurance frauds, and future speculation; protection of architectural integrity; maintenance of the existing socio-economic make-up of neighbourhood housing, with priorities given to low-income people; and maintenance of rooming houses, without conversion to large apartments. There are also issues affecting each block: planning of backyards and lanes; the right to passage and clotheslines; maintenance of green spaces; and organized parking so that people have access to green spaces.

CONCLUSIONS

The influence of tenure on the urban fabric can be seen in: the effects of a seigneurial system in the French colony, which indeed implied some form of social contract; the evolution from a benign capitalist system in the British colonial period to a malignant and malicious capitalist system in the Second World War; and the recent change to non-market housing and the redistribution of property rights from individual to collective control, which again implies a form of social contract. The influence of the "idea of the city'' held by architects and/or their clients on the urban fabric is important. In 150 years the ''idea'' has changed: farmland and leasehold; the country house and estate of colonial British immigrants; row houses and the street car suburb; ''visionary'' architecture, the automobile, and the super corporation; urban conservation by community groups and the neighbourhood movement. These specific building forms are linked to two specific forms of land holding and are based on specific economic systems.

The effect of industrialization and our capacity to effect sweeping changes very rapidly through the concentration and misuse of resources demand that land tenure and building be approached in a much more thoughtful and informed manner. Leonardo Benevolo, an architect and urban historian, discussed the split which occurred in the late 1840's between humanists and technocrats, with the technocrats prevailing, in his book *The Origins of Modern Town Planning,* published in the 1960's.[36] I believe that both his book and this analysis show the need for guidance from those who are detached from the processes described. Urban historians, among others, can provide that guidance. They are needed to be able to assess the proposals of architects and urban planners. The plans of Le Corbusier were dogma in schools of architecture and planning. Their fallacies and serious social implications should have been the subject of debate immediately, not fifty years later. To my knowledge, they still have not been analyzed by historians of urban development.

The solution chosen for Milton-Park brings solutions to basic problems of the urban environment. Collective tenure eliminates the concept of housing as a commodity and thus eliminates speculation. It also permits each individual an active role in the decisions about his home and neighbourhood. It would be irresponsible to make idealistic claims for the solution chosen in Milton-Park. If it answers some basic problems, it poses others. For example, not-for-profit housing cooperatives place housing under the control of resident-owners, but how will the governance by cooperative societies of small and large sectors of the city work and be affected? What other solutions exist or can be developed in order to finance them beyond capricious governments and those seeking tax shelter? These questions require serious analysis and, possibly, new political structures, not hopeful assertions or denials.

Other issues urgently require serious study. It is now easy to see the relationship of Le Corbusier's proposals of 1925 and the enormous concentrations of capital in post-Second World War corporate mergers and multinational corporations. Perhaps they were *avant la lettre,* but they cannot have been innocent of the alliance of government and capital, and this model and its implied political, economic and social structures still dominate urban planning and development. The economic model and structures that can change these unacceptable practices must be analyzed and put forward. The future of projects like Milton-Park must be based on these studies. These are some of the questions that economists and urban historians must be concerned with if they are to provide the tools of analysis that guide action.

NOTES

1. This word denotes the process which, after purchase and renovation, results in a change of residents from those who have low income to those with higher incomes.
2. Terrier de l' le de Montréal, concession n° 944-cl, AVM.
3. Jacques Ducharme, "Les revenus des Hôpitaléres de Montréal au XVIIIe siècle" in Michel Allard, ed., *Hôtel-Dieu de Montreal* (1642–1973), (Montreal, 1973) p. 232.
4. Ibid.
5. Greffe Pierre Panet, 23 mars 1771; Simon Sanguinet, fils, 12 février 1776; 17 février 1778; 23 juillet 1785, ANQM.
6. Greffe Louis Chaboillez, 7 novembre 1791; Simon Sanguinet, fils, 13 mai 1783, ibid.
7. Greffe Henry Griffin, 7 mars 1816, ibid.
8. Notman Photographic Archives, Montréal Cards, no. 30, Musée McCord.
9. "Un apercu du développement de la propriété foncière à Montréal, la carrière de Pierre Foretier de 1760 à 1815," conférence de Alan Stewart et Hélène Dumais du GRBPGM présentée à la Réunion annuelle de la Société pour l'étude de l'architecture au Canada, 1980.
10. Terrier du Faubourg Saint-Laurent, bo te no. 9, emplacement no. 362, AVM.
11. Notman Photographic Archives, Montréal Misc. Bldgs., U.A.S. office 1929, no. 24, 579-view, Musée McCord.
12. John Adams, *Map of the City and Suburbs of Montreal* (New York: Engraved by Jas. D. Stout, 1825). James Cane, *Topographical and Pictorial Map of the City of Montreal* (Montreal, 1846).
13. *Le monastère du Bon-Pasteur: Histoire, Relevé et Analyse*. Rapport préparé par le Groupe de recherche sur les bâtiments en pierre grise de Montréal sous la direction de Phyllis Lambert pour le Ministère des Affaires culturelles, Direction générale du Patrimoine, Service de l'Inventaire des Biens culturels, 1978.
14. D.-B. Viger, *Mémoires* (1827), and various notarial acts.
15. In March 1841, Dr. Beaubien became the Administrative Executor controlling the Fief Closse (Protonotaire de Terrebonn, St–Jerome, Greffe J. J. Girouard, 16 juillet 1842, no. 161. Expertise des biens des successions Pierre Foretier et de Thérèse Legrand) "Puis le 18 mai 1842, M. Joseph Bourret, Louis Hypolite Lafontaine et Pierre Beaubien sont devenus adjudicataires dudit Fief

(Lagauchetière) au décret et ont pris titre du shériff le 23 décembre 1842 et on prêté foi et hommage le 15 mai 1844.'' Terrier de l' le; Boite 12, no. 948 D et C. AVM. Research, Robert Marshall, GRBPGM.

16. Salle 16. Accumulated biographies. AVM. Research on Foretier, Beaubien, Bourret, Lafontaine is part of on-going work for publication by the GRBPGM, Phyllis Lambert, Director. For relationship between land speculation and political office, see Paul-André Linteau, *Maisonneuve: Comment des promoteurs fabriquent une ville 1883-1918* (Montréal, 1981).
17. ANQM Greffe Casimir–Fidéle Papineau 16 Février 1864 No. 4053. Cession pour l'énlargissement, ouverture et prolongation des rues Sherbrooke, Ste-Famille, Bagg, Hôtel-Dieu et St–Urbain, par les [. . .] Soeurs Hospitaliéres [. . .] de l'Hôtel-Dieu [. . .] à la cité de Montréal.
18. Analysis of lot divisions and building construction here and below as well as population characteristics are drawn from the Rolls of Evaluation (tax rolls) of the City of Montréal Atlases of Montréal: Charles E. Goad. *Atlas of the City of Montreal.* (Montreal 1880). Charles E. Goad, *Atlas of the City of Montreal* (Montreal, 1880 revised to June 1890). A. R. Pinsoneault, *Atlas of the Island and City of Montreal and Ile Bizard* (Montreal, [1907]).
19. Statistics are from a survey made by the Société d'amélioration du Milton-Parc, 1982, and those published in, Société du Patrimoine Urbain de Montréal, *Action Plan* (Montréal, 1er trimestre 1980), pp. 33–61, drawn from Statistics Canada's ''Population and Housing Characteristics—Montreal'' from census between 1951 and 1976.
20. ''Widening of Park Avenue to Finish Within Six Weeks,'' *The Montreal Star,* 16 April 1931.
21. ''Park Pine Project Sparks Council Fireworks,'' *The Herald,* Montréal, 7 September 1956.
22. ''Work Starts in Two Weeks, Pine Park Contract Let,'' *The Gazette,* Montréal, 18 September 1959.
23. ''Notre historique Mont-Royal coûtera cher en ronds-points,'' *La Patrie,* 10 mai 1959.
24. The objections of Parks Director Claude Robillard were reported in ''Big Cut into Park Approved,'' *The Gazette,* 20 June 1959.
25. ''Le carrefour à voies étagées des avenues du Parc, et des Pins.'' *Architecture-Bâtiment-Construction* (Octobre 1961): 38–40. ''L'étagement des voies de l'avenue du Parc et de l'avenue des Pins,'' *Cités et Villes* (juin 1961): 28–30, p. 54.
26. See William Zeckendorf, *The Autobiography of William Zeckendorf* (New York, 1970), for an account of the buildings on C.N.R. land. See also Robert W. Collier, *Contemporary Cathedrals: Large Scale Developments in Canadian Cities* (Montréal, 1974) and James Lorimer, *The Developers* (Toronto, 1978).
27. I am indebted to Ray Affleck for information on the roles of those involved in the construction of Place Ville Marie, Place Bonaventure, and Concordia Estates, in Milton-Park.

28. Lorimer, *The Developers* (Toronto, 1978) p. 129.
29. Humphrey Carver, *Cities in the Suburbs* (Toronto, 1962, reprinted 1974), p. 44.
30. Le Corbusier et Pierre Jeannert, *Oeuvre Complète de 1910–1929* (Zurich, 1956) pp. 109–17.
31. The architect of the first scheme, conceived as a superblock with much denser development, was Harry Meyrowitz. In conversation with me, Harry Meyrowitz has pointed to Radburn, New Jersey as the model for the superblock. The major concern in Radburn, designed in 1928, was the separation of pedestrian and vehicular traffic. The designers Clarence S. Stein and Henry Wright were themselves inspired by Ebenezer Howard's *Garden Cities of Tomorrow* first published in 1893. In his book *Toward New Towns for America* (Cambridge, 1978) published in 1950, Stein wrote:

> We believed thoroughly in green belts, and towns of a limited size planned for work as well as living. We did not fully recognize that our main interest . . . had been transferred to a more pressing need, that of a town in which people could live peacefully with the automobile — or rather in spite of it. (p. 37)

A succession of architects followed Meyrowitz: when ARCOP resigned, Dimitri Dimakopoulos continued, and he was followed by Eva Vecsei who began her involvement in the project working for ARCOP on La Cité.

32. A private bill, an Act respecting Concordia City Properties Limited, *Statutes of Québec*, 1969, Ch. 126, p. 1077, was presented and passed by the Quebec Legislature. It erased existing servitude on laneways and restricted land use to "first class dwelling houses with stone foundations and stone facades," established by the original owners.
33. Interview with the chairman of the City Planning Department, Aimé Desautels, Jeanne-Mance Street Committee File, typescript, 8 July 1969.
34. Information on restructuring Milton-Park as a community collectively owned and controlled is based on my knowledge of the project in my capacity as president of Héritage Montréal, and president of the Société du Patrimoine Urbain de Montréal (later the Société d'amélioration de Milton-Parc) which I formed in order to provide the needed management skills in holding the land, acting as interim landlord, forming cooperatives and bringing together the architectural skills.
35. Société du Patrimoine Urbain de Montréal, *Action Plan* (Montreal, 1980).
36. Leonard Benevolo, *The Origins of Modern Town Planning* (translated by Judith Landry from *Le Origini dell' Urbanistica Moderna*) (London, 1967).

7

The Land Development Process in Edmonton, Alberta, 1881–1917

John Gilpin

The process of urban land development is a subject which has only recently received the attention of Canadian urban historians.[1] Important themes in this small but growing body of literature include urban boosterism and local markets. The bulk of the literature on this theme deals with western Canadian cities reflecting their more recent history as frontier urban communities. An overview of urban boosterism in this region has been provided by Alan Artibise, while R. Rees, M. L. Foran, and Norbert MacDonald have provided studies of Saskatoon, Calgary and Vancouver.[2] Institutional and individual participants in the land development process have also been the subject of some analysis. The role of government and its efforts to attract business, industry and railways to its area has been discussed by E. H. Dale, who studied the promotional efforts of successive town and city councils in Edmonton between 1892 and 1966, while studies dealing with this aspect of Hamilton's history have been prepared by R. D. Roberts and Eric W. Ricker.[3] The role of transportation companies in shaping the urban system and their role in influencing the internal structures of urban places have been discussed in Pierre Berton's history of the Canadian Pacific Railway (C.P.R.), Frances N. Mellen's study of the development of the Toronto waterfront between 1850 and 1912, Max L. Foran's study of land development patterns in Calgary between 1884 and 1945, and Deryck Holdsworth's study of the C.P.R. land subdivisions in Vancouver.[4] The role of land speculators has been discussed in detail by Michael Doucet in his thesis on land development in Hamilton as well as in a recent article dealing specifically with land speculators and their effect on the physical development of Hamilton.[5] In this essay, he demonstrated how land speculation was dominated by members of the elite and how the impact of speculators diminished very quickly as time passed.

Less well developed themes in the literature include urban form and urban land ownership patterns. Isobel Ganton, in her study of the subdivision process in the Toronto area between 1851 and 1883, concluded that these early subdivisions had a long-term effect on the development of Toronto; that the timing of subdivision activity corresponded to periods of economic prosperity and depression and population growth; and that the location and nature of subdivisions reflected the strong influence of man made constraints.[6] Walter G. Hardwick's study of Vancouver showed that subdividers had broken the various sections of the city into areas of small, medium and large lots aimed, respectively at low-, middle-, and upper-income groups.[7] The urban land owning class was an aspect of Michael Katz's study of Hamilton in the mid nineteenth century.[8] He concluded that Hamilton reflected the situation in various American cities in which land ownership was concentrated in a small group.

In addition to the studies of specific themes and cities noted above, the literature has also produced one notable attempt to create an overall conceptual framework for land development in the nineteenth-century city.[9] Michael Doucet's descriptive model carries the land development process from the initial acquisition of property through to its actual utilization. It identifies the individual actors in this process, such as farmers, speculators, subdividers, land agents and tradesmen. This model, therefore, calls for an integrated and systematic approach to the land development process. The following outline of the land development process in Edmonton is a preliminary step towards the application of this approach to a western Canadian city. The sources of land development data used includes registered plans, certificates of title, and land company records, as well as such traditional sources as newspapers, Henderson's directories and Goad insurance maps.

Edmonton was one of five dominant cities to emerge in the Prairie West between its acquisition by Canada, in 1870, and 1921. The development of these cities took place within the context of the overall urbanization and industrialization of Canadian society. Between 1870 and 1921, the urban portion of Canada's population increased from 18.3 per cent to 49.5 per cent. The application of technology to Canadian society produced national transportation and communication systems as well as new building methods. By 1917, travel between Canada's major urban centres was facilitated by 38,369 miles of railway track, a large portion of which was located in the West. Travel within Canadian cities was also improved through the introduction of electrically-powered street railway systems. The use of structural steel lead to the construction of high-rise office towers.

The chief beneficiaries of these trends were Montreal and Toronto, both of which rapidly outdistanced their nearest rival. By 1921, Montreal's population, exclusive of several contiguous cities, was 618,506 and Toronto's was 521,893, while Quebec City's was 95,193 and Hamilton's was 114,151. The growth of these first two cities was also affected by the policy adopted by the dominion government for the settlement of the West, a policy which concentrated on railway construction and tariffs to protect the infant industries of central Canada. These industries would supply the necessary goods and service to the agrarian West. Phenomenal growth rates were also evident in western Canadian cities. By 1921, Winnipeg was the third largest city in Canada, with a population of 179,087, and Vancouver was fourth with 117,217. They were followed in eighth and tenth places by Calgary and Edmonton.

The context for Edmonton's development as an urban community was the Edmonton Settlement (Map 1). The river-lot plan was a rural type of survey which had been used elsewhere in the West to accommodate existing agricultural communities, principally Metis. The Edmonton settlement, however, was never used intensively for agricultural purposes nor was there a substantial Metis community at this location.

The principal geographical features of the settlement were the North Saskatchewan River and its valley, which ranges in width from one-half to one mile and averages 160 feet in depth. The valley thus effectively separated the southern and northern portions of the settlement. Two fords provided access between the two portions of the settlement, but they could not be used during spring break-up or periods of high water. Nine flood plains located on the valley floor provided sites for development, in addition to the upland portions of the individual lots. The geography of the Edmonton settlement thus presented a number of potential problems and added costs for its conversion into an integrated urban community.

The settlement as defined by the 1883 plan consisted of forty-three lots located on both sides of the river, primarily to the east of the Hudson's Bay Company (H.B.C.) reserve. These lots ranged in size from 48 acres to 704 acres. The smaller lots were located in a cluster immediately to the east of the H.B.C. reserve. Ultimately this location would be the urban focus for the settlement. The H.B.C. reserve dominated the settlement by virtue of its size and by the presence of the H.B.C. fort, which had been the focus for economic activity in the region since its establishment in 1795. It was anticipated that the H.B.C. reserve would be the location of any urban development in the Edmonton settlement.[10] Claimants to land in the settlement included the Methodist Church; former servants of the Hudson's Bay Company such as John Walter and Malcolm Groat; Metis such as Lawrence Garneau; and government officials such as Edmonton Crown Timber Agent Thomas A. Anderson, who was also a member of the Winnipeg merchantile firm of Merrick and Anderson. Despite the variety

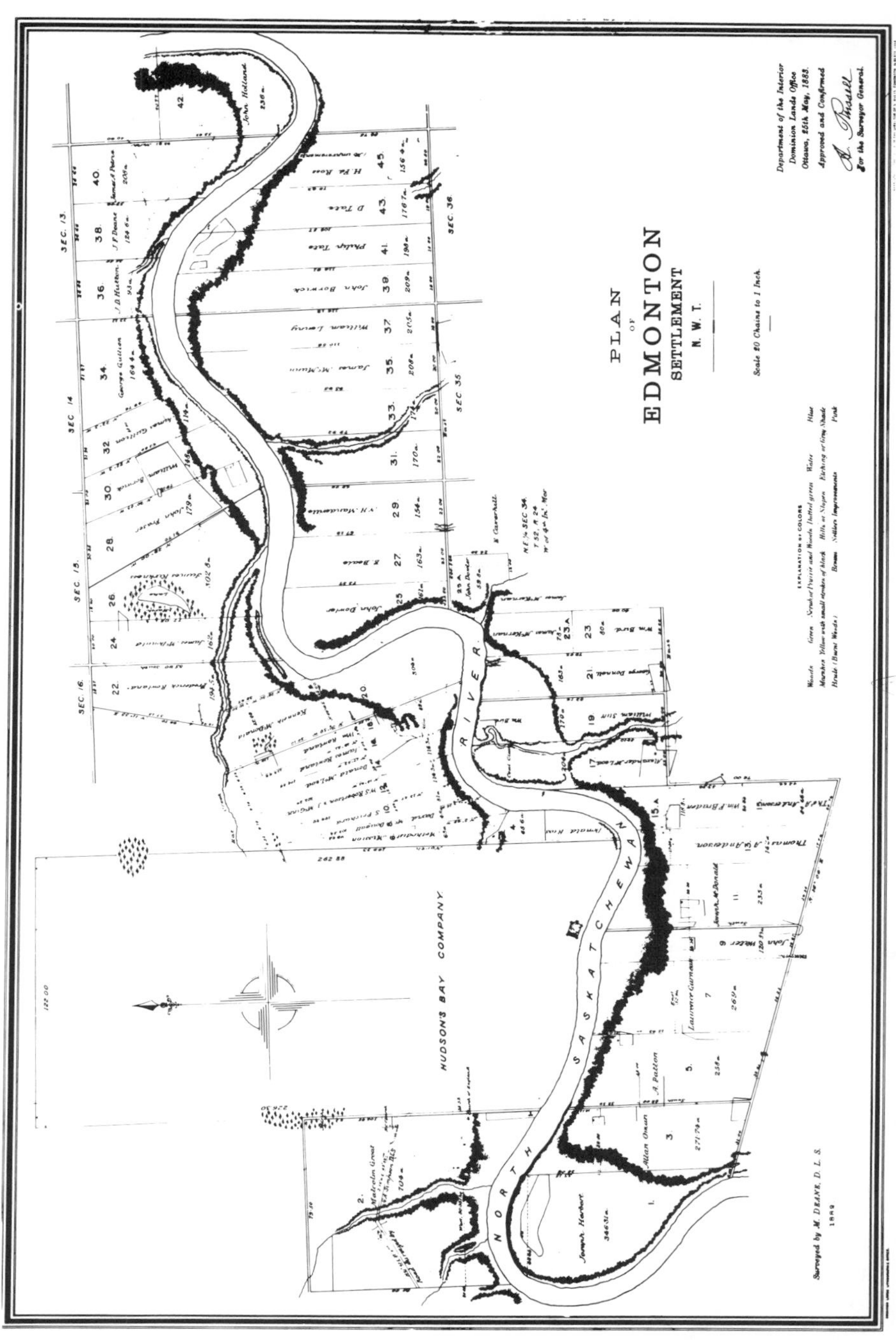

Map 1: The Edmonton Settlement, 1883.

of people who claimed land, few were agriculturalists interested in using their property. The majority were interested in the exchange value of their claims in terms of their potential for conversion into urban subdivisions.

The city building process in Edmonton was officially inaugurated on 29 October 1881 with the H.B.C.'s announcement published in the *Edmonton Bulletin* heralding the creation of the "City of Edmonton." According to the H.B.C. advertisement, the townsite was:

> situated at the head of navigation on the North Saskatchewan River; the centre of the Gold, Coal, Timber and Mineral region of the great North-West, and surrounded by the richest wheat-producing country in the world.
>
> The four great highways leading from Winnipeg, the great Bow River grazing country, the Peace River country and British Columbia via the Jasper Pass Centre on the Town site.
>
> It is the terminus of the C.P. telegraph line, the North-West mail route, and the projected Saskatchewan branch of the C.P.R.[12]

The H.B.C.'s enthusiasm for its new townsite was initially shared by Frank Oliver, editor of the *Edmonton Bulletin:*

> There is a possibility . . . that the syndicate have decided to build the C.P.R. via Edmonton, crossing the river here, and uniting with the H.B. Co. in building upon their property the metropolis of this far North-West. If this surmise should prove correct, and it is at least reasonable, all the booms that have taken place yet in Manitoba or elsewhere will be as nothing compared to that which the tumble-down walls of Fort Edmonton will see during the next year or two.[13]

This announcement was followed by the calling of a public meeting, at which time the company explained its intentions to the citizens and invited their participation in certain aspects of the town's design.[14] Terms of the land sales were to be one-third cash down and the balance in two equal annual installments. Land purchasers were also required to erect a building inside of eighteen months from the date of purchase on at least every second lot. Lots would also be given for schools and churches and "liberal inducements in the shape of lots will be given to parties starting manufactures."[15] The people at the meeting were also requested to select the location of a market square and choose the main street. Initially, one thousand lots were created for immediate sale.

Edmonton's first legal subdivision found a ready market when offered for sale in October 1881. Initially, company officials in Edmonton conducted the land sales. The *Edmonton Bulletin* reported that "the moment the sale opened there was a rush for lots that would have surprised even a Winnipeg auctioneer, and in three or four days $12,000 worth, or about 400 lots were sold subject to building erections."[16] H.B.C. Land Commissioner Brydges, however, considered the price too low and ordered that sales from the Edmonton office stopped four days after they began. Henceforth land sales in the Edmonton townsite were to be conducted from Winnipeg.[17] Brydges's initial strategy to raise the price of the lots was to sell blocks of land to a Winnipeg land broker and a land company. W. W. Ross and his business associate Walker, Stuart and Co. obtained 320 lots at $40 each, and the Scottish, Ontario and Manitoba Land Co. obtained 300 lots at $110 per lot. The increased interest in Edmonton lots by May 1882 prompted Brydges to subdivide additional land and dispose of the lots by auction. The price rose as high as $163.00 per lot. The net result of the land boom was the creation of a plan consisting of 2,288 lots.[18] The plan ignored the geographical realities of this portion of the reserve by imposing a strict grid pattern. Portions of some road allowances and a number of the lots were impossible to develop because of the steepness of the valley wall. An existing system of trails which facilitated access between the flats and the top of the valley was ignored.

Interest in the Edmonton townsite, however, did not endure beyond the spring of 1882. The initiatives with respect to the design of the town were forgotten, with the exception of the location of the main street. This rapid decline of interest in Edmonton real estate was, in part, a result of the failure of the alliance between the H.B.C. and the C.P.R. to develop a townsite on the reserve. The C.P.R. chose a more southerly route, thus allowing it to avoid dealing with the various land speculators who had gathered to welcome them to the Edmonton settlement. The response to the collapse of the land boom in Edmonton clearly reflected the lack of local participation, a result of the decision to conduct land sales from Winnipeg. As the *Edmonton Bulletin* observed:

> Outside of the boom the prospects of Edmonton are second to those of no place in Manitoba or the North West except Winnipeg. The boom as far as it has gone has left a large amount of money here of which every dollar has been invested and if it has burst utterly and lots can not now be sold in Winnipeg for a cent a piece the matter will concern very few of the people here. They have not been in the real estate business. The boom started suddenly and went ahead too rapidly for them to invest.[19]

Frank Oliver clearly resented the fact that the Winnipeg business community was monopolizing the benefits to be derived from land speculation.

Thus, the H.B.C. had not only failed to create the "City of Edmonton" but had also prevented Edmonton's business community from playing a prominent role as land brokers. The events of 1881–82 left a legacy of suspicion in Edmonton of Winnipeg real estate brokers and the Hudson's Bay Company. The H.B.C. reserve was no longer given the same deference as the logical location for the development of an urban community. The H.B.C. had thus lost its best opportunity to play a dominant role in the Edmonton land development process.

The frustration expressed by Frank Oliver with respect to the H.B.C. land boom was only one aspect of the land issue as it emerged in the 1880's. Other local concerns included the failure of the dominion government to prepare a legal survey of the settlement and issue certificates of title to the appropriate owners based on this survey; the creation of a land registration office; and the introduction of the Torrens system of land registry. These concerns were taken care of by the creation of the Edmonton Land Registration Office in 1885 and the passage of the Territories Real Property Act in 1886, which introduced the Torrens system of land registry and provided the first regulation concerning the subdivision process.[20]

Despite the collapse of the Hudson's Bay Company land boom in the spring of 1882, the unresolved issue of land tenure, and the retarded growth of the institutions to facilitate real estate transfers, the large scale subdivision of land at other locations in the settlement continued throughout the 1880's. This development was spurred on by the failure of the H.B.C. land to receive the benefit of a railway and the corresponding decline in the perception that the reserve was the future urban focus of the Edmonton settlement. During the winter of 1882–83, river lots 10, 12, and 14 were subdivided. The largest subdivision, which covered lots 12 and 14, created 1,594 lots, the majority of which were 33′ × 100′ in size.[21] The river lot 10 subdivision plan created an additional 489 lots, also 33′ × 100′.[22] The street pattern of this latter subdivision did not complement the adjacent street pattern in river lots 12 and 14. Unlike the H.B.C. reserve, the local business community had an interest in these subdivisions through ownership and/or through their role as land brokers. John Cameron and Walter Scot Robertson, who were in partnership with Winnipeg merchant Alexander MacDonald, owned river lots 12 and 14. Land in these two subdivisions was handled by a variety of local realtors. The subdivision of these properties was a less spectacular venture, which provided more direct economic benefits to the Edmonton business community in the form of real estate commissions. These subdivisions were also a less deliberate effort to create a townsite, since no public meeting was called to consult the citizens with respect to the location of the main street or a market square.

The problems resulting from this approach to the land development process were noted by Frank Oliver in the *Edmonton Bulletin* of September 1886. He observed that:

> Edmonton possesses one of the finest town sites in the North-West all our residents claim and visitors admit. At the same time it must be acknowledged that by the system or lack of system pursued in surveying it into blocks and lots its natural beauty and utility could not have been turned to less advantage.[23]

A specific example of poor design was the imposition of a grid pattern over the southern portion of the H.B.C. reserve, which made access from the town to the steamboat landing and the upper ferry crossing circuitous and difficult. The eastern townsite lacked a wide straight main street and a proper access road to the industrial area located on the flats in River lot 20. "It is evident that if business is to be done free access must be had to the river at both ends of Town on the easiest possible grades, . . . short narrow or crooked streets are a drawback to business and keep down the value of property."[24] Oliver's proposal to remedy this problem was to have the owners of land in the eastern part of the town come together and settle "on a general plan that would give a straight wide Main Street and a system of survey conforming as far as possible with that of the H.B. and to the natural features of the place as well."[25] No action was taken on this suggestion. A number of owners were non-residents and thus were not available to respond to Oliver's advice. The high rate of non-resident ownership thus mitigated against any kind of community action which was designed to modify the subdivision process in such a way as to deal with the unique aspects of Edmonton's site.

The separation of the east and west end townsites was not bridged until 1888 when the Methodist Church subdivided river lots 6 and 8.[26] These subdivision plans created 174 lots which were equal in size to lots in the H.B.C. reserve, but the street alignments added further confusion to the street pattern in this area. By 1888, these subdivisions, prepared without any consultation with residents, brought the cumulative total of urban lots in the Edmonton settlement to 4,545. The estimated population of Edmonton in that year was 350.

The subdivision activity which took place in the Edmonton settlement between 1881 and 1888 insured that there would be plenty of choice for those seeking land for commercial, industrial, residential, and institutional purposes. Nevertheless, a considerable degree of continuity between pre- and post-boom land use patterns is evident, since no incentives to alter land use patterns, such as railway construction, were in place. The speculation seen in the creation of subdivisions was thus not evident in the latter stages of the land development process. Investment in land development, which totaled $182,260.00 by 1887, was for specific commercial, residential, industrial, and institutional structures.[27] The buildings were constructed by a small group of contractors who built on commission. Edmonton's central business district thus remained in the southern end of river lot 10, while industrial land use remained in river lots 18 and 20 and adjacent to the North Saskatchewan River. These locations had originally been selected because the H.B.C. had not subdivided any of its property until the fall of 1881. The only exception to this continuity was the H.B.C. success in attracting the small amount of institutional land development, which included Edmonton's first school, the Roman Catholic Mission, and a Presbyterian Church. The advantage possessed by the H.B.C. was its ability to provide the owners with legal certificates of ownership which the claimants to land outside the reserve were temporarily prevented from doing.

The only company created specifically for the purpose of constructing buildings for resale was the Edmonton Building and Investment Company. This company, which was incorporated by letters patent issued in 1889, had the power to acquire real estate, erect buildings thereon and lease or sell the same.[28] The majority of the shareholders were Edmonton merchants and did not include any of the tradesmen building on commission. No records have survived to indicate whether the company was successful in the attainment of this goal.

The commercial, residential, industrial, and institutional structures built in the 1880's used an estimated 5 per cent of the land created for building purposes. In addition to the gross underutilization of the townsite in terms of building sites, the opening of road allowances and the creation of other public works required by an urban community were virtually nonexistent.

The fact that little effort had been made towards the creation of a municipal government which could regulate site development reflected the view of Edmonton residents that the arrival of a railway and the economic development that would follow was the necessary prerequisite to incorporation and the deliberate effort to create an urban community. The Calgary and Edmonton Railway, which was incorporated in 1890, was expected to play this role. The railway, however, chose to locate its northern terminal on the south side of the river, where a new townsite consisting of 1,280 lots was created.[29] Initially the railway townsite attracted some investment in industrial plants and commercial structures. Like the H.B.C., however, the railway company did not have a long-term commitment to urban development in the Edmonton settlement. By 1893, the townsite administrators Osler, Hammond, and Nanton had stopped actively promoting the new metropolis.

The lack of aggressiveness by the railway townsite administrators was in marked contrast to the response to this new townsite from the northside business community, which immediately formulated a self-defence policy. The view of the northside, as expressed by Frank Oliver, was that the railway townsite was a conspiracy involving another group of Winnipeg land speculators who wanted to monopolize the real estate benefits of Edmonton's progress.[30] They were determined to prevent a repetition of what had happened in 1881–82. This strategy included the incorporation of Edmonton as a town in 1892 (Map 2). Since it was felt that its land owners would use their influence to inhibit the growth of the north side, the boundaries of Edmonton were drawn to deliberately exclude the railway townsite. The newly created town council also initiated a programme to construct a bridge across the North Saskatchewan River, thus allowing Edmonton to enjoy the benefits of the arrival of the railway.

Edmonton's business community responded with other programmes to meet the challenge of the railway townsite. The Edmonton Street Railway Company, the Edmonton District Railway Company, the Edmonton Electric Light Company and the Edmonton Telephone Company were created in close cooperation with the town council, which either purchased shares in some of the companies or entered into long-term service contracts. These organizations succeeded in providing the townsite with only a very rudimentary utility system or totally failed to progress beyond the incorporation stage. Progress towards the development of Edmonton as a regional transportation centre was only made after William MacKenzie and Donald Mann acquired the charter of the Edmonton District Railway Company in August 1898. The company was reorganized as the Edmonton, Yukon and Pacific Railway in August 1899 and construction was under way by 1901. The acquisition of the charter by MacKenzie and Mann coincided with the construction of the long awaited low-level bridge which was opened in 1902. The entry of the E.Y. & P. into Edmonton was governed by an agreement negotiated with the town council.

The impact of this strategy on the land development process was to preserve the viability of the northside subdivisions, create additional nodes of industrial land use in the river valley, and fragment institutional land use. It also generated some genuine economic growth. This growth increased the rate at which land was being utilized, thus establishing some equilibrium between land subdivision and utilization which had been totally absent in the 1880's. This was particularly true of the two subdivisions created by the H.B.C. in 1899 and 1902, which accommodated the expansion of the central business district and a residential area to the west. These subdivisions thus reduced the disjointed nature of urban development in the Edmonton settlement. The industrial development spread to the

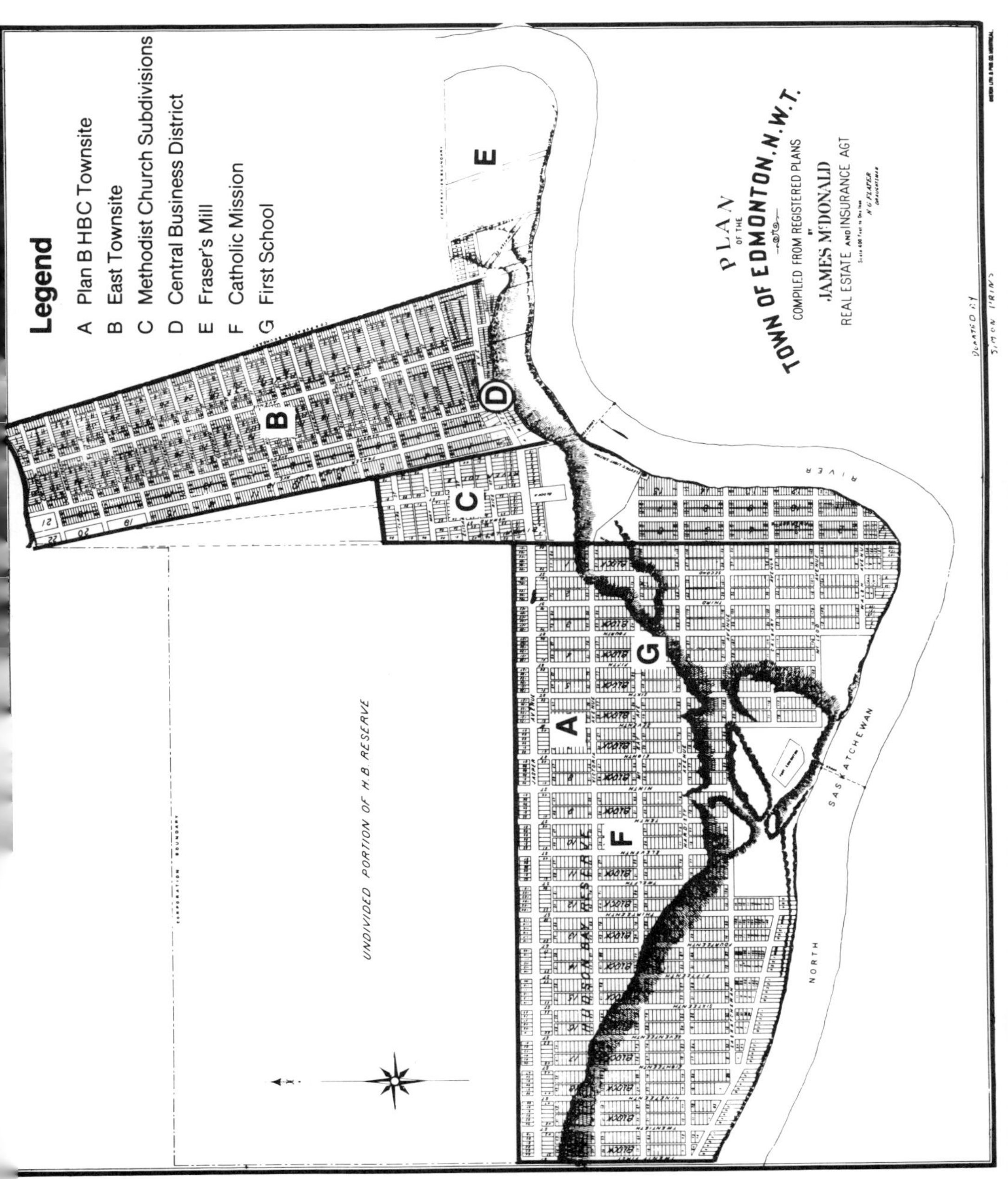

Map 2: Plan of Edmonton, 1892.

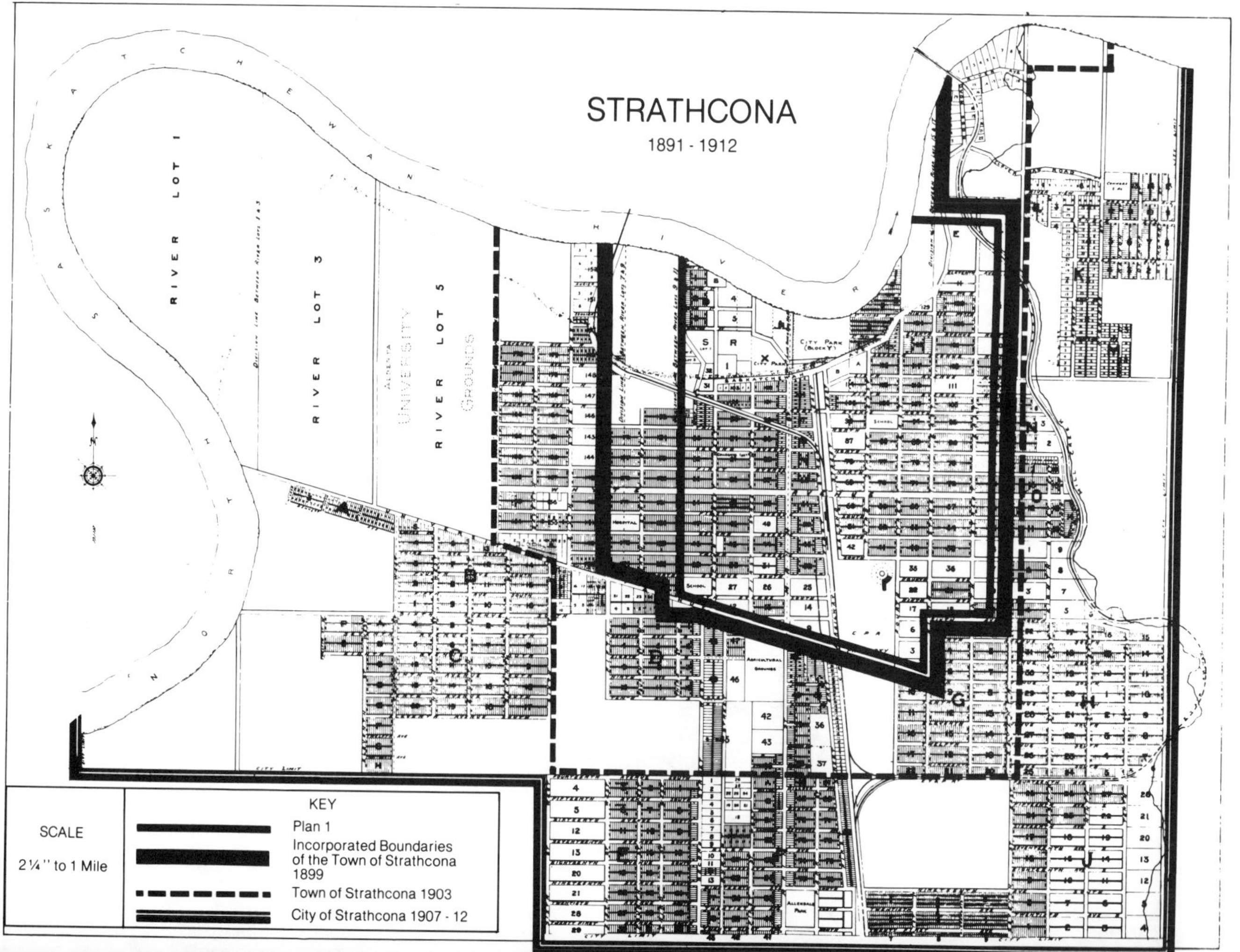

Map 3: Strathcona.

other flood plains, primarily as a result of the construction of meat packing plants and plants related to the manufacture of building products such as bricks and lumber. In addition to the expansion of the original urban node on the north side was the construction of various institutional buildings to the east of the reserve, a result of the Edmonton business communities control of the municipal government and school board. The H.B.C. reserve, however, was the site of the first hospital and Edmonton's first federal public building, which was located on a plot of land donated by the company. Despite the shift away from speculative subdivisions, at least one Edmonton businessman continued to be involved in this activity; in 1893, the Ross estate in river lot 4 was subdivided.[31]

Land development between 1891 and 1902, therefore, occurred within the context of a number of rivalries, the most significant of which was between the north and south sides for control of the Edmonton settlement. This rivalry was resolved by the turn of the century in favour of the north side and the Edmonton business community, because of their initiative with respect to incorporation and negotiation of a terminal agreement with the E.Y.& P. Thus the stage was set for the next step in the land development process.

In 1903, a terminal agreement was negotiated with the Canadian Northern Railway (C.N.R.). This was a three-party agreement which involved joint purchase of 68.88 acres of H.B.C. reserve by the town of Edmonton and the Canadian Northern Railway for use as yards and a station. The C.N.R. made no other land purchases in the Edmonton area for urban land development. The C.N.R. mainline was located some distance to the north of any buildings with the exception of Queen's Avenue School. Thus the entry of the railway did not necessitate the reorganization of the built-up area. In March 1906, a terminal agreement was also negotiated between the Grand Trunk Pacific Railway and the city in which the city provided some free land for right-of-way. The Grand Trunk also purchased 640 acres to the north of the H.B.C. reserve for use as yards and future industrial sites. The location of the Grand Trunk Pacific right-of-way would eventually lead to the creation of the villages of West and North Edmonton.

These railway agreements created a second land boom reminiscent of the winter of 1881–82. Between 1903 and 1914, a total of 274 new subdivisions were created, which were located as far as seven miles from the central business district (Map 5).[32] This represented an 1,800 per cent increase in the number of subdivisions on the north side alone compared with an 800 per cent increase in the total population of Edmonton between 1904 and 1914. These subdivisions were located on both sides of the river, with the greatest concentration being to the north east of the central business district.

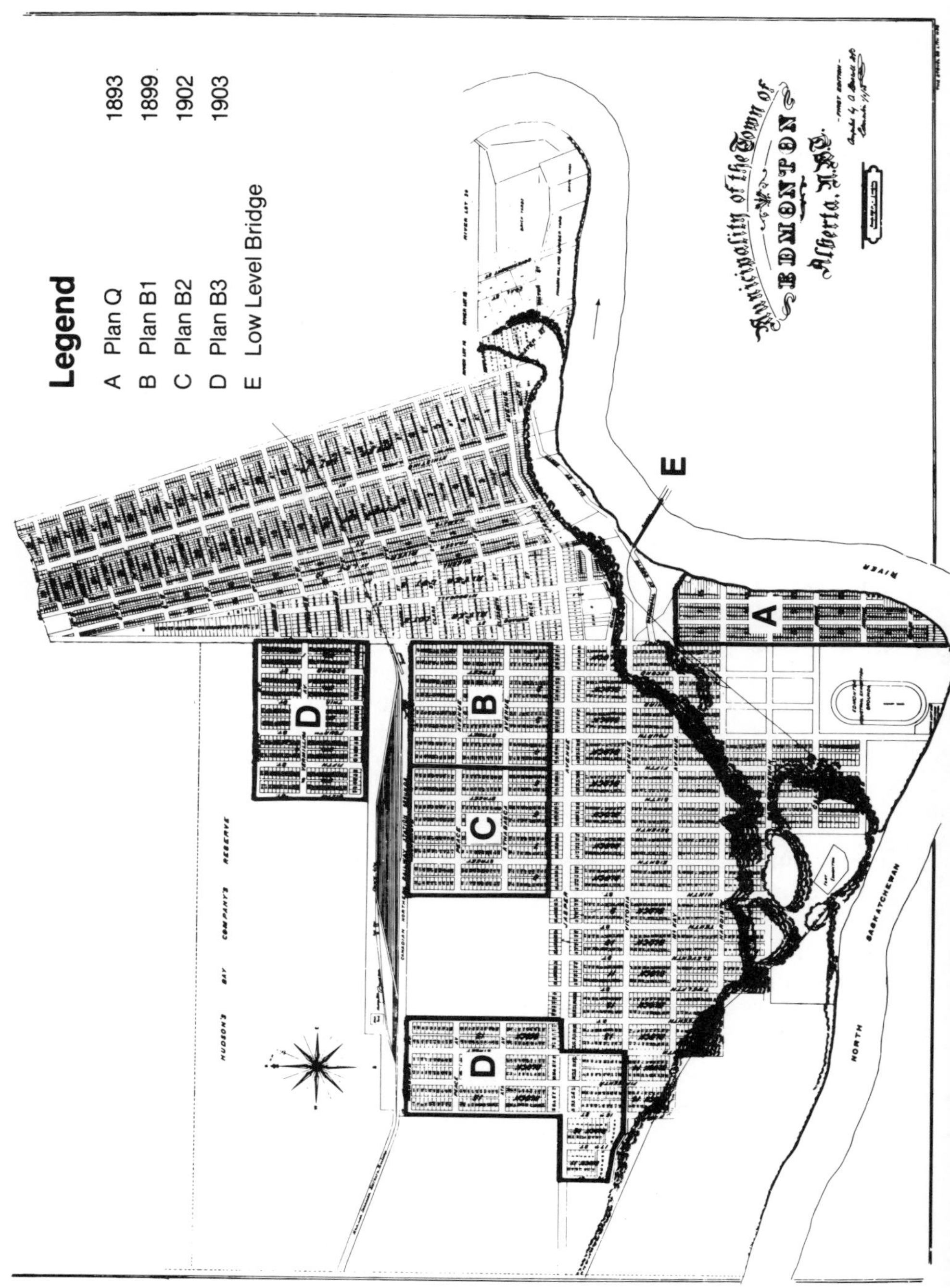

Map 4: Municipality of Edmonton.

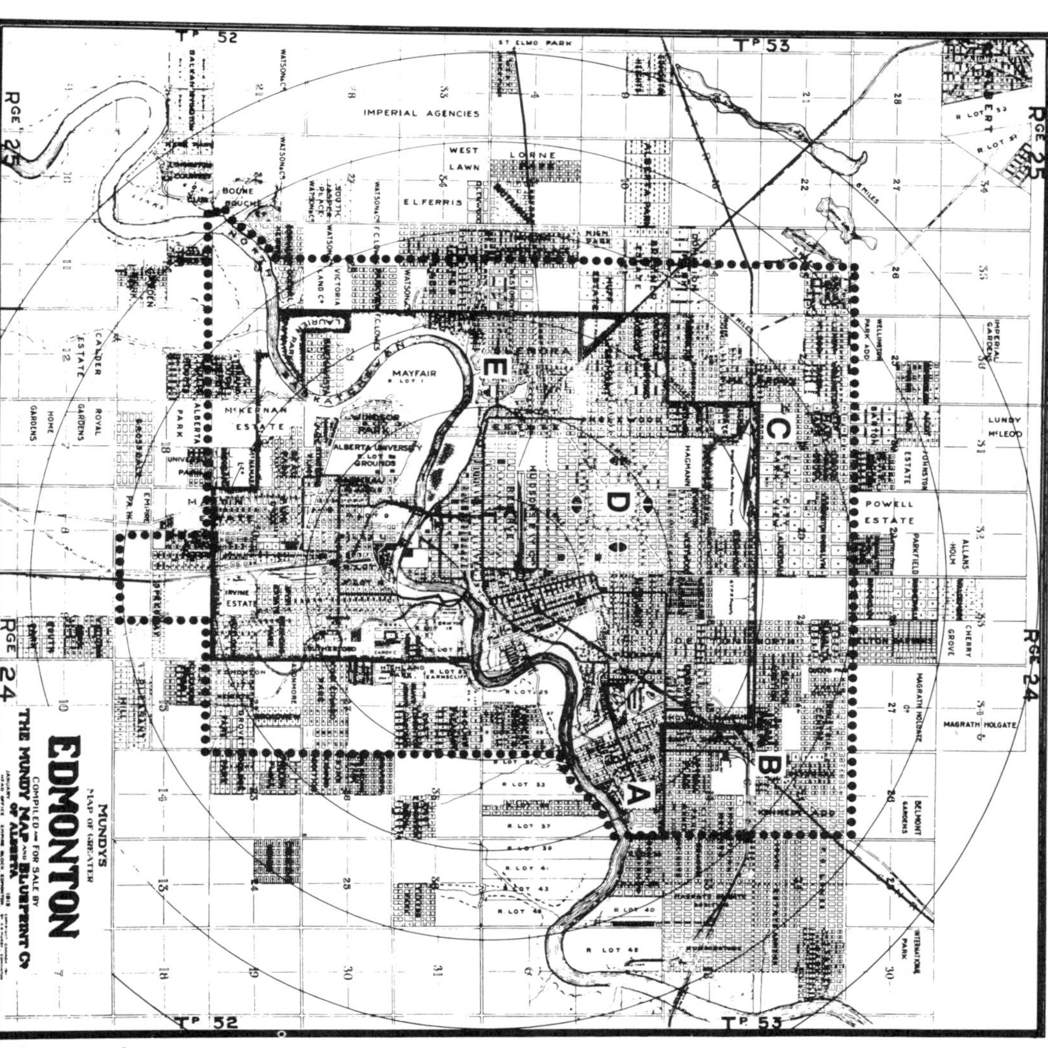

Legend

Boundary •••••• 1917

A Highlands

B North Edmonton

C West Edmonton

D HBC Subdivision 1911

E Glenora

Map 5: Map of Edmonton.

The creation of this blueprint for a "Greater Edmonton" was to a large extent under the control of Edmonton's business community. The participants included a number of Edmonton's well established mercantile companies which reorganized in order to participate more actively in the land development process.[33] In 1909, the firm of McDougall and Secord Ltd. was created for the purpose of carrying out a number of objectives. One of these was the purchase, lease, and acquisition of land for speculation and development. As part of this reorganization, their mercantile, northern freighting, and wholesale and fur trade businesses were sold. Members of Edmonton and Strathcona's professional elite also expanded their involvement in the land subdivision process. Alexander Cameron Rutherford, who had established himself as a lawyer in Strathcona in 1894 and premier of Alberta from 1905 to 1910, became a major subdivision promoter in the area to the east of the railway townsite.

In addition to the reorientation of Edmonton's established business community, eighteen new land companies were incorporated for the purpose of creating and marketing new subdivisions. A limited amount of foreign capital was also attracted to the Edmonton real estate market for investment in the creation of new subdivisions. The Edmonton-Strathcona Land Syndicate was an English company incorporated in London on 19 November 1908 for the purpose of acquiring and developing land throughout the empire. The company's subdivisions, called Mayfair Park and Windsor Terrace, were located in River lot 1. American investment in the creation of new subdivisions was provided by Alexander M. Harroun and Ora L. Harroun, both of the city of Chicago.[34] On 17 February 1908, they registered a plan for Capital Hill. On 9 July 1908 George E. Roberts, a farmer from Carroll, Iowa, registered a plan for Woodcroft.[35] The actual registration was handled by Edmonton attorney John R. MacIntosh, president of the Sherbrook land company, which also owned a subdivision in the west end.

The physical characteristics of these new subdivisions were consistent, based on examination of maps and various registered plans. These subdivision plans ranged in size from one fully subdivided block containing thirty-six lots to plans which contained over 100 blocks arranged in a grid pattern, each containing thirty-six lots. The majority of the lots were 33 feet in size, with the exception of those in the H.B.C. subdivision, which were 50 feet. A second approach which was less common was the creation of large blocks which could be resubdivided at a later date. The Elm Park subdivision was an example of this approach. Irrespective of the approach used, developers continued to ignore the geographical realities of the site. An example of this approach was the Spruce Centre subdivision in river lot 19, which incorporated a creek into the principal road allowance.

The ultimate fate of the bulk of the property created was its acquisition by the city of Edmonton through tax sales which began in 1917. Following the city's acquisition of the property, some of the subdivision plans were cancelled, allowing the land to revert back to agricultural use or to permit its replotting. This process of rationalizing the great plan constituted the next period in the land development process, and many subdivisions were never integrated into the city fabric. For portions of the river valley as well as the H.B.C. reserve, this reversal of the land subdivision process was permanent.

Closely related to the phenomenal increase in the rate of land subdivision was an enthusiastic political response to the pace being set by the land promoters. This response was evident in Edmonton's annexation policy and the extension of urban service to these new areas. The objective of the annexation policy was to achieve the political consolidation of the Edmonton settlement and keep pace with the subdivision process as well as with trends in the expansion of the built-up area. Edmonton's first annexation bid was made in 1903 when a city charter was under discussion. Its primary objective was the industrial plants in Cloverdale at the north end of river lots 17 and 19. Edmonton, however, had to be content with 3.79 square miles of undeveloped land located primarily to the north and east of the original townsite, since Strathcona annexed this territory before Edmonton could act. Edmonton's most ambitious bid to achieve these goals was made in October 1911. Included in the area to be annexed were the villages of West and North Edmonton as well as the city of Strathcona. These annexations were made despite warnings from the city engineer that problems would be created[36] and only after agreements with the city to ensure services to the village of West Edmonton.

Commensurate with this process of political consolidation was the attempt to provide urban services to this new area. A vast system of sewage, water, electric light and street car extensions was initiated. The expansive tendencies of the civic administration was also evident in the decision in 1906 to purchase a site for the west end park and a site for the exhibition grounds, which were to be located in the east end. Both sites were located beyond the existing boundaries of the city. This latter decision was made despite the fact that a more central location on the H.B.C. reserve was favoured over the site purchased.

The positive response of the civic administration was equalled by that of the Edmonton Public School Board, which adopted a policy of purchasing land in the new subdivisions in advance of settlement. This policy reflected, in part, the high cost of purchasing additional land to expand the size of the grounds of existing schools in the pre-1903 townsite. The development of this strategy was first suggested by the board's building committee in 1906.[37] Its application was first made in Norwood, where the school site was bought from McDougall and Secord. This policy ensured that each new subdivision would have at least one customer and thus encouraged the subdivision process. This practice was institutionalized in 1912 when the province changed the land subdivision regulations to require subdivision owners to provide school sites.

The enthusiasm of the city council and the school board reflected the influence which Edmonton's "land men" had on these organizations. Examples of this overlap included John A. McDougall, Robert Lee and P. T. Butchard. John A. McDougall was Mayor of Edmonton in 1908. Robert Lee who was a member of the real estate firm of Crafts, Lee and Galliger served as an alderman in 1908 and as mayor in 1909 and 1910; he also served on the Edmonton Public School Board. The Great West Land Company which was promoting the Westmount subdivision was owned by the Butchards. P. T. Butchard, president of the company, served as chairman of the Edmonton Public School Board in 1910 and 1911.[38]

During the period from 1903 to 1914, the emphasis in the land development process was on creating a grand design for a greater Edmonton through new subdivisions and boundary and utility system extensions. The actual utilization of the land proceeded at a slower pace despite the issuance of a record number of building permits. The peak years were 1912 and 1913, when a total of 5,287 permits were issued, compared to 1,570 for the period from 1914 to 1917. Land utilization at this time was also distinctive because of the appearance of speculative building and the significant contributions of non-Edmonton companies as well as the provincial and federal governments. These investments introduced the first major changes in Edmonton's morphology since the initiation of the city-building process in 1881.

These changes included the terminal facilities of the Grand Trunk Pacific Railway, which were located on 640 acres of land situated at the north end of the H.B.C. reserve. The residential community which developed around this installation was incorporated as the village of West Edmonton in 1914 and annexed by the city of Edmonton in 1917. It was to remain isolated from the original portion of the built-up area until the 1940's.

A new industrial area located at the junction of the Canadian Northern and Grand Trunk Pacific railway lines in the northeast sector of the expanded city also developed. The principal industries of North Edmonton were the Burns and Co. and Swifts packing plants. In 1913 H. P. Kennedy, a Toronto-based investor, purchased the North Edmonton subdivisions of Industrial Heights and Kennedale, to which he was able to attract the Western Foundry and Machine Co., the Edmonton Casket and Box Co., and the Weber Lumber Co.

A clearly defined warehouse district also emerged during this period as a result of the construction of the Revillon Building, Shaw Block, Armstrong Block, and the Great West Saddlery Company Block, amongst others, on a portion of the H.B.C. reserve located adjacent to the new Canadian Northern Railway yards. Contributions to the existing built-up area by the Grand Trunk Pacific Railway included the MacDonald Hotel, while the Canadian Pacific Railway contributed a north side terminal building and an office block. The provincial government contributed a two million dollar legislative building and a court house while the federal government contributed a post office to the central business district. The contributions of the Edmonton business community included the Tegler and McLeod Blocks, which were the two largest office buildings in the central business district. Robert Tegler was the promoter of the Belgravia subdivision, while Kenneth McLeod was a contractor who had been involved in construction work since his arrival in Edmonton in 1881. This building represented a major shift by McLeod into the construction of buildings on a speculative basis. The construction of the Tegler building proved that profits from subdivisions were being reinvested in land development in the central core. The Edmonton business community was also active in residential construction in the form of both apartments and single-family, detached residences. Major apartment blocks were built by Rene LeMarchand, the Arlington Apartment Co., and the Edmonton Home Builders Limited. LeMarchand, as well as a number of the shareholders of the latter two companies, were major participants in land subdivision activity.

Residential land was not greatly affected by the arrival of the railway, since the land adjacent to the river valley and its various ravines continued to attract Edmonton's business and political elite. As a result, Edmonton's mansion district stretched from Glenora in river lot 2 through the southern portion of the H.B.C. reserve to the Highlands subdivision in river lot 34. No one subdivision emerged as the dominant elite neighbourhood, despite efforts by both west end and east end land developers to promote that objective. Edmonton continued to some degree to be a river valley city, despite the arrival of two transcontinental railways and a corresponding reorientation of the community to the north east. No residential monuments equivalent to Mount Royal or Shaughnessy were created by the railway companies.

The land development process in Edmonton between 1881 and 1917, like other western Canadian cities at this time, reflected many of the characteristics of land development in the nineteenth century. The rectangular grid and lot system was used extensively; the marketing of new subdivisions depended on boosterism; and the speculator played a prominent role, as did transportation companies and the local government. The creation and utilization of urban land took place in a cyclical manner only slightly modified by municipal and provincial regulations. It also operated independent of the communities' need for land, thus creating a high volume of unoccupied space. The regulations and institutions which were created simply facilitated the activities of those individuals and companies who participated in the real estate market. The idea that it was necessary for the various levels of government to intervene to protect the public interest was never seriously considered. The positive role of the government with respect to land speculation was also indirectly evident in improved communication systems, such as the telegraph, which permitted international participation in urban land development in the Canadian West. Urban land development in the mid-nineteenth century in such places as Hamilton appears to have operated within the context of a more local market. Edmonton, along with other prairie cities, therefore, represents the progressive amplification of the role of land speculators as a result of these communication improvements.

Edmonton is, however, unique with respect to one very basic aspect of urban land development in the West. Its development was not dictated by the real estate interests of a railway company or the Hudson's Bay Company. This was a result of poor timing on the part of the H.B.C. and the entry of railways after a critical period in the formation of the community. A conflict ensued between the vested interests of the frontier business community, who had a long-term interest in their investment, and the two corporate owners, who had a short-term interest. This created a very competitive real estate market. As a result, the resolution of such questions as where the main townsite would be or where the exclusive residential area would be were resolved over a longer period of time, thus fragmenting land use patterns. This competition maximized the disruptive effects of the geography of the Edmonton settlement. The nature of the Edmonton real estate market along with boosterism thus helps explain the fact that Edmonton was Canada's largest city in area and had the lowest population density by 1921.

NOTES

1. For an excellent review of this literature, see Michael Doucet's article "Urban Land Development In Nineteenth-Century North America: Themes in the Literature," *Journal of Urban History* 8, no. 3 (May 1982): 299–342.
2. A. F. J. Artibise, "In Pursuit of Growth: Municipal Boosterism and Urban Development in the Canadian Prairie West, 1871–1913," in G. A. Stelter and A. F. J. Artibise, eds., *Shaping the Urban Landscape* (Ottawa, 1982); R. Rees "The 'Magic City on the Banks of the Saskatchewan': The Saskatoon Real Estate Boom 1900–1913," *Saskatchewan History* 27 (1974): 51–59;

M. L. Foran "Urban Calgary 1884–1895," *Histoire sociale/Social History* 5 (1972): 67–70; Norbert MacDonald, "A Critical Growth Cycle for Vancouver, 1910–1914," *B.C. Studies* 17 (1968): 26–42.

3. R. D. Roberts, "The Changing Patterns in Distribution and Composition of Manufacturing Activity in Hamilton Between 1861–1921" (Master's Thesis, McMaster University, 1964); Eric W. Ricker, "Consensus and Conflict: City Politics in Hamilton at Mid-Century," in I. Winchester, ed., *The Canadian Social History Project Report Number 5* (Toronto, 1973), pp. 163–241.
4. Pierre Berton, *The Last Spike* (Toronto, 1971); Frances N. Mellen, "The Development of the Toronto Waterfront During the Railway Expansion Era 1850–1912" (Ph.D. Diss., University of Toronto, 1975); M. L. Foran, "Land Development Patterns in Calgary 1884–1945," in G. A. Stelter and A. F. J. Artibise, eds., *The Usable Urban Past* (Toronto, 1979), pp. 293–315; Deryck W. Holdsworth, "House and Home in Vancouver: Images of West Coast Urbanism, 1886–1929," in G.A. Stelter and A. F. J. Artibise, *The Canadian City,* (Ottawa, 1984), pp. 187–209.
5. Michael J. Doucet, "Building the Victorian City: The Process of Land Development in Hamilton, Ontario, 1847–1881," (Ph.D. Diss., University of Toronto, 1977) and "Speculation and the Physical Expansion of Mid-Nineteenth Century Hamilton," in Stelter and Artibise, *Shaping the Urban Landscape*.
6. Isabel Ganton, "The Subdivision Process in Toronto, 1851–1883," in Stelter and Artibise, *Shaping the Urban Landscape*.
7. Walter G. Hardwick, *Vancouver* (Don Mills, 1974).
8. Michael B. Katz, *The People of Hamilton, Canada West: Family and Class in a Mid-Nineteenth-Century City* (Cambridge, 1975).
9. See Doucet, "Urban Land Development."
10. *Edmonton Bulletin,* 4 February 1882.
11. Despite the opinion expressed in this advertisement, Brydges later expressed the view that Edmonton's "connection by a branch with the main line is entirely problematical. And as you know our land is situated on the north side of the Saskatchewan River, and would not therefore be touched by the railway even if the line passed through the Rocky Mountains by the Yellow Head Pass." Brydges to Colvile 27 May 1882, *The Letters of Charles John Brydges 1879–1882,* ed. Hartwell Bowsfield. (Winnipeg: The Hudson's Bay Record Society, 1977) vol. 31.
12. *Edmonton Bulletin,* 29 October 1881.
13. *Edmonton Bulletin,* 3 February 1882.
14. *Edmonton Bulletin,* 29 October 1881.
15. Ibid.
16. *Edmonton Bulletin,* 3 February 1882.
17. Brydges to Colvile, 27 May 1882, *The Letters of Charles John Brydges 1879–1882*.
18. Province of Alberta, Attorney General's Department, North Alberta Land Registration District, Edmonton, Plan B.
19. *Edmonton Bulletin,* 17 June 1882.

20. Canada, Law, Statutes. An Act Respecting Real Property in the Territories 49 vic., ch. 26. The subdivision regulations were contained in section 6 of the Act. This section required that all subdivision plans were to be certified by a licenced surveyor and prepared using a certain scale depending upon the area of the subdivision. The owner was also required to sign the plan before the registrar or a justice of the peace. The Land Titles Act passed by the Province of Alberta in May 1906 contained provisions relating to land subdivision which were very similar. No legislation was passed to regulate the subdivision process until the Town Planning Act of 1913.
21. The subdivision plan was described in detail in the *Edmonton Bulletin* on 23 December 1882. It was later registered at the Land Titles Office as Plan D.
22. Land sales in the Pritchard Estate were noted as early as February 1883, however it was not registered as Plan A until 1886.
23. *Edmonton Bulletin,* 22 September 1886.
24. Ibid.
25. Ibid.
26. Province of Alberta, Attorney General Department, North Alberta Land Registration District, Edmonton, Plans E and F.
27. *Edmonton Bulletin,* 31 December 1887.
28. *Edmonton Bulletin,* 11 May 1889.
29. For a detailed account of the land development policy of the Calgary and Edmonton Railway, see John Gilpin "Urban Land Speculation in the Development of Strathcona (South Edmonton), 1891–1912," in John E. Foster, ed., *The Developing West,* (Edmonton 1983), pp.179–200.
30. *Edmonton Bulletin,* 18 July 1891.
31. Province of Alberta, Attorney General Department, North Alberta Land Registration District, Edmonton, Plan Q.
32. This statistic is based on the 1914 Henderson's Directory, Mundy's Map of Greater Edmonton compiled by the Mundy Map and Blueprint Co. in 1912 and various subdivision plans on file at the North Alberta Land Titles Office, Edmonton.
33. David Leonard, *A Builder of the North West: The Life and Times of Richard Secord* (Edmonton: Secord, 1981), p. 126.
34. Province of Alberta, Attorney General Department, North Alberta Land Titles Office, Edmonton, Plan 6878V, 9 November 1908.
35. Ibid. Certificate of Title 246-0-4.
36. *Edmonton Bulletin,* 15 November 1912.
37. Edmonton Public School Board, *Annual Report* 1906.
38. Province of Alberta, Consumer and Corporate Affairs Department, Corporate Registry, Corporate Access Number 20000147.

8

An Entrepreneur in the Halifax Building World: The Role of John D. Nash

Susan Buggey

Building requires land assembly, capital, and acumen, as well as design and construction. In many nineteenth-century towns, therefore, building was carried out not only by artisans but by entrepreneurs whose principal occupation was not that of builder. Such activity is difficult to trace in Halifax because assessment records are sparse and property documents are accessible by owner rather than by site location. Nevertheless, individuals do stand out. This examination of the career of auctioneer John D. Nash demonstrates the diversity and complexity of the entrepreneur's involvement in the mid-nineteenth-century Halifax building world, but it does not show convincingly that entrepreneurs outside the city's social elite contributed substantially to the speculative building stock in the Nova Scotian capital.

The literature of entrepreneurship in nineteenth-century Canada has focused primarily upon those areas of growth which have been seen to contribute to our national emergence: commerce, transportation and, to a lesser extent, industrialization. Characteristically, the scale was large, the financing complex, and the principal actors the wealthy, interconnected, social and political elites or foreigners. While recognizing that property was a measure of wealth and that these entrepreneurs were often substantial landholders, this literature has given little attention to their dealings as urban land speculators, developers or landlords.[1] Where urban land speculation has been studied, it has been largely in the industrialized and expansionist final decades of the century in new suburbs or new western cities, where it constituted an integral aspect of urban emergence.[2] If building has rarely been a focus of Canadian business history, on the other hand, its treatment in the architectural and heritage literature has addressed the character and history of buildings rather than the building process or the role of building in nineteenth-century urbanization.[3] Between these two approaches falls our need to understand the nature of the physical evolution of cities, including the incidence and processes of subdivision and the nature of the building industry in terms of its character, organization, and impact. Some recent studies by geographers, such as Michael Doucet's for Hamilton, David Hanna's for Montreal, and Jeanette Rice's for Kingston, have begun to address this lacuna by examining land development processes in these cities in the nineteenth century.[4] Such studies have yet to be carried out for urban centres in the Atlantic provinces. In their absence, this paper undertakes to examine the role of one entrepreneur who maintained a high profile in the Halifax building world in the mid-nineteenth century.

The study of building in nineteenth-century Halifax is difficult. Between 1835 and 1880 there are city property assessments for only three years: 1836, 1841 (for one of six wards), and 1862. The entries in these surviving lists are made street by street, giving proprietors' and tenants' names often indistinguishably and without building numbers, so that it is difficult to know where buildings begin and end and what pattern of recording has been used on the streets. The building act of 1861 provided for a building inspector — the so-called city architect — and this office was duly filled. But no documents survive, such as written notices of any intended building and the written reports on the erection, alteration, and repair of every building in the "brick district."[5] It is with such documents as these that the studies of building trends, patterns and cycles in Britain have been so usefully carried out.[6] Moreover, outside a few government structures, there are virtually no surviving building contracts for Halifax. Land titles are a significant source of information, but, unlike Ontario, where they are organized by section and lot number, in Halifax they are accessible only by indexes of grantee and grantor, with date of registration of the record. Such documents clearly show subdivision of property when the items are located, but some transactions are entered in the names of executors, trustees or assignees rather than of owners, and some were apparently never registered. Furthermore, most deeds and mortgages use a generic phrase referring to "all buildings, tenements and appurtenances thereto belonging" and thus provide no specific information regarding structures on the property. Consequently, only when a property was resold at a price difference not accountable by market factors can the deeds be used to identify construction and changing property values. In addition, iconographic evidence for the period is scarce. The scale of Church's 1865 map of the *City of Halifax* makes it difficult to correlate his representations of individual structures with those on Hopkins's detailed 1878 *City Atlas of Halifax,* which provides the first particularized record of buildings in the city.[7] In this context, newspaper data assume critical importance for the study of building in mid-nineteenth century Halifax. These sources are, however,

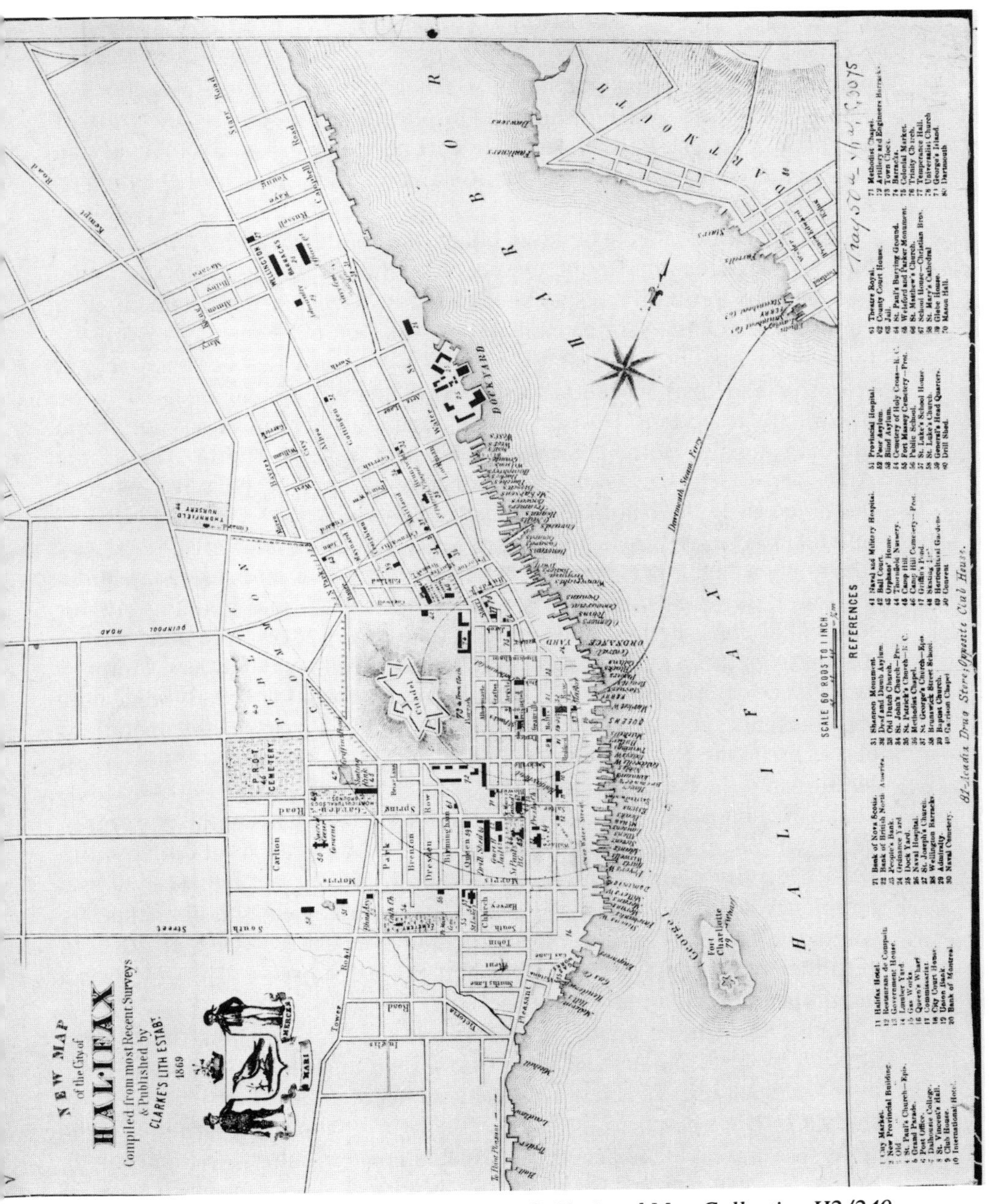

Map 1: The city of Halifax, 1869 (source: *PAC, National Map Collection H2/240 Halifax/1869*).

partial, incomplete and ambiguous, a result of their creation in contexts of selectivity, haste and familiarity. Despite these limitations in terms of available sources, it is worthwhile to undertake the study of evolving patterns of development, construction and building industry behaviour in the city.

Amidst a fin-de-siècle building boom, the Halifax *Evening Mail* glanced back a quarter century to a previous peak in the building cycle and found two citizens primarily responsible for the extensive development then current in the Nova Scotian capital: one was Colonel Bennett H. Hornsby; the other was John D. Nash.[8] The *Mail*'s choice was a curious one, for Hornsby had died in 1880, Nash in 1875, and neither appeared to be historically important. Hornsby was a speculator, of proportions familiar in building annals. Born in Kentucky, he had come to Halifax during the American Civil War as an agent for a southern tobacco firm. When it dissolved in 1868, Hornsby remained in Nova Scotia. There he plunged into local development. Amidst prosperity and an expansionist mood, he, like many a developer, purchased a peripheral estate property (John Hill's Willow Park), laid it out into streets, subdivided it into building lots for residential construction, and initiated building. Because the area lay too distant from the centre of the town to attract buyers and builders, Hornsby established an omnibus service which operated from 1873 to 1895. He used the mortgages on his sales at Willow Park to extend his operations elsewhere in the city. By the mid-1870's, he claimed to be one of the largest land owners in the city, worth between $150,000 and $200,000. R. G. Dun's evaluator described him as "a Keen shrewd man" with "the rep. of being vy. sharp as a dealer." When the real estate market collapsed in 1875, Hornsby's fortune plummeted with it. Halifax nevertheless viewed him generously: "Hornsby wanted to make money, but he also honestly wanted to improve Halifax, especially the North End. . . . He really tried to help the working classes to secure homes for themselves. . . . [He was a man] ahead of his time."[9]

John D. Nash, in contrast, was a man very much *of* his time. Nova Scotian by birth, he arrived in Halifax in the mid-1830's and lived there until his death in 1875. Nash was an auctioneer by trade. Surprisingly little study has been given to auctioneers in light of their role in nineteenth-century commercial society,[10] but Nash's position, character, and role in Halifax clearly warrant study. Unlike Montreal,[11] auctioneering firms in mid-nineteenth-century Halifax were long-lived. At least four — Deblois & Merkel, William Ackhurst, W. L. Evans and Edward Lawson — shared Nash's longevity of twenty-five to thirty years, while at least two others — James Cogswell and William M. Allan — operated as prominent firms for at least ten and fourteen years respectively. Most, like Nash, lacked substantial means, but Ackhurst, like Nash, was an enduring city alderman who, after six years' service, was nominated, though not elected, as mayor.[12] As an auctioneer, Nash's activities were diverse and gave him broad exposure to situations, opportunities and trends within the Halifax market. Principally, he auctioned a wide variety of goods, including dry goods, foodstuffs, household furniture, specialty and damaged items as well as property, on his own account, on others' account, and occasionally on account for an institution or government office, over a period of thirty years. He was equally as willing, if less frequently engaged, to negotiate the private sale of goods and property. He also acted, when required, as a commission merchant, a trustee in assignments, a manufacturer's agent, and an attorney representing foreign business interests in Halifax. In addition, Nash was a broker and the principal auctioneer of bank, insurance and utility stocks for twenty years; this was a lucrative, virtually monopolistic line which he continued until 1874.[13] Clearly, Nash was not primarily a builder. Rather, he represents that class of nineteenth-century entrepreneur who, though not himself a builder, had close connections with builders and was actively involved in the building world. Much of Nash's success, as well as his failures, can be attributed to the fact that he found speculation and improvement irresistible.

While Nash shared Hornsby's penchant for speculation, he was essentially a practical man. If not always regarded as entirely principled, he was noted as generous and trusted. His role in the Halifax building world was more diversified, more enduring and more intimately linked to city life than Hornsby's. Where much of Hornsby's activity was a reflection of his own opportunism, Nash's involvement in the building of Halifax provides a statement of its mid-century evolution. Nash's role can be defined in three contexts: as an entrepreneurial builder, as a land speculator, and as an auctioneer dealing extensively in property sales. In each of these areas, his activities mirror a larger Halifax building role. Because of the nature of the existing records, it is sometimes difficult to determine whether his role in particular cases was that of building entrepreneur, himself commissioning a structure on a lot for subsequent rental or sale; of developer, transforming an estate lot into building lots; of speculator, purchasing and holding land in anticipation of a lucrative sale for building; or of broker, providing a marketing facility between owners or between builder and dwelling owner. Nash appears to have played all of these roles at various times, apparently defining his part in particular instances by opportunity, convenience, or viability.

Lewis Fischer has provided us with a model of entrepreneurial behaviour which incorporates environment within the identified behavioural pattern.[14] Nash's most recognized building in Halifax largely fits within this

Fig. 1: Nash's Victorian buildings, Hollis Street, Halifax.

model. In 1857, following the first of the city's major mid-century fires, Nash made a significant entrepreneurial statement by erecting a solid, albeit plain, four-storey brick building, ten bays wide, with fashionable ground floor shop fronts on property purchased in the burnt district. This Hollis Street property, the Victoria Building, was Nash's most successful building venture. Both its size and its timing were an expression of building confidence in the face of a faltering blow to the commercial community. Its facilities were rented to numerous tenants providing various goods and services to the city. Finally, it was sold after six years, in an advantageous if complex transaction, into experienced financial hands.[15] Nash's judicious risk in erecting the building, his recognition of the potential of his market, his skillful promotion of the building to enhance his own profile and profits within that market, and the building's novel design and grand scale, all accord with five of the six qualities of Fischer's model of entrepreneurial behaviour. In the absence of more substantial information about Nash's financing, his relationship with partners, and the extent of his indebtedness, it is impossible to assess his individual responsibility in the project, outside of noting the popular acceptance in the press of Nash's responsibility for this enhancement of Halifax's urban fabric.

Nash's other notable building venture, the initiation in 1862 of fourteen brick houses as "good substantial tenements for the masses," reinforced his record for "enterprise and public spirit in erecting buildings at once useful and ornamental" in the city.[16] The actual extent of Nash's role in this project is unclear. Although he received the public credit for it, no property on the South Common was registered in his name at the time, and his subsequent purchases there appear to have been mere brokerage operations. Because of his frequently precarious financial situation, however, Nash did not always register his property in his own name. His Hollis Street lands, for example, were formally entered in his name at least six years after purchase, and then only when his holder's circumstances became more critical than his own.[17] A construction contract for the brick houses on the South Common was apparently let to the respected builder Henry Peters in 1865, and street directory evidence confirms household occupation in the area, although on a smaller scale than Nash's intended project, later in the decade.[18] Despite a favourable social climate and a convenient location, the economic reality of constructing solid housing stock on speculation appears to have limited Nash's penchant for improvement.

In addition to construction contracts directly with builders, Nash was actively involved in financing building in other ways. In some cases he sold lands for building purposes, repurchasing them for subsequent sale once structures had been erected on them. In other instances, he purchased built properties from builders and found new owners for them.[19] Nash was also actively involved in the building industry through the supply of construction materials: in the early 1860's through a steam-powered, cabinet-making establishment operated from his own premises; in the mid-decade through promotion of an hydraulic limestone discovered at Truro; and in the late 1860's through a brick and pottery manufacturing company, in which he cooperated with Halifax's prominent real estate agent, W. Myers Gray.[20]

Examination of the extent of Nash's building ventures does not support the hypothesis that local entrepreneurs were principal contributors to speculative building stock in mid nineteenth-century Halifax.[21] And if Nash's direct participation in building appears insufficient to account for his reputation in the nineteenth-century building world, it is evident that he was also involved in local land speculation. From 1840 to the late 1850's, he concentrated his activities, sometimes in partnership, in the most rapidly expanding part of the city, the North Suburbs. His purchase and subdivision of two-thirds of an acre on Lockman Street into thirteen small building lots proved premature, even for a site only one mile from centre town and convenient to the Dockyard. His only substantial return derived from a consolidated portion which he sold as a good-sized town lot fitted up with a new dwelling house.[22] In this, Nash's experience mirrors that of other Halifax entrepreneurs undertaking to subdivide estate properties. Colonel Bazalgette's south end estate, Belvedere, for example, was offered for sale in 1854 in eighty-two building lots; only the homestead portion and fifteen lots were sold, and ten years later only five buildings had been erected. When J. Scott Tremain's North West Arm estate, Belmont, was offered for sale two years later, it failed to subdivide and was purchased intact by barrister J. W. Ritchie, who used it as his residence into the 1870's. Similarly, carpenter W. G. Anderson's attempt to sell eighty building lots in Cambridge subdivision in 1853 saw little development; Nash himself purchased ten of these lots from painter Joey Metzler seventeen years later, at which time only one contained a structure, and it appears Nash did not add any further buildings during his five-year ownership.[23] Although he reaped a 19.8 per cent gross return on the portion of his Lockman Street subdivision for which measurable data exist, he did not repeat the attempt. His subsequent buying pattern reflected a continuing commitment to fringe areas with development potential, but it was limited to properties already subdivided and only rarely to more than three or four lots in any area.[24]

Although Halifax's fringe areas were expanding slowly in the 1850's and 1860's, Nash's speculative investments in them were generally profitable. Rarely was this a result of substantially rising market prices on the land he held. One exception was his purchase of lots in the new suburb of Campbellton, a growth area stimulated by erection of the British Army's Wellington Barracks and the opening of the Nova Scotia Railway's depot at Richmond. Nash's lots, which he mortgaged at 80 per cent of the purchase price to cover a debt, were situated between lands purchased concurrently by builders. Three years later he sold his property to them at a mark-up of 43 per cent.[25] Normally, Nash reaped his return by mortgaging his properties heavily and recycling the mortgage funds. In 1869, for example, he again bought fringe area lots, in the recently subdivided Robie's Fields, which he mortgaged to the seller for their full purchase price. The following year he bought a further ten building lots in the same vicinity which he mortgaged for a total of 104.3 per cent of their purchase price. Even after he sold off much of his heavily mortgaged property in 1871, commitments outstanding against his remaining lands three years later were reported to have totalled over $30,000.[26] Mortgages were a customary form of investment for Halifax money. Nash's mortgagers represent the propertied, monied class who formed the core of such investors, putting their money not in building per se but in that age-old symptom of wealth: property. They included widows, spinsters and businessmen well-known in Halifax for their investment in local property — the Artz, Cogswell, Forman, and Young families. None of Nash's registered mortgagers resided outside the city, nor did any of his personal real estate sales attract absentee speculators.

While Nash's land speculation afforded him a substantial investment in potential growth areas in the city, it does not appear to have justified his sustained reputation for large scale speculative investment. His position in the Halifax building world derived neither from entrepreneurial building nor from his personal land speculations. Rather, it was a function of his position as a broker and auctioneer which gave him the knowledge, the connections, and a continuing role in the Halifax building world of the mid-1800's.

Nash's practical knowledge of real estate apparently gave him his start in this lucrative field. Although R. G. Dun's representative did not specifically note real estate as a substantial element of Nash's business until the late 1850's, his active participation in the formation of the Nova Scotia Benefit Building Society and Savings Fund in 1849 attested to his early involvement in the field.[27] Building societies, initiated in England in the late eighteenth century, were a well-established medium for facilitating building and home ownership by those outside the monied classes through a long-term, low-cost mortgage tied to a small monthly premium purchase of society shares. Nash himself occasionally made use of the building society's mortgage funds, including its first offering in 1850, to finance his own purchases of property, but his substantial role in the organization was the encouragement of sufficient initial subscribers to create a functioning society. Evidence of the building society's utility in the Halifax market is provided by its average seventy-three mortgages let per year over the twenty-five year period from 1852 to 1876; its sustained level of activity through the early years of the 1870's recession; and its low level of retirement of mortgages, at only nineteen per year. By 1876, nearly fifteen thousand shares had been issued, and the society's funds totalled four million dollars.[28]

Much of Nash's promotion of Halifax property in his role as an auctioneer and real estate broker fell naturally in the realm of boosterism. Auction was a traditional means of facilitating the exchange of urban property in the nineteenth-century British North American city, and mid-century sales in Halifax prove that this mechanism fluctuated in popularity not only with the availability of property in the market but also with the demand for commercial and residential property. Many sellers opted first for private sale, sometimes employing an auctioneer as real estate broker, before resorting to sale at auction. When a property was offered at auction, reserves were rarely specified. Most real estate sales involved developed properties changing hands from owner to owner. Nash's role as a real estate broker kept him familiar with builders, clients, markets, and trends. His keen sense of marketing gave him a substantial profile in the successful promotion and sale of Halifax properties of all types.[29] By the mid-1850's, his share in the real estate market was well-established, although other firms led the field with the most numerous and most prestigious sales. By the late 1860's, Nash held an increasingly respectable share of the field, and by the early 1870's, he was the clear leader. In September 1872, he reported having sold over one million dollars' worth of real estate in the previous three years.[30] Until the downturn in the property market the following spring, his principal auction business remained focused upon real estate.

Auction was used extensively not only to sell developed property but also to dispose of estates at the time of subdivision, and it in this aspect which is of particular pertinence to this study. The mid-nineteenth-century saw large scale subdivision of fringe area properties into building lots; Nash acted in three contexts in relation to such sales. First, he was a purchaser, occasionally on his own account but much more frequently on account of others for whom he acted as agent. The latter purchases were never registered in Nash's name and are therefore traceable only when auction sales were reported in the public prints. For example, his purchases of eleven lots at the auction of Smith's Fields, the prominent south-end property subdivided by Smith's executors in 1862 totalled 1352, or 12.6 per cent of the total reported sale, and were second in number and value only to purchases by W. M. Richardson.[31] Such sales give an inflated idea of Nash's actual participation in land speculation; they undoubtedly contributed to his sustained reputation for large-scale activity in this area. Nash's second role in estate subdivisions was as auctioneer at the principal and subsequent land sales on behalf of owners, trustees or assignees of the property. These latter men had themselves prepared the plan of subdivision, had streets and building lots surveyed, and brought the estate to market. Nash's 1870 sale of Skimming's Farm, between Quinpool Road and the North West Arm, appears to have been of this type.[32] His third role incorporated his part as auctioneer and included a more active involvement in the sale, with varying responsibility for development of the plan, arrangement of the subdivision, and promotion of the sale. It is often difficult in Nash's sales to determine precisely the extent of the role he did play, but his auction of eighty acres of McNab's Island for summer residences in 1872 appears to belong to this third type. Nash had had connections with the proprietors of the island as early as 1857, and the timing, persistence, and promotional character of his advertisements suggest that he was probably one of the "party who ha[d] it divided and laid off into suitable Building Lots." The sale itself was organized by Nash as a Saturday picnic which he turned into a popular public outing. The first round sale disposed of thirty-three lots of a half acre to two acres each for a total of $13,265; a second round ten days later sold a further thirteen lots for $4,700 for a total sale of $18,000.[33]

Nash's prominence in the Halifax building world cannot be attributed solely to his activities, diverse as they were, within this sphere. His political and social activities were essential assets in the role he played. As a city alderman for many years, he was a civic colleague of the several builders who also served in the city's directorship in the 1850's and the 1860's. He was not only a member of various council committees responsible for the physical character of the city but also strongly endorsed a number of issues affecting it — and the building community — including more effective fire protection, wider publication of the building act, and promotion of the street railway. In addition, his attempts to alter the building act were matters of direct concern to builders.[34] As a city councillor, Nash had strong Conservative connections. Former mayor Samuel Caldwell was holder of his principal property in the late 1850's and early 1860's; P. C. Hill, sometime mayor and M.L.A., was his largest creditor and held 25 per cent of Nash's outstanding debt at the latter's death. He was, as well, an ardent supporter of Confederation, active, as were Halifax's leading builders, in promoting the celebration and acceptance of federal union.[35] Nash gained further influence from his participation in the closed fraternities of freemasons and oddfellows. He was a sometime master of St. Andrews Lodge, but his brothers stood indebted to him particularly for the rescue of their Masonic Hall, which he effected in January 1874 when a Supreme Court judgement foreclosed their overdue mortgage and sent the property to sale at public auction.[36]

Nash did not belong to Halifax's social and political elite. His background, his trade, and his precarious financial position excluded him from the city's dominant social environment. Nevertheless, his active role as a promoter of Halifax, his solid political connections, his fraternal associations, and his membership in the local Methodist church placed him in contact with the propertied members of this elite.

This examination of John D. Nash's role in the mid-nineteenth-century Halifax building world was undertaken to test the hypothesis that E. W. Cooney's third type of builder — not a craftsman but perhaps a merchant, erecting complete buildings on the basis of contracts with master craftsmen in the various trades[37] — was active in the Nova Scotian capital. It was evident that Nash carried out some building of this type, including a few well-known projects. The press bespoke large scale activity in this field on Nash's part, primarily in the late 1850's and early 1860's. Extensive property transactions through a lengthy career suggested that such activity should be traceable and could well exist over a longer time frame. In truth,

Nash's building activity proved elusive: partly because of his own practice of not registering all of his property investment in his own name; partly because existing property records are sometimes incomplete in terms of prices and at other times suggest that the transaction forms part of a larger debt relationship; and partly because of the inherent ambiguity and flamboyance of newspaper records. Nash's role in the building world conforms rather to the North American pattern noted by Michael Doucet that "on this side of the Atlantic speculation tended to be in land rather than in dwellings."[38]

NOTES

1. See, for example, T. W. Acheson, "The Great Merchant and Economic Development in Saint John," *Acadiensis* 8, no. 2 (1979): 3–27; Peter A. Baskerville, "Entrepreneurship and the Family Compact, York-Toronto, 1822–55," *Urban History Review* 9, no. 3 (1981): 15–34; J. K. Johnson, "The Businessman as Hero: The Case of William Warren Street," *Ontario History* 65 (1973): 125–32; E. J. Noble, "Entrepreneurship and Nineteenth Century Urban Growth: A Case Study of Orillia, Ontario, 1867–1898," *Urban History Review* 9, no. 1 (1980): 64–89; Jacob Spelt, *Urban Development in South-Central Ontario* (Toronto, 1972); Gerald J. J. Tulchinsky, *The River Barons: Montreal Business-Men and the Growth of Industry and Transportation, 1837–53* (Toronto, 1977). One exception is Paul-André Linteau and Jean-Claude Robert, "Propriété Foncière et Sociale à Montreal: Une Hypothèse," *Revue de l'Amérique française* 28 (1974): 45–65.
2. See, for example, Ruban Bellan, *Winnipeg: First Century An Economic History* (Winnipeg, 1978), chapter 3. For the most recent example, see Paul-André Linteau, *Maisonneuve ou Comment des promoteurs fabriquet une ville 1883–1918* (Montreal, 1981), section 1.
3. See, for example, Eric Arthur, *Toronto No Mean City* (Toronto, 1974) and Martin Segger and Douglas Franklin, *Victoria: A Primer for Regional History in Architecture, 1843–1929* (Watkins Glen, NY, 1979).
4. Michael Doucet, "Building the Victorian City: The Process of Land Development in Hamilton, Ontario; 1847–1881," (Ph.D. Diss., University of Toronto, 1977); David Hanna, "Creation of an Early Victorian Suburb in Montreal," *Urban History Review* 9, no.2 (1980): 38–64; Jeanette Rice, "From Crown to City: The Urban Land Development Process in Kingston, Ontario, 1800–1900," (Master's thesis, Queen's University, 1980).
5. Public Archives of Nova Scotia (hereafter PANS), RG 35A, vols. 3 & 4; Nova Scotia, *Statutes,* 24 Vic. c.45.
6. The literature on the role of the building industry in British society is extensive. The older literature, focusing on building cycles, is noted in H. J. Dyos, "The Speculative Builders and Developers of Victorian London," *Victorian Studies* 13 (1969/70): p. 335n1. The debate, focusing more on housing and on urban fringes, has been continued recently in the *Journal of Historical*

Geography 4 (1978): 175–91, 5 (1979): 72–78, and in *Business History* 21 (1979): 226–46. A cursory overview of the findings is provided in C. G. Powell, *An Economic History of the British Building Industry 1815–1979* (London, 1980).

7. *City of Halifax, Nova Scotia, 1865;* H. W. Hopkins, *City Atlas of Halifax, Nova Scotia* (Halifax, 1878).
8. Halifax *Evening Mail,* 28 February 1896.
9. On Hornsby, see Phyllis R. Blakeley, *Glimpses of Halifax 1867–1900* (Halifax, 1949), p. 104; R. G. Dun & Co. Collection, Canada, vol. 11, p. 353, Harvard University, Graduate School of Business Administration, Baker Library (hereafter HUBL); PANS, RG 47, vols. 5–7; Nova Scotia. Crown Lands Department (hereafter NS Crown Lands), A-22, Plan Subdivisions of Willow Park by Bennett H. Hornsby, 28 June 1872; Halifax *Herald,* 24 October 1896.
10. For a contemporary description of the auctioneer's trade, see Edward Hazen's *The Panorama of Professions and Trades or Every Man's Book* (Philadelphia, 1837; facsimile reprint, 1970), p. 118.
11. G. J. J. Tulchinsky, *River Barons,* p. 23.
12. Halifax *Evening Express,* 18 September 1867.
13. The portrait of Nash's business activities is based primarily on auction sale notices in Halifax newspapers, 1855–75. On the Stock Exchange, see Halifax *Morning Chronicle,* 6 March 1875, and *Halifax and Its Business: containing Historical Sketch, and Description of the City and its Institutions* (Halifax, 1876), p. 154.
14. Lewis R. Fischer, " 'An Engine Yet Moderate:' James Peake, Entrepreneurial Behaviour and the Shipping Industry of Nineteenth Century Prince Edward Island," in L. R. Fischer and E. W. Sager, eds., *The Enterprising Canadians: Entrepreneurs and Economic Development in Eastern Canada, 1820–1914* (St. John's, 1979), pp. 99–118.
15. Halifax *Novascotian,* 15 June, 28 September, 20 November 1857; *Evening Express,* 30 January 1861, 23 May 1862; PANS, RG 47, bk. 141 f.451, bk. 186 f. 248.
16. Halifax *British Colonist,* 27 May 1862.
17. PANS, RG 47, bk. 137 f.315.
18. *Evening Express,* 14 July, 24 November 1865; *McAlpine's Halifax City Directory for 1869–70 . . .* (Halifax, 1869).
19. See, for example, PANS, RG 47, bk. 76 f.370, bk. 90 ff.175, 434.
20. PANS, RG 47, bk. 130 f.569; *Evening Express,* 19 June 1863, 6 February 1867.
21. For the classification of builders by type and examination of the categories identified in England, see E. W. Cooney, "The Origins of the Victorian Master Builders," *Economic History Review* 8 (1955): 167–76.
22. Nash's activity can be traced in PANS, RG 47, bk. 70 f.182; bk. 72 f.156; bk.73 f.532; bk. 75 f.142; bk.76 f. 370; bk. 81 f.4; bk. 83 f.56; bk. 84 f.541; bk.91 f.259; bk. 101 f.549.

23. NS Crown Lands, C-7, "Plan Shewing a Division of Belvidere late the property of Col. Bazalgette, 1854"; Halifax *British North American,* 6 September 1854; *Novascotian,* 11 September 1854; *City of Halifax, 1865;* Halifax *Acadian Recorder* 17 May 1856; John W. Regan, *Sketches and Traditions of the Northwest Arm* (Halifax, 1908), p. 53; NS Crown Lands, C-11, "Cambridge"; PANS, RG 47, bk. 170 f.273.
24. See above, note 22.
25. PANS, RG 47, bk. 128 ff.335, 400, 402; bk. 141 f.256.
26. PANS, RG 47, bk. 167 ff.167, 168; bk. 158 ff.591–92; bk. 170 ff. 218, 273; RG Dun & Co. Collection, Canada, vol. 11, p.406, HUBL.
27. RG Dun & Co. Collection, Canada, vol. 11, p.225, HUBL; Nova Scotia Savings, Loan & Building Society (hereafter NSSLBS), Minutes, 20 June & 1 August 1849, 20 February & 6, 12 August 1850, MG 3, vol. 1824, PANS.
28. Ibid.; PANS, RG 47, vols. 3–7; *Annual Reports,* 1857–76, NSSLBS, MG3, PANS.
29. See, for example, Nash's auction sale ads in *Morning Chronicle,* 1, 2, 18 October, 1, 6 November 1872.
30. *Acadian Recorder,* 11 September 1872, cited in P. R. Blakeley, *Glimpses of Halifax,* p.104n.
31. *Evening Express,* 4, 6 June 1872.
32. PANS, RG 47, bk. 171 ff.67–73, including plan.
33. *Morning Chronicle,* 2, 14, 16, 18, 23 October 1872.
34. See, for example, *Evening Express,* 31 January 1862, 16 October 1867.
35. PANS, RG 47, bk. 137 f.315; Halifax County, Court of Probate, Estate no.2214; *Evening Express,* 1 May, 26, 28 June 1867.
36. PANS, RG 47, bk. 192 ff.137, 138, 156–63; bk. 199 f.66.
37. E. W. Cooney, "Origins of the Victorian Master Builders," p. 168. The application of Cooney's classification of builders to Halifax has been examined in Susan Buggey, "Building Halifax 1841–1871," *Acadiensis* 10, no.1 (1970): 90-112.
38. Michael J. Doucet, "The Role of the *Spectator* in Shaping Attitudes toward Land in Hamilton, Ontario, 1847–1881," *Histoire Sociale* 12, no. 24 (1979): 433–34

9

Suburban Street Railway Strategies in Montreal, Toronto, and Vancouver, 1896–1930

Christopher Armstrong and H. V. Nelles

Why were Canadian street railway systems generally smaller and more compact than their U.S. counterparts? And why were some much smaller than otherwise might be expected? The matter is of more than passing interest. The consequences of controlled access to public transportation during this phase of urban development included high population densities, housing problems, class intermingling, delayed and attenuated suburbanization, and, ironically, the persistence of public transit into the automobile era; they are of lasting significance. In pursuit of their own private interests, Canada's street railway magnates unwittingly helped shape a distinctive urban environment.

An 1898 Massachusets street railroad commission studying transit regulation in North America and Europe wondered in passing why Montreal, a city of 300,000, had only eighty-two miles of street railway. The suggestion was that Montreal lacked "important suburban villages surrounding."[1] In Toronto, no fewer than three major investigations between 1910 and 1915 documented the stubborn refusal of the street railway company to extend its system to serve the city and its suburbs adequately.[2] As a result, Toronto had the lowest ratio of miles of streetcar track per capita and the most congested service of all North American cities of comparable size. Moreover, suburban and interurban railroads failed to expand to fill the need. John F. Due commented in the mid-1960's on the surprisingly underdeveloped state of the Canadian intercity electric railway industry before the First World War. Construction lagged and Canadian systems never attained American levels of route ramification. The densely populated Toronto area presented a special puzzle: "It is difficult to explain the limited development," Due wrote, "except to some extent in terms of the domination of the transportation picture in the area by Sir William Mackenzie, who was interested in so many things he had relatively little time or money for electric railroads.'' Mackenzie's bad relations with the city also played a part, Due added as an afterthought.[3]

Yet this personal explanation of stunted development has its limitations. Sir William Mackenzie interested himself in street railroad construction in England, Europe, South America, Mexico, the United States, and in other Canadian cities. His difficulties with the city of Toronto arose in large part from the notably inadequate service of his Toronto Railway Company and its subsidiaries. The protracted mutual antagonism between the city council and the street railway company which bedevilled transit development in Toronto, when described by Michael Doucet recently, prompted the pointed challenge from a critic: ''Why did the Toronto Railway Company reject expansion?''[4] Among Canadian cities, only Vancouver with its 249 miles of integrated urban and regional electric railroad in 1922 achieved something like U.S. levels of development and service.[5] Different underlying strategies were plainly at work. Thus a general treatment of the Canadian street railway industry must come to terms with this apparent paradox: why did the locally-owned companies of Toronto, and to a lesser extent Montreal, follow policies of containment and restricted development, while the foreign-owned British Columbia Electric Railway in Vancouver pursued a more expansionist strategy?

No sooner had the street railroads of Montreal, Toronto and Vancouver completed the reconstruction and electrification of existing routes in the central city than an insistent clamour arose for extensions and improved service. Every frantic real estate developer wanted a car line to his subdivision; commuters demanded more frequent, better equipped cars; municipal authorities sought additional downtown routes to relieve traffic congestion. Journalists, urban reformers, and ambitious municipal politicians rushed to lead these popular crusades for expansion of the wonderfully fast trolley system. The city councils, having learned from years of fighting with the old horsecar companies, quite properly believed that the franchises thrashed out in the early 1890's with the electric railroads gave the municipalities the upper hand in deciding routes, standards of service, and extensions. At first the problem semed straightforward enough: petitions from ratepayers would be referred to the city engineer for study; upon receipt of a favourable report from him and a two-thirds vote of council, new routes could simply be ordered up from the private street railroad contractor.[6] However, it would never be that easy.

Inevitably, the street railroad owners saw things differently. They greeted the demands for immediate extensions not only with skepticism and a good deal of foot dragging but also with private alarm. No company could meet all of these requests and survive, but to ignore public pressure completely was to court disaster as well. Though it may be difficult to appreciate in retrospect, the street railroad proprietors of the late 1890's considered themselves in an extremely risky situation. They had just committed quite a lot of someone else's money to their capital-intensive undertakings. As it turned out, electrification cost more than expected, and initial earnings proved disappointing. To complicate matters, a deep commercial depression had settled upon Canada in the mid 1890's; business was sluggish, even the street railroad business. In Toronto, Winnipeg, Halifax, and a few other cities, the companies struggled with the added burden of not being able to operate their cars on Sunday.[7] In the United States, several street railroads, some of them in the largest cities, hovered on the brink of bankruptcy as a result of overeager expansion and mergers. Under the circumstances, Canadian traction entrepreneurs believed they needed some time to get their companies established as going concerns, to begin to earn the interest on borrowed money and, of course, to turn a neat capital gain on the speculation for themselves. But by the end of the century, they had yet to arrive at that point.

Therein lay the conflict of perceived "rights," which would confound transportation development and poison municipal affairs with fruitless controversy for a generation. The cities believed they had a right based upon their jurisdiction and their franchises to regulate street railroad service to meet demand. The owners of the street railroads thought they had an equally legitimate claim to maximize income from their commercial property. Some held to this view more firmly than others. The risk in the street railway business arose not so much from the difficulty of meeting operating expenses with earnings as from turning these somewhat unconventionally but legally capitalized companies into successful stock promotions. Making a profit was relatively easy; making a large enough profit to accommodate a mountain of common stock was another matter. Thus, at the end of the nineteenth century, when mayors came around to their offices with wads of resolutions from city council demanding extensions, the street railroad men had many other things on their minds, such as: eliminating competition; protecting their territory from incursions by outside roads; forestalling the union; establishing profit-generating management procedures, like those being discussed at the annual conventions and in the trade journals; and making a capital gain on the original speculation. The legitimate imperatives of capitalist accumulation were at odds with the public right and politically sanctioned demand for additional service.

Before analyzing this conflict, it might be helpful to examine the tradeoffs the companies had to negotiate in coming to a decision about extensions. From a company perspective, the danger posed by expansion was all too clear. Construction of suburban lines used up capital which might be more profitably applied elsewhere. In the less densely populated outlying districts, company cars had to run further, carrying fewer fares than in the core districts. This increased operating and maintenance expenses, occupied scarce manpower and equipment in less remunerative service, and in general lowered net receipts per car mile, one of the basic measures of street railroad efficiency and profitability. Balanced against this, however, was the possibility of private gain on the side for the owners from real estate speculation. That was always a temptation. Then there was the general concern about the timing of going to the capital markets: would conditions be right to maximize returns?

To refuse an opportunity or an order to build a line opened up the chance of competition: from nuisance companies which would have to be bought out later; from potentially dangerous opportunists already poised on the outskirts of the city; or, ultimately, from the municipal government. On the other hand, expansion could preempt the most likely routes, foreclose competition, and thus protect and extend monopoly; this might be thought of as the telephone strategy. As municipalities grew more demanding, company lawyers delivered comforting opinions concerning the legal rights of companies to manage their affairs more or less as they pleased, and the courts, at the very least, offered time-consuming procedures and, at the most optimistic, held out the possibility of establishing greater independence from political interference. If pressed too hard, the companies could test the limits of their power. That would necessarily mean outright defiance of public opinion and elected officials. The public and its tribunes could, if necessary, be damned, but that entailed certain risks. The indeterminate dangers of fighting city hall and the benefits to be gained from negotiated compliance had to be compared. Some traction managers, taking the long view of the situation, conceived a strategy of forestalling an eventual municipal takeover upon the expiry of the main franchise by perpetuating private ownership through long-term agreements with the suburban governments. Other executives chose to face the consequences and the possibilities of a public takeover when that time came. In short, street railroad companies generally preferred to move slowly, on their own timetables, expanding their systems as population growth, money markets, stock prices, retained earnings and agreeable opportunities allowed. This was invariably much slower than impatient ratepayers, straphangers, real estate drummers and irate municipal politicians believed necessary.

The dilemma posed by the issue of expansion could be presented schematically as follows:

TABLE 1

THE TRADE-OFFS OF EXPANSION

Reject		Approve
	Advantages	
short run profit		real estate speculation
independence		monopoly and security
		goodwill
	Risks	
competition		lower rate of return
public ownership		

Every decision concerning expansion or new routes involved calculations of this sort. The outcome depended upon how the individual companies weighed these factors. Assessing the risks required more than narrow business judgement. City councils, of course, were not similarly constrained when expanding their own territory through annexation or ordering the street railway to serve new areas. Municipal goals were quite different and the political calculation of costs and benefits of quite another order.

The Toronto and Montreal street railways operated under approximately similar terms: each franchise expired on a specific date; each company owed the city annual payments for paving, snow clearing and the use of the streets; and each paid an escalating percentage of gross income to the city as a rental. The Toronto franchise was exclusive; the Montreal agreement was not. Though quite separate entities, the two companies were linked at the beginning by common underwriting syndicates and shared directors. H. A. Everett, William Mackenzie and James Ross built both systems. Rodolphe Forget took charge of the Montreal property, and William Mackenzie became the moving spirit behind the Toronto enterprise. James Ross was for a time a director of both companies and his protegée, Charles Porteous, instituted similar management and accounting procedures in the Montreal and Toronto operations.

By contrast, the British Columbia Electric Railway franchise, acquired by R. M. Horne-Payne of the British Empire Trust Company of London in 1897, covered not only Vancouver but also Victoria and New Westminster. At first the company operated under separate agreements for each street in Vancouver, but in 1901 the company and the city successfully renegotiated a comprehensive franchise and revenue-sharing agreement similar to, but less onerous than, those prevailing in Toronto and Montreal. Apart from geography and foreign ownership, the key factor that distinguished the Toronto Railway Company and the Montreal Street Railway from the British Columbia Electric Railway was that the former were exclusively downtown operations whereas the latter was an integrated regional transportation, gas and electric utility.

Profits concerned the professional managers of all three systems all of the time. But in the late 1890's, profit maximization verged upon an obsession. Even by 1900, in the opinion of most of the directors, these companies still had a long way to go before they could be considered successful promotions. Thus, in the late 1890's the question of system expansion hinged upon profitability more than any other factor.

Charles Porteous's intermittent correspondence with James Ross and William Mackenzie gives a hint of the constant straining that went on during difficult economic and political times to wring the utmost surplus from the Toronto Railway Company. Ross and Mackenzie were frequently away on business and it fell to Porteous to oversee their various investments. In June of 1895, for example, Porteous prepared a comparative statement of earnings and expenses for the previous month for the Montreal, Toronto, and Minneapolis street railroads, in which Ross and Mackenzie held a major interest. This table set out gross earnings, itemized labour costs, energy charges, maintenance accounts, office salaries, general expenses and the number of miles run. The most important line indicated expenses as a percentage of earnings, the ratio which street railroad promoters considered to be one of the most important indicators of managerial efficiency. During May of 1895, the percentage of operating expenses to revenue for these three companies was: Montreal, 48 per cent; Toronto, 45 per cent, and Minneapolis, 41.5 per cent. In 1896 Porteous began a major campaign to reduce operating expenses even further in Toronto, and in January of 1897, he planted a professional administrator in the office of the Winnipeg Electric Street Railway to tighten discipline, "re-order the office affairs of the company," and eliminate the habitual "loose and unbusinesslike manner" about the place.[8]

Strict control over the number of miles run was one of the keys to keeping operating costs low. The object was to increase earnings per car mile as much as possible. "In looking over the May statement I notice that earnings per car mile are down to 14.41¢," Porteous wrote to James Gunn, the superintendent of the Toronto Railway Company, in 1896. "This is very low, showing that our present service is too good for the business offering. We must try and cut it down on the least profitable routes," and Porteous went on to give Gunn specific instructions as to where to make those reductions. Old horsecar men like James Gunn had difficulty adjusting to the close accounting methods of the new generation of street railroad financiers. In due course he was adjudged "not up to Modern Street Railway management" by Porteous and replaced by F. L. Wanklyn, who understood the imperatives of the business. Wanklyn was so good that he quickly moved on to take charge in Montreal, where he also acted as a management consultant to a number of the foreign and domestic utilities being organized there.[9]

His successor in Toronto, E. H. Keating, the former city engineer, also had to be tutored by Porteous, but his connections with the city council were thought to compensate for these temporary inadequacies. In June of 1898, Porteous reported that "Keating has allowed the mileage to run up, and the rate per Car Mile to run down. I drew his attention to this and some other matters in the June report." To Keating Porteous wrote: "You have 6 lines where your earnings per car mile are under 12 cents, these should be looked after first. Compare with Montreal where the average earnings per car mile were 18.37 cents against Toronto 14.92 cents. It is the half cent per Car Mile that makes the difference between the road being run economically or otherwise." In another letter that same year Porteous counselled firmness on the matter of extensions: "I fully appreciate the pressure on the part of the people of Toronto and the Council to complain of insufficient service, but I came to the conclusion during my time in Toronto that most of it really came from a few confirmed kickers and over-zealous Aldermen always ready to connect their names with complaints against the company."[10]

R. M. Horne-Payne and Rudolphe Forget ran their Vancouver and Montreal properties with a similar concern for earnings per car mile and operating costs. Horne-Payne kept the local managers of the British Columbia Electric Railway on an extremely short financial leash, especially on the matter of extensions. In Montreal, company accountants calculated earnings per car mile on each route to two decimal places. The resulting rations of operating expenses to income, which are not strictly comparable and must be read with some caution, are as shown on page 194. These publicly-reported figures show Toronto to have been consistently more effective in controlling costs and thus, from a financial point of view, more efficient than Montreal and Vancouver. This pattern would hold true for the next decade and a half. The owners and operators in Montreal and Vancouver, by comparison, were slightly more prepared to trade off short run profitability for other advantages. The narrow policy being pursued in Toronto had its costs, as Porteous observed in 1899 as he inspected the worn out track and poorly maintained cars.[11] There would be serious long-run implications as well.

The urgency of squeezing out the maximum arose not simply from a

TABLE 2

OPERATING EXPENSES AS A PERCENTAGE OF REVENUE

YEAR	MONTREAL	TORONTO	B.C.E.R.
1892	82.7	71.9	
1893	79.0	59.1	
1894	71.2	54.0	
1895	59.2	49.3	
1896	56.5	50.9	
1897	55.0	48.8	
1898	52.1	47.4	68.0
1899	55.2	48.8	60.6
1900	56.3	51.0	56.4

Source: Montreal Street Railway, *Annual Reports; Canadian Railway and Shipping World,* various years.

need to meet interest payments on borrowed money. Rather, the slightly unorthodox method of financing companies of this sort provided a compelling incentive to hold the line on costs. The real money to be made on these properties was to be had from the capital gain on the common stock, which had been acquired for next to nothing. Every nickel pared from expenses was available for bond interest, dividends on the common stock, sinking funds, reserve accounts, and depreciation funds, all of which served to enhance materially the value of the equity. Thus, in managing a utility of this sort, financed in this way, every action had to be considered in light of how it would affect the price of the shares.[12] Compared with the enormous capital gains to be made from stock operations of this kind, urban real estate speculation was a rather minor league affair.

Of course, all of the capitalists involved in these companies owned real estate, often in several cities, but they were not primarily or even secondarily real estate speculators or developers. The street railway operators appear to have left the tricky and time-consuming business of suburban land development to smaller fry, preferring instead to take more certain and more substantial profits from their tightly controlled monopolies. Perhaps they had all been traumatized by the collapse of real estate prices in Canadian cities during the depression of the early to mid-1890's. At any rate, they stood aloof. Porteous, for example, was genuinely surprised by the building boom which began in Toronto in the summer of 1899, especially the suburban construction quite far removed from Toronto Railway Company lines. "Building is going up everywhere," he wrote to James Ross, "and curiously largely in the residential suburbs. Real estate has not advanced in price as much as might be expected, due they state to Loan Companies being free sellers of fore-closed properties that they have had for years."[13] This is not the correspondence of men intimately involved in the real estate business. They are for the most part spectators, not speculators.

Confronted by this cold indifference to their needs, real estate promoters and suburban governments (dominated as they were by developers) attempted to entice the street railways with construction subsidies and lenient franchises. Generally speaking, the major companies resisted this temptation during the first decade or more of operations. In Vancouver, for example, when the local management recommended that the company accept the astonishing offer of several land developers to pay for the construction of a line down their street, the London directors turned the proposal down flat.[14]

At first, other ambitious promoters, encouraged by the equipment manufacturers and the local governments, hastened to fill the vacuum. Early in the 1890's, several groups of lawyers and company promoters in Toronto got up companies to build lines on the northern and western outskirts of the city, but these ventures collapsed with the real estate boom.[15] The Metropolitan Railroad began as an adjunct to a real estate development on north Yonge Street about the same time. The manager of this company received a monthly salary and a 2½ per cent commission on any land sold by him belonging to the company or its principals, Charles Warren, Robert Jenkins, H. C. Boomer, and Nicholas Garland.[16] This company electrified its line up Yonge Street to Glen Grove in 1891; gradually its owners were lured further into the country: to York Mills, Richmond Hill, Newmarket, and eventually to Lake Simcoe. The investors were attracted by municipal bonuses, alluring franchise terms, and contractor's profits. But these extensions were never justified by the traffic available, and only the southernmost section, a commuter line that connected with the Toronto Railway, ever earned its expenses.[17]

The Montreal Park and Island Railroad, which by the late 1890's operated forty miles of track in the northern and western suburbs, regularly accepted subsidies from interested parties to build its lines. In 1895, for example, it received $5,000 from the Consolidated Land Company for one extension and an unspecified amount from property owners along St. Lawrence Street.[18] These subsidies lowered construction expenses, but operating and maintenance costs were correspondingly increased. A bigger, longer system was unlikely to be profitable. Certainly the relatively slow growth of population on the urban fringe during the recession of the 1890's undermined the already precarious finances of these marginal enterprises.

If the downtown companies refused to build extensions into the suburbs, they naturally ran the risk of competition. During the 1890's, the principal street railroads were forced to tolerate a certain amount of controlled competition from the likes of the Montreal Park and Island, the Toronto Suburban, Metropolitan, and Toronto and Mimico railways. In the meantime, they conducted a determined campaign to neutralize threats from the municipalities and these outlying rivals. The main line of defence was the private bills committee of the provincial legislature, where corporate interests always saw to it that they exerted considerable influence. This was the committee that "knocked out" offensive sections of threatening private bills and pulled the teeth of restrictive municipal legislation. Here the Hamilton Radial Railway lost the authority to run into Toronto, the Metropolitan failed to obtain permission to operate its cars on Toronto Railway Company track, the municipality of Ste. Cunegonde met opposition to its by-law taxing street railways, and the city of Vancouver discovered it could not go into competition with its utilities without first buying them out.[19] In each case, and in many others, lawyers and kept politicians protected company interests in the relative obscurity of this legislative committee.

Competition was a much more serious problem in Montreal, where the company did not possess an exclusive franchise. In 1893, the Montreal Street Railway came to an agreement with the rival Montreal Park and Island Railway allowing the latter to run its cars into the city centre on the former's track. When the two companies negotiated this contract, they also privately divided the territory between them, a pact which effectively relegated the Montreal Park and Island Railway to the unprofitable margins. Thereafter, whenever the Montreal Street Railway wanted a route assigned to its competitor, it simply bought the privilege with minor concessions.[20]

With an exclusive franchise in Toronto, William Mackenzie could adopt a hard line policy of no connections and no running rights towards suburban roads. When the Metropolitan Railroad tried to connect its line to the Canadian Pacific Railway at Summerhill and sought legislative approval to obtain through routes into the city on Toronto Railway Company track, Mackenzie mobilized both his own forces in the private bills committee and those of the indignant city council, which interpreted the action as an attempt by Metropolitan to seize control over city streets without civic approval.[21] Mackenzie thus stonewalled his rivals and even enlisted municipal help in doing so, whereas in Montreal and Vancouver the companies had to negotiate.

Ironically, the process of social learning made governments unwitting allies in this game of stalling on extensions and marginalizing competition. It took a while, but gradually governments began to learn about this new kind of street railroad business and eventually attempted to regulate what came to be seen as its abuses. To begin with, both the cities of Toronto and Montreal drove hard bargains with the companies seeking electric railway franchises, especially on the revenue sharing provisions. They were able to do this because they had studied practices elsewhere, and the eager franchisees bid each other up in order to win the lucrative concessions. On other matters, councils were less prescient. In 1895, the province of Ontario passed a general statute governing the chartering of all new street railroads. Its provisions, of course, were not retroactive. A bemused Charles Porteous noted at the time: "It might be called an Act to prevent the building of Electric Rys so stringent are its provisions against overcapitalization, for the payment of stock in cash, purchase of materials etc. Dividends are limited to 8 per cent. Fares are restricted and Sunday running forbidden." Legislation of this sort took all of the fun and most of the profit out of street railroading. Latecomers to the business faced regulations blocking opportunities from which existing companies had already profited. Thus, as governments got tougher with capitalists, based upon the accumulated experience with the industry, their regulations constituted unintended barriers to entry which served to further reduce the prospect of serious competition for the established enterprises. As Porteous wryly observed: "To the Toronto Ry it is beneficial as it makes suburban lines an impossibility."[22]

In small, controlled doses, however, competition had its uses. It muffled the antimonopoly cry. It meant unprofitable districts were served — by someone else. The residents of Côte St. Laurent were rebuffed in their petition to the Montreal Street Railway for service in 1897; they were told that the company's agreement with the Park and Island Railway prevented it.[23] When these suburban street railways collapsed, as several did, the urban street railroad proprietors could use these failures to illustrate their case against overambitious expansion.

As soon as the Metropolitan Railroad Company electrified its line in North Toronto, Charles Warren, the president, entered negotiations with William Mackenzie to take the company off his hands. A dissident shareholder in Metropolitan and a sceptical Toronto Railway board of directors prevented a formal amalgamation in September of 1892. Nevertheless, Warren tried repeatedly in the 1890's to sell his company to Mackenzie — who was tempted — only to be turned down.[24] The other directors of the Toronto Railway Company continually badgered Mackenzie to put all thought of further acquisitions out of his mind for the time being. "I hope you talked over the Metropolitan matter with Mackenzie before he left," Charles Porteous reminded James Ross in 1897, "and that he will not spend Toronto Railway money in buying this property, which must sooner or later fall into our hands on our own terms.''[25] The Metropolitan, like most suburban lines in the late 1890's, was in serious financial difficulty. Lines of this sort only barely paid their current operating expenses and sometimes failed to earn even their bond interest, as these fragmentary income/expense ratios suggest:

TABLE 3

OPERATING EXPENSES AS A PERCENTAGE
OF SUBURBAN STREET RAILROAD REVENUES

YEAR	METROPOLITAN	PARK AND ISLAND
1893	86.0	
1894	83.0	
1895	81.6	
1896		86.0
1897		80.8

Source: Metropolitan Railroad, *Minutebooks,* 1889–1905; Montreal Park and Island Railway, *Minutebooks,* 1888–1906.

When the Montreal Park and Island Railway failed in 1898, Charles Porteous was positively exultant. This rival's misfortune thoroughly justified the policy Porteous and Ross had been advocating of limited extensions in Montreal and Toronto. His letter to Ross on this occasion offers considerable insight into the attitude of influential street railway owners towards system growth and competition:

> I hear that they ran beyond gross receipts $24,000 in working expenses for the past year, and that every year for the past few years the deficit has been larger than this. They have never made a dollar of interest on their $1,400,000 of bonds. I learn there had been an illegal issue of bonds, over which there is likely to be trouble.
>
> This object lesson before the people of Canada is going to prevent them putting money into suburban roads, and make those who have it there feel blue. Something like this is what I have been waiting for for some years. It removes all danger at other points. The tale at other points will be the same with variations. There has only been one good done by this profligate building of suburban Railways, namely, to put a barrier around urban properties, with plenty of danger signals both to the investor and the urban roads themselves, as to the danger of premature expansion. *Leave them alone* should be our policy, to die a natural death. There is no danger from them for ten years to come.[26]

Following this disciplined approach to extensions, the Toronto Railway Company increased its track mileage only 7 per cent between 1895 and 1900 and only 4 per cent over the next five years.

Nevertheless, a clear monopoly meant greater security. Thus the tactical value of competition had to be weighed against the strategic advantages of monopoly. The Montreal Street Railway was obliged by its nonexclusive franchise to purchase its active and dormant competitors if it wished to secure a *de facto* monopoly. In 1893, it bought the franchise for the town of St. Henri from the Standard Light and Power Company, and in 1907, the company secured the rights of the Longueil Tramway Company for a mere $6,400.[27] Formation of the British Columbia Electric Railway in 1897 amounted to a consolidation into one company of all the operating companies in the Lower Mainland. There was little need for acquisitions of traction franchises after that point. The creation of a regional monopoly of the B.C.E.R. type was the ultimate goal of operators like Mackenzie and the Forgets, but they were constrained in the 1890's by their less impetuous associates and by extremely unfavourable economic conditions. As time passed, these constraints were gradually relaxed. Mackenzie in particular itched to take over the suburban lines. In the late 1890's he did buy two small companies, over the mild objections of his colleagues. He also coveted the Toronto Junction and the Metropolitan lines to complete his monopoly. Mackenzie eventually acquired the Metropolitan in 1904, but only after James Ross's departure from the board of the Toronto Railway Company. He nevertheless kept this group of suburban street railway lines separate and distinct from his major property, the Toronto Railway Company. As of 1904, Mackenzie completely controlled the traction business in the Toronto region and through the radial lines stretching outward from the eastern, western and northern boundaries.[28]

The Montreal Street Railway approached the wreckage of the Park and Island company with extreme caution. First it simply leased the line from the receivers. Then after three years, the property was formally acquired by the Montreal Street Railway as a subsidiary. With the purchase of the Montreal Terminal Railway in 1907, a small line serving the eastern tip of Montreal Island, the Montreal Street Railway also exercised an effective monopoly of the traction business in its region.[29] Nonetheless, the suburban lines had to work harder for their income. For example, in 1902 the suburban lines around Toronto ran their cars 7 per cent of the distance of the Toronto Railway Company but carried only 3.9 per cent of its passengers. The same year in Montreal the outlying companies travelled 8.8 per cent of the mileage of the Montreal Street Railway carrying only 3.6 per cent as many passengers.[30]

The building of a regional monopoly was always a major objective, but circumstances during the 1890's militated against it in Toronto and Montreal. The British Columbia Electric Railway held rights to the entire region but moved with glacial caution to occupy the ground. System building was pursued more energetically during the second decade of electric railway operations. By then the surprising growth of the cities and more bouyant financial markets had begun to justify a more positive outlook towards extensions in Toronto, Montreal, and Vancouver.

As the cities expanded their boundaries to encompass the spreading population, they expected the street railway companies to service the newly incorporated territories on the same terms as the older parts of the city. In some cases, the street railways were already present in the annexed districts, having penetrated the nearer suburbs for their own reasons. More likely, the suburbs were reserved for separate subsidiary companies. In any event, the main companies demonstrated a marked reluctance to expand their operations when called upon. At first the two parties could talk. Charles Porteous, for example, had some success in convincing the city of Toronto that the Dovercourt extension being urged upon the company was premature.[31] To facilitate communication, the Toronto Railway hired a former city engineer as general manager and later took on former mayor R. J. Fleming in that capacity. It was their job to say no as palatably as possible. But in time the municipal authorities, pressed as they were by angry ratepayers, grew tired of excuses, however politely phrased, and began to insist upon extensions. As the cities became more insistent, the companies had to decide whether to remain intransigent or to comply — for a consideration.

To a degree which seems astonishing in retrospect, street railroad companies generally preferred to fight the municipalities, often over the smallest matters, rather than give ground.[32] Extensions proved to be the most contentious of issues. After years of quarrelling about the subject, all semblance of civility passed out of the relationship between the companies and the cities, and every negotiation became a test of who was in charge. Companies could be quite brazen in their defiance if they wanted. The Montreal Street Railway, for example, promised to construct three lines through the suburb of Maisonneuve in order to obtain a strategic franchise and then flat outright refused to build two of them once the agreement had been signed.[33] After grudgingly providing service to Mount Royal Ward, the Montreal Street Railway then demanded a premium over the regular fare.[34] Under such circumstances, the cities had no choice but to take the companies to court, a riskier business than it might seem. The cities quickly learned that courts tended to construe contracts extremely narrowly, which favoured the company contentions. If the court ruled against the company, then the judgment could always be appealed, which bought more time and frequently meant vindication. There were no more litigious partners in the history of commerce than street railroads and cities.

Toronto offers the most extreme case of bluff intransigence on the part of the company and furious litigation on the part of the city. William Mackenzie's lawyers advised him in 1898, at the beginning of the extension agitation, that the city had no right under the 1892 agreement to order the company to build lines in territory not yet annexed. By that time Mackenzie had begun to surround the city with a ring of suburban railroads — eventually united as the Toronto and York Railroad in 1907 — none of which paid any operating fees. Mackenzie preferred to leave suburban service to these roads and to collect another fare from the passengers as they changed at the city limits to his Toronto Railway Company. This uncompromising policy, combined with a general indifference on the part of the main company to overcrowding and inadequate equipment, quickly poisoned all relations with the testy city council. The unedifying tale of these disputes has already been recounted by Michael Doucet and need not be repeated here. Concerning the controversy over extensions, however, two things stand out: first, when an out-of-court settlement lay within reach the company backed out, and second, when the city pressed its suit to the ultimate arbiter, the Judicial Committee of the Privy Council, it lost.[35] Usually the courts took a very broad view of the companies' rights over their "property," and a very narrow interpretation of the civic right to interfere in what was deemed to be the public interest. The legal regulatory process thus offered every incentive to the company managers to stall, refuse compliance, and then let the city bear the costs of a suit.

Ready consent to municipal requests never seems to have entered the minds of the managers of these street railways. In truth, they were overwhelmed by the sudden growth of the cities after 1898. Years of caution led them to be extremely defensive about the adequacy of their systems. When Charles Porteous proffered his advice about being "caught napping," it was ignored. Instead, the Toronto Railway management chose to tough out the criticism, deny any difficulties, refuse cooperation, shrug off complaints, and to do the bare minimum to improve service. It was a dangerous game.

In Vancouver, and to a lesser extent Montreal, the companies took a different tack. There management was disposed to consider meeting the city councils part way if in return the city would give the company something it badly needed. In essence, the companies in Vancouver and Montreal chose to barter extensions and service improvements for longer franchises. Invariably the negotiating took place largely on the companies' terms, and the cities did not distinguish themselves in the bargaining process, but these rare moments of agreement contrasted sharply with the permanent state of seige which paralyzed transit matters in Toronto.

The British Columbia Electric Railway managed to obtain an extremely favourable consolidated franchise from the Vancouver city council in 1901. The Montreal Street Railway tried much the same thing in 1911 when it approached the city with an offer to break the deadlock over suburban extensions. After a failed attempt to amalgamate the street railway with the Montreal Light, Heat and Power conglomerate in 1910, the former was acquired from the Forget group in 1911 by A. E. Robert, a utilities speculator, and J. R. McConnell, an industrialist and newspaper proprietor. The new owners renamed the company the Montreal Tramway, swallowed up all of the suburban lines in the consolidation, and completely recapitalized the swollen enterprise.[36] The problem, however, was that Robert and his associates had reorganized a company whose principal franchise would expire in 1922. Almost immediately they set about trying to renegotiate the franchise with the city. Extensions were offered and promises of better service made if the city would agree to extend the terminal date of the franchise by twenty years. The city, in high dugeon over the audacity of the new owners, refused to negotiate, even though it agreed in principle that a new franchise was necessary. There matters stood for years. During the impasse — during which the city even refused the company permission to relieve congestion in the core area — conditions deteriorated to the point that in 1916 the province of Quebec empowered a commission to investigate the situation and restore order. From that body the Montreal Tramways Company obtained the security of a franchise that lasted until 1953 and received one of the first service-at-cost contracts on the continent (which protected it against inflation). In return the company would build long overdue extensions, upgrade its downtown service, and abide by the regulatory rulings of what was to become a permanent Montreal Tramways Commission.[37] Since this settlement was imposed upon the city by order of the provincial government, it was much less than a mutual agreement. Still, in Montreal as in Vancouver earlier, negotiations between the two parties did produce new contracts beneficial to the company and the city, especially the former. If the companies wanted something badly enough, they were prepared to make deals. Grudges and mutual suspicion made the bargaining process difficult but not impossible.

The Vancouver and Montreal owners seem to have worried more about public ownership than their Toronto counterparts; right from the very beginning they took precautions to prevent it. "The cry for municipal ownership is strong in this country, particularly in new communities," Johannes Buntzen advised his London board in 1899.[38] Both he and his successor, R. H. Sperling, made defence of the company against municipal insurgency a top priority in recommending policy to the English directors. Together, they were always more than a step ahead of the Vancouver municipal reformers. Since the English owners were primarily interested in the long-term income and investment potential of the company, they too paid a good deal of attention to the problem of franchise security. All through this period, the British Columbia Electric Railway took many steps in clear anticipation of public pressure.[39]

However, the most imaginative and far-seeing policy to forestall recapture of the franchise by the city involved a programme of strategic suburban extensions. In the midst of one of the periodic public ownership campaigns in 1906, R. H. Sperling developed the notion that construction of four key suburban lines running directly into the downtown on private rights of way might be an effective means of precluding a municipal takeover when the franchise expired. His plan had other attractions: the outlying municipalities, eeager for development, would give the company forty-year franchises, in some cases perpetual rights. The municipalities and real estate developers would also assist by contributing most of the land needed for the private right of way; they would subsidize construction as well. Geography helped. A narrow neck of land connected the peninsular downtown to the suburbs, allowing for a natural funnelling of traffic into a central depot.[40] The London board weighed the costs of premature expansion against the strategic advantages and authorized the programme:

> Sooner or later, in the opinion of the Board, we must secure a system of trunk lines on our own right of way, and we are now called upon to make an effort in this direction, both from the point of view of price and because the local authorities and government are not likely in the future to be more favourable to us than they are at present, and in all probability will be inclined to actively oppose such developments as we get nearer to 1919.
>
> Again, although at the present moment there is a tendency to divide up the municipalities, the Board consider on studying the history of other cities, that it is almost certain within a very few years a movement will set in to consolidate all of these districts into one big city of Vancouver, in order to secure better credit and other advantages. Once Vancouver is consolidated, or the movement towards consolidation is well on foot, it will be too late to attempt such a plan as the one now under consideration.[41]

During the trying negotiations with the suburban councils and the provincial government, the London board continually impressed upon the local managers the long-term objectives of the exercise. For example, when the municipality of Point Grey insisted upon a clause in its franchise giving the municipality the option of buying the lines in 1919, the London directors refused. R. M. Horne-Payne instructed the company secretary to remind the local negotiators: ''the only reason for our desire to build the line in Point Grey is on account of its value to us in negotiating with the city in 1919. We are not at all anxious to construct the work immediately and will do so only on condition that Point Grey give us the 40 years unconditional franchise we ask. If Point Grey persists in refusing our terms we must leave them alone, and when they see us extending the lines to Burnaby and South Vancouver, the landowners in Point Grey will very soon come to their senses and agree to our terms.''[42] And they did.

The policy was adopted by the company in 1909, and the British Columbia Electric Railway had successfully encircled the city of Vancouver with long-term franchises on private rights of way. The company's owners had learned from the Detroit experience, where the city found it could not fully recover the street railway when it wanted to, because the private company would continue to carry suburban commuters into the city on its separate lines. Municipal ownership meant a fragmentation of an integrated system under those circumstances.[43] Moreover, in their eagerness to obtain transportation and the higher land values it entailed, the real estate fraternity and suburban councils had given the company most of the land it required and paid a good portion of the capital costs.[44] Fully ten years before the city could do anything to acquire its street railway, the company had constructed elaborate defence works. If the city chose to take over the downtown lines in 1919, it would find itself in possession of a worn out plant handling only local traffic. Meanwhile the still lively and operational British Columbia Electric Railway Company would be carrying commuters into the downtown via its untouchable private rights of way from suburbs where its franchises would not expire for another thirty years. From this position of strength, the company was able to thwart with relative ease a major effort by the combined municipalities to impose a uniform consolidated franchise upon it in 1912–13, all the while giving the impression of bargaining in good faith.[45]

It is doubtful that the Montreal Street Railway directors thought this carefully about the problem of franchise security. Nevertheless, the board of that company adopted a policy of selective suburban expansion which had the same practical effect. In 1897, for example, the municipalities of Côte St. Paul, Verdun and Longue Pointe were told that the company would consider extensions if and only if it received a thirty-year franchise, exemption from taxation for twenty years, a right of way furnished by the municipalities, the right to charge an additional fare, and no restrictions on the frequency of service.[46] The company demanded and received similar exacting terms from other towns into which it cautiously spread its lines.

A committee of the Montreal city council investigating the street railway situation in 1915 discovered no less than twenty franchises governing the Montreal Tramway Company, each with different expiry dates, tax exemptions, terms, and renewal procedures.[47] Three years later, the provincial Tramway Commission considered the possibility of municipal ownership only to dismiss the idea. The commission concluded that the proliferation of complicated suburban franchises was one of the factors — apart from the more serious problems of municipal corruption and bankruptcy — which made municipal ownership impractical: "Montreal lacks the means to acquire the tram system of the whole company and there is no sense in the acquisition of that part of the system within the city. To do so would require buying the whole system and trying to reach terms with the surrounding municipalities."[48] Rather than propose such an expensive and legally complex situation, the commission recommended the imposition of a service-at-cost contract upon the company and all the municipalities it served. The suburban strategy helped the private companies in Vancouver and Montreal retain ownership of their properties even after the main franchise expired.

However, in Toronto, something like a zero-sum game developed as both the company and the city dug in their heels at a very early date. Protracted litigation, pettiness on both sides, and the absence of an effective third party mediator helped produce quite a different outcome to this struggle in Toronto than in Vancouver, Montreal and most U.S. cities. The city of Toronto did not take its court setback with much grace. It simply refused to believe that the franchise of 1892 gave William Mackenzie's company the right to refuse building new lines into annexed territory. The Toronto Railway Company was not particularly magnanimous in victory. Management continued to pursue with single-minded determination and notable success a policy of profit maximization. The data summarized in the accompanying tables 4, 5, 6, and 7 indicate that Toronto was consistently the most profitably operated franchise before the First World War. These tables also show how quickly the Vancouver company moved after 1901 to improve its market coverage once funds became available in London. But in Toronto, the population depended more upon the street railway (Table 8), endured a more crowded service, and suffered the inconvenience and additional expense of not having an integrated core to suburbs service despite the fact all of the companies were presided over by the same man. Long before the issue of extensions into the suburbs was finally settled by the Judicial Committee of the Privy Council, a deeply offended sense of civic populism had arrived at the conclusion that if transit

TABLE 4

GROSS REVENUE PER CAR MILE IN CENTS

Year	British Columbia	Montreal	Toronto
1901	21.1	17.8	16.8
1902	20.7	18.7	17.2
1903	23.1	19.2	18.1
1904	23.0	20.0	19.0
1905	22.0	20.0	19.0
1906	25.0	20.0	21.0
1907	29.7	22.8	22.8
1908	30.3	25.9	24.3
1909	30.3	26.3	25.3
1910	34.0	27.4	26.8
1911	33.5	29.0	28.1
1912	33.6	29.0	27.8
1913	34.2	41.9	28.5
1914	30.8	37.2	27.7

Source: Calculated from *Canada, Department of Railways and Canals, Railway Statistics* (Ottawa, various years), Electric Railway Statistics.

TABLE 5

OPERATING EXPENSES AS A PERCENTAGE OF GROSS REVENUE

Year	British Columbia	Montreal	Toronto
1901	68.0	57.5	52.7
1902	70.0	55.8	52.0
1903	69.3	59.2	56.6
1904	64.8	61.0	56.3
1905	65.0	61.7	58.5
1906	64.5	59.1	54.1
1907	58.3	60.8	51.8
1908	62.9	58.1	54.7
1909	63.5	58.1	49.9
1910	63.3	56.4	51.2
1911	68.9	57.0	50.4
1912	70.1	57.0	52.4
1913	77.5	59.7	52.2
1914	77.1	59.7	52.2

Source: Calculated from *Canada, Department of Railways and Canals, Railway Statistics* (Ottawa, various years), Electric Railway Statistics.

Note: Year ends 30 June. Data submitted for Montreal Tramways after 1911 spurious.

TABLE 6

OPERATING EXPENSES PER CAR MILE IN CENTS

Year	British Columbia	Montreal	Toronto
1901	14.3	10.2	8.8
1902	14.5	10.4	8.9
1903	16.0	11.4	10.2
1904	15.0	12.0	11.0
1905	14.0	12.0	12.0
1906	16.0	12.0	11.0
1907	17.3	14.1	11.8
1908	19.6	15.0	13.4
1909	19.3	15.3	12.6
1910	21.5	15.4	13.7
1911	23.1	16.5	14.1
1912	23.5	16.5	14.6
1913	26.5	25.0	14.8
1914	23.7	22.2	14.4

Source: Calculated from *Canada, Department of Railways and Canals, Railway Statistics* (Ottawa, various years), Electric Railway Statistics.

TABLE 7

NET REVENUE PER CAR MILE IN CENTS

Year	British Columbia	Montreal	Toronto
1901	6.8	7.6	8.0
1902	6.2	8.3	8.3
1903	7.0	7.9	7.9
1904	8.0	8.0	8.0
1905	8.0	8.0	7.0
1906	9.0	8.0	10.0
1907	12.4	8.7	11.0
1908	10.7	10.9	12.8
1909	11.0	11.0	12.7
1910	12.5	12.0	13.1
1911	10.4	12.5	14.0
1912	10.1	12.5	13.2
1913	7.7	16.9	13.7
1914	7.1	15.0	13.3

Source: Calculated from *Canada, Department of Railways and Canals, Railway Statistics* (Ottawa, various years), Electric Railway Statistics.

Note: Year ends 30 June. Data submitted for Montreal Tramways after 1911 spurious.

TABLE 8

DAILY RETURN TRIPS AS A PERCENTAGE OF THE LABOUR FORCE

	1901	1911
Montreal	40.6	63.1
Toronto	52.5	83.9
Vancouver/Victoria	29.7	76.6

Source: Canada, Department of Railways and Canals, *Railway Statistics* (Ottawa, 1901, 1911); *Canadian Railway and Marine World,* 1901, 1911; population data for the metropolitan areas from George Nader, *Cities of Canada,* vol. 2 (Toronto: Macmillan, 1976), pp. 126, 203, 381; and Patricia Roy, *Vancouver: An Illustrated History* (Toronto: James Lorimer, 1980), p. 168; labour force estimates from Frank Denton and Sylvia Ostry, *Historical Estimates of the Canadian Labour Force* (Ottawa: Dominion Bureau of Statistics, 1967), Table 10. Daily return trips were calculated by dividing the total paid fares by 6.5 days (338 per year) per week to obtain the total trips. Victoria had to be included with Vancouver because the passenger data submitted by the company in its annual return did not break the total down by city. The index is only suggestive of the potential importance of public transportation to working commuters in each city.

were to be improved, the city would have to do the job itself.

Both the Toronto Railway Company and the Toronto city council must share responsibility for the early appearance of public ownership. As in most cities, exasperation with fruitless discord and frustration with over-burdened transit facilities led counsellors to advocate everything from punitive regulation to expropriation.[49] Usually such rhetorical assaults broke rather harmlessly against the fortress-like legal position of the company or its unaffordable size. In Toronto, however, company obduracy coincided with a populist moment in civic affairs, something for which the company and its president, William Mackenzie, helped inspire. Recent experience with other utilities provided a precedent for action on the street railway front. In 1907, the ratepayers of the city of Toronto approved construction of a civic electrical utility to operate in competition with the private Toronto Electric Light Company as part of a province-wide municipal electrical cooperative.[50] Unquestionably, this civic uprising on the electrical question imparted a good deal of momentum to discussion of street railway matters. Ironically, the company's very determination to confine itself to the 1891 boundaries of the city made the achievement of public ownership easier.

Before the Judicial Committee of the Privy Council handed down its decision in the Toronto Railway case in 1910, the city had received ratepayer approval to build a street railway system on routes declined by the private company. Moreover, the city had begun to investigate the cost and legal technicalities of building underground subways to compete directly with the Toronto Railway Company in the built-up districts.[51] Thus 1910 marked a decisive point at which serious negotiations between the city and the company might have been resumed: the company had been vindicated by the courts, and the city council's public ownership response gave it impressive bargaining strength. But the opportunity was shunned by both sides. The city's offer to lease the new lines to the company was rebuffed; the company, true to form, steadfastly refused to negotiate transfer privileges, connections, or through running rights with the proposed municipal utility. Instead, Mackenzie offered to sell the Toronto Railway Company to the city at a price to be determined by arbitration. The city, somewhat startled by the proposal and bent upon its immediate objective of building a separate civic railway, answered with a plainly objectionable offer: it would pay the value actually sunk in the company's plant plus a small consideration for the time remaining in its franchise.[52] With yet another example of deadlocked negotiations between the city and the company fresh in their minds, the ratepayers of Toronto went to the polls in January 1911 and voted overwhelmingly to finance the construction of a municipal street railway. A year later, the publicly owned Toronto Civic Railway actually commenced business on five routes in the neglected eastern and northern portions of the city.[53] The persistent refusal of the Toronto Railway Company to build its lines into the new suburbs, its determination to press its rights in the courts, and its unwillingness to enter into serious negotiations with the city created a vacuum which was filled not by private but by much more dangerous public competition.

From 1911 onward, it was only a matter of price and time before the entire street railway system in Toronto came under public control. Mackenzie seems to have been willing to part with his property in Toronto as well as in Winnipeg if satisfactory terms could be arranged. Further talks in 1913 and throughout 1914 came very close to producing a municipal takeover of both the street railway and electrical utilities Mackenzie controlled.[54] However, the onset of a world war with its restrictions on public borrowing and a closing off of access to British capital required that these matters be postponed for the duration. The ascendancy of a *guerre à l'outrance* faction on city council in 1915 halted negotiations when agreement seemed near.[55] Thus a resolution of the complex and impassioned Toronto utilities situation was deferred until the street railway franchise expired, at which time the city acquired both the private street railway and the electrical utility as part of a purchase agreement negotiated by the provincial Hydro-Electric Commission with the Mackenzie estate.[56]

One of the reasons public ownership made easier progress in Toronto than in the other cities is that the provincial government facilitated rather than obstructed the municipal insurgency. The province removed restrictions on public-private competition, sanctioned the construction of a civic car line, and much later played a key role in the takeover of the Mackenzie utilities empire in Ontario. Perhaps part of the explanation for this unusual municipal-provincial partnership can be found in the fact that the Ontario legislature was physically located in Toronto, where the cabinet and the legislative committees came under direct and continuous pressure. Municipal politicians in Vancouver and Montreal had to travel to Victoria and Quebec, far removed from the scenes of daily battle, where their pleas were heard by a more reserved, dispassionate audience. Moreover, both the British Columbia Electric Railway and the Montreal Street Railway did their utmost to stay on good terms with their respective provincial governments.[57] In Toronto and in Winnipeg, Mackenzie was either less skilful or unlucky — probably both. Since Mackenzie and his companies were the main antagonists in a provincial-municipal movement to build a publicly-owned electrical distribution cooperative, the usual close relationship between the provincial government and the private interests became clouded. In Ontario, the provincial government was inexorably drawn into a partisan role in these conflicts rather than a mediating role. This was true also of its regulatory body, the Ontario Railway and Municipal Board, which consistently sustained city complaints against the Toronto Railway Company. In short, for reasons having to do with the dialectics of provincial politics on the energy question, the upper level of government in Ontario tended to facilitate rather than interfere with municipal public ownership initiatives. Proximity and a broadening populist ideology combined to create a much more conducive setting for public ownership in Toronto than in Montreal or Vancouver. Mackenzie was either mistaken in his calculation of the political risk his strategy entailed, or he was operating the Toronto Railway Company rationally with the short-run intention of selling, a policy he pursued successfully in Winnipeg.

At the outset, the three street railroad systems in Vancouver, Toronto, and Montreal followed similar plans. They all made profit maximization their first priority in the 1890's, and they all strove towards regional monopoly during the first decade of the twentieth century. But in other important respects, the companies came to different conclusions concerning the pros and cons of suburban expansion. The Vancouver and Montreal companies were rather more inclined than their Toronto counterpart to negotiate with their respective cities if desirable objects could be secured in the process. These two companies acted on long-term strategies of franchise proliferation and suburban extensions to secure their property against a partial or a comprehensive municipal takeover. The Toronto Railway Company, on the other hand, pursued profit maximization more singlemindedly, placed a higher value upon demonstrating the fullness of its legal rights, resisted negotiation with the city even when such talks might have proven mutually beneficial, and consistently discounted the threat of public ownership. As a result, the Toronto company was the first to encounter significant competition from the public sector and was the first to fall under complete municipal ownership in 1921. Mackenzie's strategy was rational insofar as profit maximization was concerned, if he planned all along to promote in order to sell. This may well have been his objective. But by the time he showed an interest in selling, the poisonous political situation scared off all private buyers and effectively prevented meaningful negotiations with the most likely public buyer.

Unquestionably, the slow growth of Canadian cities in the 1890's helped these companies establish firm control over their territories with a minimum of private competition (Figure 1). Suburban stagnation in particular during this crucial interval blighted the hopes of the struggling independent lines on the outskirts (Figure 2). The stronger urban companies could entertain such hobbled competition with equanimity, simply waiting for the day when these suburban lines would fall into their hands at distress prices. Then, as soon as the suburban land boom, stimulated by vigorous economic growth, picked up during the first decade of the twentieth century, the eastern companies quickly moved in on their weak rivals. The Vancouver company already held rights to the territory. It responded with an ambitious programme of suburban extensions which, as we have seen, had a deeper purpose. Transit operators in the large cities in the United States usually faced stiffer competition, partly because suburbanization had begun sooner.[58] Such private competition and route proliferation provided better service, but it also exacerbated the problem of overcapitalization, especially during mergers. Philadelphia is the most outstanding example of this phenomenon.[59]

Just as company strategies differed, so too cities behaved in different ways in the face of the transit crisis. Quite apart from matters of geography, some city councils were more capable than others of mounting an effective opposition. In Vancouver, the shrewd managers of the British Columbia Electric Railway were generally able to hoodwink, outmaneuvre — in short, outsmart — an indignant but directionless municipal government. In Montreal, the street railway company always managed to maintain enough influence on city council, even reform city councils (the general manager

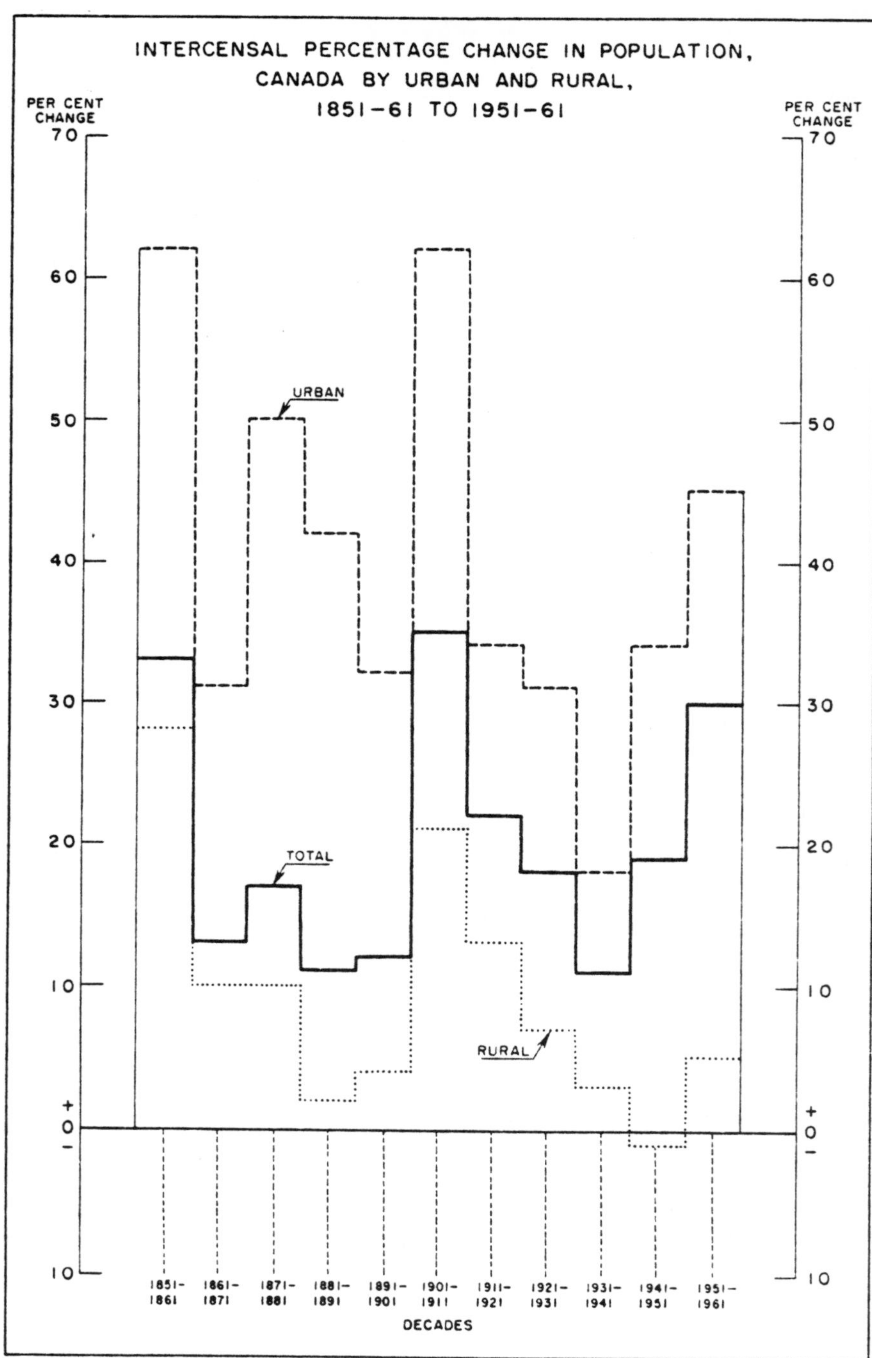

Fig. 1: Urban growth in comparative perspective (source: *Leroy O. Stone,* Urban Development in Canada [*Ottawa: Dominion Bureau of Statistics, 1968*], *p. 137).*

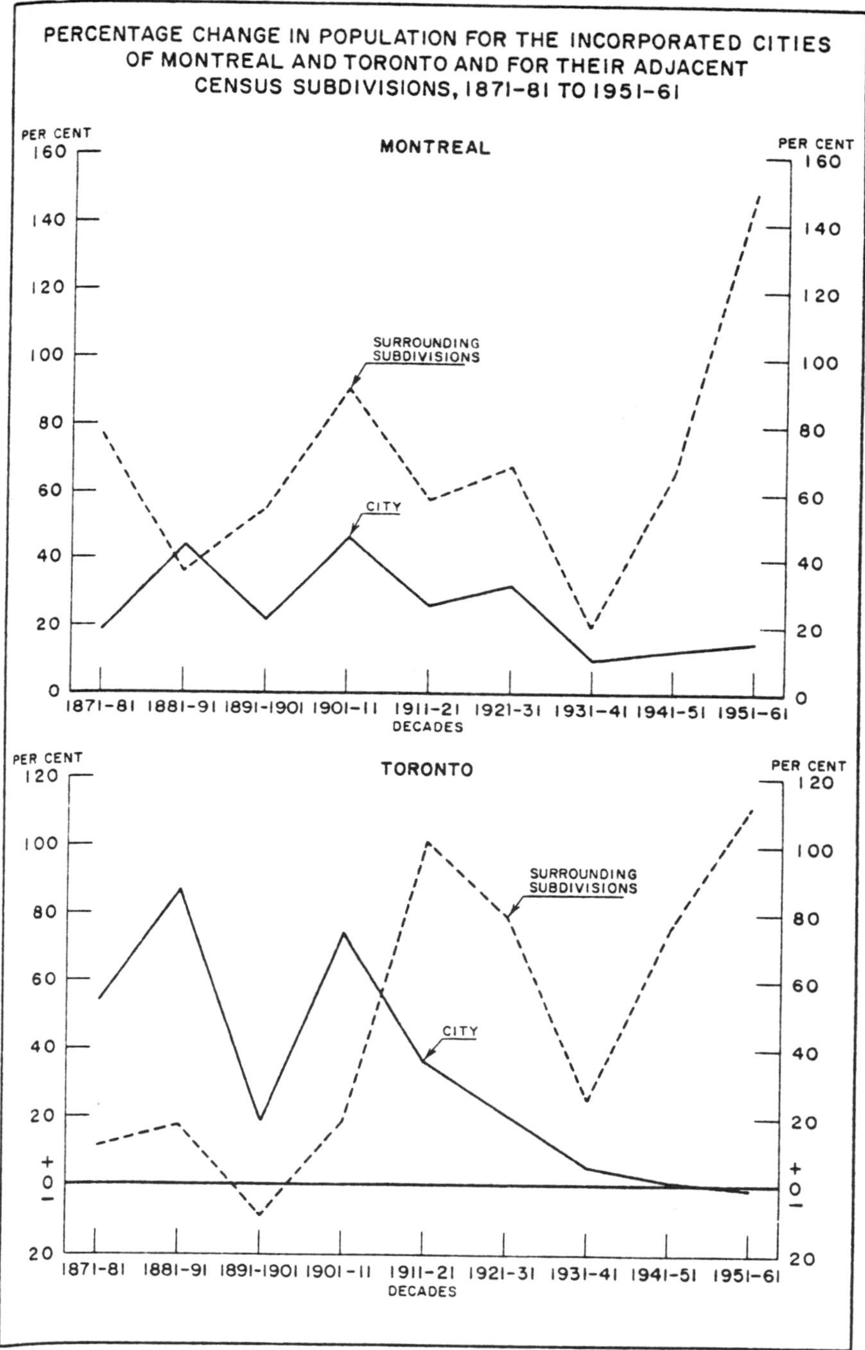

Fig. 2: Suburban growth in Montreal and Toronto (source: *Leroy O. Stone,* Urban Development in Canada, *p. 27*).

of the company was even elected to council as a reformer!), to stay out of deep trouble. Only after the Robert-McConnell reorganization did Montreal Tramways fall into dangerous disfavour with the francophone majority on council, which was slowly returning to power after an anglophone reform interlude.[60] When the possibility of a serious threat loomed during the First World War, the city of Montreal found itself in receivership, unable to manage its routine affairs much less finance the purchase of a giant corporation. In those delicate circumstances, the city rather than the company had to come to terms. Toronto was a different matter. Its finances were in better order. It had annexed land early enough that it was in fact larger than its street railway. The company's decision to restrict its lines to the old municipal boundaries only served to make public competition and then eventual takeover easier. Municipal reform in the late 1890's had provided council with a strong board of control which supplied the needed executive leadership through the twists and turns of a complex relationship. Moreover, an aroused civic populism gave public ownership a legitimacy and momentum in Toronto it lacked in Vancouver and Montreal. In making a direct challenge to the private company, the city received cooperation from the province rather than obstruction or third-party mediation. It would seem, therefore, that Toronto was a more fiscally capable, politically aggressive, and provincially reinforced adversary to its transit company than were the cities of Vancouver and Montreal. It is nevertheless surprising that the Toronto Railway Company so gravely miscalculated by pursuing its strategy of restricted extensions, that it seems to have discounted the seriousness of the municipal threat, especially since its general manager throughout this period was himself a former four-term mayor of the city.

NOTES

1. Massachusetts General Court, *Report of the Special Committee Appointed to Investigate the Relations between Cities and Towns and Street Railway Companies* (Boston, 1898), pp. 134–35.
2. Jacobs and Davies Inc., "Report on Transit to the Mayor of the City of Toronto," 25 August 1910, City Council Papers, Toronto City Archives [hereafter TCA]; Brion Arnold and John W. Moyes, "Report on the Toronto Railway Company and Portions of the Toronto and York Radial Railway Company and the Toronto Suburban Railway Company situated within the limits of the City of Toronto," September 1913; *Report of the Civic Transportation Committee on Radial Railway Entrances and Rapid Transit for the City of Toronto* (Toronto, 1915), 2 vols.
3. *The Intercity Electric Railway Industry in Canada* (Toronto: University of Toronto Press, 1966), p. 82.

4. Michael Doucet, "Mass Transit and the Failure of Private Ownership: The Case of Toronto in the Early Twentieth Century," *Urban History Review* (1977): 3–33; Donald F. Davis, "Mass Transit and Private Ownership: An Alternative Perspective on the Case of Toronto," ibid. (1978): 60–98.
5. Due, *Intercity Electric Railway Industry,* pp. 101–7; Patricia Roy, "The British Columbia Electric Railway Company, 1897–1928: A British Company in British Columbia," (Ph.D. Diss. University of British Columbia, 1970).
6. This was the Toronto procedure. For details, see *The Charter of the Toronto Railway Company Together with Subsequent Statutes, Agreements and Judgements* (Toronto, 1906), Toronto Transit Commission Archives.
7. For treatment of the Toronto sabbatarian struggle, see C. Armstrong and H. V. Nelles, *The Revenge of the Methodist Bicycle Company* (Toronto: Peter Martin Associates, 1977).
8. Porteous Papers, Vol. 25, Porteous to W. G. Ross, 13 August 1896, Public Archives of Canada [hereafter PAC]; Vol. 19, Porteous to D. B. Hanna, 4 January 1897, Confidential; Porteous to Wm. Whyte, C.P.R., Winnipeg, 23 January 1897.
9. Ibid., Vol. 19, Porteous to James Gunn, 18 June 1896; Porteous to Mackenzie, 11 January 1897. Note Porteous's interesting use of the upper case throughout this correspondence.
10. Ibid., Vol. 20, Porteous to E. H. Keating, 23 June, 14 November 1898; Porteous to James Ross, 21 June 1898.
11. Ibid., Vol. 21, Porteous to James Ross, 6 October 1899.
12. The appointment of Wanklyn, for example, "had a good effect on the price of the Stock and public feeling, and it will give the property better support from Mr. Angus and the Montreal men." Ibid., Vol. 19, Porteous to Mackenzie, 11 January 1897.
13. Ibid., Vol. 21, Porteous to James Ross, 6 October 1899.
14. Patricia Roy, "Direct Management from Abroad: The Formative Years of the British Columbia Electric Railway," in Glenn Porter and Robert Cuff, eds., *Enterprise and National Development* (Toronto: Haakert, 1973), pp. 101–21.
15. Minute Book of the Davenport Electric Railway and Light Company, and Minutebook of the Weston, High Park and Toronto Street Railway Company, Baldwin Room, Toronto Public Library.
16. Metropolitan Railway Company Papers, Minute Book, 2 July 1892, Ontario Hydro Archives. Charles Warren of the Imperial Lumber Company was both president of the railway and its contractor. On the line's profitability see Due, *Intercity Electric Railway,* pp. 82–87.
17. Metropolitan Railway Company, Minute Book, 3 March 1897, 28 March 1900.
18. Montreal Park and Island Railway Company, Minute Book, 22 April, 8 June 1895, Montreal Urban Transportation Community Archives [hereafter MUCTCA].
19. Porteous Papers, Vol. 24, Porteous to James Ross, 23 March 1896; Vol. 19, Porteous to James Ross, 5 March, 1 April 1897; MUCTCA, Montreal Street Railway Minute Books, 28 November 1895 MUCTCA.

20. Montreal Street Railway Minute Books, 11 July 1893. For the territorial agreement between the Montreal Street Railway and the Park and Island Railway see the latter's Minute Books, 13 July 1893, and for subsequent horse-trading, 28 May 1894.
21. Board of Control Minutes, 26 March, 1 April 1901; Minutes, 1901, Appendix C, Mayor's Message; Appendix A, Board of Control Report No. 8, 20 April 1901; Minutes, 1902, Appendix C, Mayor's Message, TCA.
22. Porteous Papers, Vol. 25, Porteous to James Ross, 23 April 1895. For a full account of this legislation see E. H. Bronson Papers, Vol. 702, E. H. Bronson to A. G. Blair, 12 February 1897, PAC.
23. Montreal Street Railway Minute Books, 26 June 1897.
24. Metropolitan Railway Minute Book, 19 September 1892; 27 March 1893; 9 March 1894. When Mackenzie turned down the offer, the owners tried to sell the railroad to the municipality of North Toronto, also in vain.
25. Porteous Papers, Vol. 19, Porteous to James Ross, 5 March 1897; Vol. 29, Diary, 23 February, 21 November 1898; Vol 20, Porteous to W. D. Mathews, 21 October 1898; Porteous to Mackenzie, 21 October 1898.
26. Ibid., Vol. 20, Porteous to James Ross, 7 June 1898: Montreal Park and Island Railway Minute Book, 7 June, 15 September 1898.
27. Montreal Street Railway, Minute Book, 20 October, 3 November 1893; 7 April 1894, 7 January 1907.
28. Metropolitan Railway Company, Minute Book, 17 August 1904.
29. Montreal Terminal Railway Minute Book, 18 September 1907, MUCTCA; Montreal Park and Island Railway Minute Book, 30 July 1901.
30. Canadian Railways and Canals Department, *Railway Statistics* (Ottawa, 1901, 1911).
31. He used the argument that suburban extensions would disperse population and thereby reduce the City of Toronto tax base. Porteous Papers, Vol. 25, Porteous to Mackenzie, 13, 20 April, 4 May 1896; Porteous to James Ross, 5, 26 May 1896.
32. The Toronto Railway Company began arguing that curved track in its switches and turnouts ought not to be counted in the track mileage figures. In Toronto and Montreal both the city and the companies pressed frivolous appeals to regulatory decisions and court orders.
33. Paul-André Linteau, *Maisonneuve* (Montreal: Boreal Express, 1981), pp. 76–8, 128–35.
34. Montral City Archives [hereafter MCA], Minutes, 29 June, 5 November 1908.
35. Doucet, "Mass Transit and the Failure of Private Ownership"; Board of Control Report, 6 May 1904, TCA; Committee on Legislation Report, 28 March 1905; Mayor's Message, 8 January 1906; Board of Control Papers, Box 17, W. C. Chisholm to the Mayor and Board of Control, 3 November 1906; Box 18, James Fullerton to W. C. Chisholm, 29 April 1907; Box 19, Ontario Railway and Municipal Board File, 22 May 1907; Board of Control Papers, 11 January, 1 April 1910, Report of the Privy Council Decision.
36. Montreal Street Railway, *Annual Report,* 1910; Minute Book, 2, 22 November

1910, 10 January 1911; Montreal Tramways Company, Minute Book, 26, 29, 30 September, 16 November 1911, MUCTCA; Montreal Tramways Company, Annual *Report,* 1912.

37. MCA, Council Papers, Vol. 17, Special Committee on the Montreal Street Railway, 1910; Minutes, 9 January, 23 February 1911; Board of Commissioners Reports, Vol. 16, 23 February 1911; Vol. 18, 20 October 1911; Commission des Tramways de Montréal, *Rapport sur le contract,* 28 janvier 1918.
38. Vol. 41, Buntzen to Secretary, 3 August 1899, University of British Columbia Library, BCER Papers, (hereafter BCER).
39. Roy, "The British Columbia Electric Railway," pp. 92–115; C. Armstrong and H. V. Nelles, "Some Aspects of the British Columbia Electric Railway's Relations with the City of Vancouver and the Province," pp. 1–27.
40. BCER, Vol. 40, R. H. Sperling to George Kidd, 16 February 1909.
41. Ibid., Vol. 40, "Report of the BC Electric Railway Company's Position with regard to the City of Vancouver, 1909"; F. Hope to R. H. Sperling, 26 March 1909.
42. BCER, Vol. 16, George Kidd to R. H. Sperling, 26 March 1909; Roy, "Direct Management from Abroad," pp. 114–17.
43. BCER, Vol. 40, Hope to R. H. Sperling, 26 March 1909 for the lessons R. M. Horne-Payne drew from his knowledge of the situation in Chicago, San Francisco, Detroit and St. Paul.
44. Armstrong and Nelles, "Some Aspects of the British Columbia Electric Railway's Relations with the City of Vancouver and the Province," pp. 28–47.
45. Roy, "Direct Investment from Abroad," pp. 116–17; Roy, "The British Columbia Electric Railway Company," pp. 86–115.
46. Montreal Street Railway Minute Book, 13 October 1892, 21 January 1897.
47. MCA, Council Papers, Minutes, Tramway Committee Report, 8 January 1915.
48. Commission des Tramways de Montréal, *Rapport,* pp. 11–12.
49. Council Minutes, 9 January, 11 September 1905; Report of the Committee on Legislation, 29 January 1906, TCA.
50. H. V. Nelles, *The Politics of Development* (Toronto: Macmillan, 1974), pp. 256–306.
51. Council Papers, Box 21, No. 470, Annual Report of the City Engineer, 13 December 1907; Minutes, 1909, Appendix A, Report of the Special Committee on Street Railway Service, 17 November 1909; Appendix C, 1909, Return of the City Clerk Re: Plebiscite on Civic Street Railway, 1, 4 January 1910, TCA. The ratepayers voted 19,376 in favour and 10,696 against with affirmative majorities in all wards.
52. TCA, Council Papers, Board of Control Report, 9 September 1910; 21 October 1910; Minutes of the Board of Control, 20 October 1910; Minutes, 1910, Appendix C, Return of the City Clerk on a bylaw to spend $1,157,293 to build and equip the Civic Railway, 4 January 1911.
53. Doucet, "Mass Transit and the Failure of Private Ownership"; L. H. Pursley,

Toronto Trolley Car Story (Los Angeles: Railfare Publications, 1961), pp. 7–15.

54. Council Minutes, 1913, Appendix C, Mayor's Message Re Street Railways, 13 October 1913; Minutes, 1914, Appendix A, Mayor's Message, 9 February, 1914, 21 September 1914, TCA.
55. Doucet, "Mass Transit and the Failure of Private Ownership," pp. 17–25.
56. Ibid., pp. 28–29; Board of Control Minutes, Report No. 26, 3 December 1920 gives the details of the "Clean Up Deal," TCA. See also C. Armstrong and H. V. Nelles, "The Rise of Civic Populism in Toronto," in V. Russell, ed., *Forging a Consensus* (Toronto, University of Toronto Press, 1984) pp. 192–237.
57. See for example, Patricia Roy, "The Fine Arts of Lobbying and Persuading: The Case of the B.C. Electric Railway," in David S. Macmillan, ed., *Canadian Business History* (Toronto: McClelland and Stewart, 1972), pp. 239–54.
58. Toronto, Montreal and Vancouver did not experience the same sort of suburban growth as Boston and Philadelphia did, for example, in the 1870's and 1880's; see S. B. Warner Jr., *Streetcar Suburbs* (Cambridge: Harvard University Press, 1978), *The Private City* (Philadelphia: University of Philadelphia Press, 1968), and Theodore Hershberg, ed., *Philadelphia* (New York: Oxford University Press, 1981), pp. 128–203.
59. Cheape, *Moving the Masses,* pp. 155–207.
60. "Municipal Reform in Montreal, "*Canadian Magazine* 12 (1911); Bureau of Municipal Research, *Report on Montreal,* 1917–18 (Toronto, 1918); Michel Gauvin, "The Montreal City Council and the Committee of Citizens, 1906–1914," (Master's thesis, University of Ottawa, 1973); C. Armstrong and H. V. Nelles, "The Great Fight for Clean Government," *Urban History Review* (1976).

10

Single-Sector Communities in Northern Ontario: The Creation and Planning of Dependent Towns

Oiva W. Saarinen

In many regions of Canada and the United States, the single-sector community has played an important role in moulding settlement patterns and fostering the creation of distinctive economic and sociocultural settings. Such communities have been given varying names, such as, resource, single-enterprise, company, single-industry, and single-sector.[1] The survival of these communities depends upon a highly specialized economic base linked to the fortunes of either a single company or a single economic sector. The term single-sector has been adopted for this paper because it is sufficiently broad in scope to encompass the majority of communities included by the other names used. Single-sector communities can be found across the continent, from the eastern New England textile town to the resource settlements associated with the Great Lakes district and beyond to townsites found in the Canadian and American West. At the local level, single-sector communities exist in a variety of geographical settings ranging from the unplanned "squatters'" locations found in Minnesota to the formally planned "model" locations such as those in New England and in Ontario.[2] These localized settings have provided the framework for numerous studies concerning their sociocultural characteristics.[3] The continuing importance of this type of settlement to the contemporary landscape is obvious: in Canada approximately 25 per cent of all Canadians residing outside of metropolitan areas still live in such economic and sociocultural environments.[4] It is clear, therefore, that single-sector communities warrant serious consideration if the process of Canadian-American urban development is to be fully understood.

It is the purpose of this paper to provide a number of spatial and historical perspectives regarding the single-sector community as it relates to Northern Ontario. Since the latter part of the nineteenth century, Northern Ontario has served as one of the major resource regions in Canada. For the

Fig. 1: Northern Ontario.

purpose of this study, Northern Ontario encompasses the Northeastern and Northwestern Ontario Planning Regions (Figure 1). This resource area has acquired national and international significance as a source of forest and mining products; as well, its hinterland location has resulted in the development of a broadly-based system of transportation links with eastern and western Canada as well as with the United States. The resource and transportation functions, in turn, have necessitated the creation of supporting communities, many of which are single-sector in terms of their economic structure. This examination of single-sector communities includes four sections. The overriding impact of the natural environment as it pertains to the geographical factors of size and distance is first, followed by a review of the economic sequences associated with the exploitation of this natural environment. The spatial patterns which have evolved as a result of these exploitation sequences is then discussed, and the paper concludes with an assessment of the attempts by various authorities to create well-planned communities in this northern setting.

NATURAL SETTING

The scholar J. W. Watson has referred to geography as being a "discipline in distance."[5] The concept applies equally well to the framework of community development in Northern Ontario. Of the many variables that have influenced the planning of settlements in the region, that of geographical size and distance has been a major element conditioning all aspects of the development process (Table 1). Northern Ontario is equivalent in size to many country jurisdictions found in the world today; even at the level of the constituent districts, the size-distance factor remains of considerable importance. The distance of Northern Ontario from the continental heartland adds yet another frictional barrier. The area is characterized by spatial extensiveness and geographical isolation. Indeed, the latter is the basic precondition for the analysis of single-sector communities within an Anglo-American heartland-hinterland context.[6] The natural environment has similarly contributed to the formation of a random rather than systematic network of resource communities, a result of the unique locational features of the mining and forest industries. This randomness has been given added emphasis because of the existence of a restricted agricultural base and limited urban centres.

SEQUENCES OF ECONOMIC DEVELOPMENT

The economic development of Northern Ontario has traditionally been identified with the exploitation of natural resources, the local transformation of these resources to a semifinished state, and the transportation of these semifinished products to markets located elsewhere. For this development to occur, it was imperative first to create a transportation network in order to overcome the size-distance barrier and to open the hinterland to external capital and entrepreneurship. Public and private initiatives were also required to generate an adequate power base. Once the transportation and power requirements were put into place, it then became possible for an industrial economy to be forged, based upon the exploitation of mining and forest-based resources.

As Nelles has observed, railways more than anything else served to open

TABLE 1

NORTHERN ONTARIO LAND AREAS

LAND DIVISION	AREA		
	Square Miles	Square Kilometers	Approximate Geographical Equivalent
Algoma District	19,771	51,207	Costa Rica
Cochrane District	55,918	144,827	Wisconsin
Kenora District	153,220	396,838	Newfoundland
Manitoulin District	1,420	3,679	French Polynesia
Nipissing District	7,022	18,187	Fiji Islands
Parry Sound District	3,815	9,880	Cyprus
Rainy River District	6,493	16,817	Hawaii
Sudbury District	17,715	45,882	Denmark
Thunder Bay District	42,281	109,507	Tennessee
Timiskaming District	5,517	14,288	Northern Ireland
Northern Ontario	313,172	811,112	Finland and Sweden Turkey France and West Germany Texas and Louisiana
Ontario	354,223	917,434	
Northern Ontario as per cent of Ontario Land Area	88.4	88.4	
Canada	3,560,238	9,220,974	
Northern Ontario as per cent of Canadian Land Area	8.8	8.8	

Source: Statistics Canada, *1976 Census of Canada,* Supplementary Bulletins: Geographic and Demographic, Population, Land Area and Population Density, Census Divisions and Subdivisions, pp. 1–61; and Rand McNally, *Goode's World Atlas.*

up Northern Ontario for development.[7] In the period between 1882 and 1932, four major railway networks were erected in the region: Canadian Pacific; Canadian National; Algoma Central; and Ontario Northland. The first railway to appear on the scene was the mainline of the Canadian

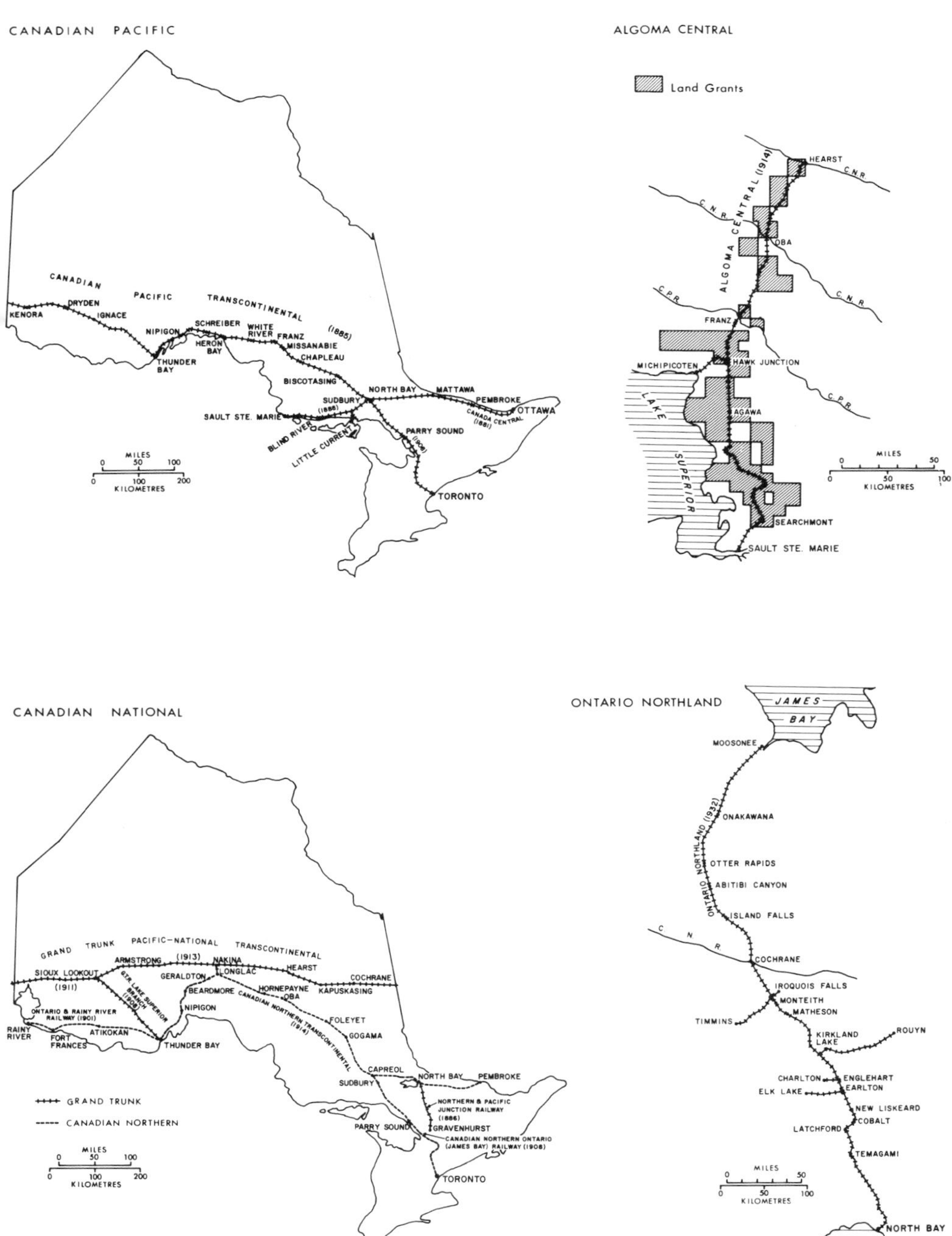

*Fig. 2: Major railways (*source: see notes 8–11*).*

Pacific Railway (C.P.R.) constructed in 1882–85 (Figure 2).[8] Later the C.P.R. built lines from Sudbury to Sault Ste. Marie in 1888 and to Toronto in 1908. By the end of the first decade of the century, the C.P.R. had succeeded in transforming the southern wilderness of the Precambrian Shield into an accessible resource frontier. Unlike the C.P.R., the Canadian National Railway (C.N.R.) was never conceived at the outset as a planned national network.[9] It evolved after the First World War as an amalgam of those railways throughout Canada on the verge of economic collapse. The network in Northern Ontario involved two main transcontinental lines: The Grand Trunk Pacific-National Transcontinental line completed in 1913, and the Canadian Northern built in 1914. The former was significant as it opened new territory north of Nipigon and the Great Clay Belt for exploitation, whereas the latter served to penetrate the tract of the Precambrian Shield lying between the two transcontinental lines already constructed. The C.N.R. likewise acquired ownership to two smaller lines linking Toronto with Sudbury and North Bay. The two remaining railway lines differed from the C.P.R. and C.N.R. in that one was associated with a private industrial enterprise while the other emerged as Ontario's first publicly-owned facility. The Algoma Central Railway (A.C.R.) was incorporated in 1899 to supply raw materials for the Clergue empire in Sault Ste. Marie.[10] By 1914, a line linking Sault Ste. Marie to Hearst in the Great Clay Belt had been completed. In the meantime, the province of Ontario had established the Temiskaming and Northern Ontario Railway (now the Ontario Northland Railway) in 1902.[11] Intended as a colonization instrument, the railway ran north until it eventually reached Moosonee in 1932. The latter was particularly noteworthy as it completed the historic goal of connecting Toronto not only with Sudbury but also with the entire northern resource frontier. Thus the stage was set for the emergence of Northern Ontario as part of the metropolitan hegemony of Toronto.[12]

As Figure 2 suggests, these lines of steel prompted the rise of numerous single-sector settlements, the majority of which consist of very small "station stop" clusters. At some of the main points, however, communities of more substantial size have arisen, such as Nakina and Hornepayne. The railway lines have also been important for many of the resource-based townsites since they often provided the locational "raison d'être" for their precise geographical setting, such as Sudbury.

Hydro-electric power provided much of the supporting base for the economic development of Northern Ontario.[13] While some of the required power was developed by the private sector, it was the province of Ontario that gradually began to assume the dominant entrepreneurial role. As early as 1895, the forest industry began to establish its own hydro-electric facilities in conjunction with allied mill projects. After the turn of the century the mining industry followed suit. Recognizing the need for additional power supplies, the government of Ontario decided to engage itself directly in this sector by creating the Ontario Hydro-Electric Power Commission of Ontario in 1906 (Ontario Hydro after 1974). The commission soon embarked upon the construction of transmission systems and generating stations; as well, it acquired control over many of the previously-built, private hydro-electric stations. A major step was taken in 1933 when the commission acquired the huge Abitibi Canyon facilities. Since then, Ontario Hydro has constructed numerous generating and distribution systems throughout Northern Ontario. While the hydro-electric network was economically significant, the resulting settlement impact has been minimal. Only in a few instances, such as Fraserdale and Otter Rapids, have hydro-electric facilities been accompanied by townsites of any size. On the other hand, hydro-electric sites frequently served as important siting factors for resource communities associated with the pulp and paper industry.

The emerging railway network and the development of hydro-electric power provided the foundation for the exploitation of the forest and mining resources of Northern Ontario. A forest industry based upon logging, wood processing, and pulp and paper production was the first to develop.[14] While the production of squared timber originally played a prominent role in supporting the growth of the province, sawn timber gradually became the central product. Towards the end of the nineteenth century, Ontario experienced its great "pine era," at which time sawmilling operations could be found in the Ottawa Valley, Algonquin, Muskoka, and Parry Sound districts. After 1900, however, the pine era declined and the main sawmilling areas shifted northward into the North Bay, the north shore of Lake Huron, and the Rainy River-Thunder Bay regions. More recently, this sector has shown an increasing concentration further inland, as at Hearst.

The forest industry underwent dramatic changes in 1895 when pulp processing was first introduced in the north at Sault Ste. Marie. This shifting of the pulp industry into Northern Ontario was primarily influenced by the presence of extensive pulpwood resources. The subsequent prohibition of pulpwood exports from Ontario Crown land in 1900 and the elimination of tariffs on newsprint entering the United States in the period between 1909 and 1913 encouraged the construction of additional mills. During the early years of the century, the majority of the pulp and paper mills were closely tied to inland waterpower sites found in close juxtaposition with the railway network; after the Second World War, the locational emphasis changed to sites found along the northern shores of Lakes Superior and Huron (Figure 3).

The basis for the development of the mining wealth of Northern Ontario rests with the existence of a widely dispersed belt of rocks situated within

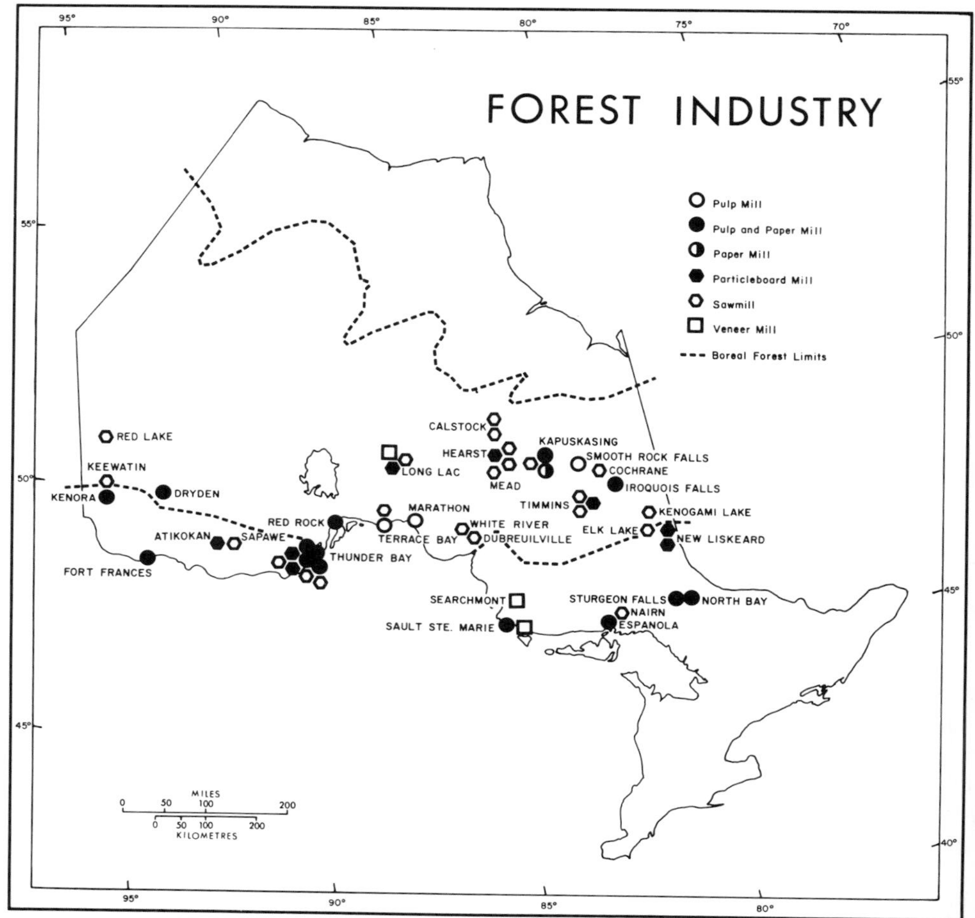

Fig. 3: Forest industry in Northern Ontario.

the Precambrian Shield known as "greenstones."[15] The first major indication of the mining potential of the north came in 1866 with the discovery of gold near Madoc and silver at Silver Islet near Thunder Bay. This was followed by the discovery of the Sudbury Basin nickel-copper deposits in 1883. By the end of the 1880's, iron ore production had started at Michipicoten (Wawa). Mining activity was greatly intensified after the turn of the century, as "boomtown" camps came into being at Cobalt, Porcupine, and Kirkland Lake in Northeastern Ontario. After the First World War, the focus of mining activity shifted westward to areas such as

Red Lake, Pickle Lake, Geraldton, and Steep Rock Lake near Atikokan. Beginning in the 1950's and continuing into the 1960's, new mining activity again returned to Northeastern Ontario, notably in the Elliot Lake, Timmins, Kirkland Lake, and Timagami districts. As was the case with the forest industry, the exploitation of minerals stimulated the formation of numerous single-sector communities scattered throughout the Shield (Figure 4).

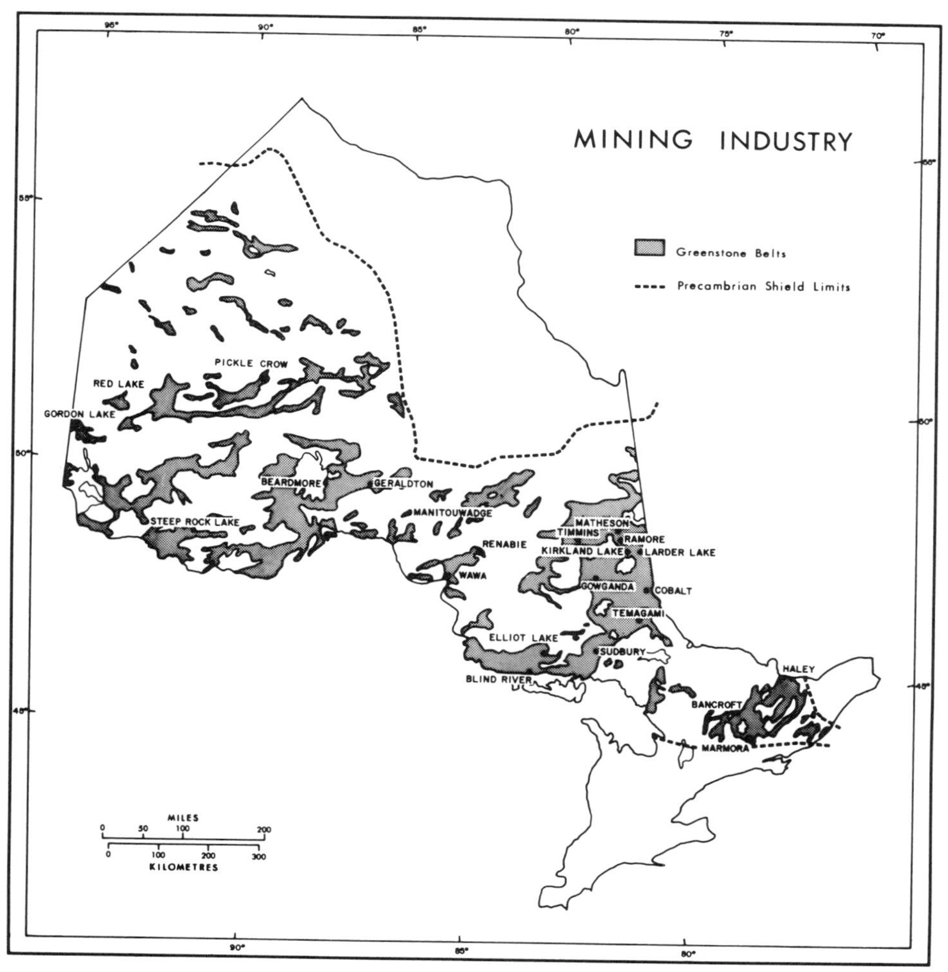

Fig. 4: Mining Industry in Northern Ontario.

PATTERN OF URBAN DEVELOPMENT

There is a close correspondence between the natural environment and the pattern of urban development in Northern Ontario. Owing to the conditioning effects of resource availability, the urban pattern tends to be random and spatially dispersed, with clustering occurring only in special areas, such as the Sudbury Basin, or where single-sector communities are surrounded by an agricultural hinterland, as is the case with Kapuskasing.[16] This close dependency upon the natural environment has given the northern communities a number of common structural features which include small populations, slow growth rates, isolation, limited hinterlands, a narrow economic base, and poorly-developed physical and sociocultural infrastructures. As well, the functioning of the urban network as a whole has been seriously influenced by powerful exogenous forces, instability and uncertainty, and weak spatial interaction among the constituent communities. These elements have all combined to create poor future growth potentials.

According to one recent federal study, the urban network in Northern Ontario is characterized by the presence of many single-sector settlements. As shown in Table 2, the study identified thirty-six communities with populations in excess of 500 that exhibited single-sector dependency.[17]

TABLE 2

SINGLE-SECTOR COMMUNITIES IN NORTHERN ONTARIO

Community	Activity	Population 1976
Atikokan	Mining	5,803
Beardmore	Forestry	650
Capreol (Sudbury Basin)	Mining	4,089
Dryden	Forestry	6,799
Ear Falls	Mining	1,982
Elliot Lake	Mining	8,849
Espanola	Forestry	5,926
Field	Forestry	801
Geraldton	Forestry	3,127
Hearst	Forestry	5,195
Hornepayne	Transport	1,694
Ignace	Mining	1,983
Iron Bridge	Restaurant & Accommodation	790
Iroquois Falls	Forestry	6,887

TABLE 2 (*continued*)

Community	Activity	Population 1976
Kapuskasing	Forestry	12,676
Longlac	Forestry	1,934
Manitouwadge	Mining	3,551
Marathon	Forestry	2,283
Mattawa	Forestry	2,849
Nakina	Transport	620
Nipigon	Forestry	2,724
Onaping Falls (Sudbury Basin)	Mining	6,776
Pickle Lake	Mining	508
Red Lake–Balmertown	Mining	4,893
Red Rock	Forestry	1,694
Sault Ste. Marie	Steel	81,048
Schreiber	Forestry	2,010
Smooth Rock Falls	Forestry	2,446
Spanish	Utilities	1,082
Sturgeon Falls	Forestry	6,400
Sudbury CMA*	Mining	156,840
Temagami	Mining	1,327
Terrace Bay	Forestry	2,098
Timmins	Mining	44,747
Virginiatown	Mining	1,189
Wawa	Mining	4,272
TOTAL*		398,542

*Includes Sudbury, Copper Cliff, Coniston, Levack, Lively, Falconbridge, and Garson.

Source: Department of Regional Economic Expansion, Government of Canada, *Single-Sector Communities,* pp. 69–71.

The population of these settlements totalled almost 400,000, a figure equivalent to two-thirds of the total urban population and roughly one-half of the total population. These generalized figures, however, mask important differences between the northwest and the northeast, as the latter has a single-sector dependency that is three times greater than the former. This fact suggests that the pattern of urban development is markedly different for the two areas. In the northwest, for instance, the metropolis of Thunder

Bay has succeeded in acquiring a broad regional dominance. Because of its strategic location on the Great Lakes, it now features a low specialization index with considerable strength in the transportation and tertiary sectors.[18] Kenora, the second largest settlement in the northwest, has similarly branched out from the forest industry into tourism, transportation, and the provision of trading services. In the northeast, by comparison, there is no such clearcut metropolitan dominance by Sudbury. In this region the only major communities that do not reflect single-sector dependency are North Bay and Kirkland Lake. While the former is distinguished for its public administration and defence functions, the latter has come to serve as a central-place node.[19]

The majority of the single-sector communities in Northern Ontario are relatively small; only Sudbury, Sault Ste. Marie, Timmins, and Kapuskasing have populations in excess of 10,000. These small population sizes, in turn, have been a major factor in the generally poor past growth performances in terms of population, employment, income, and participation rates.[20] The 1981 census information confirms that the past pattern of slow population growth is continuing. Between 1976 and 1981, Northern Ontario had a growth rate of only 0.3 per cent which compared poorly with the provincial figure of 4.4 per cent.[21] Isolation and the lack of strong agricultural hinterlands have likewise contributed to the creation of limited urban fields. Françoise Ricour-Singh has concluded that Northern Ontario, aside from Thunder Bay, is featured by the existence of numerous small centres whose influence extends no further than their immediate hinterlands; even in the east-west line from North Bay to Sault Ste. Marie she noted that the resulting hinterlands are essentially discontinuous.[22] Another structural aspect is the reliance upon a narrow economic base, which has given many of the settlements a "company town" character. Despite attempts to offset this aspect of corporate dominance through municipal incorporation and the sale of company real estate interests, a company town atmosphere still prevails in many of the communities today.[23] The narrow economic base has also resulted in a simplified occupational structure with an under-representation of the middle class.[24] Unfortunately, northern communities continue to be hindered by a physical and sociocultural infrastructure that compares poorly with the rest of the province.[25] Historically, this infrastructural weakness has been reinforced by the existence of a punitive provincial taxation system for mining communities and a tendency for industrial operations to locate outside of municipal jurisdictions.

Externality in one form or another has been an integral aspect linked with the urban network since the nineteenth century. In part this has been caused by the geographical separation of the resource base from its supporting market areas. As Weller has noted, "all the key segments of the region's economy are . . . based upon the needs of another region.''[26] Aspects of this underlying staple orientation have been discussed by other authors.[27] In addition, a large part of the decision-making authority with respect to the determinants of urban growth resides elsewhere. This tradition of outside authority developed early, as much of the initial entrepreneurial thrust for the opening of the north came from the United States. After the Cobalt boom, Toronto began to loom large as an alternative control point for the northern development process. As Stelter has written: ''in several respects, all the communities of the nickel belt were subject to a complex system of outside forces beyond that of the American and British based companies. They all fell within the metropolitan hegemony of Toronto, 250 miles to the south.''[28] As previously noted, the orientation of the railway network contributed significantly to the emergence of the region as a hinterland for Toronto. This reliance upon external markets and outside authority accounts for the economic vulnerability of the north and the lack of certainty in terms of long-run planning. In the absence of endogenous demand, the trend has been for a ''boom and bust'' cyclical pattern to emerge for both urban and economic development. Elliot Lake is a good example. Beginning with a boom in the 1950's, the community later experienced a severe setback in the 1960's. This was followed by recovery in the 1970's; even today, however, rumblings are being heard about the possible termination of contracts signed between Ontario Hydro and the local uranium companies in 1978.[29] It is no surprise, therefore, that the economics of resource extraction have led to a negative atmosphere in the north, involving feelings of exploitation and alienation and a sense of powerlessness regarding local destinies.

Small populations, limited complementarity, the importance of Toronto, and distance have all combined to narrow the potential for spatial interaction among the northern communities. Thus the northern urban network lacks regional cohesiveness. This lack of regional cohesiveness has made it difficult for full-fledged urban systems to develop. Ricour-Singh, for example, is cautious in referring to Sudbury and Thunder Bay as the focal points for urban systems.[30] Recently, the provincial and federal governments have attempted to create stronger links in the north through the creation of Norontair and the establishment of C.B.C. radio and television stations. The potential for the future growth of the urban network appears to be weak. This weakness is a result of: the increased capital-intensive nature of the mining and forest industries; substitution effects; limited opportunities for alternative employment outside of the public sector; the greater profitability of other resource areas such as Alberta and the southern United States; and the inability to capitalize upon economies of scale because of dispersion factors.[31]

SINGLE-SECTOR COMMUNITIES AND URBAN PLANNING

Northern Ontario provides useful insight into a century of planning activity as it relates to single-sector communities. Beginning with the opening of the Sudbury basin in 1883, the region has provided the setting for a variety of public and private community planning projects which have achieved varying degrees of success. According to McCann, such single-sector communities in Canada have generally been planned within the framework of three planning philosophies: additive, holistic, and comprehensive.[32] Under the additive approach, town development proceeded haphazardly with little regard for orderly growth other than through the use of the ubiquitous grid street plan. Such an approach was common prior to the First World War. Between the First and Second World Wars, holistic planning was introduced, whereby concern for physical arrangement and zoning of land uses, the provision of open spaces, and the accommodation of orderly expansion on the basis of a predetermined plan were in evidence. The subsequent adoption of comprehensive planning with its greater emphasis on social and advanced physical principles made its appearance in the post-Second World War period. This paper uses the above classification with some modifications. The first involves the addition of an "unplanned" category. The second relates to the inclusion of an overriding thread after the additive phase linked to the utilitarian principle. Third, the classification illustrates the importance of foreign models from such countries as Great Britain and the United States. The latter was particularly noteworthy, as planning for single-sector communities could be traced back to the early nineteenth century in New England and to the Lake Superior mining region after the 1840's.[33] Finally, reference is also made to the various sponsors of community planning activity (Figure 5).

Resource communities prior to the First World War were either unplanned or were planned in simple additive fashion. Unplanned communities sprouted early in the Sudbury and Cobalt mining camps. In the Sudbury Basin, the small company towns which appeared at the site of mines and smelters after 1883 were merely appendages, hardly more than collections of hastily constructed bunk houses scattered randomly around local operations. These appendages were similar in form to the early unplanned or squatters' locations found in the mining regions of Michigan, Wisconsin, and Minnesota.[34] Many of the original settlements such as Victoria Mine, Blezard Mine, Worthington Mine, Murray Mine, and Gertrude Mine eventually disappeared.[35] Fostered by the presence of numerous constraints, including competing mining companies, topography, lack of faith in the future, and inaction on the part of the Temiskaming & Northern Ontario Railway Commission, Cobalt too evolved as an example of un-

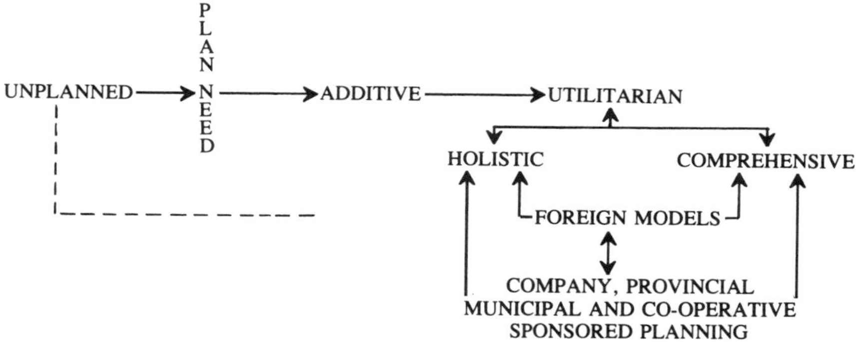

Fig. 5: A framework for the planning of single-sector communities in Northern Ontario.

planned development until its pioneering phase was brought to an end by the fire of 1919.[36]

The prewar years, however, were accompanied by numerous examples of additive planning. Such planning featured a predetermined layout usually prepared by surveyors for railways, governments, companies and for private subdivisions. These early layouts lacked distinction and were based on simple variants of the gridiron system. The C.P.R., for instance, prepared numerous plans of this kind, including those for Sudbury in 1886 and Ignace in 1887.[37] In line with its philosophy of encouraging settlement, the land department of the Temiskaming and Northern Ontario Railway surveyed lots along its route which became sites for stores, offices, and houses in settlements such as Englehart and Cochrane. Cochrane's townsite, distinguished by an ordered layout of generous proportions, was planned to conform with Premier Whitney's belief that the settlement would eventually become the "Metropolis of the North."[38] In 1896, Dryden was laid out in grid form to serve the anticipated needs of the surrounding agricultural area.[39] Stimulated by the possibility of employment opportunities and a dissatisfaction with the existing order, land surveyors began to assume a more prominent role in the laying out of new townsites after the Cobalt boom. Thus the mining communities of Porcupine, Timmins, and Kirkland Lake came to acquire layouts which reflected some ordering principle under the guiding hand of the surveyor.[40] A similar pattern occurred within the forest industry as evidenced by the layout prepared for Espanola in 1903.[41] The conspicuous role of the surveyor at this time was prompted by the belief that the profession was the best qualified to deal with the problem of laying out new townsites in the north.[42] The position of the surveyor was enhanced by the powerful role played by the profession in creating the Town Planning Institute of Canada in 1919.[43] Aided considerably by the influence of the Association of Ontario Land Surveyors and its standing committee on town planning, the surveyor continued to play an influential role in the shaping and enlargement of single-sector settlements up to the Second World War period. The growth of Sudbury between the war years, for example, was largely planned by surveyors through the medium of private subdivisions. While additive planning was responsible for bringing about a greater semblance of order, the designers' neatly-drawn maps frequently conflicted with the natural topography. Michipicoten City in the early gold-mining district of Wawa was a good example of this deficiency, as it was laid out in 1903 "with a ruler and without any regard to land contours, hills, rivers, or swamps."[44]

The development of both holistic and comprehensive planning was based on a strong utilitarian ethic dictated by the fact that single-sector communities were simply a form of human investment required by companies in order to achieve a profit on their operations in frontier areas. Many of the communities fell under the influence of corporate administrations dominated by engineers who advocated a form of engineering functionalism in all aspects of decision making. Proclaimed as the dominant men of the north, engineers proceeded to adopt the American city efficiency model, with its emphasis on the development of urban centres as "optimally efficient units."[45] This utilitarian approach to community development, however, was frequently tempered by the aesthetic impacts of the American city beautiful and British garden city planning philosophies. After the Second World War, the rise of the planning profession also added a new dimension to the townsite development process.

The introduction of holistic planning around the First World War resulted from four major influences. The first was related to the devastating impact of repeated fires and typhoid epidemics in many of the northern townsites. Among the major fires which attracted attention at the time were the Cobalt Fire of 1909, the Porcupine and Cochrane Fire of 1911, and the Matheson Fire of 1916.[46] The second involved the Townsites Resolution passed by the Haileybury Board of Trade in 1912. The resolution condemned the lack of urban planning in the north and called for the imposition of proper regulatory controls.[47] The third influence arose out of the realization that mining camps founded at Sudbury or Timmins could no longer be thought of simply as "five year wonders."[48] As well, the rise of the forest industry and its reliance upon trees as a renewable resource gave added emphasis to the long-term viability of future northern townsites. The fourth influence was the acceptance of the fact that planned communities offered companies the best means of bringing qualified labour into Northern Ontario. As stated by S. D. Clark:

> As individual enterprises grew in size, however, and large numbers of workers were required, an increasingly high price was paid for the failure to build up a stable work force. An acceptance of responsibility by these larger employers for the welfare of the community in which they operated was a reflection of their realization that if workers were to be persuaded to remain in the North, they had to be given a stake in it. Very early in the development of many of the industrial communities of the North, the problem of attracting trained personnel had led to the providing of company houses and recreational facilities for senior company officials . . . . From the provision of such amenities, it was a short step to the company's acceptance of at least some responsibility for the providing of homes and various community services for the body of its workers. Thus, emerged, in various degrees of completeness, the company town.[49]

The laying out of the townsite of Iroquois Falls in 1915 marked the transition towards holistic planning in Northern Ontario; with the creation of the Kapuskasing plan in 1921 the transition was complete. This transitional period was important; it heralded the first real attempt to introduce model company towns along the lines of those founded earlier in New England.[50] While the two townsite plans were similar in that they portrayed innovative planning features, they differed somewhat in terms of the imprint of foreign models. The Iroquois Falls townsite was developed by the Abitibi Power and Paper Company headed by the American entrepreneur Frank Anson.[51] Under Anson's supervision a townsite plan was worked out and implemented in cooperation with A. P. Melton and L. Schlemm, the latter a landscape engineer from Montreal.[52] (While there have been some assertions that Thomas Adams was involved in the planning of the townsite, this was not the case.[53]) The plan was framed partly around the philosophical and paternal premises of garden city ideology; as well, some of the design elements reflected the utilitarian spirit of the city efficient movement. As one journal noted at the time, the plan for Iroquois Falls was both "utilitarian and aesthetic."[54] The importance of the garden city philosophy underlying the planning of Iroquois Falls was clearly indicated in an article written in the *Broke Hustler,* the local company magazine, which surveyed the evils of overcrowding in Great Britain and outlined the subsequent creation of the garden cities of Port Sunlight,

Bourneville, and York as model communities for the working classes. The article also stated:

> We here in Iroquois Falls, are, very fortunate in the respect, as the Abitibi Power & Paper Co. when plans were laid down for the Mill, conceived the idea of building a Garden City for their employees, replete with all modern conveniences and with spacious parks, recreation grounds and boulevards and where every house has its lawn, flower garden and vegetable garden, and where we can all breathe the invigorating air of the Northland. A town which in a year or two time bids fair to be the most modern working class town in the whole Dominion of Canada.[55]

At the same time, the utilitarian principle was asserted through compactness and the adoption of an efficient street and back lane layout.

The plan for Iroquois Falls (Figure 6) represented a major change from the straightforward layout of the additive town and included several aspects of holistic planning such as a more varied street arrangement, zoning, and the use of open space in various forms. While adhering to the gridiron system, the street network was changed where necessary to provide for a more graceful appearance. This adaptation to the environment was absent during the additive phase. The street pattern was used to girdle the townsite and to emphasize the compact nature of the built-up area. Where possible, back lanes were used for the provision of more efficient servicing. The link to the British tradition was given reinforcement through the use of street-names such as Argyle, Buckingham, Cambridge, Devonshire, Essex, and Fyfe. Zoning was in evidence. The heart of the plan consisted of a small civic centre which included a park and space for public buildings. South of the civic centre and opposite the railway yards, a number of rectangular lots were laid out for business purposes with the idea that the better class of businesses would face the centre. The overall arrangement was designed so that children would not have to pass through the business district on their way to school. Considerable thought was given to the maintenance of a rural atmosphere and the provision of open space. A main feature in this regard was the introduction of a combined educational and park complex in the northwestern part of the townsite intended to contain sports facilities, recreational parks, and childrens' gardens. The intention was clearly to give the townsite a "village green" and "cottage" appearance. After 1919, both Anson and Schlemm enhanced the aesthetic character of the townsite through an intense greening program which, according to the mayor, resulted in the formation of another "Garden of Eden."[56] Much of the

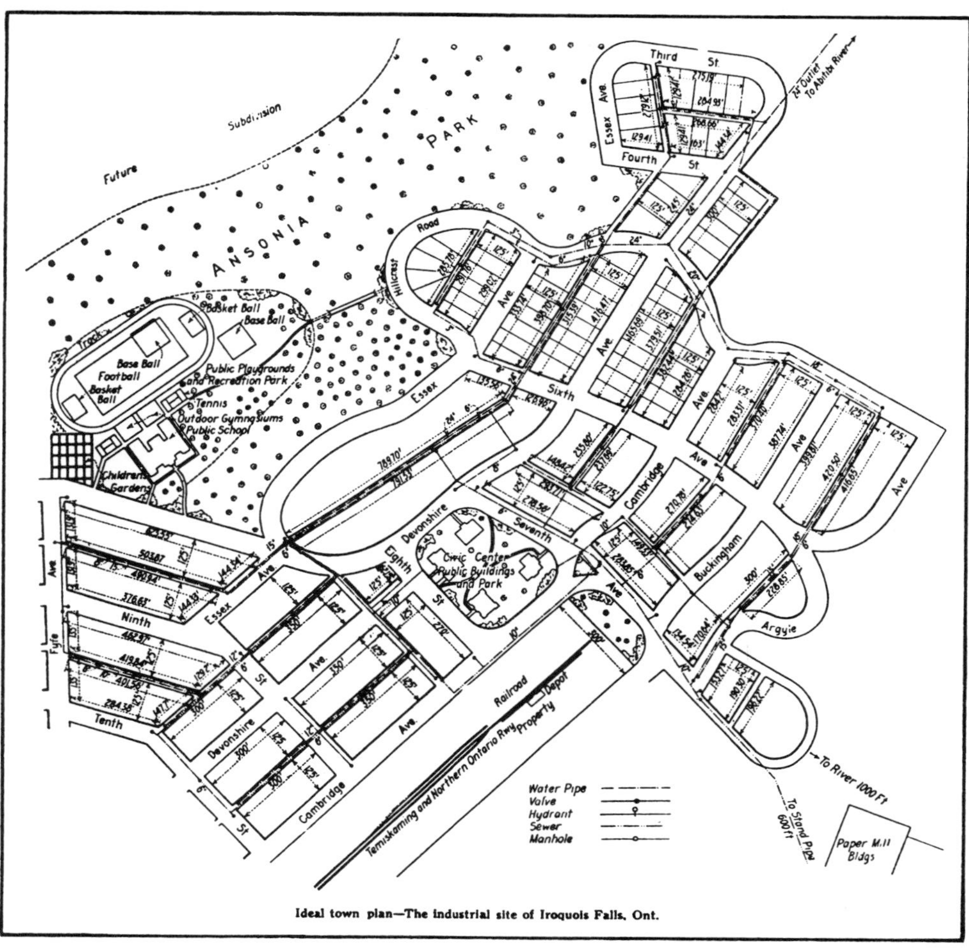

Ideal town plan—The industrial site of Iroquois Falls, Ont.

Fig. 6: Iroquois Falls, Ontario (source: *see note 54).*

planning done by Schlemm was repeated in much the same way at Pine Falls, Manitoba.[57]

From a social planning perspective, the town of Iroquois Falls did not fully reflect the "Garden of Eden" atmosphere. In fact, it was established at the outset as a full-fledged company town where "everything in the town was owned and operated by the company with the exception of the Royal Bank.[58] While the Province of Ontario had originally retained 25 per cent of the land as required under existing legislation, much of it had been turned over to the school board for a school site and playground.[59] Consequently, the provincial role within the townsite proved to be negligible. The closed and paternalistic nature of the town quickly became a bone of contention between the company and its workers. As L. R. Wilson, an executive of the company, wrote later in his memoirs:

> the Company owning the entire town made it extremely interesting and valuable experience.... However, there were always differences between us and one of the sore points with the Union was the closed town and the Company control. We finally incorporated the town, let the residents elect their own Mayor and Council and run it as any town. We did, however, take the mill out of the town, for we did not want the Council to have the right to tax the property.[60]

Nevertheless, Iroquois Falls continued to be criticized by outsiders for its company orientation. The situation forced the local company magazine to rise to the defence of the company town by quoting a favourable commentary from the *Porcupine Advance* which concluded that the benefits of such a relationship outweighed its drawbacks. Stating that Iroquois Falls had none of the undesirable features of other unrestricted townsites based upon promiscuous private ownership, the *Advance* affirmed that the community represented "one of the Wonder Towns of the Great North.[61] The tradition of the closed company town continued until the post-Second World War period; as late as 1953 the company still owned 99 per cent of the housing stock in the townsite.[62] The company then began to grant its employees the option of purchasing their rented homes.

Founded in 1921, the town of Kapuskasing was the most thoroughly planned resource community in Canada prior to the Second World War. Its original plan marked the culmination of the holistic planning phase in Northern Ontario. Kapaskasing differed from Iroquois Falls in that it was a government planned community which attempted to bring about a diversified rather than company-controlled settlement. Much of the impetus for the planning of the townsite was derived from personal initiatives undertaken by E. C. Drury, who served as the premier of Ontario from 1919 to 1923. In many respects, the planning process quickly became the "personal charge" of the premier.[64] According to a memorandum of agreement signed between Ontario and Spruce Falls Limited in 1921, the government assumed the responsibility for creating a noncompany town along model lines; this action eventually forced Iroquois Falls to proclaim itself as Northern Ontario's "original" model town. The basis for the government's negative attitude towards the company town is not clear. It is possible that this attitude was rooted in the events which surrounded Drury's first visit to Northern Ontario in 1919. It was on this occasion that Drury toured the settlements of Cochrane, Timmins, Smooth Rock Falls, and Iroquois Falls. In the light of his subsequent actions, it is clear that Drury was unimpressed with the prevailing atmosphere in Iroquois Falls and the nature of the relationship between company and worker in northern resource communities.[65] While Drury's objective was not fully achieved, Kapuskasing never did acquire a reputation for being a closed company town, despite the fact that the Spruce Falls Company eventually managed to own more the one-half of the housing stock. As well, Drury's contention that the Great Clay Belt would provide some basis for alternative employment proved to be correct.

The plan for Kapuskasing was prepared under the supervision of J. A. Ellis, director of the Bureau of Municipal Affairs (Figure 7).[66] He was assisted by a team which included a consulting architect, town planners, landscape architects, and engineers. The spatial organization of the plan was framed within a utilitarian philosophy with some adherence to the city beautiful and garden city traditions. In accord with the political realities of the day which supported utilitarianism, the plan gave support to the principle of efficiency, the extensive use of zoning, and the elimination of land speculation and unplanned suburban development. A. V. Hall, an associate town planner for the Kapuskasing project, formally acknowledged the utilitarian approach advocated by the province:

> Through these channels it seemed possible, without great expense, to direct the layout and physical growth of the town by recording in the preparation of plans, bylaws, and the reports for use of the new municipality, the provision for the present and for the future as far as could be foreseen at the time of planning, and as far as economical and legal limitation would seem to permit, at the same time keeping in mind not only the interests of the developing company, but also those of the settlers who have become already established throughout the Township of O'Brien . . . . The purpose in including within the municipal corporate limits an area so much larger than was obviously required for the town site, was to insure the municipality control by means of taxation, by-laws, and like restrictions, of the development of land, business, health conditions, for some distance around the townsite itself.[67]

An editorial in the *Housing and Town Planning Journal* in 1922 placed the utilitarian premises of the plan into a broader perspective by suggesting that the Kapuskasing project really represented an attempt on the part of the province "to lead a movement for the better beginning of town building so that the economic waste of bad planning . . . may be discouraged by the provision of something more intelligent, as well as more efficient, for

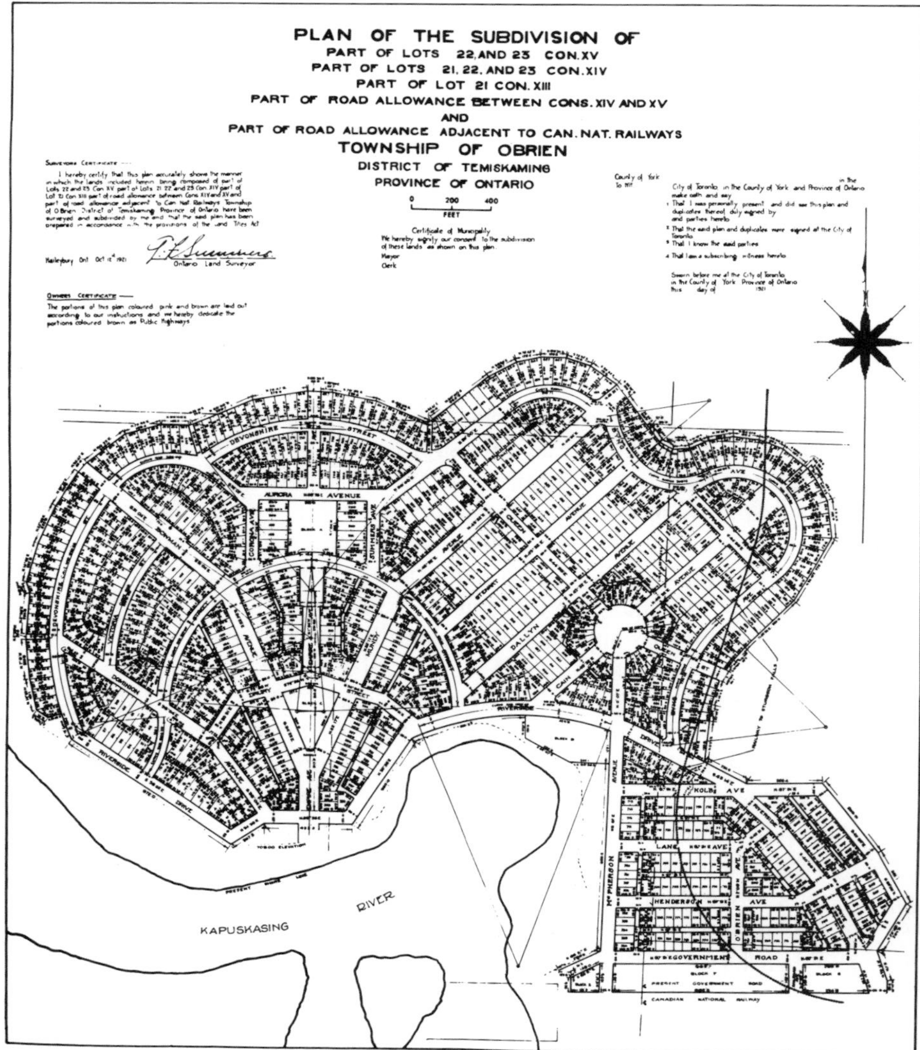

Fig. 7: Original townsite plan for Kapuskasing, Ontario (source: *Office of Land Titles, District of Timiskaming*).

everybody concerned.''[68] The statement implied that the Kapaskasing project was intended as a planning model for all communities in Ontario. The principle of zoning was used extensively to divide the proposed community into four major land use categories: business, industrial, residential, and greenbelt. General plans were prepared to illustrate the land use provisions for each of the above categories. To encourage the continued use of zoning, the consulting architect drafted a number of by-laws for adoption by the municipality. Within the residential areas, provisions were made for the differentiation of housing according to economic status, a feature which had previously been incorporated in the planning for the forest community of Temiskaming in Quebec.[69] This planning aspect was made clear in an internal memorandum by Ellis:

> It is proposed that the business centre of the town will be located near the head of the bridge and the Company will build a hotel or staff-house there. The boarding houses for unmarried men will be erected on the street going east around the bay. The first class houses will be erected in the district immediately west of the head of the bridge. The second class houses will be located on the street behind the boarding houses. . . . The lots have a frontage of fifty feet. For the first class houses the depth is one hundred and forty feet, for the second class, one hundred and twenty feet.[70]

Owing to the prevailing political mood, the plan did not make explicit reference to any form of city beautiful influence; however, its impact was evident in the use of vistas and variation in the street pattern, the adoption of the parkway concept, and the impression of civic grandeur generated by the overall design.[71] The introduction of the broad vista of moderate length with a visual focus appeared in the form of Empire Avenue, which led to a triangular parcel of land intended for public buildings. Diagonal streets and a traffic circle, possibly borrowed from the Goderich example in Ontario, were likewise used for stimulative effect. Another city beautiful feature was the integration of the parks along the Kapuskasing River as a parkway belt. To preserve the visual impact of the parkway, only lots on one side of Riverside Drive were permitted. From a wider perspective, the collective impacts of the plan including the Empire Avenue vista, the diagonals and the traffic circle, the parkway, and the greenbelt, provided the plan with a "civic grandeur" layout (Figure 8). The greenbelt, intended for agricultural and park uses, served to link the plan with the British garden city tradition; it was also intended to provide a mechanism for controlling land speculation and uncontrolled suburban development.[72] The latter was a holistic planning aspect that was not considered at Iroquois Falls.

While holistic planning principles did manage to provide attractive physical cores for both Iroquois Falls and Kapuskasing, they proved insufficient to prevent the appearance of unplanned fringe settlement. At Iroquois Falls, fringe settlement occurred in part because of the inability of the original plan to accommodate growth. The pattern of peripheral growth started as early as 1915, and by 1921 the population of the fringe actually

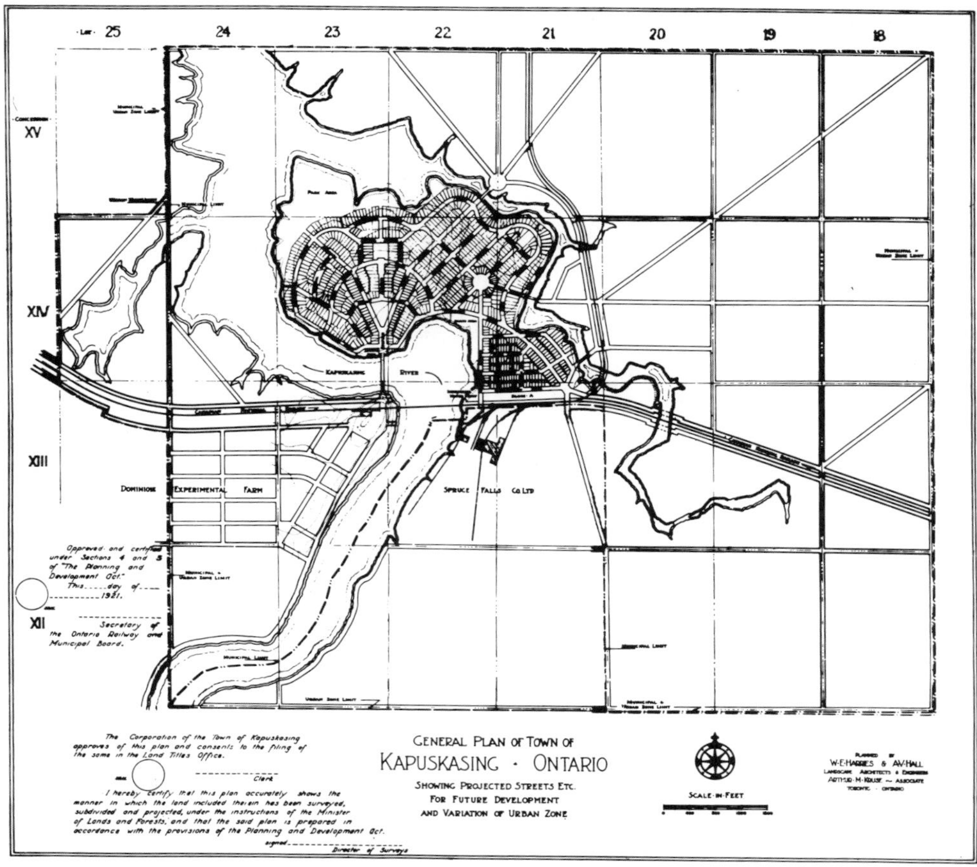

Fig. 8: Proposed general plan for Kapuskasing (source: *see note 66).*

exceeded that of the townsite proper. In contrast to the core, which was Anglo-Saxon, the outlying areas were characterized by Francophones who resided on small, privately-owned lots within a rigid gridiron system. The parallel evolution of both the core and the periphery eventually gave rise to problems related to schooling, transportation, assessment, and the provision of services. The problems were compounded by a deep social rift between the two residential areas. The deep nature of the rift was evidenced by the fact that it was not until 1969 that the planned town of Iroquois Falls was amalgamated with its less attractive fringe; thus, the new municipality managed to emerge only as a weak testimonial to the high aspirations of Anson in 1915. Despite the existence of a greenbelt designed to avoid such an occurrence, a similar pattern developed at Kapuskasing. This unplanned settlement took place via the route of unregistered land transactions during the 1920's. For a variety of reasons, including low taxes, the lack of municipal regulations, cheap land, and difficulties in obtaining accommodation in the townsite, the demand for lots in the periphery continued to grow. In 1928, the town of Kapuskasing used financial arguments to legally divorce the fringe settlements from the municipality. The process of physical separation was again a result of cultural differences that existed between Anglophones living in the core and Francophones residing on the periphery. According to S. D. Clark, the partitioning of the population was based upon class rather than ethnic differences, linked to the urban and rural origins of the two groups.[73] After 1958, the province of Ontario deemed it necessary for legal, health, and safety reasons to begin a major experiment in suburban neighbourhood rehabilitation. Following implementation of the project, the peripheral area was annexed to the Town of Kapuskasing in 1964. This innovative project eventually proved an unqualified success (Figure 9).[74]

The advances in holistic planning established by the Iroquois Falls and Kapuskasing examples served as partial models for the planning of other single-sector communities in Northern Ontario during the interwar period. In many cases, however, new townsites were still brought into being and older ones expanded in the additive style. The main emphasis during this period was to build the physical plant of the townsite at the lowest possible cost, a tendency consistent with utiliarianism and "the engineer's view of the overall aim of engineering."[75] While frequently lacking innovative physical design principles, the planning did use many of the elements previously incorporated at Iroquois Falls and Kapuskasing. The social aspects of the company town, with its structured housing and spatial segregation between core and periphery, were continued as well.

The single-sector communities of the Sudbury Basin typified the above trends.[76] In 1913, the Coniston and Levack townsites were laid out in predetermined gridiron style by company officials; as the mining companies owned the land, a company town orientation was immediately established which included residential segregation according to occupational status. The two townsites developed as neat and functionally efficient urban settings with sharply contrasting regional environments. Whereas Levack was surrounded by attractive tree-lined hills, Coniston, a smelter town, was soon accompanied by a rocky landscape devastated by sulphur fumes. Copper Cliff differed from the above two townsites in that it became the local headquarters for Inco after 1929. Copper Cliff, originally unplanned, moved into the additive phase around 1910; five years later, the environmentally harmful roastyards were moved away from the townsite. With the location of Inco's headquarters in the townsite, the community

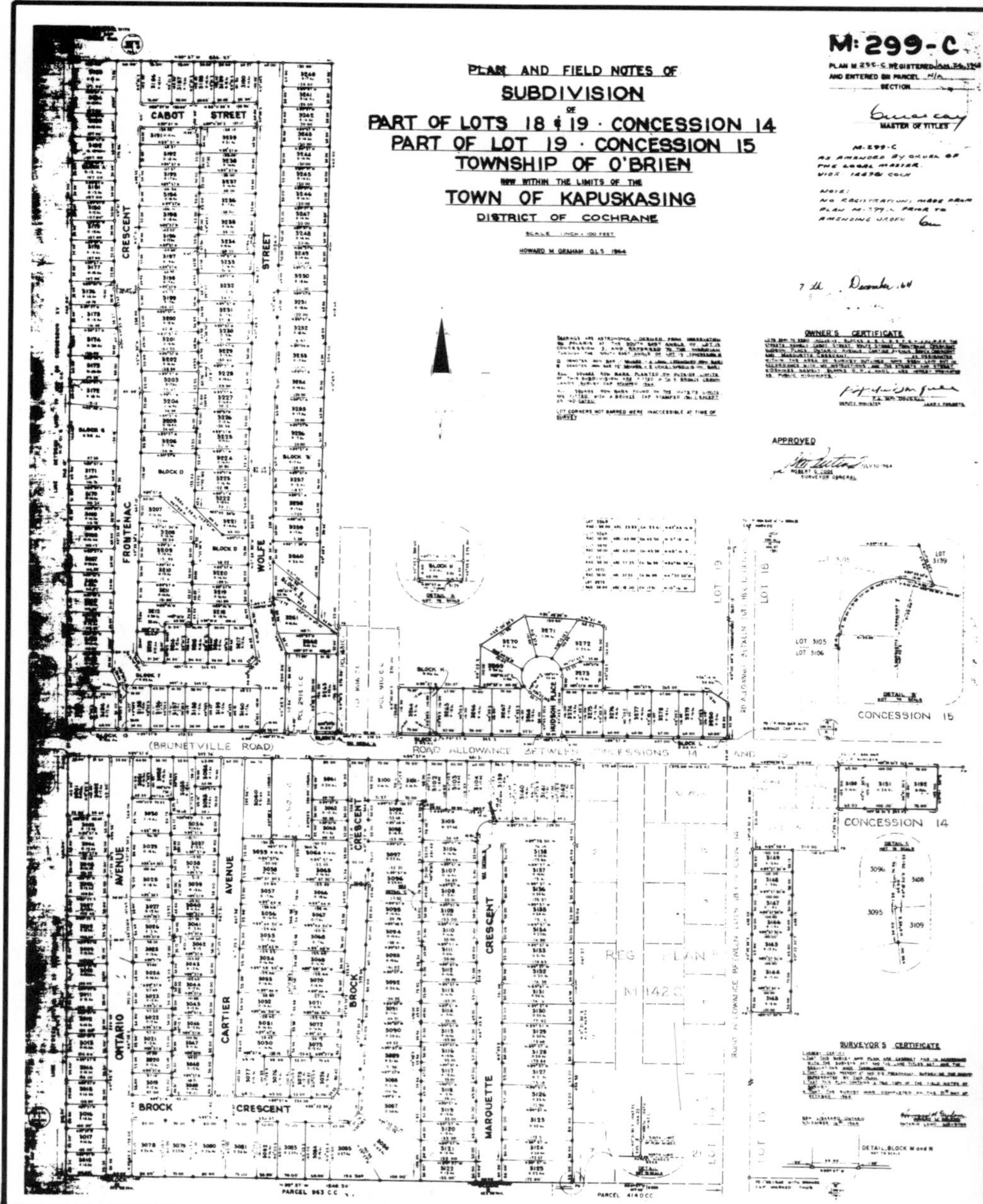

*Fig. 9: Subdivision plan for Brunetville neighbourhood, Kapuskasing (*source: *Office of Land Titles, District of Timiskaming).*

emerged as a sort of company "showcase," with comfortable homes, well-kept streets and parks, and numerous recreational facilities. The community also evolved towards company-town status via the acquisition of properties and the construction of homes by Inco. An employee's position was then rigidly correlated with the proper form of housing. A highly paternalistic attitude prevailed in all the Inco towns, with the company providing all the essential services and even controlling political representation: until the 1950's, the normal electoral process consisted of the acclamation of company executives. Resistance to the status quo was muted by the reliance of residents upon the company for housing and employment; equally important, the existence of Sudbury nearby offered residents the option of travelling to a less socially restrictive urban environment. The company town setting was expanded in 1929 when Falconbridge Nickel Mines appeared on the scene. Ernie Neelon, an engineer, was hired by the company to plan the Falconbridge townsite as another corporate "showcase" in the Sudbury Basin.[77] Like Copper Cliff, Falconbridge acquired a layout that was not particularly distinctive but nonetheless exhibited a land use pattern that was efficient in terms of servicing; spacious lots and wide streets were added to give the townsite a pleasing outward look. In similar fashion, the principle of company home ownership and spatial segregation was adopted.

Another feature of single-sector community development in the Sudbury Basin that was common to Iroquois Falls and Kapuskasing was the existence of peripheral settlement. In the Sudbury Basin communities, the fringetowns were occupied by both immigrant and Francophone workers. In Levack the periphery was known as Little Warsaw; in Coniston two immigrant areas developed, one dominated by Italians and the other by Poles. At Copper Cliff, a district known as Little Italy emerged; another area to the south was frequented by East Europeans and Finns. As early as 1929, squatters appeared at Happy Valley, south of the Falconbridge townsite. The above patterns aptly demonstrated the reality of Walker's dictum that segregation by class and race was not only desirable but necessary for company towns in North America.[78] In contrast to the above immigrant groupings on the periphery of the company towns, the Francophone population in the Sudbury Basin revealed a locational preference for residential sites in Sudbury and in the agricultural "Valley." These two areas served as the Francophone fringetowns for the Inco and Falconbridge company towns. This spatial partitioning of the population in the Sudbury Basin was a deterrent to the sociocultural and political development of Sudbury, as the company towns attracted virtually all of the white collar employees associated with the mining industry. As Donald Davis has shown, this phenomenon of the company town as the home of the economic "elite" also had its parallel in the American urban experience.[79]

The political setting of single-sector communities in Northern Ontario was greatly improved in 1943 when the province introduced the concept of the "improvement district." Set up as an interim form of government to bridge the gap from company control to democratic local government, this form of municipality was intended to apply to isolated communities in the north that were temporarily incapable of being run as self-governing units. The governing body of such an improvement district consisted of a three-member board appointed by the province. These boards exercised all the normal functions of a municipality; however, they were directly responsible to the province rather than to the residents of the improvement district. The objective of the board was to operate the townsite on behalf of the province until a capability for self-government was shown. Improvement districts were used to good effect around the Second World War period at Atikokan, Virginiatown, Longlac, Marathon, Red Rock, and Renabie.[80] Planning in these communities continued to reflect the utilitarian approach of the interwar period.

After the Second World War, other single-sector communities emerged. They illustrated a number of innovative and more comprehensive approaches to urban planning which used advanced physical designs and incorporated social and environmental concerns. Terrace Bay, Manitouwadge, and Elliot Lake serve as models of the new planning approach; more recently, such an approach has been applied as a form of community expansion and revitalization at Hornepayne. Terrace Bay was developed as a sulfate pulp mill townsite along the north shore of Lake Superior in 1946 by the Kimberly-Clarke Pulp and Paper Company. The plan for the new community was undertaken by the planner E. G. Faludi, who introduced a number of distinctive planning features, many of which served to set the townsite aside from the typical interwar townsite (Figure 10).[81] First, the industrial operations were located about one and one-half kilometres away from the residential areas, reducing their dominating effect over the townsite and minimizing the presence of pungent odours from the sulfate pulp mill.[82] Second, mature trees were left to grow in clumps rather than being ripped up during the laying out of streets and subdivisions. This policy was adopted at the suggestion of the planning consultant despite strong objections by engineers.[83] The decision proved to be correct, as Terrace Bay continues to serve as one of the finest examples of the integration of the human and natural environments in Northern Ontario. Third, the commercial, recreational, and educational focal points were located so as to serve the townsite at equal distances from the periphery; this has given the community a favourable pedestrian orientation. Fourth, natural parks and play areas provided a continuous park system through the

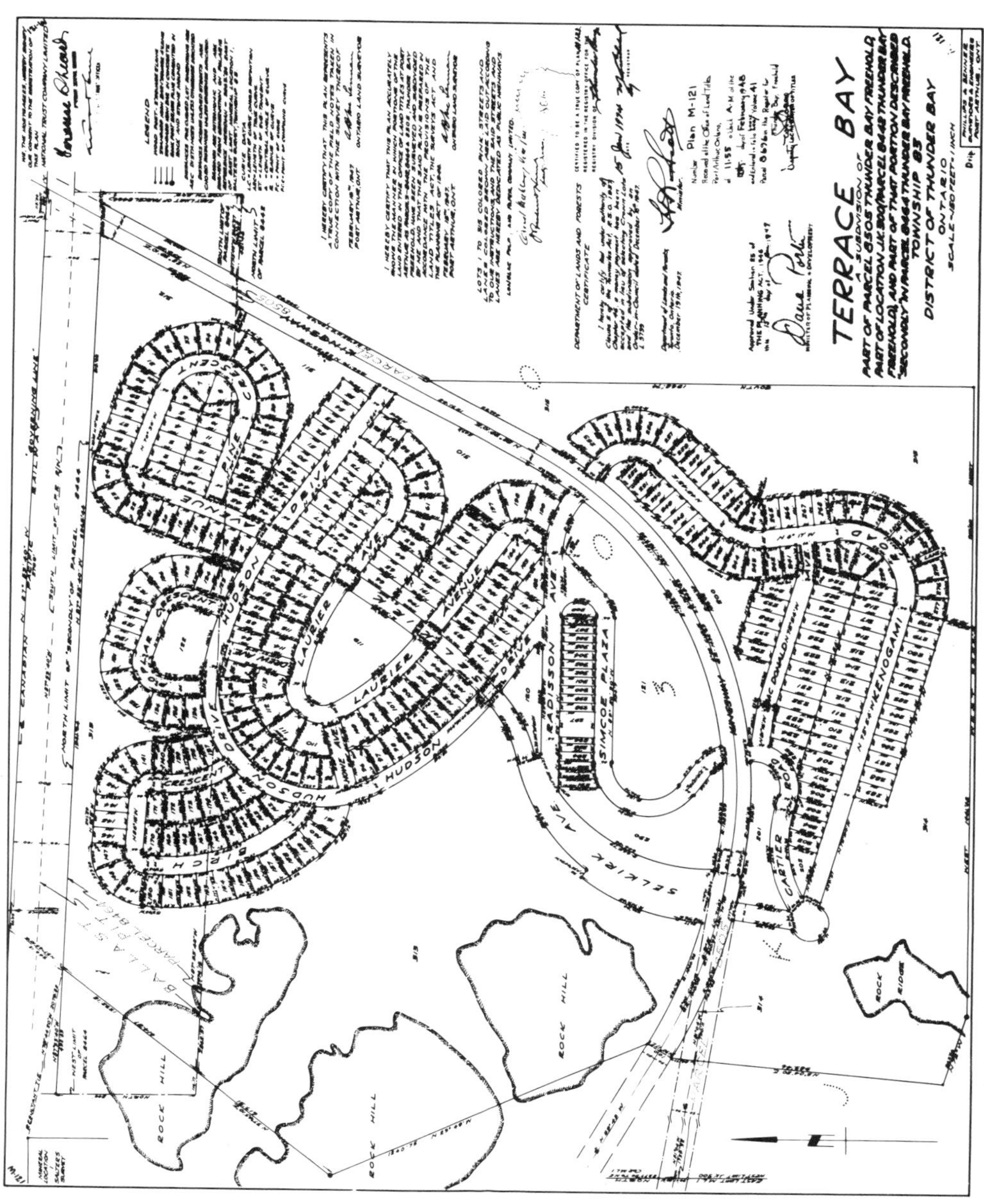

Fig. 10: Townsite plan for Terrace Bay, Ontario (source: *Land Registration Office, District of Thunder Bay*).

town and between neighbourhoods; these, in turn, were blended into a protective greenbelt where no fringe development was permitted. Fifth, special plans were made to offset the impact of the TransCanada Highway which bisected the townsite. These included a subway for the safety of school children, the location of the main shopping plaza on an adjacent side street to avoid traffic congestion, and the provision of a greenbelt between the highway and the residential areas. Sixth, the plan accommodated eight contiguous and partially self-contained residential areas framed within a street network that utilized curvilinear, loop, and cul-de-sac patterns. Seventh, an attempt was made to vary the style of the dwelling units on the basis of family composition and architectural variety rather than on the basis of occupational status. Greater attention was given to the provision of more efficient and attractive terrace housing. By using these measures, Faludi sought to improve the social life of the community by eliminating the spatial segregation common to other single-sector towns. These varied initiatives at Terrace Bay incorporated many of the concepts previously used by the American planners Clarence Perry, Clarence Stein, and Henry Wright.[84]

In the early 1950's, comprehensive planning proceeded along a different path at Manitouwadge and Elliot Lake, where the province again became actively involved in townsite planning. The Manitouwadge project commenced in 1953 with the discovery of copper and other minerals northeast of Lake Superior and the formation of Geco and Wilroy Mines.[85] Realizing its limited expertise in the area of townsite planning, officials of Geco Mines requested the Ontario government to take the initiative in designing the community.[86] The province agreed to accept this responsibility since it corresponded to its policy against the formation of more company towns. In 1954, the legislature amended the Mining Act to permit the reservation of surface rights of mining claims by the province for townsite development purposes. To formulate policy with respect to new towns in the north, a cabinet committee and an administrative subcommittee were created. The subcommittee recommended that the Department of Planning and Development should be given the responsiblity of locating, surveying, and designing all future towns in Northern Ontario. It was on this basis that the Community Planning Branch began to plan the Manitouwadge townsite in the fall of 1954, with $600,000 from the government.

Following the location of the townsite, an improvement district was formed which covered twelve square miles and included the mining properties. Some 1,600 acres were given to the municipality. The plan contained many of the design features already incorporated at Terrace Bay; as well, the neighbourhood concept was developed further, with each of the residential areas having its own centre, consisting of a local shopping area and school and church sites. These neighbourhood centres were all grouped around a commercial core. Attempts were made to preserve and to integrate as much of the natural beauty as possible. The appearance of the townsite was controlled by a zoning bylaw which made it obligatory for houses to be varied in external design and colour while conforming to a staggered system of setbacks from street lot lines; also, a unified architectural scheme for the town centre was introduced. An additional feature linked to the town centre was the separation of pedestrian from automobile traffic (Figure 11).

The concept of a preplanned community under government supervision and administered as an improvement district was also adopted at Elliot Lake following the discovery of uranium in 1953.[87] In 1954, twelve planners associated with the Community Planning Branch of the Department of Municipal Affairs were assigned the task of implementing Elliot Lake's first planning phase. With the assistance of the consulting firm of Marshall, Macklin, and Monaghan, a townsite was selected in rugged terrain. According to Don Taylor, the director of the Community Planning Branch of the Department of Municipal Affairs, the site selection process reflected a compromise between two broad locational pressures.[88] While planners were concerned that a southern location on or near Highway 17 would give rise to development pressures at the various minesites, it was also felt that a townsite situated close to the mines would lose the high accessibility afforded by the TransCanada Highway. The province decided in favour of an area of some 5,000 acres situated to the east and south of existing Elliot "Lake" and thirty kilometres north of the highway. This decision to locate the townsite in the interior effectively guaranteed the community a continued form of single-sector status. The selection of the townsite was followed in 1955 by the creation of the Improvement District of Elliot Lake, encompassing 396 square miles, including the mining properties. Surface rights to the land were secured through provincial legislation. The conceptual plan was completed in 1956; it originally included provisions for the construction of two subtowns to be known as the eastern and western townsites. Only the former, however, was actually built. The plan relied heavily upon the neighbourhood principles used at Terrace Bay, Don Mills, Kitimat, and Manitouwadge. As was the case at Terrace Bay and Manitouwadge, the residential areas were based on the idea of a heterogeneous mixing of the population. To offset a company town atmosphere, the houses erected by the mining companies were offered for sale to employees on a buy-back basis. A major design feature was the location of an automobile-oriented town centre on the eastern periphery of the townsite and adjacent to Highway 108, which served to connect the minesites directly to Highway 17 further south (Figure 12).

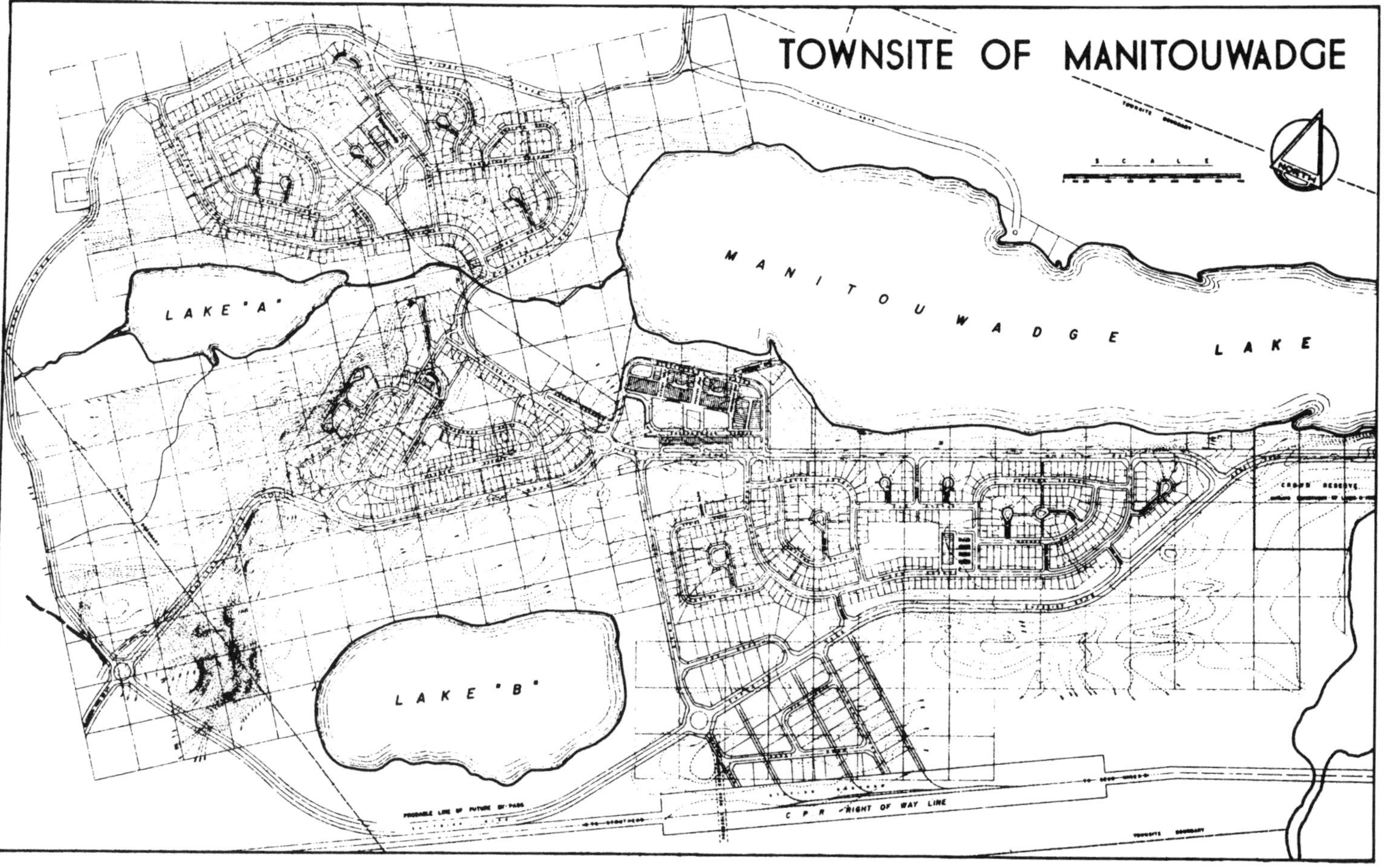

Fig. 11: Townsite plan for Manitouwadge, Ontario (source: *Township of Manitouwadge*).

Fig. 12: Aerial photograph of Townsite No. 1 for Elliott Lake, Ontario (source: *Ontario Ministry of Natural Resources).*

Construction of the townsite began in 1956; by 1959 the first planning phase had been essentially completed. It was at this point that Elliot Lake acquired its peak population of approximately 25,000. The construction of the townsite within this three-year span was a remarkable technological achievement; unfortunately, the same cannot be said of the attempt by the government to create a comprehensively-planned community. Virtually all of the professional planning assessment of the first phase was negative. The noted planner, Norman Pearson, was the sharpest critic; he viewed Elliot Lake simply as a typical southern Ontario subdivision transplanted into the north and lacking many of the distinctive features common to European new towns of the same period. Another planner, Anthony Adamson, went so far as to call Elliot Lake a form of ''miserable little suburbia.'' To others, the curvilinear pattern was confusing and illustrated a can-of-worms layout. When questioned recently by the author regarding the layout of the community, Taylor acknowledged the lack of any innovative concepts aside from the introduction of a parking-oriented town centre.[89] In many respects, the Elliot Lake plan reflected an underlying subservience to the automobile; only recently have neighbourhood shopping facilities been introduced, and even today the original townsite lacks bus service. Concern for social and environmental planning was minimal. As late as 1979, the local newspaper was still able to make the comment that for entertainment ''there were only four things to do in Elliot Lake—watch a stripper, watch a stripper, watch a stripper, or go to the Lake Theatre.''[90] With respect to environmental planning, Joan Kurisko asked in her novel, ''How could anyone have faith any more when the sewage disposal plant in a model town was located upstream of the water supply?''[91] It is clear that the first planning phase for Elliot Lake marked a major attempt that fell far short of the full potential offered by previous Canadian and international experience.

Elliot Lake's first boom phase was brought to an abrupt end in 1959 when the Atomic Energy Commission of the United States announced that there would be no further stockpiling of uranium beyond 1963. The decision had a profound negative effect upon the local economy; as the community lacked alternative forms of employment, the inevitable result was a bust period which lasted until the turn of the 1970's. It was also during this period that the municipality finally acquired township status. While some economic growth took place in the early years of the 1970's, the process of full recovery was not set into motion until 1977–78, when Ontario Hydro signed major contracts with Denison Mines and Rio Algom. The contracts, the largest uranium transactions ever negotiated, brought forward the need for a second planning phase. This second phase proved to be lengthier and more complex than originally envisaged, largely because of disputes regarding financial accountability and the need to resolve environmental concerns. Despite the fact that it was known as early as the turn of the decade that the uranium industry would soon be greatly expanded, nobody came forward to accept full responsibility for the associated urban planning process. The township took the position that the taxpayers should not be forced to pay for townsite expansion costs, especially in light of the costs it had assumed during the 1960 bust period. The province claimed that the onus for housing construction resided with the companies, since they were the ones for whom the housing was primarily intended. In turn, the mining companies felt that considerable financial assistance had to come from the two senior levels of government. In the meantime, the housing problem in Elliot Lake had become one of a housing shortage. It was 1975 before any action was undertaken to resolve the housing issue. In this year, the first construction of new housing since the late 1950's began. The consulting firm of Marshall, Macklin, and Monaghan was hired to proceed with a search for a second townsite. A decision was reached quickly to locate the new townsite immediately south of the existing community. A plan for Townsite No.2 was given tentative approval by the government in 1977. The continued affirmation by the province that planning was a local responsibility did little to clear the uncertainty which clouded the financing of the townsite. The uncertainty did not begin to clarify itself until Ontario Hydro agreed near the end of 1980 that it would provide the sum of $20 million for the development of the townsite and the design of the sewer and water treatment plants. The financing was formally agreed upon in the form of a municipal by-law which charged the town with the responsibility for assuming three-quarters of the costs of erecting the sewage and water treatment plants in return for the conveyance of land in the first two neighbourhoods in Townsite No. 2 to the two mining companies for residential construction purposes. It is clear, therefore, that while the planning process had been officially vested in the municipality, the development of the new townsite fell under the control of the two uranium companies. In effect, the establishment of Townsite No.2 marked a return of the company town to Northern Ontario. For example, in 1981 some 3,000 of the 5,000 dwelling units (60 per cent) in the town were owned by the two mining companies. The companies, of course, did not hesitate to take advantage of this new reality as evidenced by the "special considerations" given to them in the form of preferential building permits.

While the above-mentioned financial disputes were taking place, the planning process became engulfed in the environmental hearings conducted by the Environmental Assessment Board of Ontario (A.E.B.) between 1976 and 1979. The hearings were held to determine whether or not expansion of the uranium industry at Elliot Lake could be done in an environmentally acceptable manner; the fact that expansion was already taking place was of little consequence. The link between urban and environmental planning was brought to a quick head by news that some of the existing residential areas in Elliot Lake were experiencing radon gas problems. The A.E.B. responded to this news by refusing to allow any further urban development in the town until the issue was resolved. As well, the Ministry of Housing was directed to study the feasibility of locating the expanded labour force along Highway 17 rather than in the immediate Elliot Lake vicinity. The study came out in favour of retaining growth at Elliot Lake, provided that the radon gas problem could be solved. Special measures were implemented to reduce the problem to acceptable levels, thus permitting occupation in the new residential areas situated in the original townsite. In its final report of 1979, the A.E.B. gave its approval to the expansion of uranium production and concluded that the planning process was proceeding in an acceptable manner.[92] At the same time, however, the A.E.B. expressed a number of strong reservations. For instance, it concluded that housing and population projections were exaggerated in order to exert pressure on the town and the province to expedite housing and related services. The board also concluded that there was a serious lack of planning provisions for the non-mining sector. Criticism was expressed about the serious lack of social planning. Nevertheless, in the latter part of 1979, the province gave its approval to the community planning process.

Construction of Townsite No. 2 began early in 1981, and by the end of the year homes in the first neighbourhood were ready to live in (Figure 13). By 1982, work was actively taking place on the completion of the second neighbourhood. The development to date, unfortunately, appears to be a virtual replica of the undistinguished planning which occurred in the 1950's. According to one official from the consulting firm of Marshall, Macklin, and Monaghan, this duplication can be attributed directly to officials from the two mining companies who thought that the new townsite should be similar in appearance to the original one. This was done despite attempts on the part of the consulting planners to encourage visits by mining officials to model single-sector communities such as Leaf Rapids in Manitoba or Fermont in Quebec, where distinctive planning concepts had been implemented. Instead, the mining officials opted for visits to some of the newer southern Ontario residential developments. As was the case in the 1950's, it appears as though the second planning phase at Elliot Lake marks the loss of yet another golden opportunity to develop a truly distinctive northern community. In this connection the words of A.E.B. are revealing:

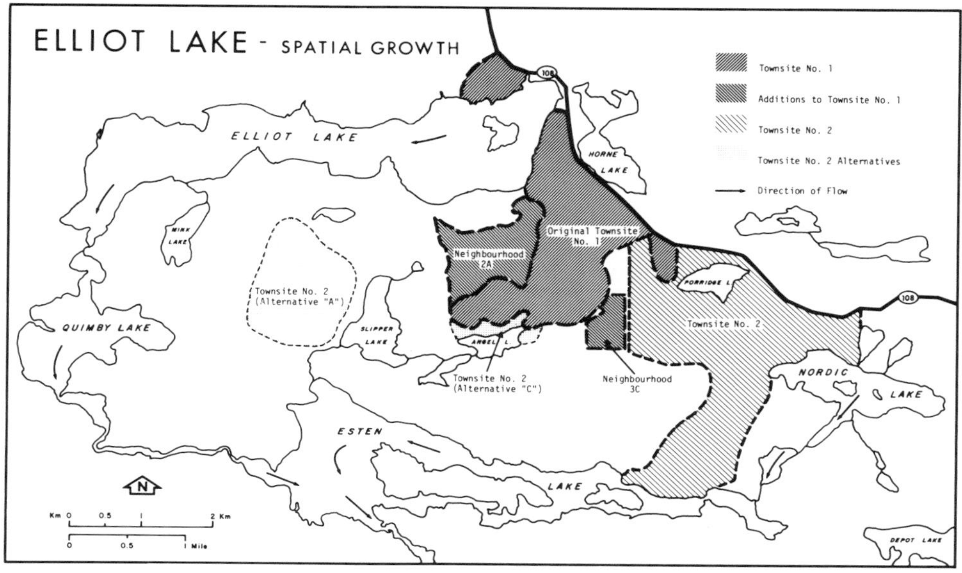

Fig. 13: Spatial growth of Elliott Lake, Ontario.

> The future expansion of Elliot Lake should have provided a rare opportunity to take an imaginative approach towards the physical and social environment. The Town and its planners, in the Board's opinion, by physical infrastructure but also social needs, goals and objectives for the people, have only partially expressed what the community of Elliot Lake *should* be like in the future.[93]

Perhaps the most interesting experiment with respect to comprehensive planning in single-sector communities during the past two decades has taken place in the railway centre of Hornepayne, situated in the township of Wicksteed. Hornepayne is a C.N.R. divisional point on the transcontinental line, midway between Winnipeg and Montreal, and has a population of around 1,800. The only other form of local employment involves timber cutting in the outlying areas. Until recently, the C.N.R. had experienced major problems related to a high turnover of its staff. This turnover was caused by the fact that Hornepayne had very poor facilities for housing, with the local Y.M.C.A. providing the main source of accommodation. As other community facilities were lacking, the townsite could be said to be "sociologically bankrupt." The C.N.R., in an attempt to overcome its employee-related problems, approached Hallmark Hotels Ltd. in the middle 1970's. Hallmark was a small company that previously constructed small lodges and hostels for the C.N.R. along its railway lines. The company president, E. L. Balmer, soon conceived of a project which he felt would be the basis for a new lifestyle for Hornepayne residents and, at the same time, would reduce many of the labour problems being experienced by the C.N.R. According to Balmer, his proposal for a new town centre evolved out of the spirit of the Toronto reform movement of the early 1970's as well as from his personal interest in "domed city" ideas.[94] The proposal was drafted in 1975 and it received the endorsment of the C.N.R. Owing to its radical nature, the uniqueness of the legal arrangements, and the high degree of cooperation required between the private and public sectors, it took three years to finalize the project. It was at this time that the Hornepayne project was compared to that which was being implemented at Leaf Rapids in Manitoba under government sponsorship. A visit to the Manitoba town served to reinforce much of the basic concept; as well, it confirmed Balmer's contention that certain facilities such as curling rinks and movie theatres were not financially viable options for such a small settlement. Balmer also left Leaf Rapids convinced of the need for intimate and relaxed surroundings in any town centre project.

The project, known as the Hallmark Hornepayne Centre, took two years to construct and was partially opened around the turn of 1980–81. Due to the unsettled state of the economy, the centre is not yet fully occupied. The project consists of one huge building serving as a complete community under one roof. The building contains both the Centre Inn and the Town Centre. The Centre Inn includes a thirty-five room hotel along with restaurants and bars. The Town Centre Inn includes a shopping mall, medical centre, social services centre, dental clinic, high school, municipal-high school library, indoor swimming pool, gymnasium, Ontario Provincial Police headquarters, sixteen senior citizen apartments, twenty regular apartments, and 112 residential units for C.N.R. employees. The building has been framed with both utilitarian and aesthetic considerations in mind. The efficiency principle has been expressed through the concepts of clustering, integration, and shared space. The idea of clustering was used to provide the community with a functional and highly visible form of urban presence, one which contrasted sharply with the rest of the townsite. Through integration, it has become possible to provide both visitors and residents with multiple attractions on a day and night basis. Great care has been taken by means of architectural design to enhance the internal and external visual setting. The shared space concept has been extensively used to increase utilization of facilities and to reduce operational costs. For example, the first floor of the library serves as a municipal facility during the daytime hours while the second floor serves as a school library during the evenings, in like manner both the gymnasium and swimming pools serve as municipal and educational resources. Thus, it has been possible for the centre to derive much of its revenue on the basis of rental charges shared by more than one body. The cost of the project has been estimated to be in the order of 13 million dollars.

The impact of the Hornepayne Centre was both immediate and positive.[95] For adult residents, the building offers a new life style which has proven to be especially attractive during the long winter months. Visitors now prefer to stay at Hornepayne overnight rather than to drive in from elsewhere. For high school students, the project has provided them with a small but well-equipped educational facility; as well, it has offered them opportunities for apprenticeship programmes and parttime employment. For senior citizens the facility offers easy access to municipal and commercial services. The C.N.R. is likewise pleased, as the centre has reduced turnover and minimized the need for isolation pay. Overall, the Hornepayne experiment is significant in that it offers a fresh approach to the construction of new or expanded single-sector communities. Equally important, it suggests that the cooperative partnership approach, involving corporate commitment, government assistance, and private developers, may provide a satisfactory entrepreneurial framework for the promotion of improved living and working conditions for Northern Ontario communities.

SUMMARY AND ASSESSMENT

When examined from an historical perspective, attempts to create planned single-sector communities in Northern Ontario have passed through several stages. Beginning as unplanned communities in the 1880's, these settlements later moved on to the additive stage, characterized by a simple level of spatial order within a gridiron system which featured rectangular streets and parallel lots. The imprint of the surveyor was strong during this formative planning era. After the First World War, it became clear that the single-sector community was to remain as a permanent phenomenon of the northern resource frontier. For a variety of reasons, including the isolation brought about by northern size-distance factors, the general lack of a complementary agricultural base, and the presence of a weakly-developed urban network, the need arose for better-planned communities that could operate as independent and self-contained urban units. Such an approach was also required in order to attract qualified labour. As the majority of single-sector communities were adjuncts to corporate balance sheets, the planning process proceeded within a utilitarian framework. Thus compactness and the efficient delivery of basic services rapidly became the norm. Many of the communities also acquired aesthetic and land use features derived from the city beautiful and garden city planning traditions. Iroquois Falls and Kapuskasing served as examples of the new planning style. Built in holistic fashion, they reflected the presence of several planning innovations, including the use of zoning, a greater variety in street patterns, more attention to recreational and open space, the civic square, a more attractive "cottage" type of development for residential areas, and the greenbelt principle. The basic elements of the company town, with its emphasis on company home ownership and internal and external forms of social stratification and segregation, were similarly set into motion, especially at Iroquois Falls. Owing to the involvement of the provincial government, Kapuskasing never did evolve into a full-fledged company town. These two communities served only as partial models for the single-sector communities built during the interwar period. While many of the larger single-sector communities such as Sudbury or Timmins continued to reflect the additive tradition, smaller company towns such as Copper Cliff and Falconbridge acquired a form of "engineering functionalism" which resulted in the formation of neat and compact environments with little to distinguish them from typical southern Ontario suburbs.

Comprehensive planning did not begin to emerge until after the Second World War; it made its initial appearance at Terrace Bay. Relying upon American planning philosophy, the planner E. G. Faludi promoted the concept of the neighbourhood and the open town centre. Steps were taken to remove many of the company town elements associated with the traditional single-sector community. These precendents were subsequently refined by government planners at Manitouwadge and at Elliot Lake during the 1950's. In the 1970's, comprehensive planning at Elliot Lake was continued in much the same fashion as previously, with the exception that planning was officially vested with the municipality rather than with the province. In practice, however, real control remained in the hands of the uranium companies. Thus Elliot Lake gradually came to acquire some of the company town characteristics that prevailed during the interwar era. During the middle and late 1970's, comprehensive planning took a major step forward with the introduction of the closed town centre concept at Hornepayne, under an innovative cooperative setting involving a remarkable blend of public and private enterprise. In contrast to the Elliot Lake example, the Hornepayne project holds considerable promise for the development of new townsites as well as for redevelopment of existing single-sector communities.

NOTES

1. See Gilbert A. Stelter and Alan F. J. Artibise, "Canadian Resource Towns in Historical Perspective," in Gilbert A. Stelter and Alan F. J. Artibise, eds., *Shaping the Urban Landscape: Aspects of the Canadian City Building Process* (Ottawa: Carleton University Pres, 1982), pp. 413–44; Institute of Local Government, Queen's University, *Single-Enterprise Communities in Canada* (Kingston: Queen's University, 1953); James A. Allen, *The Company Town in the American West* (Norman: University of Oklahoma Press, 1966); Rex Lucas, *Minetown, Milltown, Railtown: Life in Canadian Communities of Single Industry* (Toronto: University of Toronto Press, 1971); and Department of Regional Economic Expansion, Government of Canada, *Single-Sector Communities* (Ottawa, 1979).
2. See Arnold R. Alanen, "The 'Locations': Company Communities on Minnesota's Iron Ranges," *Minnesota History* 48, no. 3 (Fall, 1982): 94–107; John S. Garner, "The Architecture and Environment of the Model Company Town in New England," paper presented at the Canada-American Urban Development Conference held at the University of Guelph, 1982; and O. W. Saarinen, "Provincial Land Use Planning Initiatives in the Town of Kapuskasing," *Urban History Review* 10, no. 1 (June, 1981): 1–16.
3. See Royal Commission on Corporate Concentration, *The Social Characteristics of One-Industry Towns in Canada*, (Ottawa: Queen's Printer, 1977); and Stanley Buder, *Pullman: An Experiment in Industrial Order and Community Planning 1880–1930* (Toronto: Oxford University Press, 1967).
4. Department of Regional Economic Expansion, *Single-Sector Communities*, p. 1.
5. J. W. Watson, "Geography—A Discipline in Distance," *Scottish Geographical Magazine* 71, no. 1 (1955): 1–13.
6. See L. D. McCann, "Canadian Resource Towns: A Heartland-Hinterland Perspective," in Richard E. Preston and Lorne H. Russworm, eds., *Essays on Canadian Urban Process and Form II* (Waterloo: University of Waterloo, 1980), pp. 213–66; and John H. Bradbury, "Towards an Alternative Theory of Resource-Based Town Development in Canada," *Economic Geography* 55, no. 2 (1979): 147–66.
7. H. V. Nelles, *The Politics of Development: Forests, Mines & Hydro-Electric Power in Ontario, 1849-1941* (Toronto: Macmillan, 1975), p. 117.
8. A summary of the historical development of the C.P.R. is found in Pierre Berton, *The National Dream* and *The Last Spike* (Toronto: McClelland and Stewart, 1971, 1974); W. Kaye Lamb, *History of the Canadian Pacific Railway* (New York: Macmillan 1977); and Harold A. Innis, *A History of the Canadian Pacific Railway* (Toronto: University of Toronto Press, 1971).
9. This information on the C.N.R. has been derived from A. W. Currie, *The Grand Trunk Railway of Canada* (Toronto: University of Toronto Press, 1957); T. D. Regehr, *The Canadian Northern Railway: Pioneer Road of the Northern Prairies, 1895–1918* (Toronto: Macmillan, 1976); G. R. Stevens,

vols.1 and 2, (Toronto: Clarke, Irwin & Company, 1960–62); and G. R. Stevens, *History of the Canadian National Railways* (New York: Macmillan 1973).

10. Evolution of the Algoma Central Railway is traced in J. Konarek, "Algoma Central and Hudson Bay Railway: The Beginnings," *Ontario History* 62 (June, 1970): 73–81; and O. S. Nock, *Algoma Central Railway* (Sault Ste. Marie: Algoma Central Railway, 1975).
11. For a review of the history of the Ontario Northland Railway, refer to Albert Tucker, *Steam Into Wilderness: Ontario Northland Railway, 1902–1962* (Toronto: Fitzhenry & Whiteside, 1978).
12. The importance of the metropolitan hegemony of Toronto with respect to the Sudbury Basin is outlined in Gilbert A. Stelter, "Community Development in Toronto's Commercial Empire," *Laurentian University Review* 6, no. 3, (1974): 4–53.
13. See Nelles, *The Politics of Development*, and Ontario Hydro, *Gifts of Nature* (Toronto: Ontario Hydro, 1979), pp. 18–40.
14. Aspects of the forest industry in Northern Ontario are covered in Ontario Ministry of Natural Resources, *The Forest Industry in the Economy of Ontario* (Toronto: Ministry of Natural Resources, 1981); and R. S. Lambert, *Renewing Nature's Wealth: A Centennial History* (Toronto: Queen's Printer, 1967); and Nelles, *The Politics of Development*.
15. The mining history of Northern Ontario is reviewed in L. Carson Brown, *Ontario's Mining Heritage* (Toronto: Ontario Department of Mines, 1967); and John Carrington, *Risk Taking in Canadian Mining* (Toronto: Pitt Publishing Company, n.d.).
16. This distribution is noted in Ontario Economic Council, *Northern Ontario Development: Issues and Alternatives 1976* (Toronto: Ontario Economic Council, 1976), p. 3.
17. Department of Regional Economic Expansion, *Single Sector Communities*, pp. 69–71.
18. See D. Michael Ray, ed., *Canadian Urban Trends: National Perspective*, vol.1 (Toronto: Copp Clark, 1976), p. 100.
19. Ibid., 96, 98.
20. These urban characteristics are discussed in Michel Boisvert, *The Correspondence between the Urban System and the Economic Base of Canada's Regions* (Ottawa: Economic Council, 1978), p. 7; L. S. Bourne and G. Gad, "Urbanization and Urban Growth in Ontario and Quebec: An Overview," in L. S. Bourne and R. D. Mackinnon, eds., *Urban Systems Development in Central Canada* (Toronto: University of Toronto Press, 1972), p.23; and Government of Ontario, *Statistical Profiles of Northeastern and Northwestern Ontario Regions* (Toronto: Ministry of Treasury and Economics, 1979).
21. Statistics Canada, *1981 Census*, Population: Geographical Distributions.
22. Statistics Canada, *Poles and Zones of Attraction*, by Francoise Ricour-Singh, (Ottawa: Statistics Canada, 1979), p. 44 and conclusion.

23. Institute of Local Government, *Single-Enterprise Communities in Canada*.
24. Gilbert A. Stelter and Alan F. J. Artibise, "Canadian Resource Towns in Historical Perspective," *Plan Canada* 18, no. 1 (1978): 8.
25. See, for example, Mick Lowe, "Why Inco Must be Nationalized," *Maclean's* 19 July, 1982, p. 7.
26. G. R. Weller, "Hinterland Politics: The Case of Northwestern Ontario," paper presented at the 1976 Annual Meeting of the Canadian Political Science Association held at Laval University, Quebec City, p. 6.
27. Derek Hum and Paul Phillips, "Growth, Trade and Urban Development of Staple Regions," *Urban History Review* 10, no.2, (1981): 13–24.
28. Gilbert A. Stelter, "Community Development in Toronto's Commercial Empire," p. 4.
29. "Paying the Price of Hydro Excesses," *Toronto Star*, Saturday, 24 July, 1982, p. B5.
30. Statistics Canada, *Poles and Zones of Attraction*, p. 44. Refer also to Boisvert, *Correspondence Between the Urban System and the Economic Base*, pp. 164 and 166.
31. See Boisvert, *Correspondence Between the Urban System and the Economic Base*, pp. 110 and 135; and Wallace Clement, *Hardrock Mining: Industrial Relations and Technological Changes at Inco* (Toronto: McClelland & Stewart, 1981), pp. 70–93.
32. McCann, "Canadian Resource Towns," p. 235.
33. Arnold A. Alanen, "The Planning of Company Communities in the Lake Superior Mining Region," *Journal of the American Planning Association* 45, no. 3, (1979): 258–59.
34. Alanen, "The Locations," p. 97.
35. Douglas Baldwin, "The Development of an Unplanned Community: Cobalt, 1903–1914," *Plan Canada* 18, no. 1 (1978): 17–29.
36. Stelter, "Community Development in Toronto's Commercial Empire," pp. 8–9.
37. Gilbert A. Stelter, "The Origins of a Company Town: Sudbury in the Nineteenth Century," *Laurentian University Review* 3, no. 3, (1979): 8–9; and E. Barr and B. Dyck, *Ignace: A Saga of the Shield*, (Winnipeg: Prairie Publishing Company, 1979), p. 33.
38. Michael Barnes, *Cochrane: The Polar Bear Town* (Cobalt: Highway Book Shop, 1976), p. 4.
39. George Wice, *Carved from the Wilderness: The Intriguing Story of Dryden* (Dryden, n.p., n.d.), p. 16.
40. Association of Ontario Land Surveyors, *Biographies, Gordon Foster Summers*, (Toronto: Association of Ontario Land Surveyors, 1955), pp. 135–36; and S. A. Pain, *Three Miles of Gold: The Story of Kirkland Lake* (Toronto, Ryerson Press, 1969), pp. 45–46 and 56–58.
41. Eileen Goltz, "Espanola: The History of a Pulp and Paper Town," *Laurentian University Review* 6, no. 3 (1974): 83, 91.

42. H. T. Routley, "The Development of Townsites in New Ontario," in *Annual Report no. 37 of the Association of Ontario Land Surveyors* (Toronto, 1922), p. 173.
43. Walter Van Nus, "The Plan Makers and the City Architects, Engineers, Surveyors and Urban Planning in Canada 1890–1939," (Ph.D. Diss., University of Toronto, 1975), p. 91.
44. Agnes Turcott, *Land of the Big Goose: A History of Wawa and the Michipicoten Area* (Dryden: Alex Wilson Publications, n.d.), p. 70.
45. Thomas I. Gunton, "The Ideas and Policies of the Canadian Planning Profession, 1909–1931," in Alan F. J. Artibise and Gilbert A. Stelter, eds., *The Usable Urban Past: Planning and Politics in the Modern Canadian City* (Toronto: Macmillan 1979), pp. 180-82; and P. J. Smith, "The Principle of Utility and the Origins of Planning Legislation in Alberta 1912–1975," ibid., p. 202.
46. Tucker, *Steam into Wilderness*, pp. 54–70.
47. Routley, "Development of Townsites," pp. 168–70.
48. Michael Barnes, *Gold in the Porcupine* (Cobalt: Highway Book Shop, 1975), p. 45.
49. S. D. Clark, "The Position of the French-Speaking Population in the Northern Industrial Community," in Richard J. Ossenberg, ed., *Canadian Society: Pluralism, Change, and Conflict* (Toronto: Prentice-Hall, 1971), p. 65.
50. J. S. Garner, "Architecture and Environment."
51. "The Founder," *The Enterprise*, Iroquois Falls, November 1972, p. 13.
52. "Mr. Anson's Greatest Monument," *The Broke Hustler*, November 1923, and "Planning the Town of Iroquois Falls," *The Contract Record*, 28 June, 1916, p. 636.
53. See Oiva Saarinen, "The Influence of Thomas Adams and the British New Towns Movement in the Planning of Canadian Resource Communities," in Alan F. J. Artibise and Gilbert A. Stelter, eds., *The Usable Urban Past: Planning and Politics in the Modern Canadian City* (Toronto: Macmillan, 1979), pp. 275–76.
54. "Planning the Town of Iroquois Falls," p. 636.
55. Hortus, "One House: One Garden," *The Broke Hustler*, 1 May, 1920, p. 8.
56. "Touch of Magic Wand Turned Ugly Mud into this Beautiful Town," *The Broke Hustler*, 12 June, 1928, p. 1; and "Premier Drury and Colleagues Visit Iroquois Falls," *The Broke Hustler*, 13 December, 1919, pp. 1–2.
57. J. P. Mertz, "Townsite Planning at Pine Falls, Man.," *The Canadian Engineer*, 2 July, 1929, pp. 109–10.
58. L. R. Wilson, *A Few High Spots in the Life of L. R. Wilson* (Iroquois Falls: n.p., n.d.), p. 27.
59. "Housing and Taxes Discussed at Length by Town Council," *The Broke Hustler*, 6 December, 1921, p. 3.
60. Wilson, *A Few High Spots*, p. 27.
61. "The Wonder Town of the North Land," *The Broke Hustler*, 2 October, 1920, p. 2.

62. Institute of Local Government, *Single-Enterprise Communities*, p. 297.
63. For a more detailed treatment of the planning at Kapuskasing refer to O. W. Saarinen, "Provincial Land use Planning Initiatives in the Town of Kapuskasing," 1–15.
64. E. C. Drury, *Farmer Premier: Memoirs of the Honourable E. C. Drury* (Toronto: McClelland & Stewart, 1966), p. 131.
65. See "Premier Drury and Colleagues Visit Iroquois Falls," pp. 1–2; and Drury, *Farmer Premier*, p. 101.
66. Bureau of Municipal Affairs, *Report Re Housing for 1921 Including Town Planning of the Town of Kapuskasing* (Toronto: King's Printer, 1922).
67. A. V. Hall, "Considerations in the Laying Out of the Town of Kapuskasing," *The Canadian Engineer*, 43, no. 7 (1922): 260.
68. "An Experiment in Town Building," *Social Welfare* (December 1922): 56.
69. See Saarinen, "The Influence of Thomas Adams," p. 286.
70. Kapuskasing File, Memorandum by J. A. Ellis re Town of Kapuskasing Bill, Bureau of Municipal Affairs, Archives of Ontario.
71. These principles of city beautiful thought have been derived from Walter Van Nus, "The Fate of City Beautiful Though in Canada, 1893–1930," in Gilbert A. Stelter and Alan F. J. Artibise, eds., *The Canadian City: Essays in Urban History*, (Toronto: McClelland and Stewart, 1977), pp. 162–85.
72. The intent of the province to reduce speculation is revealed in Drury Papers: General Correspondence re Kapuskasing Townsite, Letter from Hon. E. C. Drury to Mr. Douglass, 7 January, 1921, Archives of Ontario.
73. Clark, "The Position of the French-Speaking Population," p. 68.
74. Saarinen, "Provincial Land Use Planning Initiatives in the Town of Kapuskasing," pp. 9–14.
75. Walter Van Nus, "Towards the City Efficient: The Theory and Practice of Zoning, 1919–1939," in Stelter and Artibise, *The Usable Urban Past*, p. 227.
76. Some of the following summary has been obtained from Stelter, "Community Development in Toronto's Commercial Empire," pp. 3–53.
77. Trent Black, et al., *Nickel Centre Yesterdays* (Nickel Centre: Northern Heritage Nickel Centre, 1976), p. 56.
78. J. A. Walker, "Planning of Company Towns in Canada," *The Canadian Engineer*, 19 July, 1927, p. 147.
79. Donald Davis, *The Price of Conspicuous Consumption: The Detroit Elite and the Automobile Experience*, paper presented at the Canadian-American Urban Development Conference held at Guelph in 1982.
80. Institute of Local Government, *Single-Enterprise Communities*, pp. 47–70.
81. E. G. Faludi, "Planning New Canadian Communities," *American Institute of Planners*, 16, no. 3 (1950): 143–47; and Faludi, "Plans for Eight Communities," *Journal of the Royal Architectural Institute of Canada*, 23, no. 11 (1946): 290–92.
82. Kimberly-Clark Pulp and Paper Company, *Terrace Bay: Scenic Centre of the North Shore* (Terrace Bay: Kimberly-Clark Pulp and Paper Company, n.d., n.p.).

83. Institute of Local Government, *Single-Enterprise Communities*, p. 82.
84. See Clarence Perry, *Housing for the Machine Age* (New York: Russell Sage Foundation, 1939); and C. S. Stein, *Toward New Towns for America* (Cambridge, MA: MIT Press, 1966).
85. Aspects of the Manitouwadge project are dealt with in L. Carson Brown, *Manitouwadge: Cave of the Great Spirit* (Toronto: Ontario Department of Mines, 1963), pp. 5–15.
86. F.H.D., ''Manitouwadge: A New Ontario Mining Community,'' *Ontario Planning Supplement* 4, no. 2 (1957): 1–10.
87. The following is largely a summary of O. W. Saarinen, *Elliot Lake: A Geographic-Planning Perspective of a Planned Resource Community*, paper presented at the Annual Meeting of the Canadian Association of Geographers held at the University of Ottawa, Ottawa, 1982.
88. Don Taylor, interview with author, 12 May, 1980.
89. Ibid.
90. ''Entertainment,'' *The Standard*, Wednesday, 4 April, 1979, p. 4.
91. Joan Kurisko, *Interlude: The Story of Elliot Lake* (Cobalt: Highway Book Shop, 1977), pp. 234–41.
92. Environmental Assessment Board, *The Expansion of Uranium Mines in the Elliot Lake Area: Final Report* (Toronto: Queen's Printer, 1979).
93. Ibid., p. 70.
94. E. L. Balmer, interview with author, 6 July, 1982. Some of the observations in the paper are based upon a visit to Hornepayne in June 1982.
95. Stephen Miko, Manager of the Centre Inn, and other Hornepayne residents, interviews with author, June 1982. For additional comments, refer to ''$13.3 Million Town Centre Opens in Hornepayne,'' *The Globe and Mail*, Friday, 15 October, 1982, p. B5.

SECTION IV

LOCAL GOVERNMENT

Introduction

The central thesis of this volume—that state and political power have a tangible effect on urban growth patterns—cannot be adequately explored without direct reference to local government. It is essential, however, to begin this examination with a brief review of the context of intergovernmental relationships in Canada. Control of urban communities—in a constitutional and legal sense—resides in the provinces. Municipalities are creations of the provinces and thus are subordinate to them. This is in sharp contrast to the division and powers between the federal government and the provinces, a relationship that in many areas gives provinces exclusive jurisdiction over certain matters. Municipalities, however, are entirely controlled by the provinces, and Canada's cities, towns, and villages have no formal constitutional rights. This fact contributes to a wide variety of municipal-provincial relationships, with variations from province to province. Moreover, even within provinces, all municipalities are not dealt with consistently; many major metropolitan centres have special relationships in the form of distinct city charters, while most smaller urban centres are generally controlled by one piece of municipal legislation. Adding to this complexity is the federal role in urban affairs, which has fluctuated greatly, especially since 1945 when Ottawa created two federal agencies to help formulate and implement urban policy—the Central (now Canada) Mortgage and Housing Corporation (C.M.H.C., 1946) and the Ministry of State for Urban Affairs (created in 1971 and disbanded in 1979).

Unfortunately, there is a paucity of historical material on the subject of local government. Certainly there has been little research interest in this area by Canadian urban historians, while political scientists and scholars of government have tended to emphasize federal-provincial relationships and contemporary issues. When they do study either provincial-municipal relations or municipal government itself, researchers usually concentrate on the post-1945 period.[1] There are several studies of municipal government (all of which include some mention of federal-provincial-municipal relationships), but because of a lack of detailed historical research, most of these surveys fail to provide convincing chronological or thematic frameworks or compelling hypotheses.[2] In contrast, this broad field is far more developed in the United States.[3]

In terms of more specific themes, the role of the federal government in urban affairs has received some attention, both in a general sense[4] and in terms of specific topics such as studies of the role of C.M.H.C., the Ministry of State for Urban Affairs, and the question of municipal finance and the provincial-federal relationship.[5] Municipal-provincial relations have received a good deal more attention, and there are numerous studies of the policies and problems of this evolving relationship. While the bulk of the material deals with Ontario, there are good studies of provincial-municipal relationships in Quebec, the Maritimes and Alberta.[6] As well, there is at least one overview of this important theme.[7]

In this section, three aspects of intergovernmental relationships are examined. In a pioneering work, John H. Taylor provides a chronology of the evolution and decline of municipal autonomy from the early 1800's through to the present. Taylor argues that municipal autonomy has evolved through several phases until, by the 1970's, municipalities had little room to maneuvre. Much of the local authority was by this time either dispersed among an array of independent boards, commissions and agencies, or powers formerly exercised by municipalities were taken over or assumed by senior levels of government. In either case, municipalities were increasingly incapable of vigorous policy making.

While the story of Canadian municipal autonomy has some similarities to the experience in the United States, the work of American historian Jon C. Teaford indicates that there are important distinctions. While both countries experienced an overall trend toward centralization, the move was less pronounced in the U.S. In that country, the ideal of local autonomy remained more powerful, and centralization proceeded at a more hesitant, uneven pace.[8]

Another theme examined in this section is metropolitan government. There are numerous studies of regional and/or metropolitan government–focusing on a tier of government that comes between municipalities and provinces—because metropolitan forms of government are common.[9] What is unique about P. H. Wichern's paper is his context: he examines the historical nature of metropolitan reform and the organization of local governments in a comparative, North American setting. He argues that the evolving political economy of urban development emphasized competition between local areas and regions for growth industries and development of space for maximum financial returns. This conflict created metropolis-hinterland disparities as well and exacerbated the negative aspects of urban life. In response, North Americans turned to "metropolitan reform" and local government reorganization, based on the analysis that fragmented local government was the primary hindrance to solving urban problems and managing urban development. The solution posited was a unification or coordination of local governments on the metropolitan government model. Surprisingly, Wichern's evidence suggests that local government structures and metropolitan reform were not crucial components in the urban development process.

The final paper, by Michael P. McCarthy, deals with a similar topic but takes a very different viewpoint. Through his examination of the politics of suburban growth, McCarthy makes an important contribution to an almost totally ignored topic: suburbanization. There are few studies of this process in either Canada or the United States, although new research is beginning to be published.[10] In any case, McCarthy's paper suggests that there are striking parallels in terms of the so-called "consolidation movement" in both countries. Certainly this theme has great potential to increase our understanding of the political-economy of urban development; it deserves far more attention than it has received to date.

NOTES

1. Two useful bibliographic surveys are D. J. H. Higgins, "Municipal Politics and Government: Development of the Field in Canadian Political Science," *Canadian Public Administration*, 22 (1979): 380–401; and Fillippo Sabetti, "Reflections on Canadian Urban Governance Research," *Comparative Urban Research* 8 (1981): 87–112.
2. The major works are: K. G. Crawford, *Canadian Municipal Government* (Toronto, 1954); D. J. H. Higgins, *Urban Canada: Its Government and Politics* (Toronto, 1977); T. J. Plunkett, *Urban Canada and its Government: A Study of Municipal Organization* (Toronto, 1968); and C. K. Tindal and S. N. Tindal, *Local Government in Canada* (Toronto, 1979). An important collection is L. D. Feldman, ed., *Politics and Government of Urban Canada*, 4th ed. (Toronto, 1981).
3. For a succinct review of the literature, see Alan F. J. Artibise, "Exploring the North American West: A Comparative Urban Perspective," *American Review of Canadian Studies* 13 (Spring, 1984).
4. D. G. Bettison, *The Politics of Canadian Urban Development* (Edmonton, 1975); K. D. Cameron, "Municipal Government in the Intergovernmental Maze," *Canadian Public Administration* 23 (1980): 195–317; Hans Blumenfeld, "The Role of the Federal Government in Urban Affairs," *Journal of Liberal Thought* 11 (1966): 35–44; and D. C. Rowat, "The Problem of Federal-Urban Relations in Canada," *Journal of Canadian Studies* 3 (1975):

214–24. There are, as well, a number of valuable reports and studies published by the Canadian Federation of Mayors and Municipalities.

5. See for example, Robert Andras, ''Formation of the Federal Ministry of Urban Affairs,'' *Community Planning Review* 21 (1971): 4–11; C. A. Curtis and C. H. Chatters. ''Municipal Finance and Provincial-Federal Relations.'' *Canadian Journal of Economics and Political Science* 17 (1951): 297–306; and Humphrey Carver, *Compassionate Landscape* (Toronto, 1975). The latter, an autobiography, contains a great deal of excellent information on C.M.H.C.
6. See, for example, A. D. O'Brien, ''Father Knows Best: A Look at the Provincial-Municipal Relationship in Ontario,'' in D. C. MacDonald, ed., *Government and Politics of Ontario* (Toronto, 1975); G. Fraser, ''The Urban Policies of the Parti Quebecois,'' *City Magazine* 3 (July 1978) 21–31; J. R. Cameron, *Provincial-Municipal Relations in the Maritime Provinces* (Fredericton, 1970): P. G. Bettison, et al, *Urban Affairs in Alberta* (Edmonton, 1975).
7. David Siegel, ''Provincial-Municipal Relations in Canada: An Overview,'' *Canadian Public Administration* 23 (1980): 281–317.
8. Jon C. Teaford, ''The Evolution of Municipal Autonomy in the United States,'' paper presented at North American Urban History Conference, Guelph, August 1982.
9. See, for example, C. R. Tindal, *Structural Changes in Local Government: Government for Urban Regions* (Toronto, 1977).
10. In Canada see John Sewell, ''The Suburbs,'' Special Issue of *City Magazine* 2, no. 6 (1977): 19-55. In the U.S., see the article by K. Jackson, ''The Crabgrass Frontier: 150 Years of Suburban Growth in America,'' in R. A. Mohl and J. F. Richardson, eds., *The Urban Experience* (Belmont, CA, 1973). Jackson is also completing a general history of American suburbanization.

11

Urban Autonomy in Canada: Its Evolution and Decline

John H. Taylor

A study of urban autonomy addresses a number of questions central to the study of cities.[1] Perhaps first among these is the role of the city in the political economy of the nation, particularly the relationships of the city (or "state") to its elites (or "capital"). The nineteenth century city and its elites identified with each other. That is, individual fortunes were perceived to be wedded to place: the essence of boosterism. But these local elites were, depending on the place, also aspiring regional and national elites. To this extent, Canada really was Montreal writ large, as Ontario was Toronto writ large. Both the growth of individual fortunes, at a micro level, and the growth of regions and nations, at a macro level, were organically linked and perhaps even determined by the growth of cities, at the meso level. In this regard, a study of urban autonomy forces the historian to confront questions about the function of the city over time. Were cities in the nineteenth century chiefly engines of economic growth, a kind of technology to be converted into twentieth century delivery systems? Was the conversion determined by secular forces? Or did it represent a failure of local imagination and initiative?

The notion of urban autonomy can be hard to understand, especially in Canada where it has never been entrenched in either historical event or the scholarly lexicon as in the United States. It often seems to be result as well as cause. But it amounts to the belief that a place can command and develop its own resources. What might be called municipal or local autonomy, the power or right of local self-government, is an aspect of some importance in the larger definition.

A comparison of the Canadian, British and American experiences indicates that there have been similar periods when senior governments "permitted" local authorities to operate more or less autonomously. Despite a rather different "intergovernmental" tradition, Canada, the United States and Britain all followed a rather similar pattern with respect to the acquisition and loss of urban autonomy. The specific constitutional or legalistic arrangements did not seem to matter in the long term as much as the *de facto* ones. The differences between the three countries with respect to autonomy had more to do with the amount of local protest generated over its loss and the level of senior government that eventually proved the most persuasive meddler in local affairs.

Though none of the three countries granted local government constitutional autonomy, by the late eighteenth and early nineteenth centuries all three provided their major centres with the legal and financial authority and instruments to pursue their own interests and generally adopted a permissive approach to their activities. In the United States

> Nineteenth-century municipalities could not claim formal autonomy nor were they immune from sporadic partisan meddling. Systematic supervision of localities was, however, alien to state government during the period, and the federal government exercised no direct authority over the cities. The lawmaking structure was, then, permissive rather than oppressive, and local leaders enjoyed broad latitude in fashioning the framework of municipal rule.[2]

And in Britain, after the reforms of the 1830's, the central government practised only ''selective interventionism,'' largely confined to the areas of health and policing.[3]

The birth of autonomous local government in Canada has usually been traced to the events of the 1840's, in particular to the Baldwin Municipal Act of 1849 and similar legislation in Nova Scotia and Quebec. Though individual charters had been given to some cities in the Canadas and Maritimes as early as the 1830's, they were spotty and to some extent intended to broaden police powers and make possible certain acts of amelioration. The agitation, though, if not the legislation, was part of a widening effort to develop the commercial city of the day into an instrument of expansion for the commercial classes. Certain groups of merchants and retailers were attempting to use the city as a vehicle or lever to expand their own fortunes, primarily, through provision of infrastructure in the form of railways, roads, harbour improvements and the like. Typically in the period of the commercial city, most municipally-related improvements were in the area of transportation. But charters were not widespread and generally not comprehensive in their powers. Rather, such legislation seems to have been part and parcel of the great economic and political events of the 1840's that created the autonomous and national, as opposed to the dependent or imperial, commercial city in Canada.

The Baldwin Act, the act incorporating Halifax, and the scattered town and city charters of the 1830's and 1840's seem to have had two overriding objectives in common. All wished to break the centralized and oligarchic type of local government, in the form of the justices of the peace and grand jury systems, and create independent centres of local power. In that sense they wanted a political reform. And all seem, with some ambivalence, to have wanted an economic independence, one not beholden to the imperial commercial system within which they then operated. In that sense they were operating within the times and were to some extent at one with the imperial reformers, who wanted to dismantle the imperial and mercantilist system, and with the colonial reformers who were agitating for political independence in the form of responsible government.

The agitation for responsible government in Nova Scotia, for example, was at least in part directly related to the emergence of a new retail class and its desire for a charter for the city of Halifax, one that would recognize its new economic importance and would wrest some of the political control from the merchants who had political and economic roots deep in the imperial system.[4] The Baldwin Municipal Act, too, seems to have stemmed from some of the same concerns. As Whebell noted, the "principle of responsible government was a facet of [the reform], but underlying it was the deeper reality of a rising middle class struggling for a share of political power. The Municipal Corporations bill of Baldwin Act was a weapon in this struggle, especially as it demolished the magistracy as a perpetual power base for the Tories."[5] It was also the occasion for the "rising middle class" to weld their futures and fortunes to those of their towns and cities and produce the phenomenon of boosterism. In both the political and the economic sense, local communities were freed from provincial and imperial control.

The development of local autonomy also appears to have meshed neatly with the desire of men such as Francis Hincks to underwrite the financing of railway construction in the 1840's and 1850's. One of Hincks's devices was his Railway Guarantee Act of 1849. A second was to encourage municipal support of railway projects, in effect a scheme to use the property tax base to underwrite railway development. Both were more or less failures and were a prelude to direct granting of Crown land to supply collateral for railway ventures. But the desire to use the municipal "state" to support railway building necessarily implied the development of that "state."[6] Hincks thus supported the passage of the Baldwin Act, as he had supported the earlier municipal legislation of Sydenham.

In this way, the opportunity arose to make supreme in local government a business group whose focus was on development of localities, regions and, in case of metropolitan centres, a nation, and the concurrent displacement of a gentility whose fortunes were tied to imperial prerogatives. To some extent this was accomplished, at least in the case of the Baldwin Act, with a new residency qualification that was attached to the property qualification in the franchise. That too, reinforced identification with place. The property franchise, nonetheless, remained intact. Control of local governments, though in theory broadened, was in reality shifted from one elite to another. There was at no time an intent to admit popular democratic control of local governments in the nineteenth century, and such tendencies were resisted in most jurisdictions until well after the Second World War.

This pattern of local autonomy adapted easily to the industrial phase of economic development in Canada, perhaps because the British municipal model of 1835, designed for an industrial society, was used in Canada, or perhaps because the newer industrial enterprises found the new system as much to their liking as the older commercial ones. There is some indication that commercial and industrial capital found itself at odds in terms of the development of some Canadian cities. Generally, though, there seems to have been an interlocking of the commercial and industrial groups, except where one group or the other attempted monopoly control of development policy, like the successful commercial group in Saint John,[7] or the power and traction capitalists of Ontario, who were defeated by provincial intervention at the behest of urban business.[8] There was a fairly fluid transition, so far as local government went, from the commercial to the first industrial state. There were areas which, in Canada, as in the United States, privatism did not handle well: for example the social ills stemming from industrial development, health problems; matters of fiscal control, and audit. The provincial governments began to intervene in these areas in the 1880's. But the essential identification by a booster elite of its fortunes with the fortunes of its place was not seriously impaired. Local governments, controlled by a small body of men operating under a property franchise, largely raised and disposed of their own funds for their own purposes and in their own interests. Political tensions were vented by various forms of what has been called elsewhere Conventional factionalism.[9]

In general, urban centres were left free in the last part of the nineteenth century to pursue their policies of growth and physical and social amelioration. Certainly the senior governments posed few obstacles to such activities. Most statutory legislation applicable to early twentieth century localities was open-ended. There was an abundance of "may" clauses and very few "must" ones. In addition, such legislation generally was not encroached upon by other statutes that were concerned with specific problems like welfare. Finally, most senior governments were noninterventionist. Local governments were, by and large, left alone to deal with both the progress and the problems of late nineteenth and early twentieth century society and economy.

Services, such as utilities and public works, were expanded in the late nineteenth and early twentieth centuries, either by the public bodies or under their franchises.[10] Social services, especially for the indigent and the unemployed, were elaborated or expanded.[11] Efforts were made in some centres to introduce planning; in many cities elaborate schemes emerged from the drawing boards of early consultants.[12] Efforts were made to provide housing, parks, and other amenities. Local governments, for all their ad hoc activities and intermittent reluctance, did make some provision for the improvement of the conditions in which their citizens lived and did business. And, significantly, the governments acted largely out of their own pocketbooks.[13] By the late 1920's, though, many local governments were finding it difficult to sustain such efforts and were beginning to call for a readjustment among all levels of government of revenues and responsibilities, including abandonment by the federal government of the income tax field.[14]

Though local governments were left largely to their own devices in this period, the beginnings of senior government intervention in local affairs was also apparent: "avec le tournant du siècle, les interventions législatives abandonnent, en effet, leur caractère essentiellement libéral pour adopter une orientation plus impérative et plus centralisée."[15] The process of intervention was haphazard, and consequent loss of local autonomy was disorganized. The process is not entirely complete even today. It appears to have taken place in two phases: the first beginning in the nineteenth century, and the second, more significant, one about the time of the First World War.

In the first phase, beginning in Ontario about 1880 and following an American pattern, "new functions of local government were assigned to newly created boards rather than to the established municipal councils."[16] Such boards included library boards, park boards, and health boards. In addition to restricting local control over certain functions, there was also the nineteenth century phenomenon of restricting local control over certain local officials, like the medical health officer, assessor, and sanitary inspectors.[17] In certain highly sensitive areas, like policing, a buffer, usually in the form of a commission, was often placed between the politicians and the functioning department. This last scheme, in various forms, was also used to control indulgent political behavior with respect to utilities or, sometimes, private enterprise.[18] Finally, there was the creation of bodies to provide a service to an aggregation of municipalities; such bodies generally had a quasi-independent status. The Vancouver Water and Drainage Districts were an example of this phenomenon with respect to physical services, as was the Montreal Metropolitan Commission with respect to the control of borrowing.[19] In this phase, certain functions or offices were removed from direct control by city council, but both the functions and the offices were retained and funded at the local level. Senior government supervision was imposed, in effect, by fragmenting or diluting local authority.

The second phase in the erosion of local autonomy, beginning about the time of the First World War, was more significant. In this phase, senior governments imposed function and office on the local authority but retained most of the control over funding and regulation. In the short period between the two wars, the practice had become solidly entrenched extending into social service and other areas. By 1940, K. G. Crawford could write:

> It has become almost a standard practice that a portion of the cost of almost every "social service" which, in its wisdom, the provincial government sees fit to undertake, shall be passed on without consultation to the municipalities and thence to the owners of real estate, whether or not the service is one which might logically be classed as a municipal service or a legitimate charge to be based on the ownership of real property.[20]

This changed relationship between local and senior governments was uneven in the quality and pace of application. But in broad terms, it tended to depend on exigencies (most notably the Great Depression); the extent and impact of the change to urban-industrial and post-industrial society in the various regions; and the composition and attitudes of governments at all levels.[22] The changed pattern of the relationship, despite its uneveness, can be seen in at least four interrelated developments of the interwar and immediate postwar period: changes in provincial statutory control; changes in administrative and regulatory control at the senior levels; changes in local finance; and the expansion of the conditional grants system.

Though it is almost unquestioned that in Canada the provinces have exclusive powers to "make laws in relation" to "municipal institutions,"[23] the sort of laws existing in the first decades of the twentieth century were generally not restrictive. An examination of provincial statutes in this period provides fairly clear evidence that the provinces conferred on local governments (at least the larger and more mature ones) almost "residual powers" to make laws affecting their communities. Indeed, such powers in at least one jurisdiction, Saskatchewan, were expanded in the first decades of the century. "The City Act" of that province, passed in 1908, asserted that a city council "may" make regulations and by-laws "for the peace, order, good government and welfare of the city," but specifically enumerated some obligatory responsibilities.[24] In 1915, these general powers were somewhat widened, mainly by removing references to specific responsibilities,[25] and thereby were made to conform to the more general practice in the Dominion. Ontario was not untypical. The "General Provisions Applicable to all Municipalities" in Ontario in 1914 were as follows:

> Every council may pass such by-laws and make such regulations for the health, safety, morality, and welfare of the inhabitants of the municipality in matters not specifically provided for by this Act, as may be deemed expedient and are not contrary to law, and for governing the proceedings of the council, the conduct of its members and the calling of meetings.[26]

Similar clauses can be found in the statutes of most of the provinces in the period. The broad, almost residual nature of local powers, and their discretionary quality, was coupled with rather limited provincial control. In the main, concurrent legislation affecting local government was aimed at preventing abuse rather than controlling function. Most of the preventative legislation was concerned with audit of local revenue and expenditure, with control over borrowing and lending, and, in some instances, with control of "public" utilities, including funding and promotion of railways.

Perhaps the most extensive set of pre-First World War statutes affecting local government can be found in Quebec. However, though extensive, the statutes were not highly restrictive. Municipal governance fell under the rubric of the provincial secretary (and later a number of other ministers). The provincial secretary "superintend[ed] the administration or the execution . . . of the laws respecting . . . the municipal system," in addition to a number of other duties.[27] Quebec municipalities were also required to inform this minister when they required an expansion of borrowing powers[28] but had to make the application to the Lieutenant-Governor.[29] The statutory limit on borrowing came into effect only when interest and sinking fund payments absorbed up to half the annual revenue of the municipality.[30] Fiscal control was exerted under "The Municipal Accounts Act" dating to at least 1909[31] and under "The Municipal Debt and Loan Act" of 1918[32] and a series of amended versions of it in the following five years.[33] These acts were concurrent with another series of acts to control aid to or sale of utilities. There were few other significant statutory or ministerial restraints on Quebec municipalities at this time.

At the other end of the statutory spectrum, New Brunswick, Nova Scotia and British Columbia had almost no explicit legislation outside of the municipal and other incorporation acts to circumscribe their local governments, apart from some control over audit. In the middle of the spectrum was Ontario, with legislation similar to that of Quebec, but less extensive.[31] Only two provinces, Alberta and Saskatchewan, had departments of municipal affairs under the direction of a cabinet minister.[35] Though statutes gave the departments of both provinces fairly broad powers of supervision, the main intent of the legislation was clearly to control finances, debts, and audit. Manitoba had what approximated a department in the form of the Municipal Commissioner's Department. It was established under "The Municipal Commissioner's Act" of 1890 and had functions similar to those of the departments in the neighbouring prairie provinces.[36]

At the time of the First World War, there was a perceptible increase in the quantity and quality of the legislation affecting municipalities. This legislation told local governments what they were required to do with respect to their omnibus powers. And, by the 1930's, as the provinces became more interventionist in the social sector and the municipalities more financially strapped, the legislation began to encroach on the powers of the local governments.

The growth of provincial statutory control as it relates to local government can be observed most clearly in four areas: general municipal supervision through departments of municipal affairs; social welfare; planning and housing; and finance and audit. In terms of general municipal supervision, every province except Prince Edward Island had by the mid-1940's fully operational departments of municipal affairs, most with extensive powers to supervise, influence and pass money on to local governments.[37] Furthermore, both prior to and after the establishment of such ministries, there was an expansion of legislation providing for greater provincial control over many local government functions. Ontario provides perhaps the most spectacular example of this phenomenon, though it was endemic in the Dominion. The Municipal Act entry in the index of the Revised Statutes of Ontario for 1950 contains cross-references to sixty-five other provincial acts affecting local government.[38] Some acts date prior to the First World War and are generally prohibitive or guiding in nature, but most date after the war and control the powers of local government. Chief among these later statues were: The Planning and Development Act (1918); The Ontario

Housing Act (1919); The Municipal Housing Act (1920); The Department of Public Welfare Act (1931); The Factory, Shop and Office Building Act (1932); The Ontario Municipal Board Act (1932); The Federal District Commission Act (1934); The Department of Municipal Affairs Act (1935); The Municipal Employees Pensions Fund Act (1937); The Department of Planning and Development Act (1944); The Municipal Health Services Act (1944); The Planning Act (1946); The Department of Reform Institutions Act (1946); The Department of Public Welfare Act (1948); The Housing Development Act (1948); The Vital Statistics Act (1948); and the Ontario Municipal Improvement Corporation Act (1950).[39]

Perhaps the most significant development in this legislative outburst focussed on those acts relating to public welfare and to the creation of provincial departments of public welfare, an area clearly within the general powers of most municipal acts and charters.[40] Of nearly equal significance was the legislation related to town planning, development control, and housing.[41] What gives all this legislation such importance is that it not only represented an interventionist commitment on the part of the senior government in certain policy areas and the concurrent growth of bureacracies to implement such policy; but it was also a commitment in most instances to three-level conditional cost-sharing as the means of funding such interventionist ventures. With these developments, and with local financial problems associated with the Depression, fiscal supervision also became much tighter.[42]

Oddly enough, despite these statutory changes, the general powers of local government remained virtually untouched. For example, the general powers of city councils in Ontario were precisely the same in 1950 as they had been in 1914.[43] But by 1950, legal power and real power were no longer coincident. Other provincial statutes now trenched on the general powers of local government, as did provincial, and federal, administrations.

While legislative changes can be charted with some degree of accuracy, changes in administrative structures and powers are not nearly so susceptible to analysis. But administrative changes were nonetheless significant insofar as they affected the loss of local autonomy. The new provincial and federal administrators were able to exert control over municipal decisions through their statutory and discretionary powers. They were also in a position to influence new policy directions that tended to concentrate authority at a central point and to homogenize the type and amount of services delivered.[44] Growth of senior government administration was particularly strong from the 1930's on, even though much of it was haphazard, often temporary, and ad hoc. Its influence could be pervasive.

In the 1930's, for example, the unemployment relief branch of the federal Department of Labour, operating on a year-to-year basis and with no recognized constitutional powers to provide relief to the indigent unemployed, could exert considerable control over provincial and local authorities in its efforts to protect the federal treasury. "These controls [were] manifested in federal approval not only of projects and contracts for public works but also of schedules of families to be assisted under the relief settlement agreements; in inspectional and investigational activities; in reporting requirements; in departmental rulings and interpretations; and in audits."[45] Provincial administrative controls over local governments could be even more direct. Grants brought bureaucracies in their train.

Along with a loss of autonomy through the growth of statutory control and changes in its quality, local government also lost much of its autonomy through the erosion of its tax base, both absolutely and in relation to services it was expected to provide. The contraction of the local tax base was mainly a phenomenon of the 1930's and 1940's when provincial authorities eliminated local income taxes, sales taxes, and personal property taxes; eliminated or reduced the local share of liquor and motor vehicle taxes; and in some instances placed restrictions on untrammelled exploitation of the property tax.[46] By the end of the 1930's the major remaining tax field left to local government, the property tax, was approaching the limits of exploitation. However, the costs of services local government was expected to provide continued to rise. The result was a growing gap between what local governments could raise on their own and the total amount of revenue they required (Table 1). The transfer payment, usually in the form of a conditional grant, was the device used to close the gap.

The federal conditional grant came into use in Canada in 1913, and until the unemployment and farm relief grants of the 1930's, it was used for only six programmes that involved relatively small amounts of money. The grant was used not for financial exigency but "to get the provinces started in certain activities having a national interest."[47] Until the Depression, its significance was far outweighed by the unconditional federal subsidies passed on to the provinces under the terms of the British North America Act and subsequent agreements. By 1934, largely because of the relief grants, conditional transfers amounted to almost $44 million while the direct subsidies came to just over $15 million.[48] Perhaps more important, the relief grants were in response to financial need more than functional need; though given to the provinces, they were in effect administered and disbursed by the local authorities. By the 1940's, they had become an important and apparently permanent feature of intergovernmental finance and policy making.

TABLE 1

MUNICIPAL REVENUES AND TRANSFERS
1926 to 1956
($ X 10_)

	1926	1928	1930	1932	1934	1936	1938	1940	1942	1944	1946	1948	1950	1952	1954	1956
Total Municipal Revenues	336	367	403	385	366	380	381	393	412	452	496	640	796	1027	1206	1463
Total Transfers*	29	32	46	48	36	37	37	36	44	65	86	138	182	228	274	361
Municipal Revenue Less Transfers	307	335	357	337	330	343	344	357	368	387	410	502	614	799	932	1102
Revenue Less Transfers as a Percentage of Total Revenues°	91	91	89	88	90	90	90	91	89	86	87	78	77	78	77	75

*Transfers from municipalities to provinces and transfers from provinces to municipalities. Municipal revenue less transfers thereby represents net available revenue obtained from local sources.

°By the mid-1970's this percentage, by some accounts, had fallen to almost 50 per cent. See David M. Nowlan, ''Towards Home Rule For Urban Policy,'' *JCS* 13, no. 1 (Spring 1978): 70.

Source: DBS, *National Accounts, Income and Expenditure, 1926–1956,* (Queen's Printer: Ottawa, 1962), Table 36, pp. 74–75.

Provincial conditional grants to local governments have a somewhat longer history than those made by the federal governments, as noted by Splane.[49] But like the federal grants, they were usually ad hoc and often temporary. Also like the federal ones, they were used for emergency purposes, or, as in the case of Ontario's housing legislation of 1919, designed to encourage local governments to move into new areas. There has been little analysis of their impact on the policy and financing of local governments, but it appears that it was slight until the 1930's.

As long as the grants were not allied with broad interventionist policies at the senior levels, as long as control remained loose, and as long as the grants were deemed temporary measures, there was no appreciable impact on local autonomy. But once the grants were allied with permanent interventionist policies, and once they became an important and permanent part of local revenues, compulsion and control by the senior governments followed. Local governments lost autonomy in two ways. They were told what to do and were given the money to do it. Or they were given the option of taking money on certain conditions or not at all. In the former case the compulsion was explicit, in the latter implicit. In either case, local autonomy was compromised. Identification of problems and the establishment of priorities could not be determined in the locality. Responsibility for problems and the power to solve them were separated. And power of elected officials at the local level was diluted or constricted by the discretionary powers of nonelected officials at the senior levels.

Changes in the relationship of the local governments with the senior ones, however inconsistent and incomplete, did not pass without some notice and alarm. One of the earliest warnings to local governments in Canada was made by an American, Mayor Joseph Carson of Portland, Oregon, in an address to the Union of Canadian Municipalities annual convention in 1936:

> I tell you gentlemen frankly, that in the United States we are facing a loss of self government. I am not in any way criticizing the present federal government in my country. What I say is that local governments, head over heels in debt and with their credit exhausted, have begged the superior governments to come in and take over our responsibilities. Now we find ourselves faced with the danger of losing our local self government rights.
>
> I warn you in Canada, whose local problems parallel our own, that cities must cease being political mendicants at the feet of federal government. For just as surely as you accept handouts from the superior authority, you will see a corresponding loss of your own local autonomy.[50]

Though the Canadian representatives to the convention paid little heed to the American guest, he clearly perceived that something was happening or had happened already to the autonomy of Canadian local government. Rather similar fears were expressed in 1938 by Commissioner Mary Sutherland in a dissenting memorandum to parts of the *Final Report* of the National Employment Commission that called for federal assumption of administrative responsibility for the unemployed. Depression exigencies, she argued, perhaps reflecting Kingsian policy, were no excuse for federal assumption:

> The fact that Municipalities and Provinces are at the moment distraught and harassed by their financial incapacity to meet their primary responsibilities is entirely beside the point. Indeed if relevancy can be claimed it should be to caution against the capitalizing of their distress and difficulties for the purpose of securing an assignment of any of their Provincial rights or powers to a central government.[51]

She also argued that alleged abuses in the delivery of relief at the provincial and local levels would not necessarily be cleaned up by federal assumption. A dominion system, she said, "is also liable to many abuses."[52] Finally, in a philosophical vein, she questioned the desirability of separating government from the individual. An individual, she argued, has a more responsible attitude toward a government he pays taxes to directly and can see functioning for him.[53] Other opinions, however, were to prevail.

The changing nature of local government was also noted, with varying degrees of trepidation, by the academic community and appears to have precipitated a debate on the relationship of local government and democracy, a debate that constituted a new rationalization for the existence of local government in a subjected form.

Among the first to make a comprehensive analysis of the changing "independence" of municipal councils was K. G. Crawford, in 1940. He concluded that the more serious encroachment was from the provincial direction:

> This is a movement which is not only increasing, but increasing at a greatly accelerated rate. It is characteristic both of legislative bodies and governmental boards and bureaux that they will endeavour constantly to widen their field of control and operation. In Ontario, the tendency toward increasing interference with municipal independence, and the imposition of financial burdens by the Province, has covered a period of many years and all varieties of governments. It is a

> trend which is not likely to be arrested until the situation becomes so acute as to overshadow other provincial issues.[54]

Crawford was followed in 1943 by Alan Van Every, who saw some potential benefit in what he termed "enlarged provincial oversight of Canadian municipalities."[55] Perhaps less sanguine was C. A. Curtis. In an article in 1942, he dealt with what he perceived to be the major problems facing local government: the inappropriate division of fiscal resources and responsibilities;[56] the fragmentation of municipal functions that inhibited the entry of good men into local politics because they would not make themselves available "unless the functions and powers of Council are worthwhile and sufficiently important;'[57] inadequate planning; irrational delineation of boundaries; insufficient housing; and the increasing impact of provincial administration and control. In an address in 1951, Curtis outlined a programme of reform.[58] A similar, tentative effort was made in the same year by Keith B. Callard.[59] Other discussions on more specific areas of concern also made their way into print: a series of articles in the 1940's on control of local finances in *Municipal Finance*;[60] A. E. Buck's chapter on the subject in *Financing Canadian Government* in 1949;[61] Eric Hardy on provincial-municipal relationships, and Fred R. MacKinnon on local government and welfare in the same volume of *Canadian Public Administration* in 1960;[62] and Lionel Feldman's discussion of legislative control in 1961.[63]

For the most part, these writers, and others like George Mooney of the Canadian Federation of Mayors and Municipalities,[64] asserted a fundamental belief in the virtue of local government on grounds that it served not only a functional good but also a political good in the sense that it was a support of and a training ground for democracy.

The view was apparently widespread in the North Atlantic community; its challenge by Georges Langrod[65] at the International Political Science Association meeting at The Hague in 1952 provoked considerable debate.[66] It precipitated what appears to have been a rather sudden change in perspective of Canadian writers in the field, notably Hugh Whalen, who in 1960 published two somewhat contradictory articles on the subject.[67] Whatever one's position in the debate, the fact that it occurred at all indicates a recognition that the place of local government in an urban-industrial society had undergone a significant and substantial change. As Whalen pointed out:

> Local self-government as it exists in most industrial democracies today can no longer be considered a major instrument of control. In an era of expanding communities, growing mass publics, and intricate and

> rapidly expanding technologies, mechanisms of democratic control must be located at the vital centres of power of each national community.[68]

By 1970, Whalen and many others had noted or accepted a diminished role for local government, and, depending on their inclinations, were offering up prescriptions either for its continued existence in an atrophied form or for its rejuvenation. Among those beginning to prescribe rejuvenation were the municipalities themselves, which, in the 1960's, broke a virtual silence that extended back to the early 1930's. Planners and economists, more recently, have also called for reversal of the drift to dimunition.

Urban autonomy emerged in Canada at about the same time as it did in the United States and Britain, roughly in the first half of the nineteenth century. It was carved away in all three countries in two qualitatively different stages: by selective interventionism at the turn of the century; and by pervasive interventionism, roughly after the First World War. What triggered that "interventionism" has been more a matter of speculation than investigation. But some comments, at least on the Canadian experience, can be made.

Two schools of explanation emerge. One proposal is that secular change of itself dictated that "mechanisms of democratic control must be located at the vital centres of each national community." And one is persuaded in this direction by the synchronic development of urban autonomy in Canada, the United States and Britain. As a general proposition, then, this explanation has much to recommend it. As an explanatory device, it parallels, in a broad sense, Marxist explanation,[69] the vital shifts in the latter analysis relating to the emergence of the commercial and industrial state in the nineteenth century and of corporations and the corporate state in the twentieth. But elaboration of the elements of that change and provision of an analytical framework, in Canada at least, have been rare.[70] Both the emergence and loss of urban autonomy was predetermined and inevitable.

Vital centres, however, can be made, and in Canada, at least, some recent scholarly work has argued that urban evolution has been a consequence of human strengths and frailties.[71] Loss of urban community has been fundamentally linked to the failure of the urban community to respond to secular change. Secular change, of itself, does not have an inevitable series of consequences, regardless of what the human actors might do.

A possible resolution of this debate might be accomplished, with more research, by looking less at the forces at work and more at the problems the cities had to face and how they responded to them. These included the development of corporate structures; the expansion of social welfare; the exhaustion of local fiscal resources; social segregation; expansion of democracy; and proletarian political organization. Probably the three most critical of these were the breaking of the booster nexus, a result of the development of corporations not identified with place; the geo-political-social identification in cities of a democratized urban proletariat; and the exhaustion of the property tax as the major source of independent municipal revenue. The opportunity was ripe for fiscal, social, and economic fragmentation and the assumption of indirect control of the cities by the provinces. And this was at a time when a minimum and equitable standard of social welfare, education and the like was becoming a strong political cry in the country and a political justification for managing the city. The era has been termed one of unstable equilibrium between the liberal decentralizers of the nineteenth century and the interventionism of the twentieth century.[72] Functionally, the cities could not manage—their mentalité and competitive instincts did not admit it—and in terms of power, their organization was morphologically incompatable with the new corporate and provincial phase.

Corporations and governments are merely *in* cities, they are not *of* cities. And the role of both grew in the twentieth century to the point that they overshadowed the industrial and commercial elites that had dominated in the century before. Most important is the fact that corporations and governments have no special loyalty to place. Their fortunes are not tied to the fortunes of a city or town, and indeed such ties can even be seen as counter-productive. The loyalty is to the organization, or at best to the corporate headquarter's city.

For the lower social classes, the case in the twentieth century was the reverse of the nineteenth, when the property franchise had effectively shut them out of local government. In the nineteenth century, their transiency and their poverty apparently gave them a relatively weak association with place, and if they did have one, it was likely with a cultural, not a class, community, for example the French in Montreal or the Roman Catholics in Ottawa. The segregation of cities in the industrial phase and the identification of class and culture with discreet geographic or social areas within cities, coupled with the widening of the franchise—through legislation or prosperity—gave rise to organization, political as well as other. By the crisis of the 1930's, an organized proletariat was seen as having the potential to control local government.[73] It is this sort of threat that Marxist scholars in the United States see as prompting the flight of corporate capital to the suburbs; to the fragmentation of corporate and therefore working class functions; and as putting their businesses beyond the influence of a local government run by the lower classes. Some evidence of this phenomenon is seen in Canada; it perhaps proved most hurtful in Montreal. But, in general, other strategies were employed. Perhaps the most important of these was the emergence of the alphabet parties as a counter to socialist impulses in the city. The old business groups, supported by the corporate sector, successfully opposed socialist organization. Conventional factionalism stopped being factious. Provincial governments, accidentally or on purpose, did their part to mute political radicalism. Many set up regional governments or agencies that limited radical activity through the iindirect election to a regional board. Such boards also pitted the generally more conservative suburbs and rurban areas—home of the expanding white collar class—against the radical core areas. Prosperity, too, helped remove much of the potential fire in the post-Second World War period. Conservatism was bred, of course, in many cities, especially west of the Ottawa River, by the widespread nature of property ownership and the almost exclusive use of the property tax as the chief tax resource of local government. Urban voters and the city itself can become hypersensitive to the burden of property tax and its visible effect on the individual. Much social conservatism can be bred by such an identification, especially when owners are usually paying the social benefits of a non-owning group, a group which is often in a geographically different part of the city.

As for the property tax itself, it had been a most lucrative source of revenue until about the 1930's and arguably the most lucrative of all the tax bases in Canada for the previous one hundred years. Certainly by 1929, the property tax was generating more tax revenue than any other single source. But as the Depression of the 1930's was to demonstrate, it was very nearly at a point of exhaustion. Few additional demands could be placed upon it in its monolithic, regressive form without creating unwarranted inequalities, without creating a capital crisis, and without creating more of the tax dodge communities that corporations were beginning to flee to. Provincial resistance to provision of new sources of revenue meant, in effect, that future funding of local government would be in the form of transfer payments, which were, as indicated, usually in the form of the conditional grant. Intergovernmental transfers would thus effectively control interclass transfers. And senior governments effectively controlled the intergovernmental transfers. Proletarian control of a city was made redundant because the city had been made impotent. Any effort by a radical local government to develop income support policies, for example, could only be done at the expense of cutting the water off. And local health officers, operating under a provincial act, could prohibit that as part of the minimum standard guaranteed to rich and poor alike.

By the 1960's, city governments had one resource left: a bureaucracy more expert than that of the senior governments. Reliance on this liberal-professional class proved a weak reed. By the 1970's, provincial and federal governments and even some corporations had hired experts of their own and often hired away the expertise the cities had developed. The cities' last hope, that of superior knowledge and intelligence, withered.

Explanation for the loss of autonomy is complex, but if one single factor had to be pointed to, it would be the loss of identification of elite with place and its replacement by elite identification with organization. Cities as a special kind of place for doing business have ceased to exist. As a special kind of place for living, they may only now be on their way to fulfilling their potential.

Such an outcome may well have been inevitable. But there is considerable evidence to show that, however difficult, urban denizens in widely-spaced cities faced with internal fragmentation had the potential to generate an effective—or at least more vigourous—political response and failed to do so. Perhaps the difficulties were, in practical terms, so overwhelming as to be paralyzing. It remains a moot point, however, whether cities were run over or gave up.

NOTES

1. An earlier version of this paper was published in G. A. Stelter and A. F. J. Artibise, eds., *The Canadian City: Essays in Urban and Social History* (Ottawa: Carleton University Press, 1984), pp. 478–500.
2. Jon C. Teaford, "The Evolution of Municipal Autonomy in the United States," paper presented to the Canadian-American Urban History Conference, Guelph, 1982, p. 5.
3. Adrian Elliott, "Municipal Government in Bradford in the Mid-Nineteenth Century," in Derek Fraser, ed., *Municipal Reform and the Industrial City* (New York: St. Martin's Press, 1982), passim, pp. 111–55.
4. David Sutherland, "The Merchants of Halifax" (Ph.D. Diss., University of Toronto, 1975).
5. C. F. J. Whebell, "Robert Baldwin and Decentralization 1841–9," in F. H. Armstrong, et al., eds., *Aspects of Nineteenth Century Ontario* (Toronto: University of Toronto Press, 1974), p. 61.
6. My thanks to Michael Piva, whose current investigations into public finance in pre-Confederation Canada led to this important insight.
7. T. W. Acheson, "The Great Merchant and Economic Development in St. John 1820–1850," *Acadiensis* 8, no. 2 (Spring 1979): 3–27.
8. H. V. Nelles, *The Politics of Development* (Toronto: Macmillan, 1975), passim.
9. J. H. Taylor, "Mayors à la Mancha: An Aspect of Depression Leadership in

Canadian Cities,'' *Urban History Review* 9, no. 3 (February 1981): 3–14.

10. See *The Rowell-Sirois Report,* Book I, ed. D. V. Smiley (Toronto: McClelland and Stewart, 1963), pp. 142–47. Francis Hankin and T. W. L. MacDermot, *Recovery by Control* (Toronto: J. M. Dent and Sons, Ltd., 1933), claim in Chapter 5 that all but 90 of 585 waterworks in Canada to 1928 were owned and operated by public bodies, one-third in the hands of public utility commissions; and in 1929 21 of 59 electric railways in Canada were owned by municipalities in Canada, including all the major ones in Ontario and the Prairies. See also J. E. Rea, ''How Winnipeg Was Nearly Won,'' and C. O. White, ''Moose Jaw Opts for Private over Municipal Ownership of Its Electrical Utility,'' in *Cities in the West,* A. R. McCormack and I. MacPherson, eds., (Ottawa, National Museum of Man, 1975).
11. See The *Rowell-Sirois Report*; Terry Copp, *The Anatomy of Poverty* (Toronto: McClelland and Stewart, 1974); Serge Mongeau, *Evolution de l'assistance au Québec* (Montreal: Editions du Jour, 1967); Richard B. Splane, *Social Welfare in Ontario, 1791–1893* (Toronto: University of Toronto Press, 1965); Margaret K. Strong, *Public Welfare Administration in Canada* (Chicago: University of Chicago Press, 1930); John H. Taylor, ''The Urban West: Public Welfare and a Theory of Urban Development,'' in *Cities in the West*, and a large body of thesis material that has emanated from the schools of social work, particularly at the University of Toronto, and the University of British Columbia.
12. Usually this was in the form of Town Planning Commissions that were permitted under legislation passed in nearly all the provinces in the late 1910's and 1920's as a result of efforts of the federal government's Commission of Conservation. Some were anaemic ventures, like Ottawa, others quite thorough, like Vancouver, and yet others, like Calgary, which planned to establish a ''Venice of the West,'' quite utopian. Much work remains to be done on the history of planning in Canada, though a number of commendable efforts have been produced recently. See Alan F. J. Artibise, ''Winnipeg and the City Planning Movement, 1910–1915,'' in D. J. Bercuson, ed., *Western Perspectives I* (Toronto: Holt, Rinehart and Winston, 1974); and Walter Van Nus, ''The Architect and City Planning in Canada, 1890–1930,'' paper presented to the Canadian Historical Association, Annual Meeting, Edmonton, 1975.
13. See Table 1. In 1926, less than 9 per cent of local revenue was received from sources other than the local tax base.
14. Notably the Union of Canadian Municipalities. See Resolution 5 of their 1929 Annual Convention as reported in *The Municipal Review of Canada* 25, no. 9 (September 1929): 369, a resolution reiterated in its substance in the 1930 and 1931 conventions. Similar sentiments were expressed in speeches and resolutions at the annual meetings of the Ontario Municipal Association.
15. Centre de recherche en droit public, Université de Montréal, *Droit et Societe Urbaine au Quèbec, Rapport Synthese,* sous la direction de P. A. Coté, A. Lajoie, J. Leveillée, et al. (Montreal, 1981), p. 3.

16. K. G. Crawford, "The Independence of Municipal Councils in Ontario," *Canadian Journal of Economics and Political Science* (hereafter *CJEPS*) 6, no. 4 (November 1940): 543.
17. Ibid., 548–49.
18. See "The Ontario Railway and Municipal Board Act," *Statutes of Ontario* 6 Edw. VII (1906), c. 31; "The Municipal Aid (to industrial or commerical establishments) Prohibition Act," Revised *Statutes of Quebec,* 1925, c. 116, as examples.
19. The Montreal Municipal Commission. Montreal proper operated outside the commission, but most of its suburbs were embraced by it. The commission membership was dominated by representatives of the richer suburban municipalities like Westmount and Outremont.
20. Crawford, "Independence of Municipal Councils," 547.
21. Contrasts could be made here between Quebec with its generally anti-statist inclinations and the Prairie provinces, which with little historical overburden seemed quite willing to experiment and did so.
22. Note the sudden changes, especially with respect to municipal control and welfare, with the changes to Liberal governments in B.C. in 1933 and Ontario in 1934. At the federal level, quite dramatic changes can be observed in the attitudes of R. B. Bennett in January of 1935, Mackenzie King in December of 1935, and King again in the war period. For the latter evolution, see J. L. Granatstein, *Canada's War* (Toronto: Oxford University Press, 1974), esp. Chapters 6 and 7.
23. "The British North America Act," s. 92, head 8.
24. *Statutes of Saskatchewan,* 1908, c. 16, s. 184.
25. *Statutes of Saskatchewan,* 1915, c. 16
26. *Statutes of Ontario,* 3–4Geo. V, c. 43, s. 250.
27. *Revised Statutes of Quebec,* 1909, Title 11, Art.777.
28. Ibid., Arts. 5889–90.
29. Ibid., Arts. 5776–89.
30. Ibid.
31. See *Revised Statutes of Quebec* 1909, Art. 5956 (i).
32. *Statutes of Quebec,* 8 Geo. V., c. 60.
33. *Statutes of Quebec,* 9 Geo. V, c. 59; 10 Geo V, c. 67; 11 Geo V, c. 48; 12 Geo. V, c. 60; and 13 Geo. V, c. 84. These acts were administered under the terms of "The Quebec Municipal Commission Act," *Revised Statutes of Quebec,* 1925, c. 111A.
34. By 1914, the main legislation affecting municipalities was "The Municipal Act," *Revised Statutes of Ontario* (1914), c. 192; "The Ontario Railway and Municipal Board Act, *RSO* (1914), c. 186; "The Municipal and School Accounts Audit Act," passed in 1914, *RSO* (1914), c. 200; and "The Houses of Refuge Act," passed in 1912, *RSO* (1914) c. 290.
35. "The Department of Municipal Affairs Act," *Statutes of Alberta,* 1911–12, c. 11. "The Department of Municipal Affairs Act," *Statutes of Saskatchewan,* 1908, c. 15.

36. "The Municipal Commissioner's Act," *Statutes of Manitoba*, 53 V, c. 51 (1890).
37. In order: Manitoba, "The Department of Municipal Affairs Act," *Statutes of Manitoba,* 1953 (2nd sess.), c. 37; New Brunswick "Commissioner of Municipal Affairs Act," *Statutes of New Brunswick* 1934, c. 14; Nova Scotia, "An Act to Amend and Consolidate the Acts Relating to the Supervision of Municipal Affairs, *Statutes of Nova Scotia,* 1945, c. 6; Ontario, "Department of Municipal Affairs Act," *SO,* 1935, c. 16; Quebec, "The Municipal Affairs, Trade and Commerce Department Act," *Statutes of Quebec,* 25–26 Geo. V. (1935), c. 45; and British Columbia, "The Department of Municipal Affairs Act," *Statutes of British Columbia,* 1934, c. 52.
38. "The Municipal Act," Index Heading, *Revised Statutes of Ontario* (1950).
39. In order, *Statutes of Ontario,* 1918, c. 38; *SO,* 1919, c. 54; *SO,* 1920, c. 84; *SO,* 1931, c. 5; *SO,* 1932, c. 35; *SO,* 1932, c. 27; *SO,* 1934, c. 16; *SO,* 1935, c. 16; *SO,* 1937, c. 50; *SO,* 1944, c. 16; *SO,* 1944, c. 41; *SO* 1946, c. 71; *SO,* 1946, c. 22; *SO,* 1948, c. 23; *SO,* 1948, c. 44; and *SO,* 1948, c. 47.
40. Manitoba, "The Health and Public Welfare Act," 1928; New Brunswick, 1944, established a minister responsible in the field but under no specific legislation; Saskatchewan, "The Bureau of Labour and Public Welfare Act, 1934–35; Nova Scotia, 1944, a minister but no act; Ontario, "The Department of Public Welfare Act, 1931; Quebec, "The Health and Social Welfare Act, 1936; Alberta, "The Bureau of Public Welfare Act, 1939; and British Columbia, "The Department of Health and Welfare Act," 1946.
41. For example, in Ontario there were no planning or housing acts in 1914. Their proliferation is indicated above, note 37. Perhaps the earliest example of planning legislation was in Alberta under "The Town Planning Act," *Statutes of Alberta,* 1913 (1), c. 18. By the 1940's such acts existed in nearly every province, in part it seems, to provide a channel through which federal money under the National Housing Act could flow. For example, Ontario's "Housing Development Act," *Statutes of Ontario,* 1948, c. 44, provides under section 6 (1) for federal and provincial agreements "as contemplated" in section 35 of The National Housing Act, 1944 (Canada).
42. For a general overview and other references, see A. E. Buck, *Financing Canadian Government* (Chicago: Public Administration Service, 1949), pp. 298–332.
43. Compare *SO*, 3–4 Geo. V, c. 43, s. 250 with *RSO,* 1950, c. 243, s. 260.
44. A phenomenon clearly evident in the flow of regulations from the provinces to most cities with respect to relief administration in the 1930's.
45. Luella Gettys, *The Administration of Canadian Conditional Grants* (Chicago: Public Administration Service, 1938), pp. 156–57.
46. See Crawford, "Independence of Municipal Councils," *Financing Canadian Government,* 548, and Buck, pp. 321–25.
47. Gettys, *Administration of Canadian Conditional Grants,* p. 13.
48. Richard Splane, *Social Welfare in Ontario,* pp. 284ff.
49. Ibid., p. 15n30.

50. *The Municipal Review of Canada,* November 1936, p. 6.
51. Mary Sutherland, ''Memorandum of Reservations Containing the Reasons for Dissent,'' Canada, National Employment Commission, *Final Report* (Ottawa: King's Printer, 1938), p. 47.
52. Ibid., 50.
53. Ibid., 49.
54. Crawford, ''Independence of Municipal Councils,'' 543.
55. Alan Van Every, ''Trends in Provincial-Municipal Supervision,'' *Public Affairs* 6, no. 4 (Summer 1943): 211–15.
56. C. A. Curtis, ''Municipal Government in Ontario,'' *CJEPS* 8, no. 3 (August 1942): 418.
57. Ibid., 421.
58. C. A. Curtis, ''Municipal Finance and Dominion-Provincial Relations,'' *CJEPS,* 17, no. 3 (August 1951): 297–306.
59. Keith B. Callard, ''The Present System of Local Government in Canada: Some Problems of Status, Area, Population and Resources,'' ibid. 17, no. 2 (May 1951): 204–17.
60. For example, Emile Morin, ''Municipal Debt Supervision in Quebec,'' *Municipal Finance* (November 1944): 16–20; W. R. Cottingham, ''Provincial Supervision of Municipal Debts,'' *Municipal Finance,* (August 1940): 20–33; and G. A. Lascelles, ''Financial Organization of the City of Toronto, Canada,'' *Municipal Finance* (November 1942) pp. 17–22.
61. Buck, *Financing Canadian Government.*
62. Eric Hardy, ''Provincial-Municipal Relations: With Emphasis on the Financial Relationships Between Provinces and Local Governments,'' and Fred R. MacKinnon, ''Local Government and Welfare,'' both in *Canadian Public Administration,* 3 (1960): 14–23; 31–41.
63. ''Legislative Control of Municipalities in Ontario,'' *Canadian Public Administration* 4 (1961): 294–301.
64. ''The Canadian Federation of Mayors and Municipalities: Its Role and Function,'' *Canadian Public Administration* 3 (1960): 82–92.
65. ''Local Government and Democracy,'' *Public Administration* 31 (Spring 1953): 25–34.
66. See Keith Panter-Brick, ''Local Government and Democracy—A Rejoinder,'' ibid., (Winter 1953): pp. 344–48; Leo Moulin, ''Local Self-Government as a Basis for Democracy: A further Comment,'' ibid. 32 (Winter 1954): 433–37, and Panter-Brick, ''Local Self-Government as a Basis for Democracy: A Rejoinder,'' ibid: 438–40.
67. ''Democracy and Local Government,'' *Canadian Public Administration* 3 (1960) pp. 1–13; and ''Ideology, Democracy, and the Foundations of Local Self-Government,'' *CJEPS* 26 no. 3 (August 1960): 377–95.
68. ''Ideology, Democracy, and the Foundations of Local Self-Government,'' p. 394.
69. See for example, W. K. Tabb and M. Sawer, *Marxism and the Metropolis* (New York: Oxford University Press, 1978).

70. One of the few is Gilbert Stelter, ''The City Building Process in Canada,'' in G. A. Stelter and A. F. J. Artibise, eds., *Shaping the Urban Landscape: Aspects of the Canadian City Building Process,* (Ottawa: Carleton University Press, 1982), pp. 1–29.
71. See for example A. F. J. Artibise, ''Continuity and Change: Elites and Prairie Urban Development, 1914–1950,'' in A. F. J. Artibise and G. A. Stelter, eds., *The Usable Urban Past* (Toronto: Macmillan, 1979), pp. 130–54.
72. Université de Montreal, *Droit et Societe Urbaine*.
73. Taylor, ''Mayors à la Mancha.''

12

Metropolitan Reform and the Restructuring of Local Governments in the North American City

Philip Wichern

Metropolitan reform and the restructuring of local governments are significant political and historical phenomena in many countries of the world.[1] However, these subjects are usually treated in academic literature as local or national case studies within recent time frames, and the literature directly comparing various facets of Canadian and American cities also lacks the type of historical analysis which is pursued in this study.[2] Three basic questions frame this research: What is metropolitan reform? What is the comparative historical record of metropolitan reform and the restructuring of metropolitan local governments in Canada and the United States? And, what is the relationship of this record to patterns of North American urban development, especially as viewed from political economy perspectives?[3] Each of these questions is answered in successive sections by research findings drawn from a comprehensive analysis of American and Canadian sources.

Before reviewing the North American historical record, it is important to identify the nature and roots of metropolitan reform as a comparative historical phenomena. The term metropolitan reform refers to ideas and practices, both of which have a history. There is an intellectual history of metropolitan reform ideas, as well as a practical history of specific restructuring proposals and attempts at comprehensive consolidation or coordination of local government institutions in metropolitan areas. Both of these histories may be traced at least as far back as British responses to urban development and local government conditions in such areas in the first half of the last century:

> As early as 1837, the English Royal Commission on Municipal Corporations suggested that London and its suburbs might be united into one "metropolitan municipality." A Metropolitan Board of Works was established in 1855 and a metropolitan county council in 1889.[5]

These practical reforms were developed in an intellectual context, in which intellectuals of all political persuasions produced and developed "the case for consolidation of local authority in Britain":

> The hope was to create new communities which would be larger and more progressive than the old. These communities would be governed by authorities who were willing and able to act in support of economic development and deal with the problems it created.[6]

These ideas and the practical innovations impressed North American municipal reformers, especially the academics who became the champions of metropolitan reform in the 1920's.[7] However, North American metropolitan reform should be defined in terms of its own historical record—of practices and ideas. It is that record which the following section examines.

THE NORTH AMERICAN HISTORICAL RECORD

Although metropolitan reform is most often identified as an historical phenomenon of this century in North America, its roots are most properly traced to patterns of economics and land use development around North American "proximal places" in the early 1800's.[8] The most common governmental response to such urban development was the incorporation of cities and expansion of their jurisdictions by annexation and consolidation of surrounding unincorporated areas. In the United States, there was a pattern in some state legislatures dealing with urban sprawl of consolidating core cities' municipalities with surrounding areas and their often rural-oriented units of local government: New Orleans and New Orleans Parish (185); Boston and Suffolk County (1821); Philadelphia and Philadelphia County (1854); San Francisco with San Francisco County (1856); and both St. Louis and New York with their county namesakes in 1874.[9] Although city-county consolidation was proposed in the late nineteenth century for even larger urban areas with multiple counties, it was achieved only in the consolidation which created "Greater" New York City in 1898. This consolidation instituted a federated form of metropolitan government which allowed the former counties (now called boroughs) to retain local representation and some service functions.[10] During the same period, other institutions and patterns of local intergovernmental relations were being developed to handle the problems of suburban development. These included: (1) the creation of local authorities and single- (or limited-multiple-) purpose metropolitan districts, and (2) the development of patterns of intermunicipal and municipal county cooperation as well as formal agreements for the sharing of urban facilities, equipment, and personnel.[11] These patterns continue to characterize practical American responses to metropolitan conditions up to the present.

In Canada, annexation by central cities was common, but city-county consolidation was not practiced. Urbanizing areas either remained unincorporated in rural counties or parishes or were separated from those jurisdictions into incorporated municipalities as cities, towns and villages. As urban growth and industrial development occurred in Canada after Confederation in 1867 (Appendix, Table 1), many of these areas were annexed but others remained separate—a pattern which varied from city to city.[12]

These methods of nineteenth-century adaptation failed to keep pace with the rapid suburban growth which took place in the late nineteenth and early twentieth centuries as a result of the revolution in transportation technology.[13] In the United States, central cities were increasingly opposed by suburban residents and their municipal officials, as well as by rural-dominated state legislatures.[14] The suburban municipalities grew more and more capable of providing central services of a comparable quality at less cost than the central cities. As well, their citizens did not want to share central city or other suburban problems, which were widely publicized by the muckrakers and attacked by municipal reformers.[15] Some of these central cities also included a growing number of socialist mayors, with socialist majorities on central city councils, who favoured large-scale annexations or consolidations.[16] Opposition also came from hostile, rural-dominated state legislatures. They stopped their mandating of local annexations and consolidations, weakened the requirements for creation of new municipalities by incorporations, and increased the requirements for the approval of core city annexations and consolidations to include a positive vote by majorities of residents in the areas affected.[17] In Canada, central city annexations of contiguous and nearby communities was extensive: both Toronto and Montreal annexed thirty communities during the period 1880–1916.[18] But in these and most other Canadian settlements, the city annexations were not comprehensive and did leave separate municipal jurisdictions, some surrounded by the expanded cities, such as Outremont and Westmont in Montreal.[19] In addition, most developed a proliferation of separate public and private school districts, as well as other special-purpose local authorities.[20]

Municipal Reform and Metropolitan Reform

The attention of municipal reformers in the United States and Canada was not on suburban and metropolitan development. It was focused instead on the urban conditions in central cities and on the improvement of central city government through various internal changes. Although the Canadian municipal reform movement has been characterized as "saving the Canadian city with a utopian vision of tomorrow's metropolis," no tangible evidence of metropolitan concerns was found, other than Morley Wickett's 1913 proposal for a Toronto metropolitan government.[21] However, the compilation of the 1910 U.S. census statistics, according to a new category of "metropolitan district," revealed to some reformers the vast dimensions of the surburbanization trend that was taking place in the United States and to a lesser extent in Canada.[22] (Canadian census statistics did not make a comparable delineation until the 1950's, when similar changes were taking place.)[23]

What Blake McKelvey calls "The Search for Metropolitan Government" developed in the United States in the early 1920's as both an intellectual and practical political reaction to the suburban development trends recognized by the census, as well as to the obvious failures of nineteenth-century adaptation techniques.[24] Practical concerns were strongly expressed by the civic leagues and municipal research bureaus in major American cities. These good government organizations, "long advocates of planning, urged the merit of metropolitan planning, even of metropolitan government" in the United States.[25] Their national umbrella organization was the National League of Cities. In its periodical, the *National Municipal Review*, numerous American political scientists and civic reformers developed and championed the ideas of metropolitan reform. Especially noteworthy are the writings of Chester Maxey, William B. Munro, William B. Anderson, A. Chester Hanford, and Thomas Reed. The latter was still championing comprehensive metropolitan reform ideas before the U.S. Congress in 1961 at eighty years of age.[26] A classic statement of these reformers' ideas was produced by Paul Studenski in his famous, book-length report for the National Municipal League's Committee on Metropolitan Government (1930):

> The modern metropolitan region is a community composed of local communities, each with its own personality and a measure of peculiar needs. Yet, side by side with the locality needs, exists the broader metropolitan interests which the component cities, towns and villages, acting as independent organs of local government, can never serve. For this task, it is necessary that the localities be integrated in such a manner as will enable the whole region to function as a political

> unit. . . . a new form of government seems to be indicated. It is the obligation of political science to devise a form that will work.[27]

It should be noted that this is quite a different focus from that of municipal reformers: the internal organization and operations of urban governments, especially central cities, and the reduction of "boss rule." Though they are directly linked in most studies, there are historical differences, justifying a distinction between municipal reform and metropolitan reform.[28] It is clear that North American metropolitan reform developed on a more sociological idea of community than its British counterpart.

This research discovered no evidence of a similar intellectual movement in Canada, and very few practical efforts, such as Grey's proposal for Toronto.[29] In fact, the first extensive references to metropolitan problems were pragmatic concerns expressed by academic journal articles around 1940.[30] This time lag may be explained to some extent by the different growth rates in the two countries. But metropolitan growth was occurring in Canada, and many Canadian urban areas already had the "metropolitan problem" during this period. The recently published work of Harold Kaplan is suggestive, though not specific, regarding the possible reasons for this difference.[31]

The Practical Record: 1920–50

All of the intellectual effort being focused on promoting metropolitan reform led Harvard University Professor W. B. Munro to predict that "out of all this is sure to rise, in due course, some movement for unification, complete or partial, such as will insure the broad treatment of metropolitan problems by a centralized authority."[32] The actual experience with American metropolitan reform proposals in the 1920's was quite different. "The suburban passion for autonomy and the hostility of rural-dominated (state) legislatures blocked" not only proposals for comprehensive metropolitan planning and government but also compromise plans for city-county consolidations and city control over "a new water source, an outlet for its sewers, or some other regional objective."[33]

The few proposals for metropolitan government made during the 1930's in the United States were not any more successful than those of the 1920's. The Pennsylvania State Legislature repeatedly blocked attempts by Philadelphia to consolidate its city and county governments ("in the interest of economy"!), and the Massachusetts legislature rejected Joseph A. Beale's design for a federated Metropolitan Boston created out of forty-three adjoining communities.[34] The *National Civic Review* reported that over half of American cities with 200,000 or more residents were considering some form of broader government, but the only tangible results were some local arrangements for interlocal cooperation, and adoption of metropolitan county charters in Cleveland and Milwaukee, consolidating a few common functions.[35] In contrast, at least twenty-eight metropolitan special-purpose authorities were established in American metropolitan areas in the 1930's, including sanitary sewer districts and district housing authorities. The number of municipalities in metropolitan areas increased from 3,165 to 3,464, with a rise in the number of such areas to 108.[36] In the context of Depression constraints, many central cities had to reduce their staffs and cut back on services, while counties and federal-state relief agencies took over some of their functions.[37] This development further weakened the logic of the reform argument that suburban residents (and their municipalities) needed to be part of the central city in order to have central city services.

There is no pattern of metropolitan reform efforts during the 1930's in Canada. The only comprehensive reform proposal identified was that made for Toronto by David Croll in 1936 and 1937, based upon the earlier amalgamation of Walkerville and Sandwich into the City of Windsor, Ontario.[38] The most common practical efforts to respond to metropolitan problems during these years in Canada were the creation of more area-wide special purpose authorities and the making of contractual arrangements between municipalities (especially between central cities and surrounding suburbs) to supply urban public services.[39] The insolvency of municipalities in the Depression years forced provincial governments to take over some rural and suburban municipalities and to extend their supervisory functions over others through municipal boards and commissions. An example is found in Quebec, where most municipal finances were placed under supervision by the Quebec Municipal Commission. The finances of the City of Montreal and other municipalities on the island, however, were supervised by the Montreal Metropolitan Commission, which also served as an ad hoc local coordinating authority.[40]

The Second World War years in Canada and the United States brought renewed efforts at formal and informal local cooperation in providing public services as part of the war effort, but there was little or no change of practice. The 1940 U.S. census, documenting declining populations in some central cities helped to stimulate further local studies and practical efforts toward consolidations by good government groups in the United States. Professor Carl J. Friedrich won a special Boston election with a plan that would have consolidated a total of sixty-six municipalities, but nothing came of this or similar schemes in St. Louis and Pittsburgh.[41] Louisville,

Milwaukee, and Atlanta were among the few cities which annexed larger suburban areas during this period, but there were few other changes in boundaries. The plight of the central cities and "the metropolitan problem" was recognized, but the war effort and planning for postwar recovery were higher priorities.[42]

However, the immediate postwar years of American metropolitan growth were characterized by the creation of regional planning commissions, which grew from fifteen in 1945 to thirty-four in 1949, though few had any official status. The number of special districts (with single or multiple functions) in U.S. metropolitan areas increased to over ninety by 1947. Proposals for city-county consolidation again increased, but only one is known to have succeeded: in a local referendum in Baton Rouge, Louisiana, the law allowed the favourable city majority to override the opposition of parish residents.[43] Despite the record of practical failures, reformers who wrote articles for the special mid-century issue of *The American City* predicted the ultimate victory of the city.[44]

No evidence was found of attempts at comprehensive reform in Canadian urban areas during the early 1940's, although there was an increase in the number of special-purpose local authorities especially related to the war effort.[45] Perhaps the most important contribution of this era was the development of urban land use and housing plans as important aspects of the federal post-war reconstruction planning begun in 1941.[46] This and similar efforts at the provincial and local level appear to have contributed to the perceived need for metropolitan-wide planning and problem-solving and led to the revitalization of the Canadian town planning movement.[47] For example, Manitoba created a Metropolitan Planning Committee in 1944, later renamed the Metropolitan Planning Commission. This commission was an important institutional step toward the Metropolitan Corporation of Greater Winnipeg, created in 1960.[48]

After the war, Canada's largest urban areas began to experience the type of explosive suburban growth which had been common in American urban areas since the turn of the century.[49] This growth and its attendant problems were especially evident in the Toronto area, where interest in comprehensive solutions was generated in the late 1940's and early 1950's by city newspapers, civic advisory groups, and a suburban politician, Frederick G. Gardiner. "Big Daddy" Gardiner became a champion of metropolitan reorganization after several years of frustration in attempting to deal with metropolitan problems as chairman of the Toronto and York Roads Commission, as a member of a provincial committee on urban planning and development, and as a member and later chairman of the Toronto and Suburban Planning Board, created by the Ontario government under its (town) Planning Act of 1946.[50]

Comprehensive Reforms in Canada, 1950–80

The last thirty years in Canada have been an era of not only "ad hoc metropolitan reform" in at least six provinces, but also of extensive local government restructuring by every province except Prince Edward Island.[51] These reforms are attributed almost universally to the impact of urbanization on local government institutions, including the consolidation of local school boards.[52] The Canadian record from 1950 to the present is one of much more extensive local government reform in general, as well as of a greater number of specific comprehensive metropolitan reform implementations, though there are fewer Canadian metropolitan areas with fewer fragmented patterns of local government than are found in the United States.[53] When analyzing this record, one must make specific comparisons with the patterns which have been noted for the United States.

Although the type of broad interest and zealous efforts toward comprehensive reform which took place in the United States did not occur in Canada, the "metropolitan problem" was being recognized at a practical level in Toronto, Winnipeg, and other major urban areas. Metropolitan reform studies were sometimes conducted by good-government reform groups (such as the Civic Advisory Council and the Bureau of Municipal Research in Toronto). But more often, the Canadian counterparts of the American "metropolitan surveys" were the products of royal commissions or committees of review: appointed, funded, and given their terms of reference by the provincial governments. Such commissions suggested different forms of metropolitan government for Montreal, Vancouver, and Winnipeg in the late 1950's and the early 1960's.[54]

In other provinces, the process of reform was initiated through applications to provincial municipal boards. In the case of Toronto, such studies and recommendations were products of hearings conducted into amalgamation, annexation, or incorporation applications by the already established, quasi-independent Ontario Municipal Board.[55] In 1950, it was presented with a petition from the Town of Mimico and the City of Toronto to amalgamate the city and the thirteen surrounding municipalities. Its hearings lasted for two years, and it submitted its report to the government of Ontario in January 1953. The report recommended against consolidating the thirteen municipalities but did recommend a metropolitan federation as a new regional municipality which would undertake area-wide functions, leaving the local municipalities intact to continue to provide a variety of local services. The Ontario government introduced a bill incorporating the board's recommendations. The bill passed its third reading in the legislature in April 1953; the municipality of Metropolitan Toronto began operations at the first of the next year.[56]

This passage of provincial bills accomplishing metropolitan reforms without local referenda distinguishes Canadian from American local reform. In the Toronto case, this was done "before any effective opposition could be mounted."[57] Smallwood calls this pattern of review, proposal generation, and implementation the "Anglo-Canadian leadership model" of achieving metropolitan and local government reform. He contrasts it with the American "participatory democracy" approach which allows local politics and referenda to determine the pace of the process as well as its results.[58]

Although widely recognized and studied in the United States as "a sort of major breakthrough in metropolitan reform," the creation of Metropolitan Toronto was not a "radical experiment" in Canadian terms, even though it was "quite properly regarded, even within Canada, as a bold step forward in as much as it provided a new structural approach for the fastest growing metropolitan centre in the country."[59] Rather, it applied to the Toronto area the framework of county government which had existed since the early nineteenth century in rural Quebec and Ontario, as well as throughout the United States. What the Ontario government actually did was to recreate an urban county: no municipalities were abolished, and significant numbers of local authorities remained at least semiautonomous.[60]

The 1960's and early 1970's were years of not only reform in some metropolitan areas, but also of general efforts in most urbanizing provinces towards "municipal reorganization" or the "structural reform of local government." All followed the pattern of the "leadership" model which has been described. Some efforts failed: a Saskatchewan provincial plan for comprehensive local government reorganization "came to a halt in the early 1960's."[61] But in 1967, New Brunswick undertook a "radical reform" of its municipalities' organization and responsibilities (shifting several to the provincial level) as a result of a royal commission on finance and municipal taxation which reported in 1963.[62]

While completing the consolidation of its local school districts in the 1960's, the province of Ontario embarked on a wide-ranging programme of "local government reviews" in urban areas experiencing metropolitan problems (Appendix, Table 2). These studies were followed by provincial bills amalgamating municipalities in the Lakehead and Timmins areas, and the introduction of second-tier regional municipalities, along with some reductions of lower-tier municipalities, in twelve other areas.[63] A Country Restructuring Program which replaced this programme in 1974 resulted in at least one further regional government for the Oxford, Ontario, area.

After a commission review of Metropolitan Toronto in 1967,

the number of lower-tier municipalities was reduced from thirteen to six, and the powers of "Metro Toronto" were increased, but the continued pleas of the three major daily newspapers in Toronto for total amalgamation (made continuously since 1950) were not heeded.[64] Another commission review, this by former Premier John Robarts, was conducted in the mid-1970's. It revealed a number of problems and made numerous recommendations in its several-volume 1977 report, but the provincial government introduced no major changes to the system in response to the report.[65] Similar reviews were conducted for the other regional governments, but they also were mostly ignored.[66]

The Quebec government created the Montreal Metropolitan Corporation in 1959, but it was "effectively sabotaged" by Jean Drapeau, who had just been elected as head of his civic party and opposed the equal representation of the city and suburbs on it.[67] Drapeau pursued an unsuccessful annexation policy which absorbed only the "virtually bankrupt" suburbs of Riviere-des-Prairies, Saraguay, and St. Michel during the 1960's, and the province did force the merger of municipalities on Ile-Jésus into the city of Laval in 1965. The Liberal provincial government, which had also created still another study committee on metropolitan government in 1964, was defeated by the Union Nationale in 1966 without taking action on the committee's controversial recommendations. In 1969, the new government proposed its own plans for urban communities in Montreal and Quebec based on recent French innovations.[68] Opposition to these plans caused an announcement of at least a years' delay, but the politics of the October police strike crisis led to the introduction and quick passage in November and December of a bill creating the Montreal Urban Community—a second-tier federation of the twenty-nine municipalities located on the Island of Montreal.[69] The following year, a similar regional government was created for Quebec City and Hull, and a programme of regroupment of municipalities throughout the province was begun.[70] This programme resulted in the reduction of eighty urban municipalities to around twenty in 1976, reductions in Quebec City from twenty-six to thirteen municipalities, and in Hull from thirty-two to eight. But the number of Montreal Urban Community municipalities has not been similarly reduced, and the Montreal metropolitan area includes all or parts of over one hundred municipalities, as well as several Indian reserves, public and parochial school districts, and other special purpose authorities.[71] Reforms have continued in the late 1970's and early 1980's.

Another noteworthy province is British Columbia which, during the 1960's, instituted a province-wide system of regional districts designed to provide hospitals and other area-wide services to both municipalities and unincorporated areas.[72] These included the Greater Vancouver Regional

District, which rapidly developed into a regional multi-purpose government.[73] Alberta and Saskatchewan were not as active in structural reform as were other provinces, such as Nova Scotia and Newfoundland.[74] The prairie provinces' cities were smaller and expanded to encompass most suburban development. The first major consideration of reform was not undertaken until the 1970's, when Calgary, Edmonton, and other urban areas experienced rapid urban growth.

In Manitoba, after four years of study by the Greater Winnipeg Investigating Commission, the government introduced a bill in 1959 creating the Metropolitan Corporation of Greater Winnipeg. Like the regional governments previously cited, it was a second-tier combination of some area-wide, special-purpose local authorities, such as the planning commission, waterworks, and sewage authorities.[75] Like Metro Toronto, it achieved area-wide planning, financial and public works successes. Unlike all of the other regional governments, it was given a directly-elected regional council, paid by the constituent municipalities. The result was what one astute observer called "the dissonant decade."[76] Newspapers and the popular central city mayor, as well as planning groups and other civic leaders, called for amalgamation of the city and surrounding areas and the demise of "Metro." This was made part of the New Democratic Party's platform in 1969, and upon winning the election it initiated studies which resulted in the creation of the amalgamated city of Winnipeg; the legislation passed in 1971 and the city officially began operations on 1 January 1972.[77]

These reforms were criticized by some reformers as being limited to better provision of urban land development services and administration, rather than production of area-wide policies, especially planning, dealing with matters of social justice and policy at the regional level, or resolving "the metropolitan problem" of many fragmented local jurisdictions.[78] For Plunkett and other Canadian metropolitan reformers, Winnipeg's Unicity became "Canada's only real innovation in urban municipal reorganization."[79] To another, it was "the most significant innovation in the attempt to provide more effective government in a metropolitan area" in North America.[80]

However, early evaluations indicated that "Unicity" was failing to live up to its promises of reorganizing administration and fostering area-wide, integrated policy making, while decentralizing local decision making and stimulating more active citizen participation.[81] In retrospect, a champion of the reform argues that:

> the Winnipeg reorganization was old-fashioned reform. It was designed primarily to overcome problems of fragmentation and of little governmental unity in planning and administration. In these endeavors

> it met with some success; however, the reform did little to meet the problems of intergovernmental relations, citizen activism, social and economic development, decentralization of authority and power, and the need for new management techniques and reorganization.[82]

The problems were formally identified in the *Report and Recommendations* of the Committee of Review, City of Winnipeg Act (1976). The recommendations of this committee followed Plunkett and other reformers who argued that what was needed was a quasi-parliamentary form of city council which would require party politics at the metropolitan level. However, the same provincial government which had created Unicity rejected the commission's major recommendations and left the organization essentially as it was.[83] Though a satisfactory evaluation has not been made of Unicity, it is clear that it has not changed the "biases" inherent in Winnipeg local government, nor has it reduced the complexity of policy making by administrative centralization.[84] Furthermore, there remain twelve school boards and other local authorities with whom the unified city must share its jurisdiction.

The most recent attempt at metropolitan reform, and focus of reform ideas and rhetoric, was the Edmonton metropolitan area. In 1979, the city applied to the Alberta Municipal Board to consolidate the surrounding county (Strathcona) and several small suburban communities into one large city modelled on Winnipeg's Unicity. After extensive hearings, the board made its recommendations to the provincial government, which rejected the idea of comprehensive amalgamation, but allowed annexation of a large portion of the surrounding area by the city.[85]

Zenith and Decline of Metropolitan Reform in the United States: 1950–80

An expert on the subject argued that interest in the reform of American metropolitan government reached its peak in the 1950's, expressing itself in the production of 79 metropolitan surveys (of the 112 undertaken between 1923 and 1958), in numerous articles in the *National Civic Review,* and widespread references and visits to Metropolitan Toronto, which was hailed as a protoype for future American metropolitan reforms.[86]

Despite this zenith of intellectual effort and interest, the attempts to actually change local political institutions were quite limited, and almost all failed. First-time efforts were made to inaugurate metropolitan authorities in Seattle, Louisville, Nashville, Knoxville, and Albuquerque later in the decade, but they all failed to obtain the required majority support of suburban residents in referenda. Perhaps most significant were the failures of referenda in the Cleveland and St. Louis metropolitan areas in 1959. Metropolitan reform in these areas had been studied, recommended, and worked on for over a generation, and carried endorsements by leading local citizens and citizen groups.[87] The St. Louis experience provided the basis for a number of books and became a symbol of the problems of practical metropolitan reform in the United States.[88]

The only exception to this discouraging record was the 1957 Miami consolidation of some common functions of Miami and Dade Counties under a new metropolitan government, a result brought about by the City's attempt to annex the entire county after the failure of four consolidation efforts.[89] Several more consolidations of this type occurred in the 1960's: Nashville-Davidson County (1963), Jacksonville-Duval County (1968), and Indianapolis-Marion County (1969, the first city-county consolidation accomplished without a referendum since 1898).[90] Studies of these "successes" suggest that they did not go as far as Toronto in creating a metropolitan federation but rather were formal arrangements for the sharing of services between the county and the local municipalities. Differences of services and property tax rates (especially between the central city and upper class suburbs) were retained, thereby promoting patterns of racial and class stratification.[91]

The active period of the 1960's "gave way to a period of relative quiesience in metropolitan structural reform in the 1970's."[92] Today, in the early 1980's, the attempts continue in the same pattern: a few successes, but many failures.

Some of the "newer" Sunbelt cities continued to expand during this period by annexation; the twenty fastest-growing American metropolitan areas more than doubled their size.[93] But in most U.S. metropolitan areas, including many Sunbelt S.M.S.A.s, the basic pattern was one of continued fragmentation of local government and the further development of single or multiple-purpose service districts along with ad hoc cooperative arrangements and regional planning activities.[94] The latter was linked with our increasing orientation toward planning as a focus of area-wide cooperation and coordination. The Association of Metropolitan Regional Organizations had been formed in 1954, having as its members numerous planning bodies.[95] Another major development of the 1950's had been the creation of a "Supervisors Inter-county Committee" in the Detroit area, which was the first Council of (local) Governments (C.O.G.).[96] Though only eight others had been formed by 1965, by 1980 there were almost 600 operating in 250 S.M.S.A.s and 350 non-metropolitan areas.[97] This growth in C.O.G.s was stimulated by federal funding for local area planning and coordinative bodies in the 1960's, and the (A-95) requirement for such bodies to priorize requests for federal Housing and Urban Development funds. At least two of these bodies were strengthened by their state legislatures to be metropolitan multi-service districts: the Minneapolis-St. Paul Metropolitan Council, created in 1967 and Portland's Metropolitan Service District created in 1978.[98] But most of the C.O.G.s remained primarily planning and advisory bodies with only limited powers and funding.

Metropolitan Reform Ideas

Metropolitan reform ideas continued to be advanced, stimulated especially by the model of Toronto; they were outlined in the *National Civic Review*, in numerous academic books and articles, and in publications of the Advisory Commission on Intergovernmental Relations, which was created in 1959.[99] A number of books such as Luther H. Gulick's *The Metropolitan Problem and American Ideas* followed the pattern of Victor Jones's *Metropolitan Government* (1942) in trying to assess why metropolitan reform was so hard to achieve. Bollens and Schmandt's textbook, *The Metropolis* (1965) devoted fou of its nineteen chapters to the subject, including a chapter on "The One-Government Approach: Annexation and Consolidation."[100]

In 1966, the prestigious Committee on Economic Development (C.E.D.) recommended an 80 per cent reduction in the number of American local governments under "super" county governments, including amalgamation of municipal governments in metropolitan areas.[101] In 1968, the National Commission on Urban Problems (Douglas Commission) adopted a similar stance in its recommendations.[102] But in another report in 1970, the C.E.D. shifted from support of total integration to support of a two-tier federated system as "an ultimate solution."[103] New studies in the 1970's by organizations such as the League of Women Voters tended to support similar solutions, as did textbooks.[104] Reorganization of local government continued to be a major topic at national League of Cities conferences, where particular attention was given to city-county consolidation prospects in the 1980's.[105]

However, a growing body of literature in the 1960's and 1970's in the United States challenged the relevance and value of metropolitan reform as an idea, as a focus of research, and as a desirable goal of practical reform efforts. One body of literature developed extensive criticisms of metropolitan reform assumptions: that the metropolitan area was a community; that fragmented government was a problem; and that comprehensive metropolitan reform was possible or desirable in American local politics.[106] Arguments were made that fragmented service delivery systems (such as the

"Lakewood Plan" in the Los Angeles area) made centralized metropolitan government unnecessary, even if it were politically feasible, which it obviously was not.[107] From this view, the "metropolitan reform tradition" was both misguided and outmoded. Considerable analyses of recent reform attempts and the successful American reforms cited above provided further arguments against it.

As an alternative to the "flawed" metropolitan reform approach to metropolitan governance, Bish (1971) and Ostrum (1973) argued for application of "public choice theory," which characterized local governments as economic organizations which should provide public goods to citizen-consumers in the organizational forms most appropriate to the efficient supply of these various public goods.[108] From this conservative urban political economy perspective, metropolitan reform is not only unnecessary, but it is dangerously misleading because it fails to properly comprehend the nature of metropolitan government and politics. Intellectual and practical energies should be directed toward determining the most efficient sizes and institutions for each type of local public service, and developing their service delivery capabilities.[109] Though widely studied in Canada, the applications of this theory to Canadian contexts have been rare.[110]

Radical Political Economy Perspectives

While one "urban political economy" perspective was rejecting metropolitan reform as antithetical to efficient urban development and government, another body of "urban political economy" literature was linking it with urban land development, corporate concentration, and other components of North American capitalism. Not all of this literature is Marxist; an excellent non-Marxist evaluation of those relationships in the American context appears in an exhaustive multi-volume evaluation published by Resources For The Future:

> The impact of land development on metropolitan functions has for many years been a major stimulus of initiatives for metropolitan reforms. The unsightliness and inefficiency of suburban sprawl, the poorly distributed burdens of rapid population growth concentrated in jurisdictions with inadequate fiscal resources, and the growing disparities in financial capacities among neighboring jurisdictions . . . have provided major justifications for proposals for metropolitan governmental reforms. But metropolitan reforms aimed at supplying the infrastructure to serve development . . . not only serve development; they generate it as well.[111]

This reciprocal relationship was generalized more broadly within the Canadian context by a number of studies published in the 1960's, but perhaps most succinctly summarized by James Lorimer:

> Alongside the process of corporate concentration in land development has gone a parallel process of political concentration in urban government . . . one which concentrates enormous planning and financial powers into a regional, metropolitan, or single-tier city government that is difficult for ordinary city residents to influence or control.[112]

From this point of view, the metropolitan reform models, such as Metro Toronto, are merely the means for servicing suburban development:

> In establishing the Metro Government (of Toronto) the Province of Ontario provided a governmental jurisdiction to lay down suburban services. The formation of Metro also established a centralized and isolated government which could raise, at public expense, the enormous sums of money needed to collectivize these costs. . . .
>
> Of great importance in this respect was the attention paid by Metro to the problem of linking the emerging suburbs to the central city by transportation networks.[113]

Similar analyses were made of various other Canadian metropolitan areas, many having reform institutions.[114] Today, further characterizations of Canadian urban development from this perspective are appearing.[115]

These characterizations of Canadian contexts were amplified in terms of explicitly Marxist perspectives offered in the American context. Ashton characterized the "political economy of suburban development" in this manner:

> it was the decentralization of production and distribution facilities which began the movement of resources out of the city. And the political needs and power of capitl ensured that the city would not annex these new areas. The central city's tax base has been further eroded. . . . To overcome this contradiction and ensure the continued profitability of the central-city investments, capitalists must rationalize the metropolis. They must appropriate the resources of the suburbs and plow them back into the central city. But to do this means that they must break the power of the suburbs. Capital must destroy the political fragmentation which it helped create and which it has exploited so profitably.[116]

A companion article, subtitled "A Marxist Theory of Metropolitan Government" argued that

> the existence of fragmented political units encumbers the co-ordination and administration of national and multi-national corporation. . . . Some corporate leaders complain about the lack of metropolitan regional planning and appear to be increasingly in favor of regionalized political structure. Thus, a struggle may ensue between suburban subclasses, militant in their desire to preserve their local public-sector autonomy and large capitalist interests, pushing for planned, rationalized, metropolis-wide government.[117]

These assessments have been convincingly challenged as oversimplifications by a recent Canadian critique:

> "solutions" to (urban) problems are the result of political accommodation and they may be advanced from either or both sides of the political divide. Metropolitan reform . . . may be regarded as a product of class struggle and a consequence of the contradictions of capitalist society, but it cannot be attributed to the demands or requirements of any one class in isolation. Like so many other reforms in capitalist societies, it commands support from both capital and labour. . . .
>
> Metropolitan government is a product of *early* capitalism, and there are reasons for thinking that it is an archaic form of political and administrative organization. The urban system of an advanced capitalist country can only be managed by a network of agencies, many of which are larger and as many smaller than the physical metropoles. The political process within such a system is certain to be extremely complex, and is liable to burst the bounds of any simplifed structure of metropolitan government. This is what the American theorists of public choice have suggested, but their message has yet to be assimilated by Marxist analysis.[118]

It remains for further research and intellectual exchange to determine the relevance of these ideas regarding the relationship between metropolitan reform and the political economy of metropolitan land development. The research and literature on this field are growing rapidly, and it is beyond the scope of this research to provide more than references to the seminal Canadian and American literatures.[119] There is little doubt that at the present time this is one of the most interesting and important strains of thought in the continuing intellectual history of metropolitan reform.

CONCLUSIONS

The process of metropolitanization is a component of world-wide urbanization in the nineteenth and twentieth centuries, involving urban development of suburban and exurban areas beyond the geographical boundaries of central cities, in unincorporated areas, and within the boundaries of already incorporated municipalities. The local political culture, especially in western capitalist democracies with a history of quasi-independent local governments, favoured creation of new local governments and maintenance of those already existing. It was impossible for most central cities to annex all unincorporated territory and consolidate all incorporated jurisdictions to make viable the one-government pattern in the larger urban areas which were later recognized as metropolitan. The response was especially inadequate in the United States where local self-government and neighbourhood community life were values protected by local referenda requirements and restrictions on annexations and consolidations created by rural-dominated state legislatures. Early in this century, as municipal reformers attacked central cities, American White Anglo-Saxons were settling in suburban municipalities or incorporated areas serviced by predominantly rural counties. The result was political fragmentation and relatively uncontrolled urban sprawl. The situation was somewhat less difficult in Canada, where central city annexations continued until the First World War, but the basic problem of multiple local governments and city-suburban politics was not avoided.

This condition was responded to by professors and other planning-oriented veterans of municipal reform in the U.S. following its 1910 census, which made the situation very clear to them and others familiar with the statistical evidence. Their intellectual effort was part of extensive practical efforts by citizen leagues and other central metropolitan elites to resolve local metropolitan problems by advocating various forms of comprehensive metropolitan government reform. The intellectual and practical histories of metropolitan reform were traced up to the present and continue in the United States today, but neither have achieved the successes which they had promised when they began. Rather, the historical record is one of continuing idealistic rhetoric and continuing failure of practical efforts. Both these traditions have received substantial criticisms from empiricists as well as from conservative and radical political economy perspectives. A relatively few city-county consolidations which have been successfully innovated have been widely recognized, studied, and held out as models in the literature; but they do not appear to have been widely copied or to have altered the basic patterns of political economy (power, decision making), and the patterns of inequality in urban development taking place in their metropolitan areas. The more common patterns of adaptation in American metropolitan areas have been the development of ad hoc formal and informal interlocal cooperation, the proliferation of special districts, a strengthening of urban counties, and the emergence of new regional planning and coordinating institutions. All of these have added to the number of local authorities and "the metropolitan problem," but have fostered, not hindered, local development.

In contrast to the "participatory" American patterns, there has been a more recent (post-Second World War) and successful "leadership" pattern in Canada, which has resulted in a second-tier (federated) metropolitan government, except for Winnipeg, which is the North American reorganization closest to the metropolitan reformers' ideals. But even this "ideal" reform did not alter the basic local power structure, its dominance of local politics, and its support of the property industry's exploitation of the suburban and exurban development process.[120] Rather, Canadian metropolitan reforms appear to provide the regional infrastructure for serving that process and its exploitation by the dominant land developers. When these developers found their lucrative markets disappearing in Canada, they shifted their attention and investments to developing urban areas in the United States.[121]

The North American urban development process has reflected and strengthened the patterns of social segregation, as well as local governmental inequalities, and there is little evidence that any of the metropolitan or local governmental reforms considered in this study have appreciably changed this condition toward greater social justice.

Thus, the broader patterns of North American society—Canadian and American—and the political economy of advanced capitalism are reflected in the social organization found in all North American metropolitan areas, whatever the nature of their local government structure or their record of metropolitan reform. But every metropolitan area in those countries has a distinctive present pattern and past history of local government institutions, based on complex local and state or provincial responses to their "metropolitan problem" through the years. As part of this pattern, especially in the United States, there has been an intellectual preoccupation with the possibilities of comprehensive institutional reform, which even if realized, fails to solve the basic problem of an ever-expanding urban sprawl, which now is largely occurring beyond even the most liberally-defined metropolitan area boundaries. There is no sign that this pattern will change in the near future, as it is a hallmark of metropolitanization, not just in North America, but around the world.

In summary, it appears that while local government structure and metropolitan reform are not central determinants of the basic urban development processes, they are important political and intellectual links between the general society and each metropolitan area's adaptive history. As such, they appear to provide an important example of the "meso-analytical" phenomena which Pacquet and Wallot argue should be the most important priorities in comparative historical research.[122]

NOTES

1. For example, Arthur B. Gunlicks, ed., *Local Government Reform and Reorganization* (Port Washington, NY, 1981), and Donald C. Rowat, ed., *International Handbook on Local Government Reorganization: Contemporary Developments* (Westport, CN, 1980).
2. Edmund P. Fowler and Robert L. Lineberg, "The Comparative Analysis of Urban Policy: Canada and the United States," in Harlan Hahn, ed., *People and Politics in Urban Society* (Beverly Hills, CA, 1972), pp. 345–68; Michael A. Goldberg and John Mercer, "Canadian and U.S. Cities: Basic Differences, Possible Explanations, And Their Meaning For Public Policy," *Regional Science Association Papers* 45 (1980): 159–83; John Mercer, "On Continentalism, Distinctiveness, and Comparative Urban Geography: Canadian and American Cities," *Canadian Geographer* 23, no. 2 (1979): 119–39; especially 133–34; and the Mercer and Goldberg article in this volume.
3. The basic development of this research took place within the original framework for the 1982 Guelph Conference: "The Political Economy of Canadian-American Development."
4. This definition reflects the fact that governments and researchers define "metropolitan areas" in various ways and with different results as to demographic and geographic-spatial size. A good discussion of definitions and their problems in the comparative context is provided by Richard L. Forstall and Victor Jones, "Selected Demographic, Economic, and Governmental Aspects of the Contemporary Metropolis," in Simon Miles, ed., *Metropolitan Problems* (Toronto, 1968), pp. 5–69. Comparative analysis of Canadian and U.S. definitions and trends was undertaken 25 years ago by Leo F. Schnore and Gene B. Peterson, "Urban and Metropolitan Development in the United States and Canada," *Annals* of the American Academy of Political and Social Sciences 316 (March 1958): 60–68. Canadian statistical definitions are discussed by Leroy O. Stone, *Urban Development in Canada* (Ottawa, 1967), p. 129 and 237 (Appendix D); Frederick I. Hill, *Canadian Urban Trends: Metropolitan Perspective,* Vol. 2 (Ottawa, 1976), pp. 2 and 36; and "Census Metropolitan Areas" in *The Census Dictionary* (Ottawa: Minister of Supply and Services, 1982). Recent United States Census definitions of "Standard Metropolitan Statistical Areas" are discussed by John C. Bollens and Henry Schmandt, *The Metropolis,* 4th Ed. (New York, 1982), pp. 5–11.
5. Warren Magnusson, "Metropolitan Reform in the Capitalist City," *Canadian Journal of Political Science* 15, no. 3 (September 1981): pp. 558, 565–66.
6. Ibid., 561.

[notes continued p.315]

APPENDIX

TABLE 1

GROWTH DATA FOR METROPOLITAN AREAS (MA's), CENTRAL CITIES, AND RINGS, CANADA AND THE UNITED STATES (1870–71 THROUGH 1950–51)

Countries	Number of MA's	Population of MA's (millions)	Per Cent of National Population		Rate of Growth During Preceding Decade					Per Cent of Total Growth Claimed by MA's During Preceding Decade	
			Central Cities	Rings	National Total	Area Outside MA's	MA's	Central Cities	Rings	Central Cities	Rings
Canada[a]											
1871	3	0.5	5.9	6.8	—	—	—	—	—	—	—
1881	2	0.5	5.3	5.2	17.2	16.4	24.5	39.1	12.7	10.0	4.0
1891	2	0.6	8.2	4.7	11.8	8.7	37.9	75.1	0.5	33.6	0.2
1901	5	1.0	11.3	7.1	11.1	10.1	16.2	24.6	5.0	22.2	3.4
1911	6	1.9	18.4	8.4	34.2	27.2	57.8	82.8	21.5	32.8	5.8
1921	10	2.8	21.9	10.1	21.9	17.3	33.3	35.7	28.3	32.0	12.3
1931	13	4.2	26.4	13.8	18.1	10.9	30.7	29.5	33.0	39.2	22.4
1941	14	4.8	26.8	14.6	10.9	10.3	11.7	11.0	12.9	27.1	16.9
1951	15	6.2	26.5	19.0	18.6	12.7	26.5	15.6	45.7	22.8	38.1

United States											
1870[b]	21	8.3	12.9	10.6	—	—	—	—	—	—	—
1880	30	11.9	13.5	10.2	41.1	45.7	28.0	36.3	18.4	12.4	5.4
1890	44	17.8	16.9	11.4	25.5	21.8	36.1	45.6	24.0	26.1	10.8
1900[c]	52	24.1	21.2	10.7	20.7	17.2	29.0	45.7	5.2	38.5	3.1
1910	71	34.5	25.0	12.7	21.0	15.0	32.6	35.3	27.6	37.4	15.7
1920	94	46.1	28.9	14.8	14.9	8.1	25.2	26.7	22.4	46.8	20.8
1930	115	61.0	31.8	18.0	16.1	7.1	27.0	23.3	34.2	43.3	32.9
1940	125	67.1	31.6	19.5	7.2	6.2	8.3	5.1	13.8	22.8	34.9
1950	147	84.3	32.3	23.8	14.5	6.3	21.8	13.7	34.8	30.7	48.6

[a] Data for Canada from Dominion Bureau of Statistics, *Ninth Census of Canada, 1951*, Vol. 1, Table 6, pp. 6–1 to 6–88.

[b] Data for the United States (1870–90) from Department of Interior, Census Office, *Compendium of the Eleventh Census: 1890*, Part I, Table 2, pp. 7–47, Table 4a, pp. 434–36, Table 5, pp. 442–52; and Department of Interior, Census Office, *Ninth Census: 1870*, Vol. 1, Table 3, pp. 77–296.

[c] Data for the United States (1900–1950) from Donald J. Bogue, ''Urbanism in the United States, 1950,'' *American Journal of Sociology*, 9, no. 5, (March 1955) Tables 4 and 5, p. 480, reproduced by permission of the publisher, copyright 1955 by the University of Chicago; and Donald J. Bogue, *Population Growth in Standard Metropolitan Areas 1900–1950*, (Housing and Home Finance Agency, 1953) Appendix Table 1, pp. 61–71. We have followed Bogue's practice of using ''county equivalent'' metropolitan areas in New England. Retrojection of 1950 areas to earlier dates does not imply these these ares were metropolitan in character; our sole intention is to hold total area constant.

Source: Schnore and Petersen, ''Urban and Metropolitan Development in the United States and Canada,'' p. 65.

TABLE 2

LOCAL GOVERNMENT REORGANIZATIONS IN ONTARIO

Review and Year Study Instituted and Report Received	Basic Study Area (1971 municipal population)
1. (a) Metropolitan Toronto (1950–53) Implemented 1954	2,045,000 population; 240 square miles; 13 municipalities plus Metro
(b) Revision 1963–65 Implemented 1967	6 municipalities plus Metro
2. Ottawa-Carleton (1963–1965) Implemented 1969	460,000 population; 1,100 square miles; 16 municipalities
3. Niagara (1964–66) Implemented 1970	338,000 population; 720 square miles 26 municipalities reduced to 12
4. Peel-Halton (1965–66) Implemented 1973 as two separate regions	463,000 population; 989 square miles; Peel—10 municipalities reduced to 3; Halton—7 municipalities reduced to 4
5. Lakehead (1965–68) Partial implementation 1971 City of Thunder Bay	106,000 population; 120 square miles; 20 municipalities of which 2 cities and parts of 3 suburbs were amalgamated
6. Brant-Brantford (1966) Only the data book has been completed. Reinstituted 1972, but no changes made.	87,000 population; 347 square miles; 7 municipalities
7. Waterloo Area (1966–70) Implemented 1973	250,000 population; 506 square miles; 15 municipalities reduced to 7
8. Muskoka District (1967–69) Implemented 1970	30,000 population, 1,688 square miles; 25 municipalities reduced to 6
9. Hamilton-Wentworth (1967–69) Implemented 1973	393,000 population; 523 square miles; 11 municipalities reduced to 6
10. Sudbury (1968–70) Implemented 1973	158,000 population; 1,090 square miles; 15 municipalities reduced to 7
11. York—Study by county (1967–69) Implemented 1970	161,000 population; 645 square miles; 14 municipalities reduced to 9

TABLE 2 (*continued*)

LOCAL GOVERNMENT REORGANIZATIONS IN ONTARIO

12. Timmins (1972) Internal government study Implemented 1973	42,000 population; 1,225 square miles; 4 municipalities plus unorganized territory reduced to 1
13. Oshawa Area (1969–discontinued) Government proposals 1972 Implemented as Region of Durham 1973	237,000 population; 1,168 square miles; 21 municipalities reduced to 8
14. Haldimand-Norfolk Implemented 1974	84,000 population; 1,122 square miles; 28 municipalities reduced to 6

Note: In all cases of implementation except Lakehead and Timmins a regional municipality was formed in addition to those enumerated.

Source: Fyfe, "Local Government Reform In Ontario," p. 24.

---

7. Magnusson makes the stronger assertion that the English model "was at the heart of the theory of metropolitan reform which was developed by American progressives," ibid., 561, 568.
8. Gregory Singleton, "The Genesis of Suburbia: A Complex of Historical Trends," in Louis H. Massotti and Jeffrey H. Hadden, eds., *The Urbanization of the Suburbs* (Beverly Hills, 1973), pp. 29–50. On Canadian development, articles in Gilbert A. Stelter and Alan F. J. Artibise, eds., *Shaping the Urban Landscape: Aspects of the Canadian City-Building Process* (Ottawa, 1982); and George Nader *Cities in Canada,* vol. 2 (Toronto, 1975).
9. Paris N. Glendening and Patricia S. Atkins, "City County Consolidations: New Views for the Eighties," 1980 *Municipal Year Book* (Washington, DC, 1980), p. 70; National Municipal League, Committee on Metropolitan Government, *The Government of Metropolitan Areas In The United States* (New York, 1930, 1974), pp. 170–203.
10. National Municipal League, *The Government of Metropolitan Areas,* pp. 342–66; Wallace S. Sayre and Herbert Kaufman, *Governing New York City* (New York, 1965), pp. 11–17.
11. National Municipal League, *The Government of Metropolitan Areas,* pp. 256–341 and 43–64 respectively.
12. Nader, *Cities in Canada*; and Stelter and Artibise, *Shaping the Urban Landscape,* Section 3, "Evolving Urban Form."
13. Kenneth Jackson, "The Crabgrass Frontier: 150 Years of Suburban Growth In America," in Raymond A. Mohl and James F. Richardson, eds., *The Urban*

Experience: Themes in American History (Belmont, CA, 1973); on Canada, references in Alan F. J. Artibise and Gilbert A. Stelter, *Canada's Urban Past* (Vancouver, 1981), pp. xxii–xxiii and passim.

14. Jon C. Teaford, *City And Suburb: The Political Fragmentation of Metropolitan America, 1850–1970* (Baltimore, 1979), Chapters 2 and 5 especially.
15. Michael P. McCarthy, "The New Metropolis: Chicago, the Annexation Movement and Progressive Reform," in Michael H. Ebner and Eugene M. Tobin, eds., *The Age of Urban Reform* (Port Washington, 1977), pp. 43–54; McCarthy, "The Politics of Suburban Growth" in this volume.
16. McCarthy, "The New Metropolis," p. 52.
17. National League of Cities, *The Government of Metropolitan Areas,* pp. 68–75; Blake McKelvey, *The Emergence of Metropolitan America, 1959–1966* (Rutgers, NJ, 1968) p. 9.
18. Michael J. Doucet, "Politics, Space, and Trolleys: Mass Transit in Early Twentieth-Century Toronto," in Stelter and Artibise, *Shaping the Urban Landscape,* pp. 363–64; "Les Annexions à la Cité de Montréal, 1883–1918," (A map by Institut national de la recherche scientifique—Urbanisation at the Université du Quebec, n.d.); on one such community, see Paul-André Linteau, "The Development and Beautification of an Industrial City: Maisonneuve, 1883–1918," in Stelter and Artibise, ibid., pp. 304–20.
19. More thorough examinations of urban development around major Canadian cities is found in Nader, *Cities in Canada*; Stelter and Artibise, *Shaping the Urban Landscape,* especially references in Stelter's "Introduction," pp. 15–18 and 25–27, and articles in Section 3, "Evolving Urban Form."
20. Kenneth Fox, *Better City Government: Innovation in American Urban Politics* (Philadelphia, 1977); Frank M. Stewart, *Half a Century of Municipal Reform* (Berkeley and Los Angeles, 1950); Teaford, *City and Suburb,* pp. 84–85.
21. Paul Rutherford, "Tomorrow's Metropolis: The Urban Reform Movement in Canada, 1880–1920," in Gilbert A. Stelter and Alan F. J. Artibise, *The Canadian City: Essays in Urban History* (Toronto, 1977), pp. 368–92; Rutherford, *Saving the Canadian City: The First Phase: 1880–1920* (Toronto, 1974); John C. Weaver, "The Modern City Realized: Toronto Civic Affairs, 1880–1915," in Artibise and Stelter, eds., *The Usable Urban Past* (Toronto, 1979), p. 56; John C. Weaver, "Tomorrow's Metropolis' Revisited: A Critical Assessment of Urban Reform in Canada, 1890–1920," in Stelter and Artibise, *The Canadian City,* pp. 393–418, especially 411.
22. Fox, *Better City Government,* p. 150; Teaford, *City and Suburb,* p. 577; National Municipal League, *Government of Metropolitan Areas*. p. 16; McKelvey, *The Emergence of Metropolitan America,* p. 977.
23. Stone, *Urban Development in Canada,* pp. 231, 233.
24. McKelvey, *The Emergence of Metropolitan America,* p. 55.
25. Ibid., 55.
26. Teaford, *City and Suburb,* p. 171.
27. National Municipal League, *Government of Metropolitan Areas,* p. 41.

28. Fox, *Better City Government,* pp. 155–158; Teaford, *City and Suburb,* Chapter 6.
29. Timothy Colton, *Big Daddy: Frederick G. Gardiner and the Building of Metropolitan Toronto* (Toronto, 1980), p. 55. There was some consideration given to metropolitan reform in Montreal: Frederick Wright, ed., *A Symposium of Opinion on the Borough System of Government for Greater Montreal* (Montreal, 1928).
30. Robert E. L. Farris, "Interrelated Problems of the Expanding Metropolis," *Canadian Journal of Economics and Political Science* (1939): 341–47; and J. A. Watson, "Urban Developments in the Niagara Peninsula," ibid. (1943): 463–86.
31. Harold Kaplan, *Reform, Planning and City Politics: Montreal, Winnipeg, Toronto* (Toronto, 1982); Thomas I. Gunton, "The Ideas and Policies of The Canadian Planning Profession, 1909–1931," in Artibise and Stelter, *The Usable Urban Past,* pp. 177–95; Walter Van Nus, "The Fate of City Beautiful Thought in Canada, 1893–1930," in Stelter and Artibise, *The Canadian City,* pp. 176–80. At least one exception to this pattern is Montreal: Andrew Sancton, "The Impact of Language Differences on Metropolitan Reform In Montreal," in Lionel D. Feldman, ed., *Politics and Government of Urban Canada* (Toronto, 1981), p. 371.
32. W. B. Munro, *Municipal Government and Administration* (New York, 1923), p. 437.
33. McKelvey, *The Emergence of Metropolitan America,* pp. 55, 58–62.
34. Ibid., p. 103.
35. Ibid., p. 104.
36. Ibid.
37. Ibid., pp. 107, 141ff; Roscoe C. Martin, *The Cities and the Federal System* (New York, 1965).
38. Coltan, *Big Daddy,* p. 56.
39. Kenneth G. Crawford, *Canadian Municipal Government* (Toronto, 1954), pp. 126–37; Horace L. Brittain, *Local Government in Canada* (Toronto, 1951), pp. 154–55.
40. Sancton, "The Impact of Language Differences," National Municipal League, *Government of Metropolitan Areas,* pp. 332–33; and Terry Copp, "Montreal's Municipal Government and the Crisis of the 1930's," in Artibise and Stelter, *The Usable Urban Past,* pp. 112–29.
41. McKelvey, *The Emergence of Metropolitan America,* pp. 138–39.
42. Ibid., p. 138.
43. Ibid., p. 139.
44. Ibid., p. 152.
45. Brittain, *Local Government in Canada;* Crawford, *Municipal Government,* pp. 126–37.
46. Edward Sommerville, "Towards the Keynesian City: Reconstruction and the Resurrection of Town Planning in Canada, 1941–1951," a paper presented at the Guelph Conference, 1982; Kent Gerecke, "The History of Canadian City

Planning,'' in James Lorimer and Evelyn Rees, eds., *The Second City Book* (Toronto, 1977), pp. 151–52.

47. Gerecke, ''Canadian City Planning,'' p. 152.
48. S. George Rich, ''Metropolitan Winnipeg: The First Ten Years,'' in Ralph R. Krueger and R. Charles Bryfogle, eds., *Urban Problems: A Canadian Reader* (Toronto, 1971), pp. 358–60.
49. John Sewell, ''Where the Suburbs Came From,'' in Lorimer and Rees, *The Second City Book,* pp. 10–17; S. D. Clark, *The Suburban Society* (Toronto, 1966).
50. Colton, *Big Daddy,* pp. 59–61.
51. C. R. Tindal and S. Nobes Tindal, *Local Government in Canada: An Introduction* (Toronto, 1979), Chapters 3–4; Thomas J. Plunkett, ''Structural Reform of Local Government In Canada,'' in L. D. Feldman and M. D. Goldrick, eds., *Politics and Government of Urban Canada: Selected Readings,* 3d Ed. (Toronto, 1976), pp. 313–32; Donald Higgins, *Urban Canada: Its Government and Politics* (Toronto, 1977), Chapter 4.
52. This research found few references to this phenomena, such as that in Donald C. Rowat, *Your Local Government* (Toronto, 1975), p. 22.
53. Mercer, ''On Continentalism,'' pp. 133–34.
54. Plunkett, ''Structural Reform,'' p. 320; Tindal and Tindal, *Local Government in Canada,* pp. 50–54; Kaplan, *Reform, Planning, and City Politics,* Chapters 9, 11, and 14.
55. Higgins, *Urban Canada,* pp. 72–75, 138–41. At least one institutional innovation in American metropolitan reform was patterned on this board: the Minnesota Municipal Commission; P. H. Wichern, ''Grass Roots Politics On the Urban Frontier,'' (Ph.D. Diss., University of Minnesota, 1970); Albert Rose, *Governing Metropolitan Toronto: A Social and Political Analysis, 1953–1971,* (Berkeley, 1972), pp. 21–22.
56. Plunkett, ''Structural Reform,'' p. 317; James F. Horan and G. Thomas Taylor, *Experiments in Metropolitan Government* (New York, 1977), p. 115; Arnold Rose, ''Two Decades of Metropolitan Government in Toronto, 1953–1973,'' in Advisory Commission on Intergovernmental Relations, *A Look To the North: Canadian Regional Experience* (Washington, DC, 1974), p. 35; Rose, *Governing Metropolitan Toronto* (Berkeley, 1972), Chapter 3.
57. Plunkett, ''Structural Reform,'' p. 317.
58. Frank Smallwood, ''Guiding Urban Change,'' *National Civic Review,* 59, no. 4 (April 1965): 191–97; also in Robert S. Morlan, ed., *Capital, Courthouse, and City Hall,* 3d ed. (Boston, 1966).
59. Plunkett, ''Structural Reform,'' p. 318.
60. After a reduction of municipalities from twelve to six in 1967, Dominic Del Guidice and Stephen M. Zacks identified over one hundred local government units in ''The 101 Governments of Metro Toronto,'' Feldman and Goldrick, *Politics and Government of Urban Canada* (1976), pp. 285–95.
61. Plunkett, ''Structural Reform,'' p. 319.
62. Higgins, *Urban Canada,* pp. 131–32; Tindal and Tindal, *Local Government in Canada,* pp. 54–56.

63. Stewart Fyfe "Local Government Reform in Ontario," Advisory Commission, *A Look to the North,* pp. 13–32; Higgins, *Urban Canada,* pp. 143–46;Tindal and Tindal, *Local Government in Canada,* pp. 60–62.
64. Plunkett, *Urban Canada and its Government* (Toronto, 1971), p. 103; Albert Rose, *Governing Metropolitan Toronto: A Social and Political Analysis, 1953–1971.*
65. Feldman, *Politics and Government of Urban Canada,* pp. 319–20, 390–430.
66. Trevor Price, "The Political Viability of Ontario's Reformed Structures of Local Government," in *Urban Forum* 2, no 4 (Winter 1976): 30–39; Robert Matas, "Regional Structure Hasn't Met Promise," *Globe and Mail* 9 March 1981, pp. 1 and 8; "Ontario Ignores Critics over Regional Bodies," Ibid., 10 March 1981, p. 9.
67. Sancton, "The Impact of Language Differences on Metropolitan Reform in Montreal," p. 373; Jean Godin, "Local Government Reform in the Province of Quebec," Advisory Commission *A Look to the North,* p. 55–57.
68. Sancton, ibid., 374–75.
69. It should be noted that this reform left the same number of local municipalities in the Montreal area. Godin, ibid., 57–61; André Bernard, Jacque Léveillée and Guy Lord, *Profile: Montreal* (Ottawa, Information Canada, 1974), Chapter 1B.
70. Godin, Advisory Commission, *A Look to the North,* pp. 61–64; Plunkett, "Structural Reform," pp. 323–24.
71. Bernard, Léveillée, and Lord, Profile: Montreal, Part 2; *Population: Geographic Distributions,* 1976 Census of Canada (Ottawa, 1977), pp. 6–2 to 6–5.
72. David Barnes, "The System of Regional Districts in British Columbia," Advisory Commission, *A Look to the North,* pp. 109–26.
73. Paul Tennant and David Zirnhelt, "Metropolitan Government in Vancouver: The Strategy of Gentle Imposition," ibid., 127–34.
74. Plunkett, "Structural Reforms," pp. 327–28; Lionel D. Feldman and Katherine A. Graham, "Local Government Reform in Canada," in Gunlicks, *Local Government Reform,* pp. 157–58, 163–65.
75. Rich, "Metropolitan Winnipeg," pp. 360–62; Tom Axworthy, "Winnipeg Unicity," Advisory Commission, *A Look to the North,* pp. 89–91; George West, "The Relevance of Structural Reform of Local Government to the Solution of Metropolitan Problems: A Case Study of Greater Winnipeg," (Master's thesis, University of Waterloo, 1974).
76. R. H. Kent, "The Dissonant Decade: A Study of Interorganizational Conflict in Municipal Government" (MBA Research Practicum, University of Manitoba, 1970); Axworthy, "Winnipeg Unicity," pp. 91–93.
77. Axworthy, "Winnipeg Unicity," pp. 96–97; Plunkett, "Structural Reform," pp. 328–30; James Lightbody, "The Reform of a Metropolitan Government: The Case of Winnipeg, 1971," in *Canadian Public Policy* 4, no. 4 (1978): 489–503.
78. Plunkett, *Urban Canada and its Governments,* pp. 109–18.
79. Higgins, *Urban Canada,* p. 147.
80. Plunkett, "Structural Reform," p. 328.

81. P. H. Wichern, "Winnipeg's Unicity after Two Years: Evaluation Of An Experiment In Urban Government," *Papers,* Canadian Political Science Association (Ottawa, 1974); Lloyd Axworthy and Jim Cassidy, *Unicity: The Transition* (Winnipeg, 1974).
82. Lloyd Axworthy, "Canada: Winnipeg," in Donald C. Rowat, ed., *International Handbook On Local Government Reorganization: Contemporary Developments* (Westport, CN, 1980), pp. 33–44.
83. P. H. Wichern, "An Election Unlike—and Very Much Like—the Others," *City Magazine,* 3, nos. 4 & 5 (1978): 22.
84. James Lightbody, "The Reform of a Metropolitan Government," p. 491 argues that Unicity is a "challenge to the historical pattern of bias inherent in Winnipeg's local government." Evidence against this is found in Wichern, ibid., 20–28.
85. Jack K. Masson, "Edmonton: The Unsettled Issues of Expansion, Governmental Reform and Provincial Economic Diversification," in Feldman, ed., *Politics And Government Of Urban Canada,* pp. 431–47; T. J. Plunkett and James Lightbody, "Tribunals, Politics, and the Public Interest: The Edmonton Annexation Case," *Canadian Public Policy* 8, no. 2 (1982): 207–21.
86. Joseph Zimmerman, "Metropolitan Reform in the United States: An Overview," in Alan Shank, ed., *Political Power and the Urban Crisis* (Boston, 1973), pp. 355–77.
87. McKelvey, *The Emergence of Metropolitan America,* p. 163.
88. Scott Greer, *Metropolitics* (New York, 1963); Henry Schmandt, Paul Steinbicker and George Wendel, *Metropolitan Reform in St. Louis* (New York, 1961).
89. McKelvey, pp. 162–63; Horan and Taylor, *Experiments in Metropolitan Government,* pp. 87–107.
90. Horan and Taylor, *Experiments in Metropolitan Government,* pp. 3–107, see esp. 68; Zimmerman, "Metropolitan Reform In The United States."
91. Richard Hill, "Separate and Unequal: Government Inequality in the Metropolis," *American Political Science Review* 68 (December 1974): 1557–68; Thomas Pettigrew, "Racial Change and the Intrametropolitan Distribution of Black Americans," in Arthur P. Solomon, ed., *The Prospective City,* p. 52–79; and Willis D. Hawley, *Blacks and Metropolitan Governance: The Stakes of Reform* (Berkeley, 1972).
92. John Bollens and Henry Schmandt, *The Metropolis: Its People, Politics and Economic Life* (Cambridge, 1981), p. 366; Zimmerman, "Metropolitan Reform in the United States."
93. Kenneth Jackson, "The Crabgrass Frontier," p. 941.
94. Donald Zeigler and Stanley Brunn, "Geopolitical Fragmentation and the Pattern of Growth And Need: Defining the Cleavage between Sunbelt and Frostbelt," in Stanley Brunn and James Wheeler, eds., *The American Metropolitan System* (New York, 1980), pp. 77–92.
95. McKelvey, *The Emergence of Metropolitan America,* pp. 163–64.

96. John Bollens and Henry Schmandt, *The Metropolis,* p. 368.
97. Ibid., 368.
98. Ibid., 366–67.
99. Ibid., p. 533.
100. Ibid., Chapter 14.
101. Committee for Economic Development, *Modernizing Local Government* (New York, 1966), pp. 11–12.
102. Joseph Zimmerman, *Metropolitan Reform in the United States,* p. 356.
103. Committee for Economic Development, *Reshaping Government in Metropolitan Areas* (New York, 1970), p. 19.
104. League of Women Voters Education Fund, *Supercity Hometown, U.S.A.: Prospects For Two-Tier Government* (New York, 1974); John Bollens and Henry Schmandt, *The Metropolis,* 2d ed. (1970).
105. "Local Government Reorganization: The Alternatives," *National Civic Review* 68, no. 6 (June 1979): 288–98.
106. Bollens and Schmandt, *The Metropolis* (1970), Chapter 14, "The Politics Of Reform"; Elinor Ostrom, "Metropolitan Reform: Propositions Derived from Two Traditions," *Social Science Quarterly* 53, no. 3 (December 1972): 474–93; Steven P. Erie, et al., *Reform of Metropolitan Governments* (Baltimore, 1972).
107. Robert Warren, *Government in Metropolitan Regions: A Reappraisal of Fractionated Political Organization,* Institute of Governmental Affairs (University of California, Davis).
108. Robert Bish, *The Public Economy of Metropolitan Areas* (Chicago, 1971); Robert Bish and Vincent Ostrum, *Understanding Urban Government: Metropolitan Reform Reconsidered,* (Washington, DC: American Enterprise Institute for Public Policy Research, (1973).
109. A review of such studies is found in Robert L. Bish, "Public Choice Theory for Comparative Research on Urban Service Delivery," *Comparative Urban Research* 7, no. 1 (1979): 18–25.
110. The few exceptions include Mark Sproule-Jones, "The Social Appropriateness of Water Quality Management for the Lower Fraser Valley," *Canadian Public Administration* 21 (Summer 1978): 176–94; and Richard M. Bird and N. Enid Slack, *Urban Public Finance in Canada* (Toronto, 1983), pp. 30–38 and 79–98.
111. Royce Hanson, "Land Development and Metropolitan Reform," in Hanson, et al., *Reform as Reorganization* (Baltimore, 1974), p. 9.
112. James Lorimer, *The Developers* (Toronto, 1978), p. 78.
113. Michael Goldrick, "The Anatomy of Urban Reform in Toronto," in Dimitrio Roussopoulus, ed., *The City and Radical Social Change* (Montreal, 1978), pp. 265–66.
114. Henry Aubin, *City for Sale* (Montreal and Toronto, 1977); Donald Gutstein, *Vancouver, Ltd.* (Toronto, 1975); Sewell,"Where the Suburbs Came From"; Peter Spurr, *Land and Urban Development* (Toronto, 1976), pp. 81–179.
115. Noteworthy are many of the articles in Stelter and Artibise, *Shaping the Urban Landscape*.

116. Patrick Ashton, "The Political Economy of Suburban Development," in William Tabb and Larry Sawyers, eds., *Marxism and the Metropolis* (New York, 1978), p. 83.
117. Ann Markhusen, "Class and Urban Social Expenditures: A Marxist Theory of Metropolitan Government," in William Tabb and Larry Sawyers, eds., *Marxism and the Metropolis,* p. 107.
118. Warren Magnusson, "Metropolitan Reform in the Capitalist City," pp. 558–59.
119. Additions to Magnusson's citations should include: Filippo Sabetti, "Reflections on Canadian Urban Governance Research," *Comparative Urban Research* 8, no. 2 (1981), pp. 95–98; James Lorimer and Carolyn MacGregor, eds., *After the Developers* (Toronto, 1981); and Dimitrios Roussopoulos, ed., *The City and Radical Social Change* (Montreal, 1982).
120. Wichern, "An Election Unlike—and Very Much Like—the Others," pp. 22, 27; Steve Jacobs, "Wheeling and Dealing in Winnipeg," *City Magazine* 4, no. 1 (January 1979): 33–38; The Editors, "Land and Politics in Winnipeg," *City Magazine* 2, no. 8 (June 1977): 21–29; and on downtown development, David C. Walker, *The Great Winnipeg Dream: The Re-Development of Portage and Main* (Oakville, 1979). In November, 1982 the pro-developer power group lost its formal dominance of Unicity to a left-wing-parties-Independent ccoalition. The impact and length of this new regime remains to be seen.
121. Susan Goldenberg, *Men of Property: The Canadian Developers Who Are Buying America* (Toronto, 1981).
122. Gilles Pacquet and Jean-Pierre Wallot, "Canadian Cities As Social Technologies: An Exploratory Essay," in Woodrow Borah, Jorge Hardoy, and Gilbert A. Stelter, eds., *Urbanization in the Americas,* Special issue of *Urban History Review* (Ottawa, 1980), pp. 57–62, see esp. p. 58.

13

The Politics of Suburban Growth: A Comparative Approach

Michael P. McCarthy

As Kenneth Jackson has pointed out, suburbs have been with us a long, long time—back to the villages outside the walls of the medieval European city, back further to those outside Imperial Rome, even back to the estates outside the Sumerian city of Ur.[1] Of course, the greatest growth of suburbs has taken place a good deal more recently, and most historians date the rise of modern suburbs from the early nineteenth century. In what was then the dawn of Eric Lampard's "urbanizing world," significant demographic shifts from rural to urban areas began in Great Britain, Europe, and North America, as those regions industrialized.[2] Innovations in transportation helped to move the growing population beyond the confines of the traditional "walking city." One of the first forms of transport was the omnibus, the horse-drawn coach that followed a schedule and a regular route, Interestingly, it was not introduced first in a major city but in provincial Nantes in France in 1826, by a retired army officer who was looking for customers for his spa outside town. The idea proved so popular that he was soon out of the spa business and into transportation fulltime, starting another line in Paris in 1828. The idea quickly was copied in London and New York and was soon adopted everywhere.[3] By mid-century the omnibus had become a tram or trolley (a coach on rails) which proved more practical as well as more profitable. Steam railroads were also into the commuter business by then, and soon more innovations—the cable and electric trolleys, elevated and underground railways—accelerated the centrifugal movement. In the 1890's, the infant automobile gave hint of things to come in the new century.[4]

Although the majority of the newcomers to suburbia were of the middle class, blue-collar workers were also taking advantage of the new transportation and were finding suburban homes too. This was especially true in England after the passage of the Cheap Trains Act of 1883, which triggered a boom of new blue-collar suburbs around London. The cheap fare idea was also applied to New York City's elevated line to help workers in Manhattan find homes out of the congested Lower East Side. In Boston, the imaginative streetcar entrepreneur Henry Whitney also boomed cheap fares to promote his suburban properties. Many workers were also finding jobs in suburbia as industries moved from downtown locations to more spacious sites on the periphery.[5]

As the suburbs grew, there was also a good deal of annexation going on as the central city tried to keep up with the centrifugal movement. This occurred everywhere in the urbanizing world, which by the late nineteenth century included far-off Australia and even Argentina, where the federal government greatly enlarged Buenos Aires in the 1880's, with the meat-packing district of Nueva Chicago among the suburbs annexed.[6]

In the U.S., the annexation (or consolidation) movement has a long and varied history. It falls into two phases: the first peaked between 1880 and 1920 when significant consolidation took place in the older cities of the northeast and midwest (and some western cities such as Los Angeles, San Francisco and Seattle); the second phase dates from 1945 to the present, and the "young" cities of the Sun Belt states are doing most of the growing.[7]

In the first phase, there were spectacular examples of greatly expanding polities: Chicago annexed several surrounding townships in 1889, adding 125 miles to increase its size to 167 square miles. In 1898, New York created a five-county regional government of 330 square miles. Los Angeles grew from 29 to 364 square miles with the largest single annexation of 170 square miles in 1915 when San Fernando joined the city. The frequency of annexation also increased in many cities. In Detroit, Pittsburgh, Chicago and Cincinnati between 1881 and 1920, for example, annexation ranged from one annexation every 2.79 years (Detroit) to 1 every .83 years (Cincinnati). Between 1841 and 1880 the four cities had averaged one annexation every 9.7 years.[8]

Consolidation was widely supported because it offered a solution to a good many suburban headaches. By joining the central city, the suburbanites were able to take advantage of the rich taxbase downtown and get significant public services (schools, fire and police protection, and so forth) at far less cost compared with the expenses of self-supporting villages.

The high cost of staying healthy made consolidation particularly attractive. Breakthroughs in medical research in the 1870's and 1880's proved that dreaded diseases like typhoid and cholera could be checked with safe drinking water and stout sewers, both of which the cities could supply for the suburbs more inexpensively than if they went their own way and built their own systems.[9]

There was some political reform in the consolidation movement too. In Chicago, for example, the suburban middle classes were becoming increasingly reluctant to support the town government in its requests for what seemed a never ending increase in taxes. The resentment was perhaps strongest in Lake township where the Republican middle classes of Englewood battled with the Democratic working classes of the Stock Yard neighbourhoods for control of town offices. Occasionally the Englewooders won, but more often they found James "Buck" McCarthy, a former prize fighter, and other colourful Stock Yard favourites, running town affairs. In Lake View, the middle classes were unhappy with William Boltenweck, another Democratic machine politician who had a strong following in the working-class neighbourhoods west of the genteel lakefront districts. In Hyde Park, they complained about the Republican regulars who dominated town affairs, especially about the board of trustees' friendliness toward George Pullman, owner of the company town at the south end of the township, who many felt was not paying his fair share of taxes. In the other suburban townships of Jefferson and Cicero, the situation was much the same: the middle classes believed that local government was machine-ridden, inefficient, unrepresentative, and overly beholden to special interests: in short, not worth the extra tax dollars necessary for the salaries of town officials. By consolidation they would eliminate the town governments and become part of the central city's mayor-council system as additional wards created from the former towns. Politicians like McCarthy and Boltenweck might continue their careers in the enlarged polity, but most likely only as aldermen, where they would "sink to their proper level, without influence or opportunity."[10]

Most of all, annexation reflected the buoyant booster spirit of an age that could have a village paper comment, for example, that "Rogers Park, Chicago sounds better than Rogers Park near Chicago." The superintendent of schools in South Chicago asked, "Why should we hesitate to join our destiny to that city which must march on until she becomes greater than imperial Rome?" In New York, Andrew Green, the leader of the consolidation movement there, wooed suburbanites with the prospect of a great metropolis "that shall be illustrious among the cities of the world, the greatest, the best governed, the most picturesque, with all the attractions of city life that the genius of modern civilization can devise."[11] For these boosters, city and suburb were interrelated parts of a whole, parts of an emerging metropolitan vision.

In an article written in the late 1890's, Adna Weber commented on the annexation movement taking place everywhere in the world, and he joked that New York and Chicago might soon go to war over which would annex Texas. In his view annexation simply represented "the legal recognition of new economic conditions" as centrifugal movement widened the population base of the metropolis.[12] In one sense of course, it is quite true that consolidation did not alter certain aspects of life. The middle-aged commuter would continue to worry about his job, his waistline and the greeness of his lawn regardless of whether the 8:08 train he rode daily was from "Rogers Park near Chicago" or "Rogers Park, Chicago." In political terms, however, consolidation meant significant changes. The suburban commuter was now a voting citizen of the city, and in this sense, consolidation created new cities, with new constituencies and new patterns of power.

We can see the effects of "suburban power" in many cities during the progressive era.[13] In Chicago, for example, the ten new suburban wards that were added as a result of the annexation of 1889 played an important role in the successes of the Municipal Voters' League, which helped to give the city one of the best-run city councils by the turn of the century. In New York City, the middle-class suburban voters in Brooklyn, the Bronx and Queens loosened the hold of Tammany Hall on city politics and helped to elect the reformer Seth Low (a former president of Columbia University) to city hall in 1901. Low lasted only one term, losing in his bid for a second term (largely because of problems between regular Republicans and independents who had backed him as a fusion candidate in 1901), but his successor was the Democrat George B. McClellan, Jr., Princeton '86 and son of the famous Civil War general; he kept Tammany at arm's length and continued many of Low's reform programmes. Tom Johnson of Cleveland was another patrician Democrat who enjoyed the support of the suburban middle classes. (Johnson's famous tent, used in his revival-style campaign rallies, was usually pitched in the suburban wards where there were no meeting halls large enough to hold the crowds.) To be sure, progressive reform occurred also in smaller cities—little Jersey City had its reform mayor, Mark Fagan, as did Boston with Josiah Quincy—but the progressive movement seems to have been most successful in the large spread cities that were growing rapidly and that contained many middle-class suburban neighbourhoods.[14]

One obvious question is, why did the political bosses permit consolidation in the first place if the movement produced such insurgency? Suburban bosses did fight consolidation since they stood to lose most, but the downtown bosses generally backed it since they believed that "bigger is better" for machines too. As noted earlier, many working-class residents, the traditional strength of Democratic machines, also lived in the suburbs, which meant that consolidation was not simply adding Republican voters.

What was largely unexpected by bosses was the way that issues in the progressive era cut across the traditional lines of class and ethnicity that had long shaped local politics. Whether blue- or white-collar, suburbanites worried about the same issues—streetcar fares, electric bills, sewers, safe drinking water, schools, housing codes—that reflected the growing pains of an expanding metropolis. As David Thelen has pointed out, a good deal of progressive era politics were battles of voters as consumers against both machines and business interests. Annexation created ideal conditions for those kinds of politics to flourish.[15]

The decline of annexation sentiment in the 1920's was the result of many factors. By that time suburbs that were not yet part of the city had their necessary public utilities, schools and the like, so no longer were there the clear fiscal benefits of earlier times. In the dawning age of the automobile, suburbs became less dependent on rail ties to the city. The feeling of affinity with the central city also faded, in part because of the dramatic changes in the ethnic and racial composition of the central city as significant numbers of blacks and new immigrants from eastern and southern Europe arrived.[16] The growing black population in particular seems to have had a chilling effect on the annexation spirit. At the turn of the century, the number of blacks in the major cities of the northeast and midwest was relatively small, but in the next two decades it grew dramatically, particularly during the First World War, when northern cities offered many job opportunities. Race riots rocked many cities during that period as the burgeoning black community spilled out of its ghetto into new neighbourhoods. But whatever the reasons, most of the cities of the northeast and midwest cover about the same area as they did fifty years ago.

By contrast, the Sun Belt cities are growing expansively in the second phase of the annexation movement that has boomed since the end of the Second World War.[17] Some examples of growth between 1950 and 1970 include: Phoenix, from 17 to 247 square miles; San Jose, California, 17 to 117; Houston, 160 to 453; San Antonio, 70 to 183; Memphis, 104 to 217; and Atlanta, 37 to 128. In some respects, the growth simply reflects stages attained earlier in the northeast and midwest, much like W. W. Rostow's "stages of economic growth" model, as the influx of industry (and defence contracts) helped to fuel the urban growth in the Sun Belt.[18] Most of the suburban periphery was also unincorporated, so annexation was easier. Suburban areas on the outskirts of Houston, for example, are not allowed to incorporate, which makes their eventual annexation almost inevitable.[19] Like residents in the new suburbs of the late nineteenth century, Sun Belt suburbanites generally support annexation since they get better services for less cost by joining the central cit. In many ways, the Sun Belt's great spread cities, with their numerous middle-class subcommunities, also have the independent voting and consumer coalitions reminiscent of the progressive era.[20]

Comparative history, of course, is a tricky business, and at the outset, real differences between the Canadian and American experience need to be noted. In the early 1900's, for example, Canadian cities still used property qualifications which limited the electorate. Moreover, voting laws in some cities gave elites even more influence. As Alan Artibise points out, in Winnipeg after 1890, wealthy property owners were allowed to vote in every ward in which they were ratepayers, which could have given them up to seven votes by 1907. As an indication of how much Winnipeg elites took advantage of their prerogative, the voting lists in the 1910 election showed approximately six thousand repeaters.[21]

Another significant difference is the split between Anglophones and Francophones. This is most apparent in Quebec, but the issue surfaces in other provinces. To be sure, the United States has had its share of ethnic and racial conflict as minorities battled each other as well as the WASP establishment. There are also some parallels, such as the black-white tensions that date from slavery days; or the resentment of the native Americans and the Mexican-Americans, whose forefathers were pawns in imperial conquest like the Canadiens. While American minorities share some of the goals of the Francophones, such as increased cultural identity and more political rights, they have been less interested in separatist solutions. In any case, there is really nothing quite comparable in the American experience to an Anglophone Westmount refusing to join a Francophone Montreal, or a Francophone St. Boniface refusing to join an Anglophone Winnipeg.

Canadian cities were also a good deal smaller in population. At the turn of the twentieth century, for example, the two leading cities—Montreal and Toronto—had populations of 268,000 and 208,000, which were significant numbers indeed, but not when compared with New York's 3.4 million or Chicago's 1.7 million. Winnipeg had experienced extraordinary growth, from a population of 241 in 1871 to 42,340 by 1901, but these figures were also not very impressive when compared with its neighbours to the south: Minneapolis, with 202,718 and St. Paul, with 163,065. Vancouver had a population of some 27,000 compared to 80,000 living in Seattle or the 343,000 further down the coast in San Francisco. In 1901, Calgary and Edmonton were little more than cities in name, with populations of 4,392 and 4,176, although both did grow explosively in the next decade to 43,704 and 24,900.

The differences, however, seem less significant than the similarities between Canadian and American cities. On both sides of the border, new transportation technology transformed cities; we see the same centrifugal movement and variegated suburbs; both experienced the influx of immigrants from central and eastern Europe. We see also comparable growth in area of Canadian and American cities in the period from 1880 to 1930.

The booster and boomer spirit was much the same, as indicated in the slogans of proud Winnipeg, which proclaimed itself "The Bull's Eye of the Dominion," or "The Chicago of the North," or "The Heart City of North America."[22] Growth meant more impressive population and area statistics that enhanced a city's image and attracted more newcomers. For the suburbs, joining the central city meant a solution to the ever-rising costs of public improvements. Frequently, suburbs were able to make annexation agreements quite favourable to themselves. East Toronto joined Toronto in 1908, for example, under the conditions that [23]

—the city to establish a sewerage system in the town of East Toronto when petitioned for; and that the sewerage system adopted should be constructed so as not to injure the property along the lakeshore or any property in town.

—the present scavenger system be continued and extended and otherwise dealt with as the Municipal Health Office of the city shall consider advisable.

—provision be made by the city for maintaining the present electric light and water works systems until adequate substitution therefrom is made.

—the city to have the Toronto Railway Company service extended to the north part of town as part of the Toronto railway system, at single fares.

—the city take into its employ the present officials and employees.

—Ward 1 of the town shall be made and set aside as a residential district, free from factories and hotels.

The central city could profit too, especially when the suburb was a booming industrial district that would bolster the city's tax base. When Ottawa added a lumber mill district on the west side of the city in 1890, the lumber magnate John Booth recalled bitterly that[24]

> as soon as I got my property in good condition, the city saw it would help the revenue a good deal as the population was following the labor. The city fathers, who have always had a keen eye to business, decided that the lumber piles were a good thing in the city and they should no longer be out in the cold.

As a result of the annexation, Booth claimed that Ottawa taxed him "twenty-five times higher than I was taxed by the county." However, when the lumber yards caught fire and burned down parts of the city in 1900 and again in 1903, Ottawans were no longer quite so sure they wanted the lumber yards in the city after all. Cooler heads prevailed when the impressive revenues from the lumber district were noted, and the city decided that better fire prevention codes, not deannexation, was the best way to solve the problem.[25]

Ottawa also had its share of unexpected health problems as a result of suburban growth. In 1911, the burgeoning lumber mill district included the newly annexed suburb of Hintonburgh, which did not have a complete sewer system. Pollution from outdoor privies along Cave Creek polluted the Ottawa River above the city's water works and touched off a serious typhoid epidemic.[26] Winnipeg had similar problems with the North End, a booming working-class district above the C.P.R. yards which the city had annexed in 1882. Sewer systems there were primitive, the district congested, and the land low-lying, all of which made the North End a very unhealthy place by the early 1900's. Montreal and Toronto had similar headaches with their suburban working-class districts. Only by costly and time-consuming public works programmes were these cities able to solve the problem.

While generally supported by both city and suburb, annexation could be highly controversial when political power was at stake or cultural identity challenged. The most dramatic example took place in Montreal in the 1880's when Francophones successfully pushed for the annexation of several Francophone suburbs, which gave them control of the city council. As John Cooper notes in his history of Montreal, this was "the great divide" in Montreal municipal politics, as the annexations brought in "blocs of new citizens into the city and new leadership in the council."[27] Harold Kaplan points out in his recent study that the Anglophones and Francophones worked out a gentlemen's agreement to alternate mayors between the two "races" but since 1914 every Montreal mayor has been French.[28] Realizing that it would have little influence in the new Montreal, the elite Anglophone suburb of Westmount refused to join the city. (It is still separate today although part of the Montreal metropolitan government.)[29] For similar reasons, the Francophone town of St. Boniface spurned marriage with its English neighbour Winnipeg until 1971 when annexation was forced on it by the provincial government.

Aside from Anglo-French differences, ethnicity was not much of an issue. In Toronto, for example, rock-ribbed Orange Society suburbanites did not hesitate to join the city—thirty-two annexations took place between 1883 and 1914—despite the growing numbers of eastern and southern Europeans in "The Ward" downtown. One reason may be the relatively small numbers of the new immigrants; another no doubt was the fact that "The Ward" was ruled by old guard WASP politicians like the colourful

Beattie Nesbitt, who knew how to keep newcomers in their place.[30] It should be noted too that in the early 1900's, Canada enjoyed economic prosperity, and there was confidence in "melting pot" theories. But the mood changed during the First World War and the postwar period, as it did in the United States.

There are some differences in the annexation movement between the cities in the East and West. Montreal and Toronto had significant numbers living in suburbs beyond the city limits. Annexation there added voters and could affect politics downtown as it did in Montreal in the 1880's. Annexation of these populous suburbs was also in many respects an inevitable stage in metropolitan growth. Montreal's Maisonneuve, for example, was similar to Hyde Park, which joined Chicago in 1889. Like Hyde Park, Maisonneuve was a mixed residential and industrial community with an aggressive group of businessmen-realtors who worked closely with downtown officials in planning parks and highways that linked city and suburb. When the suburb could no longer shoulder the costs of maintaining its independence, it joined the city in 1918. For all practical purposes, however, Maisonneuve had long been an integral part of Montreal, and in fact since 1910, it had been surrounded by suburbs that had already joined the city.[31]

By contrast, annexation in the western cities, particularly those in Alberta, was far more speculative, as boomers added miles of empty prairie to impress out-of-town investors with the size of a Calgary or an Edmonton.[32] So few people lived in the outer districts in the early 1900's that both cities experienced fiscal problems with tax defaults. The situation was so serious in Calgary by the 1920's that the city developed a policy of limiting suburban growth. Streetcar service and public utilities were restricted to districts close to the city, for example, and residential properties in outlying areas were taxed at a higher rate. The city swapped lots it held closer in to aid investors, and it even established a special house-moving fund "for the purpose of encouraging and assisting the moving of buildings from the outer areas to the inner areas."[33] Only in the years after 1945 did the suburban districts of these cities really begin to grow.

No doubt influenced by events in Alberta, the provincial legislature in British Columbia was cool toward pellmell growth. In 1911, it refused to permit Vancouver's annexation of South Vancouver, in part on the grounds that the city had enough problems providing services for its own residents. Undaunted, the two communities sought annexation legislation in 1913 only to be refused again. Not until 1929 did the union finally take place, when the legislature was apparently more receptive to the booster arguments of Vancouver's mayor, L. D. Taylor, who was sure that "to the outside world Vancouver with a population of over two hundred thousand would be an entirely different city than Vancouver with one hundred and twenty-eight thousand."[34]

A comparison of the political leadership of Canadian and American cities during the progressive era is complicated by the fact that the suffrage laws were different. The electorate was clearly more limited in Canada, and the old stock Anglophone elites pretty much ran the show. An exception might be in Quebec, but even there Anglophones maintained considerable economic clout through their dominance in banking, as Ronald Rudin has noted in his study of the impact of Montreal banks on urban development in Quebec.[35] Limited suffrage and old WASP dominance notwithstanding, it does not necessarily follow that the urban leadership was narrow-minded or repressive. In commenting on the political leadership in cities in the West, J. M. S. Careless found it just as elitest as in the East but remarked that the leadership "seemed broadly acceptable and sufficiently effective. And in particular, it did make the municipal regime a satisfactory vehicle for community sentiment and aspirations, guarding city interests against outside forces, embodying civic pride and encouraging local development."[36]

The failure of elites to do more about public health, however, is frequently cited as an indication of their civic irresponsibility, particularly toward the working classes who suffered the most. As noted earlier, typhoid epidemics did indeed strike nearly every major city in Canada in the late nineteenth and early twentieth centuries,[37] but it is important to note that this was not simply a Canadian leadership problem but part of a public health crisis occurring everywhere in the urbanizing world. In Philadelphia, for example, the Fairmount water works had given the city a reputation as one of the healthiest cities in the world after the works opened in 1815, but suburban growth along the Schuylkill Valley above the water works increasingly polluted the water supply. By the 1890's, between 400 and 600 Philadelphians were dying of typhoid each year; a severe outbreak early in 1899 brought that year's total to 948.[38]

Although everyone believed that water pollution was the culprit, for most of the nineteenth century even medical experts did not know exactly what caused typhoid or its more virulent cousin, cholera. Bacteriology was still in its infancy and it was not until the 1880's that typhoid and cholera were identified. It took another decade for scientists to design a filter capable of keeping a water supply safe; and it was not until the early 1900's that chlorine was found to be a powerful preventative.[39] To be sure, there was some waffling among city fathers even after these scientific breakthroughs. In the early 1890's when some solutions seemed clear, the Philadelphia city council debated and delayed; it took the epidemic of 1899 to get the necessary legislation for an improved water works. But to give the Philadelphia politicians their due, the delays were largely caused by disagreements among the scientific experts about which specific filtering system would work best. The experts could also not agree among themselves on what the improvements would cost, which made it difficult for the politicians to win public support for bond issues.[40]

Another example of procrastination is the case of Ottawa. In 1910 the city's water works committee decided not to treat the water supply with chlorine, despite the recommendation of Allan Hazen, a highly regarded New York sanitary engineer who had prepared a report on the city's water supply as a consultant for the city council. Unfortunately for Ottawa, a typhoid epidemic broke out in January 1911 and eighty-three people died. In the subsequent investigation, a federal official concluded that the epidemic "could have been obviated had the hypoclorite treatment been installed forthwith after its recommendation by Mr. Hazen on October fifth, 1910."[41]

The water works committee had based its decision on a report prepared by John Grant, who was chairman of the committee and a member of the board of health. Grant, the city engineer, and the city treasurer had gone to Toronto to inspect the new chlorine treatment system there. In his report,Grant had recommended against adding chlorine because the taste and smell of the chemicals could be eliminated only if the chemicals were introduced far from the point of consumption, a procedure which was not possible in Ottawa since the water works was close to the city.[42] This was a lamentable decision, of course, but it should also be noted that chlorine treatment was a very new and somewhat controversial procedure. Toronto and Montreal had just introduced it; in the first use of chlorine in a city water system in 1908 (in Jersey City, New Jersey) court action had taken place to insure that the chemicals were effective.[43] Even after another outbreak of typhoid in 1912—this time because the chlorine treatment was not strong enough—Ottawans complained about "doped water" and "the injection of foreign substances."[44] Given the novelty of chemical treatment and the state of public opinion, it is not surprising that the Ottawa water works committee acted the way it did in response to the Hazen report.

Administrative lapses notwithstanding, everywhere in Canada in the early 1900's city fathers were seeking to upgrade health conditions. In Winnipeg, for example, the city fathers were so proud of a new sewer system that they held a gala banquet, with crisp white tablecloths and plenty of red wine, right in one of the subterranean vaults when the sewer was completed in 1912.[45] The following year the city embarked on an even more ambitious project: the construction of a 13.5 million dollar aqueduct to Shoal Lake, ninety-seven miles east of Winnipeg, that was completed in 1919. By the 1920's, Winnipeg, along with its sister cities in Canada and the rest of the advanced nations in the urbanizing world, had virtually eliminated the typhoid threat.[46] In sum, in public health matters at least, the city fathers seemed to have lived up to Careless's view that they embodied "civic pride" and "encouraged local development."

In this sense, the Canadian municipal reform movement seems similar to the American experience in that public health problems were political issues, and elites frequently found themselves leading broad-based reform coalitions. In Montreal, for example, over forty civic organizations were concerned enough about public health problems that they cosponsored an antituberculosis exhibit in 1908. When the city council ignored their request for a comprehensive public health by-law, the groups joined together as the City Improvement League and won sweeping council victories in 1909 and 1910.[47] In Winnipeg, a similar uprising took place when public health conditions reached a crisis stage in the early 1900's. Bridging their own ideological differences, a coalition of what Harold Kaplan describes as "leftists and tory reformers" won control of the city government. As a first step, they created the post of public health officer in 1905 and then embarked on an ambitious public works programme.[48] Toronto saw similar coalitions in the early 1900's, as influential figures like Charles Hastings, the medical officer of health, and the dynamic Jesse McCarthy, councilman, insurance company executive, ardent Methodist and teetotaler "but not a crank in the accepted use of the term," said the Toronto *News,* took special interest in the health needs of the city's working classes,[49]

In the modern era, the Canadian annexation experience has paralleled that of the United States in many respects. The major growth centers of the nineteenth and early twentieth centuries (Montreal and Toronto in eastern Canada; Winnipeg in the midwest; and Vancouver on the west coast) like their counterparts in the United States (cities like New York, Philadelphia, Chicago, San Francisco or Los Angeles) have not grown much, if at all, since the 1930's, while the "new" cities of Calgary and Edmonton—the equivalents of cities in America's "Sun Belt"—have continued to expand their city limits.

Although they stopped growing in area, the older cities continued to grow in population, as did their suburban neighbours. In 1953, Toronto introduced the metro idea as a way of increasing regional cooperation. Under the plan, the suburbs maintained their independence in local affairs, but a metropolitan council, with city and suburban representation, now dealt with regional issues. With especially effective leadership from the first metro chairman, Frederick G. Gardiner (1953–61), Toronto proved the metro idea could work, and Winnipeg (1960), Vancouver (1967), and

Montreal (1970), adopted similar schemes.[50]

Despite inevitable controversies and changes over the years, the metro plans by and large are working well, especially in the way they encourage grassroots participation in local and regional planning. The Canadian metropolitan governments are also a good deal more ambitious than anything found in the older U.S. metropolitan regions, where cooperation between city and suburb is largely limited to such matters as sewage, water supply, public transportation and the like. In sum, the history of Canadian and American suburban growth shows many similarities, but the problems—and the solutions—have not always been the same.

NOTES

1. Kenneth Jackson, "The Crabgrass Frontier: 150 Years of Suburban Growth in America," in Raymond A. Mohl and James F. Richardson, eds., *The Urban Experience: Themes in American History* (Belmont, CA, 1973), p. 196.
2. Eric Lampard, "The Urbanizing World," H. J. Dyos and Michael Wolff, eds., *The Victorian City* (London, 1973), vol. 1, pp. 3–53.
3. John P. McKay, *Tramways and Trolleys: The Rise of Urban Mass Transport in Europe* (Princeton, 1976), pp. 10–11.
4. Useful references on these developments are McKay, *Tramways;* Charles W. Cheape, *Moving the Masses: Urban Public Transit in New York, Boston, and Philadelphia, 1880–1912* (Cambridge, MA, 1980); and James J. Flink, *America Adopts the Automobile* (1970). An interesting case study of the auto's impact on spatial growth is Howard L. Preston, *Automobile Age Atlanta: The Making of a Southern Metropolis, 1900–1935* (Athens, GA, 1979).
5. For the railroads and working class suburbia in London, see in particular Anthony S. Wohl, *The Eternal Slum: Housing and Social Policy in Victorian London* (Oxford, 1977). Cheape, *Moving the Masses* has some discussion of these issues.
6. For suburban growth in these areas, see C. B. Schedvin and J. W. Carty, eds., *Urbanization in Australia: The Nineteenth Century* (Sydney, 1974); and James R. Scobie, *Buenos Aires: Plaza to Suburb, 1870–1910* (New York, 1974).
7. The best general reference is Jon C. Teaford, *City and Suburb: The Political Fragmentation of Metropolitan America, 1850–1970* (Baltimore, 1979). Annexation and consolidation are not quite the same in a technical sense, but I will use them interchangeably since the differences do not concern us here.
8. Frequency data from Chamber of Commerce of the United States, *Municipal Annexation of Land* (Washington, DC, 1926), p. 12. Other data from various sources including tables in Kenneth T. Jackson, "Metropolitan Government Versus Suburban Autonomy: Politics on the Crabgrass Frontier," in Jackson

and Stanley K. Schultz, eds., *Cities in American History* (New York, 1972), pp. 442–62.

9. Teaford, *City and Suburb,* p. 60, for example, notes the importance of public health issues in annexation campaigns in Chicago, Memphis and Birmingham, Alabama. For some of the recent research in a field of growing interest, see Martin V. Melosi, ed., *Pollution & Reform in American Cities, 1870–1930* (Austin, TX, 1980).
10. For more on the Chicago experience, see Michael P. McCarthy, "The New Metropolis: Chicago, the Annexation Movement and Progressive Reform," in Michael H. Ebner and Eugene M. Tobin, eds., *The Age of Urban Reform: New Perspectives on the Progressive Era* (Port Washington, NY, 1977), pp. 43–54.
11. The Green quote is from his remarks in a consolidation campaign flyer quoted by John Foord, *The Life and Public Services of Andrew Haswell Green* (New York, 1913). A recently published study on Green and New York decision making is David C. Hammack, *Power and Society: Greater New York at the Turn of the Century* (New York, 1982).
12. Adna Weber, "Suburban Annexations," *North American Review* 166 (May 1898): 612–17.
13. A major example outside the focus of this paper (but in another part of the Anglo-American world) is London, where in 1888 Parliament created a new county from parts of Middlesex, Sussex and Kent. The new London County Council was the city's first municipal legislature and became the instrument of reform in the 1890's with Fabian folk like Sidney Webb leading the way. For that story, see William A. Robson, *The Government and Misgovernment of London* (London, 1939); and A. M. McBriar, *Fabian Socialism and English Politics, 1884–1918* (Cambridge, ENG, 1966).
14. Two book-length studies that examine the impact of annexation on urban politics are Robert M. Fogelson, *The Fragmented Metropolis: Los Angeles, 1850–1930* (Cambridge, MA, 1967); and Zane L. Miller, *Boss Cox's Cincinnati: Urban Politics in the Progressive Era* (New York, 1968). For Fagan and Jersey City, see Eugene M. Tobin, "The Progressive as Politician: Jersey City, 1896–1907," *New Jersey History,* 91, no. 1 (Spring 1973): 5–23; for Quincy and Boston, see Geoffrey Blodgett, "Yankee Leadership in a Divided City: Boston, 1860–1910," *Journal of Urban History* 8 (August 1982): 371–96.
15. Thelen's views on consumer politics have been developed in his *The New Citizenship: Origins of Progressivism in Wisconsin, 1885–1900* (Madison, 1972) and *Robert LaFollette and the Insurgent Spirit* (Boston, 1976). See also a review essay by Thelen, "Urban Politics: Beyond Bosses and Reformers," *Reviews in American History* 7 (September 1979): 406–12.
16. In New York and Chicago, for example, in 1900 Germans and Irish were the two largest groups of foreign-born residents. (47 per cent in both cities.) Russians, Poles and Italians represented only a relatively small percentage of the foreign-born residents (New York 16 per cent, Chicago 17 per cent) and

blacks were less than 2 per cent of the total population. By 1920 Russians, Poles and Italians were 50.4 per cent of the foreign-born population in New York and 37.2 per cent in Chicago, with the Russians the largest group in New York (German and Irish, third and fourth after the Italians) and the Poles the largest in Chicago (Germans second, Russians third, Italians fourth and Irish sixth after the Swedes.) By 1930 the black population in New York had jumped to 4.7 per cent (12 per cent in Manhattan) and nearly 7 per cent in Chicago. Data from Walter Laidlaw, ed., *Population of the City of New York, 1890–1930* (New York, 1932); and Ernest W. Burgess and Charles Newcomb, eds., *Census Data of the City of Chicago, 1920, 1930* (Chicago, 1933).

17. A recent study that includes some discussion of annexation is Carl Abbott, *The New Urban America: Growth and Politics in Sunbelt Cities* (Chapel Hill, NC, 1981). Obviously race was not a deterrent to annexation in the Sun Belt cities of the South, which had large numbers of black inner-city residents. Perhaps because blacks were long an integral (if not integrated) part of Southern society, their presence was not a threat to white suburbanites.
18. W. W. Rostow, *The Stages of Economic Growth* (Cambridge, ENG, 1960).
19. Houston has recently passed Philadelphia to become the nation's fourth most populous city through its aggressive annexation policies. If Philadelphia (127 square miles) annexed a comparable area as Houston's vast outer suburbs, Philadelphia would have a population of 4.2 million compared to Houston's 2.9 million.
20. For an overview of the politics of spread cities—both "old" and "Sun Belt" from the 1920's to the 1970's, see Michael P. McCarthy, "On Bosses, Reformers and Urban Growth: Some Suggestions for a Political Typology of American Cities," *Journal of Urban History* 4 (November 1977): 29–38.
21. Alan F. J. Artibise, *Winnipeg: An Illustrated History* (Toronto, 1977), p. 100; for more on property and voting in Winnipeg, see "Urban History in Canada: A Conversation with Alan F. J. Artibise," *Urban History Review* 8 (February 1980): 127–28.
22. Booster descriptions from Artibise, *Winnipeg*. Edmonton boomers called their city the "St. Louis of the North" in another example of hopeful comparisons with the larger U.S. cities.
23. East Toronto *Star,* 7 February 1907; cited in Susan Ross, "The Annexation of East Toronto," (undergraduate research paper, Department of Geography, University of Toronto Archives, 1971) pp. 5–6.
24. Ottawa *Free Press,* 5 May 1900; cited in Jon Fear, "Ottawa's Lumber Interests and the Great Fire of 1900," *Urban History Review* 8 (June 1979): 52.
25. Ibid., 63–67.
26. The 1911 typhoid epidemic is discussed in two articles in the June 1979 issue of *Urban History Review:* Sheila Lloyd, "The Ottawa Typhoid Epidemics of 1911 and 1912," 66–89; and Chris Warfe, "The Search for Pure Water in Ottawa, 1910–1915," 90–112.
27. Cooper, *Montreal: A Brief History* (Montreal, 1969), p. 101.

28. Kaplan, *Reform, Planning and City Politics: Montreal, Winnipeg and Toronto* (Toronto, 1982), p. 313.
29. It should be noted that the elite Francophone suburb of Outremont did not join Montreal either, so class may be part of the story, too.
30. John C. Weaver, "The Modern City Realized: Toronto Civic Affairs, 1880–1915," in Alan F. J. Artibise and Gilbert A. Stelter, eds., *The Usable Urban Past: Planning and Politics in the Modern Canadian City* (Toronto, 1979), pp. 42–43.
31. Paul-André Linteau, "The Development and Beautification of an Industrial City: Maissonneuve, 1883–1918," in Gilbert A. Stelter and Alan F. J. Artibise, eds., *Shaping the Urban Landscape: Aspects of the Canadian City-Building Process* (Ottawa, 1982), pp. 304–20. For Hyde Park, see Jean F. Block, *Hyde Park Houses: An Informal History, 1856–1910* (Chicago, 1978).
32. For an overview, see Alan F. J. Artibise, "In Pursuit of Growth: Municipal Boosterism and Urban Development in the Canadian Prairie West," in Stelter and Artibise, eds., *Shaping the Urban Landscape,* pp. 116–47.
33. Max Foran, "Land Development Patterns in Calgary, 1884–1945," in Artibise and Stelter, eds., *The Usable Urban Past,* p. 309. For Edmonton's problems, see John F. Gilpin, "Urban Land Speculation in the Development of Strathcona (South Edmonton), 1891–1912," in John E. Foster, ed., *The Developing West: Essays in Honour of Lewis H. Thomas* (Edmonton, 1983), pp. 181–99; also John C. Weaver, "Edmonton's Perilous Course, 1904–1929," *Urban History Review* 7 (October 1977): 20–32.
34. Patricia E. Roy, *Vancouver: An Illustrated History* (Toronto, 1980), p. 117.
35. Rudin, "Montreal Banks and the Urban Development of Quebec, 1840–1914," in Artibise and Stelter, eds., *Shaping the Urban Landscape,* pp. 65–83.
36. Careless, "Aspects of Urban Life in the West, 1870–1914," in Stelter and Artibise, *The Canadian City* (Toronto, 1977), p. 133.
37. A major exception is Vancouver, which Roy notes was "unusually conscious of public health" from the city's founding in 1886. The early awareness came from the city's role as a port—officials worried about the threat of diseases aboard arriving ships—but the biggest factor in the city's success against typhoid was the availability of pure mountain water nearby. Just three years after the city's founding, the Vancouver Water Works Company was pumping water from Coquitlam River to the city through a pipeline laid across Burrard Inlet. Roy, *Vancouver,* pp. 32, 36.
38. Statistics from the Philadelphia Bureau of Health records. For the early history of the water works, see Nelson M. Blake, *Water for the Cities* (Syracuse, 1956), pp. 18–99.
39. George C. Whipple, "Fifty Years of Water Purification," in Mazyck P. Ravened, ed., *A Half Century of Public Health* (New York, 1921), pp. 163–65, 172–73.
40. In 1899, a new panel of experts produced firmer figures, and the bonds were quickly approved. For a contemporary reformer's view of the situation, see

C. R. Woodruff, ''Philadelphia's Water Supply: A Story of Municipal Procrastination,'' *Forum* 28 (November 1899): 305–14.

41. Lloyd, ''The Ottawa Typhoid Epidemics,'' p. 70.
42. Warfe, ''The Search for Pure Water,'' p. 93.
43. Whipple, ''Fifty Years of Water Purification,'' pp. 172–73.
44. Warfe, ''The Search for Pure Water,'' p. 110.
45. For a photograph of the banquet, see Artibise, *Winnipeg,* p. 103. A precedent of sorts was an outdoor banquet held by the Metropolitan Board of Works in London in 1863 on the bed of reservoir it had recently completed at Barking Fall. Priscilla Metcalf, *Victorian London* (New York, 1972), p. 81.
46. For an overview of research in this area, see Paul A. Bator, ''Public Health Reform in Canada and Urban History: A Critical Survey,'' *Urban History Review,* 9 (October 1980): 87–102.
47. Kaplan, *Reform, Planning and City Politics,* pp. 326–27.
48. Ibid., pp. 471–73.
49. Weaver, ''The Modern City Realized,'' pp. 63–64.
50. For Toronto metro politics, see Timothy J. Colton, *Big Daddy: Frederick G. Gardiner and the Building of Metropolitan Toronto* (Toronto, 1980). A useful survey of the modern city is Donald J. H. Higgins, *Urban Canada: Its Government and Politics* (Toronto, 1977).

SECTION V

CULTURAL VALUES AND URBAN DEVELOPMENT

Introduction

In this concluding section, John Mercer and Michael Goldberg put many of the issues discussed in earlier chapters into a comparative context and examine these issues for the very recent past. Their provocative hypothesis is that differences in the Canadian and American urban experiences can best be demonstrated and understood by comparing the cultural values of the two societies and then looking for the implications for urban development. Culture, in their words, constitutes the "central beliefs, values and meanings that people hold widely and which effect the way in which they have collectively organized their institutions and relations." One major theme they stress is that Canadians are not as individualistic as Americans, tending to accept collective action more readily.[1] One result for cities, they argue, is a relatively greater stress on publicly-provided goods and services such as public transport, which in turn has produced more compact, more densely populated cities. Their bold suggestions are by no means generally accepted; some commentators argue, in fact, that broad generalizations about national character "lose their glimmer upon close scrutiny and often cannot withstand the inspection of scholarly analysis."[2] But their detailed research has unearthed some very important political and economic cultural value distinctions and significant demographic and institutional differences which must be taken seriously in our attempts to understand the cities and the settlement patterns these two societies have created.

NOTES

1. This has been a major theme of many Canadian scholars, including David Bell and Lorne Tepperman, *The Roots of Disunity: A Look at Canadian Political Culture* (Toronto: McClelland and Stewart, 1979); Edgar Z. Friedenberg, *Deference to Authority: The Case of Canada* (White Plains, NY: Sharpe,

1980); Herschel Hardin, *A Nation Unaware: The Canadian Economic Culture* (Vancouver: Douglas, 1974).

2. Daniel Shaffer, "A New Threshold for Urban History: Reflections on Canadian-American Urban Development at the Guelph Conference," *Planning History Bulletin* 4, no. 3 (1982): 6–7. For other criticisms of the view that Canadian and American attitudes to the role of government have appreciably differed, see the references in Robert Babcock's essay in this volume.

14

Value Differences and Their Meaning for Urban Development in Canada and the U.S.

John Mercer and Michael A. Goldberg*

This research on the nature of cities in Canada and the U.S. rests generally upon three intellectual mainsprings. First is the notion of the North American city, a concept whose validity we wish to examine critically. Frames of reference that are continental in scale are restricted to neither urban studies nor even academe but are widely used in contemporary and historic periods. They range currently from the North American Auto Pact and defence-sharing agreements back to Manifest Destiny and American expansionism in the nineteenth century and the writings and speeches of men like Goldwin Smith.[1]

A continentalist view of urban spatial structure and the geographic development of settlement systems presupposes (but has not yet adequately demonstrated) a rather homogeneous set of characteristics and processes that describe and govern cities in both countries. If it can be shown that Canadian cities are substantially and importantly different from those in the United States, then generalization from the U.S. to Canada (certainly the prevailing direction) becomes difficult. A theoretical reformulation and the sharpening of an existing and widely-used concept should thereby be achieved; we do not *a priori* imply that the idea of the North American city is without merit but wish to test it more vigorously on an anvil of reality which, to borrow a phrase, has a greater Canadian content.

The second mainspring is the urbanization process and its relationship with the mode of production or, as some would prefer, the space-economy. It has been vigorously asserted by neo-Marxist writers in geography and other disciplines that cities and city systems in advanced capitalist countries should be expected to reveal similarities in urban form and in the underlying process of urbanization because they are dominated by a particular economic order and by associated but dependent modes of behavior. Some differences in urban form and urbanization are conceded.[2] These are viewed as arising from different national contexts but are treated as superficial configurations of no great substance, given the imperatives of capitalism. For some Marxists, the entire superstructure of a society, including culture, is treated as derivative and determined by the base which, as Raymond Williams observes, is characterized in economic terms.[3]

We wish to confront this view, by, one, documenting the extent of urban differences between these two advanced capitalist societies; two, if the differences exist, by indicating that they are of greater significance, both theoretically and experientially, than most Marxists allow for; and three, by seeking explanations which are not rooted solely in geographic-economic arrangements but which have cultural antecedents, implying a stronger historical dimension than has heretofore been characteristic of contemporary urban studies. Here we use culture as constituting the central beliefs, values and meanings that people hold widely and which affect the way in which they have collectively organized their institutions and relations, past and present. These tenets are not independent of the practice of these institutions, and thus culture must be viewed relationally and historically. culture is active, continuously being made and remade. It is not passive, inherited from tradition, nor is it superorganic in nature.[4]

The third mainspring is demystification. Through our work, we have realized that certain widely-held conceptions about American and Canadian society, economy and polity are based more on myth than reality. Some myths serve special interests and are promulgated to mask the underlying reality which, if known, might occasion reforms unwanted by these interests. It is a central purpose of academic practice to force societies to look at themselves in a more revealing way; we try to be true to that purpose in our general thrust.[5]

In this essay, the focus is upon social values as they affect the nature and organization of social life, economic enterprise and political institutions, and, in turn, urban differences. These are not the values of powerful individuals, legislators, or opinion makers, although we do not gainsay their influence.[6] Rather, they are the social values by which people live, that is, in large part, selecting and interpreting experience and events in a particular time and place. This implies that these values are widely shared; they are majority values, part of the mainstream consensus. They are not unchanging but neither are they transitory. To have explanatory worth they must have some stability, be susceptible of measurement, and be demonstrated as relevant to real urban situations.

We move systematically through a series of topics. In each case, the evidence we have documented so far is summarized, occasionally with more detailed illustrations. Equally, and at times simultaneously, we address the values which we think underlie the observed differences. This approach is consistent with our empirical analysis, which is mostly of a univariate nature. We report, however, the results of other multivariate analyses which are encouraging.

Under the general heading of social life, we treat, in order: demographic structure and change in cities; racial distributions and relations; criminal behavior; and ethnicity. Under political institutions, we consider two themes. The major theme is political culture, as manifested firstly in the organization of the state, including federalism and intergovernmental relations, and secondly, in deference, collective action, and attitudes towards private property. A secondary but important theme is the question of the appropriate roles of public enterprises and private corporations in the delivery of goods and services, almost all of which are neither purely public nor private in nature.[7]

The economic order of the two countries is characterized by a pronounced dependency by Canada upon the United States. This, together with an historic orientation to resource extraction in the Canadian economy, calls into question the notion that Canada is "advanced" in the common sense of that term, despite its membership in O.E.C.D. and presence at Economic Summits. Through a brief comparative consideration of the role of the state, economic structure, income distribution, and financial institutions, and their meaning for urban development, we attempt to explicate values and their differences. Finally, the central organizing element for the conclusion is a private-public dimension. This encompasses and parallels another dimension which ranges, at its extremes, from an excess of individualism to an over-concentration on collectivism.

Before proceeding to these substantive matters, a brief word on cities as the unit of analysis: for smaller urban places, say from 50,000 to 2,500 or 1,000 (depending on the threshold for defining urban),[8] the range of data which we wish to utilize is seriously incomplete. We therefore focus on the metropolitan centres of the two countries, utilizing the Standard Metropolitan Statistical Area (S.M.S.A.) in the United States while in Canada the nearest equivalent is the Census Metropolitan Area (C.M.A.) and selected census Agglomerations (C.A.).[9] Although this gives us access to a wide range of census and other data, provides the potential for internal analysis at the census tract level, and encompasses the vast majority of the urban population,[10] using such units is not without difficulty.[11]

DEMOGRAPHIC CHANGES, RACE AND ETHNICITY

In terms of demographic characteristics, the principal items under discussion are population, household change, and household structure. Our research has shown that former pronounced differences in the amount of population decline in metropolitan centres, especially in the geopolitically defined central city have been eroded such that both sets of metropolitan centres show considerable population loss.[12] In short, in this respect, Canadian cities are becoming more similar to those in America. The latter exhibit a considerable range of experience (from the New York, Cleveland and Buffalo metropolitan areas which declined by around 8 per cent in the 1970 to 1980 decade to metropolitan centres in Florida, Texas, and elsewhere with percentage increases exceeding 50 and 60 per cent over the decade). The Canadian experience however, is more modest. No metropolitan area grew by more than 50 per cent from 1971 to 1981, and the highest decline was just less than -5.0 per cent (in Sudbury, Ontario). The phenomenon of population decline, and an overall slowing of the metropolitan growth rate, is most dramatically evident in central city losses. The American experience has been widely documented. Even before the 1980 census was taken, Berry, among others, noted "the current nationwide trend of absolute central city population decline."[13] On this point, the Canadian experience does differ. Numerically, more central cities gained population than lost during the 1976–81 period, and in absolute terms, there was a net gain of just over 100,000 people. While there are central cities in the U.S. that are "gainers," they are being swamped nationwide by the massive hemorrhaging from America's leading urban centres.

We contend that while population decline is not unimportant (such as in terms of city-provincial/state fiscal transfers, or declining demands for specific services such as education), insufficient attention has been paid to changes in a fundamental demographic unit—the household—a unit of great significance in terms of demands for housing, consumer durables, and personal and public services. Our earlier research shows that there were important differences in the amount and distribution of household change in the first half of the decade of the 1970's.[14] We argue that the greater average growth of households in Canadian metropolitan areas, including the central cities, is a result of the continued greater attractiveness of central city residential areas in Canada. In turn, we link this to a series of variables, including neighbourhood racial change, race relations, public safety, educational quality, and the provision of municipal services under fiscal stress. There are significant U.S.-Canadian differences in these variables which, we believe, arise from institutional practice.

Preliminary 1981 Canadian census data on occupied dwellings (equivalent to households) now allow us now to make this important comparison for the past decade, treating here only the "worst case" scenario: the central city. The results are striking and confirm our expectations (Table 1). No Canadian city is yet in a loss situation in terms of net household change. Eight of America's twenty largest metropolitan areas suffered a household loss in their central cities, while another six 'stagnated" (where stagnation is defined as growing at less than 0.5 per cent per annum). Of all

TABLE 1

DISTRIBUTION OF PERCENTAGE CHANGE IN DWELLING UNITS (HOUSEHOLDS) IN CENTRAL CITIES 1970-71—1980-81

Percentage Change	US			CANADA		
	n	Per cent	Cumulative Per cent	n	Per cent	Cumulative Per cent
100 or >	1	0.4		0		
90 to 99	1	0.4	0.8	0		
80 to 89	6	2.2	3.0	0		
70 to 79	3	1.1	4.1	1	2.9	
60 to 69	7	2.5	6.6	0		2.9
50 to 59	13	4.7	11.3	0		2.9
40 to 49	19	6.9	18.2	8	23.5	26.4
30 to 39	27	9.8	28.0	7	20.6	47.0
20 to 29	50	18.1	46.1	9	26.5	73.5
10 to 19	52	18.8	64.9	7	20.6	94.1
0 to 9	72	26.1	91.0	2	5.9	100.0
0 to –9	22	8.0	99.0			
–10 or >	3	1.1	100.1			
		Median 11.5			Median 29.7 (26.7)[a]	
		Mean 22.7			Mean 30.1 (27.1)[a]	

Source: U.S. Census of Population, Standard Metropolitan Statistical Areas and Standard Consolidated Statistical Areas PC80–S1–5; Statistics Canada, unpublished data (preliminary).

[a] Since these data are preliminary, the 1971 base data have not been adjusted to ensure comparable areal units with 1981. In some cases, this will inflate the amount of change. Cities where this is a major problem (such as Winnipeg) are omitted. To compensate, the median and mean are adjusted downward by a factor of 10 per cent. The U.S.–Canadian differences remain striking.

Canadian cities, only Montreal falls into this category, language likely acting as an impediment to foreign immigration, which continues to replenish Canadian inner city areas, while fears of separatism and economic decline accelerated the out-migration of employment and English-speaking households. If the well-known and frequently advanced lag argument is to be employed here (that is, that Canada is really similar to the U.S. but just lags behind in trends), we must be prepared to accept a lag of greater than ten years, if indeed there is a lag.

Household structure also varies significantly between the two countries.[15] Households comprising families with children still at home are a consistently greater proportion of all households in urban Canada; this is especially interesting for central cities where one might expect a lower degree of familism (at least, according to social area theorists). In contrast, one and two person households are more prevalent in American cities although both countries have witnessed a dramatic increase in this type of household in recent years and a systematic decline in household size. A socio-demographic variable that undoubtedly relates to this is the divorce rate, which through the 1970's has been twice as high in the U.S. Since divorce is likely a function of social attitudes and enabling legislation, some might interpret this as evidence of higher conservatism in Canada.[16]

Race in Canada and the U.S.: Urban Differences and Social Attitudes

A persistent theme in American urban studies is that black movement into central city residential districts is strongly associated with "white flight." This term occasions academic dispute, some arguing that white families are being drawn away by the prospects of a "better" material life and jobs in suburban areas rather than leaving with ill-feeling toward the incoming non-whites. Without reviewing the evidence in detail, there is behavioural data to suggest that both views are supportable; much depends on the specific situation.[17] Whatever the underlying cause, many studies have documented the aggregate shifts: massive net white gains in suburban areas and net black gains in central cities. The 1980 census figures indicate a continuation of this trend, but with an added dimension. Detroit, a city which has had its fair share of urban ills, exemplifies the established trend; in a decade, its white population declined by 425,000 (half the white population) while the black population grew by almost 100,000 and became a substantial numerical majority. The added dimension is revealed in such instances as Cleveland and St. Louis, where not only are white losses in excess of 100,000 but reductions have occurred in the black population as well. But, while blacks are participating increasingly in the suburbanization process, it appears as if many will live in suburban districts as highly segregated as the traditional inner-city ghettos.[18]

It is common to note the significant differences between Canadian and American cities in terms of the proportion of non-whites in the population. What is perhaps of greater import is that in certain Canadian cities there are now substantial numbers of non-whites (Toronto, Montreal, Vancouver, Winnipeg and Regina), the result of foreign and internal in-migration. We can point to some differences between the two countries in how people react to the social fact of race in a residential context (Table 2). Canadians have also shown less propensity for moving if "coloured people came to live in great numbers in your area." In Toronto, Kalbach has demonstrated that the West Indian and Negro group is less segregated residentially than

TABLE 2

RACIAL CHANGE AND RESIDENTIAL RELOCATION

	Per cent Answering[a]					
	Yes, Definitely		Yes, Might		No	
	Canada	U.S.[b]	Canada	U.S.	Canada	U.S.
1963	3	20	5	25	91	55
1965		13		22		65
1966		13		21		66
1967		12		23		65
1969	4		6		90	
1975	3		6		91	

[a] The question posed was "If coloured people came to live next door, would you move your home?"

[b] The question is put only to white people in the U.S.

Source: Alex C. Michalos, *North American Social Report: Volume 5, Economics, Religion and Morality* (Boston: D. Reidel Publishing, 1982), Table 32, p. 206.

certain other ethnic groups.[19] American studies, on the other hand, have consistently demonstrated very high and persistent levels of residential segregation for urban blacks. Caution is required here, for anecdotal evidence from Winnipeg and Edmonton suggests that residential areas with increasing numbers of East Indians (Edmonton) and native peoples (Winnipeg) are being shunned by whites.[20] These kinds of evidence suggest that the Canadian value system tends to be more accepting of non-whites as near neighbours. (This is not to deny that racism and housing discrimination against blacks, native peoples and others exist in Canadian communities.[21]).

It is probable that since Canadian central cities, in general, are not physically decaying, being abandoned or torched, nor contain non-white ghettos, there is no association between these features and segregated minority residence. Regrettably, only too often is this association made by urban and suburban Americans, who blame blacks, Puerto Ricans or others. The extensive literature on white fears concerning neighbourhood quality and declining property values when black households move in suggests a basis for this judgement.[22]

We need to remember scale differences, however. Non-white people in Canadian cities have simply not been numerous enough to pose a sufficient threat (in terms of "taking over" or "engulfing" local neighbourhoods).

In the U.S., when blacks were far less numerous in northern cities prior to the massive black migrations, they were less segregated and more accepted than at later periods.[23] The sheer magnitude of black population growth meant that they must inevitably seek additional living space in cities. The exclusionary tactics of white property-owners and sporadic violence encouraged the concentration and hence segregation of blacks. (Canada too had its equivalents: housing covenants in such disparate places as Vancouver and Hamilton were employed to keep out Chinese and Japanese in the former, and a whole range of ethnic groups in the latter.[24]) Given Canada's record in ethnic and race relations, one has to admit the possibility that if non-whites were as significant an urban minority as they are in many U.S. cities, we might then find less willingness among Canadians to accept them as near-neighbours.

The American conception of social rank which ascribes a low position to black Americans is of some standing; blacks were at the low end of Bogardus's social distance scale developed in the 1920's, post-dating some of the worst race riots in America.[25] Following the Civil War, black Americans experienced social improvement, but things worsened by the turn of the century as certain states moved to erect discriminatory legislation. The conventional "melting-pot" metaphor in the U.S. conveniently ignores black Americans. The black-white dualism embedded in American social practice is manifested in the phenomenon of dual housing markets within both the private and public sectors, the phenomenon of white residential relocation in the face of black in-migration, and geographic segregation of races within cities. Thus, we would conclude that there is close relationship here between value systems and urban differences.

Crime in the City: "The Killing Ground" and "The Peaceable Kingdom"

Just as there is a popular American equation of non-white and slums, so too is there an equation between non-white and crime. Unfortunately, this is not a figment of the imagination; there are real ecological and individual associations here which cannot be ignored. But from the more distant Canadian vantage-point, crime in American is popularly perceived as something to be expected in a society which has less respect for the rule of law than does Canadian society.[26] Canadians have long viewed Americans as more lawless than themselves; crime rate comparisons and somewhat self-satisfied statements about the settling of the West are legend. But if Canadians are somewhat smug, they have good reason to be; the differences in the rates for crimes against people are considerable (Table 3).

Also, there is evidence reported in the press from American tourists to suggest that Canadian cities are safer and less stressful in terms of personal safety in public places.[27] It is tempting to conclude that this reflects a

TABLE 3

VIOLENT CRIME AND PROPERTY CRIME IN METROPOLITAN AND CENTRAL CITIES: CANADA AND THE U.S.

	CANADA (1976)			U.S. (1975)		
	Violent Crime/100,000 Pop.			Violent Crime/100,000 Pop.		
	Metro	Central City	Balance	Metro	Central City	Balance
Mean	93.3	107.4	58.8	436.4	656.0	275.4
Std. dev.	51.7	94.4	35.5	232.0	455.3	193.8
n	31	26	17	219	MDBR	MDNM 243
	Property Crime/100,000 Pop.			Property Crime/100,000 Pop.		
	Metro	Central City	Balance	Metro	Central City	Balance
Mean	5363.9	6301.2	3938.6	5249.0	6978.9	3816.5
Std. dev.	1406.5	1781.0	1842.3	1556.3	2297.8	1623.0
n	31	26	17	221	243	214

Source: Authors. Data are from Statistics Canada; *The City and County Data Book,* 1977; U.S. Federal Bureau of Investigation, *FBI Uniform Crime Data.*

Canadian value system that is deferential to authority and accepting of the rule of law, whereas violent crime in America is an outgrowth of excessive individualism and decidedly non-deferential ways of behaviour.[28] However, such a conclusion is challenged by the fact that crimes against property (so-called "victimless" crimes) are about as likely to happen in Canadian cities as they are in the U.S. For the moment, this leaves us somewhat baffled in terms of value differences as an explanation. (One interpretation might be that Canadians value people more than property and accordingly behave less violently to each other, while Americans may treat others in an indiscriminate or devalued fashion.)

Whatever the reason, fear for one's personal safety is a powerful factor in encouraging a move to what the social geographer Ley has called "the firm ground" of suburbia.[29] Both in the inner city and suburban enclaves we find "fortress" America, with elaborate surveillance and security systems; these are not unknown in Canada but they are weakly developed and far less prevalent. High levels of violent crime are a factor in accounting for household declines in the U.S. central city, and their correspondingly relative insignificance in Canadian urban centres might suggest there is less to fear.[30] A national quality of life comparison presents an interesting similarity which is scarcely what one might have expected (Table 4);

TABLE 4

LOCAL AREA SAFETY: CANADIAN AND AMERICAN VIEWS

Question: Is there any area around here—that is, within a mile—where you would be afraid to walk alone at night? [a]

	Yes		No	
	Canada	U.S.	Canada	U.S.
1965		34		63
1967		31		67
1968		35		62
1970	29		66	
1972		41		59
1973		41		58
1974	37		63	

Source: Alex C. Michalos, *North American Social Report: Volume 2, Crime, Justice and Politics* (Boston: D. Reidel Publishing Co., 1980) Chapter 4, Table 5.

[a] Question posed to representative national samples in both countries.

perhaps the question should be asked of Americans visiting Canadian cities and vice versa? This adds to the complexity and makes the link between values and urban differences more tenuous.

Ethnicity, Multi-culturalism, and the Immigrant World in the City

If certain social processes are at work to depopulate particular urban districts in America, then, in the past, waves of immigrants could be relied upon to replenish the Hell's Kitchens and other immigrant reception areas. With a few notable exceptions (such as New York, East Los Angeles, The Bay Area and Miami), this social fact is no longer as numerically important as before (although the immigrant fact is still important in other ways: visually, aurally, symbolically and spatially).[31] Canada, no less than the United States, is a nation of immigrants, but it is profoundly different from America in having two principal and founding ethnic groups. Language in parts of Canada has therefore evoked emotions which, on occasion, come close to those generated by race in America. Canada and its cities cannot be understood without accepting and interpreting one of the great Canadian dualities—English-French.[32]

The immigrant, already a nominal member of an ethnic group, arrived in a society where the group was enormously important and language was the membership card.[33] We have already shown the significant urban differences in the proportions of those foreign born and living abroad prior to the census.[34] This is consistent with national trends which show that the standardized immigration rate in Canada (1964–74) was almost four times that of the United States.[35] Even prior to 1926, Canada was, in a sense, even more of an immigrant society than the U.S.: "While the United States had ninety-two people to absorb each immigrant, Canada had only sixteen" [1912].[36] Many immigrants were British, however, and possibly more readily assimilated.

The continued high level of immigration into Canada has been a powerful feature in maintaining an effective demand for inner city residences, especially in cities like Toronto and Vancouver which continue to be leading destinations. In some instances, the extended immigrant family is ideally matched with an older housing stock, originally built for larger families than are now commonplace.[37] Is a sense of ethnic identity maintained through such immigration, and is it actively reflected in the urban landscape, as it is in the federal policy of multiculturalism? In contrast, is ethnicity fading as a relevant social fact in the U.S., and are ethnic areas in the U.S. cities aging and becoming less "ethnic"? This is a contentious area with immense measurement problems. Yet an understanding of the social geography of our two sets of cities demands an investigation.[38]

Conventional theory suggests that the pressures to conform and assimilate that were part of nation building in the United States broke down ethnicity. The ethos of individualism to which the immigrant was already receptive, having moved outside the cultural hearth, further encouraged a decline in group identity. Recently, however, a contrary view has emerged, arguing that ethnicity is persistent and important and that diversity was and is an important element of the American social experience: the "unmeltable ethnics." Alternatively, ethnicity is seen as a choice, something that can be put off or taken up again. Evidence suggesting a recent rise in ethnic awareness is linked to growing consciousness in the face of growing demands of Black Americans to be treated as an ethnic group. In a society supposedly characterised by individualism, blacks above all, are not likely to be treated on an individual basis but as stereotypical members of a group, and a subgroup at that.

In Canada, the ethnic group has always been important. The arrival of new people has been accommodated, and ethnic residential segregation is generally neither feared nor despised.[39] Indeed, immigrant Canadians may have less desire to move out of ethnic "villages" for the more heterogeneous suburbs than their American counterparts. The pitfalls of generalizing about ethnic residential segregation in urban areas are illustrated by Agocs's study of Detroit and by Driedger's work in Winnipeg.[40] Both demonstrate quite different patterns of settlement and community development, depending on which ethnic group one is dealing with. There is little evidence of any universal pattern of ethnic residence or that assimilation necessarily implies dispersal to the suburbs.[41] Reviewing a scattering of local case studies leads us to suspect that a higher degree of ethnic residential segregation persists in Canadian cities. Other than for black and Hispanic populations, segregation is generally declining for American ethnics. The ethnic community may persist, but pronounced residential clustering seems now to be less of a prerequisite.

Diversity has become firmly embedded in Canadian public policy and ethnicity and its associated diversity seem to be highly and officially valued. In the United States, apart from highly visible ethnic symbolism (such as the green Chicago River on St. Patrick's Day), ethnicity is a contested concept, one which is barely recognized by the national government.[42] As long as the principal organizational features of ethnic life in Canada are located in the central cities, there is a powerful element fostering positive household growth, offsetting suburbanization, and checking so-called counter-urbanization.[43]

Finally, a recent analysis for selected American and Canadian metropolitan areas (utilizing a number of the demographic, racial and ethnic variables discussed here) yields the following results:

(a) of the five factors (which account for 57 per cent of the total variance), four exhibit statistically significant differences between Canadian and American metropolitan centers, and
(b) of the thirteen groups produced by a cluster analysis, three contain almost 95 per cent of the Canadian cities but only 3 per cent of the American cities.[44]

These results point to social structures in Canadian metropoles independent of those revealed in their U.S. counterparts and reinforce the arguments sketched here. To summarize:

1. The value system of white Americans is such that residential integration on a local area basis is relatively rare. Black in-movement, occasioned by a search for jobs and cheap, affordable housing, helps to propel white out-migration when it is seen as the portent of an inevitable change in the local area.
2. The net migration outward is accentuated by the very high levels of crime in American central cities, these being in part a reflection of attitudes towards the rule of law, authority and public order. Historical context, daily experience and economic conditions are also relevant factors.
3. The proportionately lesser significance of immigration and the possible erosion of ethnic identity means that ethnic residential communities are

less persistent or less likely to be established in American cities than in Canada. The potential for a substantial offset to white and now black out-migration is lower in the U.S. than in Canada.

4. Canadian value systems now attach considerable worth to ethnic enclaves and diversity and appear to be more accepting of other races as near neighbours. Massive net outflows of households are as yet unknown and central city population is growing.

In short, values tolerating ethnic and racial diversity and values which contribute to a less violent milieu play a role in maintaining the superior livability of the Canadian central city.

POLITICAL CULTURE, POLITICAL VALUES AND POLITICAL INSTITUTIONS: A REVIEW OF CANADIAN AND U.S. DIFFERENCES AND THEIR IMPLICATIONS FOR URBAN DEVELOPMENT

In democratic societies, social values and broadly-based cultural norms are reflected directly in political cultures, in the political values that give rise to these cultures, and in those institutions that effect political action. The full range of political cultures, values and institutions differ significantly between the U.S. and Canada, with important implications for the development of urban areas in the two countries.

Political Culture

The meaning of the term political culture has evolved since its initial formulation by Almond and Verba two decades ago.[45] A study by Presthus, from which much of the following comparative information on political culture in Canada and the U.S. derives, speaks of political culture in the following terms:

> Political culture may be described as the orientations of individuals toward the political system including the extent to which they accept government as legitimate, feel politically efficacious, identify with the "rules of the game" governing the system, and thus participate in politics. Insofar as the structure of political institutions shapes and is shaped by these variables, it seems valid to include such structures as a part of political culture.[46]

To test these concepts, Almond and Verba surveyed the general U.S. population to obtain subjective estimates of public perceptions of the political system and of public interaction with and involvement in that system. Among the dimensions studied were efficacy (a feeling that the average citizen could influence decisions), involvement (participation in the political process), and trust (the degree of acceptance of and trust in the political systems and their operations). Several recent studies provide interesting insights into the dimensions of political culture in Canada and the U.S. along the lines initially identified by Almond and Verba. In a series of studies, political scientist Robert Presthus has drawn rather sharp distinctions between Canadian and American legislatures. Significant differences exist between the amount of contact between legislators in Canada and the U.S. and with interest groups (Table 5). First, the Canadian

TABLE 5

FREQUENCY OF INTERACTION WITH INTEREST GROUPS, U.S. vs. CANADIAN LEGISLATORS IN PER CENT

	United States		Canada	
Interaction	Federal	State	Federal	Provincial
High	72	94	42	58
Medium	25	5	29	32
Low	3	1	29	11
(n)	(100)	(149)	(141)	(127)

High = ''frequently'' (twice a week); Medium = ''occasionally'';
Low = ''seldom'' or ''rarely.''
Source: R. Presthus, ''Aspects of Political Culture and Legislative Behavior,''p.12.

political system allows for less involvement than that in the United States. Second, Canadian legislators feel less efficacious than their American counterparts (Table 6), a finding reflected in the general public as revealed by a series of public opinion polls during the 1960's and 1970's.[47] Lastly, we see that Canadians display slightly greater trust (Table 7) than do Americans toward government; of particular interest here is the much greater belief by Canadians that people in government are competent and less wasteful. This greater acceptance of government by Canadians and of its role in the economy is supported by several additional pieces of survey research data. First, the previously cited work on legislator attitudes in Canada and the U.S. showed a much greater disposition among Canadian politicians to intervene in the economy (Table 8). Second, work in the 1970's also shows a much greater willingness on the part of the sampled public in each country for Canadians to accept government involvement in the economy (Table 9).

The underlying and strong acceptance of government intervention in Canada stands in stark contrast to American attitudes and has attracted a

TABLE 6

COMPARATIVE POLITICAL EFFICACY
UNITED STATES v. CANADIAN LEGISLATORS
IN PER CENT

	United States		Canada	
	Federal	State	Federal	Provincial
Political efficacy[a]				
High	57	35	28	36
Medium	41	56	53	43
Low	2	9	19	21
(92)	(147)	(135)	(118)	

[a] "Efficacy" is based upon the following items: "The old saying, 'You can't fight city hall' is still basically true"; "Most decisions in business and government are made by a small group that pretty well runs things"; "The average man doesn't have much chance to get ahead today"; "Anyone in this country who wants to, has a chance to have his say about important issues." Although the "average man doesn't have . . ." item is often used as an alienation item, it emerged as part of this index through cluster analysis.

Source: Robert Presthus, "Aspects of Political Culture and Legislative Behavior,"p.18.

TABLE 7

POLITICAL TRUST[a]
IN PER CENT

	Canada		United States		
	1968	1965	1972	1968	1964
Government Wastes Money	46	38	68	61	48
People in Government Crooked	27	27	38	20	30
Government Run by Big Interests	90	83	59	44	30
People in Government Smart	49	57	42	39	28
Trust Government to do Right	39	39	46	37	22
Average	50	49	51	40	32

[a] For political trust questions, the entry in each cell is the percentage giving a cynical response. No political trust questions were asked in a 1970's Canadian Study.

Source: Nathaniel Beck and John C. Pierce, "Political Involvement and Party Allegiances in Canada and the United States," p.39.

TABLE 8

ECONOMIC LIBERALISM,
UNITED STATES vs. CANADIAN LEGISLATORS
IN PER CENT

	United States		Canada	
Economic Liberalism[a]	Federal	State	Federal	Provincial
High	21	25	56	63
Medium	55	53	43	37
Low	24	22	—	—
	(90)	(147)	(722)	(117)

[a] ''Economic liberalism'' is defined here by the following items: ''That government which governs least governs best'' (reverse scored); ''Economic security for every man, woman and child is worth striving for, even if it means socialism''; ''if unemployment is high, government should spend money to create jobs''; ''A national medicare plan is necessary to ensure that everyone received adequate health care''; ''More federal aid to education desirable if we are going to adequately meet present and future educational needs in this country.''

Source: Robert Presthus, ''Aspects of Political Culture and Legislative Behavior,'' p.13.

great deal of attention by researchers. The deferential character of the Canadian public has been particularly curious to American observers, given the enormous stress placed in the United States on individualism and on resistance to government intervention.[48] Interestingly, despite the lower degree of political efficacy of Canadians, they in fact, participate more broadly in politics than do Americans (Table 10), an anomalous finding for a people who view government as not being responsive and catering more to ''big interests'' than to all the people (the converse of American views).

The preceding elements of political culture differences between Canada and the United States point to additional differences in political organization between the two countries. In view of American egalitarian beliefs, evidenced in part by the efficacy findings above and by general distrust of government, it is not surprising to find striking differences in the manifestation of federalism between the two countries. So pervasive is the belief in the ''American way of life,'' that the American character has tended to coalesce about this unitary idea of government and the supremacy of the American democratic forms and institutions. This pervasiveness is so great

TABLE 9

PERSONALITY DIMENSION: INDIVIDUALIST-COLLECTIVIST PERSONALITY TRAIT

Personality Items	Mean Level of Agreement[a]	
	Canada	U.S.
The government in Ottawa (Washington) is too big and powerful	40	54[b]
The government should guarantee everyone at least $3,000 per year whether he works or not	36	14[b]
Communism is the greatest peril in the world today (M)[c]	54	70[b]

[a] 0 = Definitely Disagree; 20 = Generally Disagree; 40 = Moderately Disagree; 60 = Moderately Agree; 80 = Generally Agree; 100 = Definitely Agree.

[b] Difference is statistically significant at the 0.001 level and in agreement with the comparative literature.

[c] (M) = Males only.

Source: Stephen J. Arnold and Douglas J. Tigert, "Canadians and Americans," p.81.

that it almost obviates the federal nature of the American nation, since regional and/or state concerns appear to be truly overwhelmed by the sense of nationhood.[49] In Canada, however, one of the few unifying symbols is the perennial clash of federal and provincial governments. In short, the U.S. federation is very much a static one in the sense that the respective roles of the states and the federal government have long since been decided. The Canadian confederation, on the other hand, is dynamic and fluid, with the locus of power continually shifting among the various governments.[50]

This is a curious state of affairs considering the bases of confederation in the two countries. First, the U.S. constitution, Article 10 of the Bill of Rights, allocated residual powers to the states. In Canada, in contrast, the British North America Act of 1867, Section 91, allocated residual power to the federal government. Thus, on paper at least, the U.S. federal system is typified by strong states and a weak federal presence, not Canada. As Gibbins notes in his recent study of Canadian and U.S. federalism: "The irony is that Canadians today have a federal system not far removed in spirit from the early American model, whereas the American federal system has evolved toward the Canadian model laid out in 1867."[51] Differences in

TABLE 10

REPORTED POLITICAL PARTICIPATION
IN THE UNITED STATES AND CANADA[a]
IN PER CENT

	United States			Canada		
Political Activity	1972	1968	1964	1974	1968	1965
Read Newspapers Often	37	49	47	43	—	—
Tried to Convince Others	32	34	31	23–34[b]	—	23
Attended Rally, Meeting	9	9	9	19–32[b]	—	15
Did Party Work	5	5	5	11–17[b]	—	5
Displayed Sticker	14	15	16	16–21[b]	—	—
Voted	75	76	78	85	86	86

[a] The entry in each cell is the percentage of the sample in that year reporting that they engaged in that political activity.

[b] On these activities, the questions in the two countries were asked differently. In the Canadian study, individuals were given the opportunity to indicate the frequency with which they participated in the activity, while in the American studies the response alternatives were simply yes or no. The first figure in the Canadian percentages excludes respondents saying they ''seldom'' or ''never'' participated in the activity. The second figure excludes only those individuals who said they ''never'' participated in the activity.

Source: Nathaniel Beck and John C. Pierce, ''Political involvement and Party Allegiances in Canada and the United States,'' p.25.

evolution of these federal systems are traceable to a series of judicial decisions that over time reversed the initial intentions of the ''founding fathers'' in the U.S. and the ''fathers of Confederation'' in Canada.[52] This reversal is even more interesting in light of the legislative systems designed into each constitution: the parliamentary system and the American congressional system. If any system should have provided a forum for political brokerage and for a thriving federal system, it should have been the congressional system, not the unitary British parliamentary model with its highly centralized cabinet. It is ironic, indeed, that the U.S., with the longstanding American fear of big and powerful central governments, should have achieved its present system, and that Canada, with a more deferential attitude toward government, should have evolved its system.

There are, however, important features in the U.S. system which do provide for and thus encourage the rights of the individual. Similarly, in Canada some of the disorder that would normally ensue through the weaker federal role is offset by the nature of the legal and legislative system. These features of both countries are also essential expressions of deep-seated attitudes toward government and politics more generally.

Built into the American system of government is a much studied system of checks and balances provided by the legislative, executive and judicial branches. The federal structure itself was seen as providing a further check within the legislative sphere by splitting legislative functions among the states and the federal government. Furthermore, since it is the American people ("We the people of the United States . . .") who are popularly believed to hold ultimate power in the United States, the written constitution and certain amendments reserve to the people rights which transcend the rights of governments. This further check on government maintains much of the initial spirit of the U.S. federal system and provides for redress through the courts should the legislative or executive branches usurp too much power. This ability, potential or realized, to challenge government serves to restore balance and prevents the unlimited growth of power by any level of government. Finally, the Congress itself, with its two houses and nearly six hundred legislators, provides further centrifugal force away from a total dominance of political affairs by the federal government. The notorious weakness of U.S. political parties means that a great deal of political brokerage can take place in Congress. As well, much compromise and refinement can be introduced into legislation to weaken the tendency of the federal government to dominate U.S. political life.[53]

Turning to Canada, we see an analogous set of political institutions which provide the essential glue to keep the Canadian federation together. First the Canada Act (the new Canadian constitution) allocates powers to the federal and provincial legislatures; in so doing, it sets limits on provincial domination of the Canadian federal system. Moreover, the parliamentary system provides the federal government with a powerful and highly centralized institution, the federal cabinet, with which to challenge the ten provinces and thus provide countervailing forces. Finally, and perhaps most importantly, the overarching Canadian attitude toward collective behaviour (as compared with the strong attachment in the U.S. to the individual) provides the federal government with an element of legitimacy which would be lacking in the U.S., since federal action is the ultimate in Canadian collectivity. In fact, as Elkins and Simeon have shown, Canadians seem to feel strongly about both their own province and about the entity, Canada.[54] Table 11 illustrates this dual loyalty clearly.[55] Thus, in Canada there are a number of forces keeping a dynamic balance between central and non-central powers, although the forces and the balance itself differ markedly from those in the U.S.

TABLE 11

RELATIVE ATTRACTIVENESS OF CANADA AND THE PROVINCES BY PROVINCE/LANGUAGE GROUPS (1974)[a]

	Percentage Most Oriented to Provinces	Percentage Most Oriented Nationally	Mean Scores	Standard Deviations	N
National	4.9	18.4	3.64	1.70	2383
Newfoundland	5.9	3.9	2.74	1.47	90
P.E.I.	4.2	2.1	2.89	1.45	84
Nova Scotia	1.7	10.9	3.45	1.48	147
New Brunswick	4.3	21.5	4.01	1.65	85
Ontario	0.9	25.9	4.29	1.44	651
Manitoba	5.3	18.6	3.79	1.69	108
Saskatchewan	6.9	12.9	3.53	1.72	94
Alberta	12.0	6.3	2.72	1.68	166
B.C.	6.0	13.5	3.42	1.67	242
Quebec English	1.5	37.9	4.78	1.37	126
Quebec French	9.3	11.6	3.21	1.78	531
Non-Quebec French	1.7	20.0	3.61	1.65	59

[a] This index compares "Canada in general" to "your province in general," "Canada as a place to live" to "your province as a place to live," and "Canadian government" to "government in your province." The range is 0–6, with zero being most favourable to your province, and six being most nationally oriented. Percentages do not add to 100 per cent because of the omission of scores 1–5.

Source: David J. Elkins and Richard Simeon, "Small Worlds: Provinces and Parties in Canadian Political Life," p.17.

Deference, Collective Action and Private Property: Transcendant Differences in Political Values Between Canadians and Americans

"Peace, Order and Good Government," were the rationale for the British North America Act's distribution of powers to the federal and provincial parliaments.[56] In contrast stands the American "Life, Liberty and the Pursuit of Happiness." Many authors have pointed to this difference as an indicator of deep-seated attitudes toward government in the affairs of citizens.[57] The deference to authority that Canadian society has exhibited over the past century or more has been traced all the way back to the country's conservative antirevolutionary roots and the United Empire

Loyalists.[58] The relatively greater deferential behaviour of Canadians has a number of implications for the structure and conduct of government and politics in Canada as compared with the United States.

First, Americans, going back to Thomas Jefferson and other drafters of the U.S. Constitution, feared bureaucratic and government control of their "life, liberty and pursuit of happiness." The Jeffersonian model, and the one operating in many places in the U.S. today, solved the problem through the election of an extraordinary range of public officials. For instance, it is still commonplace to elect judges, assessors, controllers, treasurers, sheriffs, and even county clerks in many American states. The theory of such practices is that bureaucracies will be accountable to the public through the election of these officials.

Canada demonstrates a Britannic continuity by establishing powerful and generally well-staffed bureaucracies which are subservient to political masters, be they municipal councils or provincial or federal ministers of the Crown. This relatively greater role played by bureaucrats in Canada would be anathema to most Americans, as would be the broad discretionary powers wielded by senior Canadian bureaucrats.

The greater acceptance of the actions of nonelected public officials is matched in Canada by much greater freedom of action in the absence of the constraints of a binding written constitution. The recently proclaimed Constitution Act of 1981 is a step toward providing Canadians with some of the procedural and substantive protection accorded American citizens, which, if taken to the U.S. limit, would surely curtail both legislative and bureaucratic autonomy.[59] There are several factors, however, that are likely to militate against the evolution of the new Canadian Charter of Rights and Freedoms into a northern version of the U.S. Constitution, all of which relate closely to the very deference under discussion. First, there is the historic unwillingness of the Canadian judiciary to interpret issues broadly, unlike their American counterparts. As a result, it is reasonably likely that Canadian legislatures will be handed back highly contentious issues for legislative, not judicial, action. Secondly, the Canadian Charter of Rights and Freedoms is a compromise (to be expected in such a federal-provincial environment) and is not necessarily binding on the provinces. Third, the long history of litigiousness that has characterized the U.S. constitutional battles is lacking in Canada. It is not unreasonable, therefore, to expect that, given greater deference, greater conservatism of the judiciary, and greater willingness of parliaments in Canada to cope with issues, the political route to social change will continue to dominate. This contrasts with the U.S., where the judiciary has played a central role in bringing about social and political change in the absence of action by federal or state legislatures.

Of particular interest for the present discussion about values and the development of Canadian and American cities is the role of property rights in the two countries. In Canada, as one would expect, property rights are not vested with the individual but rather with the Crown, just the opposite of the U.S., where the Fifth and Fourteenth Amendments to the U.S. constitution guarantee property rights. Interestingly, in the above mentioned Canadian Charter of Rights and Freedoms, property rights (as distinct from human rights) were explicitly not protected, thus leaving intact the whole set of institutions which govern urban development in Canada. The level and range of controls are much more stringent and far-reaching in Canada, as is the degree of discretion of interpretation and enforcement by local and provincial officials. For example, the British Columbia Limited Access Highways Act gives the minister of highways the right to expropriate up to 5 per cent of an individual's property fronting on a provincial limited access highway without any right to compensation. Such an act is unthinkable and also unconstitutional in the U.S. Similar discretion can be exercised on zoning, historic and heritage building designation, agricultural lands, and even building design. The only control is self-imposed by the provincial or local government. There is no appeal to a higher authority, even under the new Charter of Rights and Freedoms. Such a state of affairs would be unacceptable in the United States, where individual rights and particularly those related to personal and real property are sacrosanct.

In short, it is clear that Canadians do not dread government involvement and are willing to tolerate a much broader range of government controls and interventions in markets and in the lives of citizens than would be tolerable in the U.S. One area where this is especially apparent is in the quasi-public sector of Crown corporation, the so-called "public enterprise" about which Herschel Hardin writes so convincingly.[60] The range of "public enterprises," from the mammoth Air Canada and Canadian National Railroads down to Regina's collectively-owned Saskatchewan Roughriders football team, is vast. In between are at least four provincially-owned railroads, a provincially-owned national airline (owned interestingly enough by "Conservative" Alberta), a municipal telephone system (in Edmonton), a municipal power company (New Westminster, BC) and on and on. Such diversity and depth of involvement by the public sector in the national and regional economies would likely be unsettling to most Americans. While public enterprises are not unknown in the U.S. and may be more powerful and efficacious than is commonly recognized,[61] the prevalence and visibility of Crown corporations mark Canada as having a distinctive public sector within a North American context.[62] It points towards a very different political environment within which Canadians see their governments functioning at all levels as compared with that which Americans perceive. Of particular importance is the acceptance of government involvement in the economy not just through regulation and taxation as in the U.S. but also through direct government action through Crown corporations. It will not be at all surprising as a result, when we turn in the next section of this paper to explore economic values and institutions, to find that there is a very different kind of economy in Canada, in part as a result of this greater willingness on the part of Canadians to accept government as an active element in the economy and the marketplace. Before moving on to explore these economic issues, we summarize some of the previous discussion on political culture and values in Canada and the United States and sketch out some of the implications of these differences for urban development in the two countries.

Implications of Differences in Political Culture, Values and Institutions For Urban Development in Canada and the United States

Three themes that emerged above have implications for the course and outcome of urban development in Canada and the United States:

1. greater acceptance of government involvement in economic affairs in Canada;
2. greater role of federal government in U.S. vis-à-vis the states as compared with that of the Canadian federal government vis-à-vis the provinces; and
3. greater stress on the pursuit of individual goals in the U.S. and a correspondingly greater interest in collective action in Canada.[63]

Given the possibility of greater public involvement in urban development in Canada, we should expect to see considerably greater attention paid to planning and development controls. In the absence of constitutional protection of property rights, governments at all levels in Canada should possess greater ability and willingness to intervene. The result of such planning involvement should be more compact and better planned cities in Canada. Costs of development should be higher in Canada, since municipalities and provinces have the legal right to pass on servicing and development costs to developers as well as the right to set high servicing standards. Such higher costs need not be uneconomic, however, as higher quality urban development with greater satisfaction and lower maintenance costs can ensue from such policies.[64]

The greatly restricted role of the federal government in the Canadian confederation is particularly important when looking at urban development. Much of the initiative for urban policy in the United States has come from the federal government; U.S. federal policies of freeway building, urban renewal and urban public housing have left considerable marks on the U.S. urban scene, with only modest evidence that such federal interventions have been positive and much to suggest they have been negative.[65] In Canada, because of the highly restricted federal role in urban development, cities and provinces have been left to fend for themselves, with few if any of the problems faced by American cities, such as urban blight, loss of middle income and family households, and federally subsidized population redistribution away from existing large metropolitan areas in the Canadian industrial and economic heartland.[66] All this is not to say that the Canadian federal government is without an important role or that it has not attempted to expand its role. Simply put, under the terms of the B.N.A. Act and its judicial interpretations, federal urban policy-making has had to be minimal and in close cooperation with the provinces and the cities, or else they would be precluded from even that role.[67]

Finally, the recurring myth of individual action in the U.S. had led to what Warner has called "The Private City," and, more generally, privatism with respect to the development and maintenance of cities. This contrasts with relatively greater stress in Canada on publicly-provided goods and services. The dramatic differences in public transit patronage and automobile ownership between Canada and America highlight Warner's thesis. It also implies that Canadian cities should be more compact and should have a considerably different rent/density gradient from their American counterparts, since extensive expansion has not been subsidized through federal highway programmes in Canada, and since Canadians expect and receive considerably higher levels of public transit service.[68] An interesting extension of the American stress upon the individual as opposed to the society or group is seen in the number of governments in the U.S. It is somewhat ironic that a country with a long history of disliking government should have so many governments, largely comprised of special-purpose districts and small municipalities. Consider that in 1979 there were 79,913 governments in the United States for 223,880,000 people, or one government per each 2,801 Americans. In Canada, in 1978, there were 4,740 governments for 23,483,000 people, or an average of one government per 4,954 Canadians. In other words, there were nearly 80 per cent more governments per capita in the U.S. than in Canada.[69] Such fragmentation in the American urban system has provided individualized services to residents but has also made it difficult to deal effectively with regional (as opposed to local municipal) concerns, as would again be expected given the private and individualistic ethics.[70]

In many U.S. municipalities, the scope of public service is limited, and private contracting for what in Canada would be public services is more widespread, especially in suburban districts (garbage collection, even fire and protection services are cases in point), while the relative absence of public parks in these districts is compensated for by large private lots complete with a range of recreational paraphernalia.

ECONOMIC INSTITUTIONS AND VALUES IN CANADA AND THE UNITED STATES

Following from our previous discussion of greater willingness to accept government involvement in Canadian life, we begin our exploration of economic institutions and values with a review of the respective roles of government in the Canadian and U.S. economies and then move on to examine some key differences in the economies of the two countries. Implications for urban development of these differences in ''economic culture'' will also be examined.

The Public Enterprise Economy and Public Involvement in Economic Affairs

One dimension that stood out in our previous discussion was the extent to which Canadians accepted government action in general and government involvement in the economy specifically. This is an excellent point of departure for the present discussion of economic institution and values differences in the two countries. One dramatic measure of the involvement of Canadian governments in the Canadian economy is available from the *Financial Post 500*.[71] Of 400 top industrial firms in 1981, 25 were controlled by the federal or provincial governments. Of the top 50 industrials, ranked by sales, 7 were either wholly-owned or controlled by the federal or provincial governments. For financial institutions, 9 of the top 75 were federally or provincially-owned or controlled. Moreover, the most profitable company in terms of aggregate profits was Hydro-Quebec, with 1981 profits of $559,000,000. In short, Canadian governments at all levels exhibit little reticence about involvement in such diverse enterprises as railroads, airlines, aircraft manufacture, financial institutions, steel companies, oil companies, and selling and producing atomic reactors.

Statistics about the roles of the various levels of government in Canada and the U.S. in their respective economies support these initial impressions about Canada's greater involvement. Consider aggregate spending by all levels of government in 1977 in Canada (the most recent year for which consolidated government financial statements were available): total government spending by all levels equalled $89.514 billion out of a Gross

National Product (GNP) of $209.379 billion or 42.8 per cent of GNP.[72] In the U.S., for 1980, the equivalent figures are US$959 billion in government spending out of a U.S. GNP of US$2,626 billion or 36.5 per cent. In other words, the share of Canadian government spending was about one-fifth greater than the corresponding U.S. share. Turning to employment, a somewhat different picture emerges. While federal civilian employment is roughly equivalent (2.9 million in the U.S. compared with 279,000 in Canada), total government employment by all levels of government is not similar. There was a total of 704,000 public employees in Canada in 1978 (including military) compared with an equivalent figure of 17,322,000 in the U.S. in 1980, or nearly 2½ times as many public employees per capita in the U.S. as in Canada, reflecting in part a much larger military establishment but also, as noted earlier, much greater numbers of local governments.

Combining these figures with the qualitative dimension provided by the previous information from the *Financial Post 500* for 1981, it is clear that there is quite a different role for government in the economies of the two countries. The causes for these differences are undoubtedly related to the previously discussed Canadian tolerance of government involvement. They are also related to the very different economic processes at work in the two countries, in particular the buffering by government necessitated by Canada's "openness" to world economic events. Accordingly, we next explore the different structures of the U.S. and Canadian economies to gain additional insights into the differences in economic "culture" in the two countries.

Economic Structure: Openness, Assymmetry and Scale Effects

Two aspects of the Canadian and U.S. economies stand out immediately as different: the dependence on and structure of international economic relations; and the scale of economic activity. We begin first with scale. As a rough rule of thumb in economic matters, Canadian economic magnitudes are one-tenth of their U.S. equivalent. Thus, 1979 GNP in Canada was CDN$260.5 billion, which, using an exchange rate of CDN$1.00=US$0.8536, equalled US$22.4 billion. In 1979, U.S. GNP equalled US$2414 billion or 10.8 times the Canadian figure (subject to variations in the exchange rate). Similarly, U.S. population was 224,567,000 in 1979 compared with Canada's 23,672,000 people in the same year, (that is, the U.S. was 9.53 times as large in terms of people).

These enormous differences in scale have enabled the United States to develop a very broadly-based and more self-sufficient economy which contrasts markedly with that in Canada. Despite the triteness of the phrase, it is not inaccurate to continue to typify Canada as a "hewer of wood and drawer of water," given that Canadian exports are still dominated by resource-based raw and semi-finished materials. Correspondingly, Canadian imports are disproportionately composed of manufactured goods. In marked contrast, the U.S. trade with foreign countries shows exports dominated by manufacturers and resource-based and semi-finished materials dominating imports. For example, in 1978, exports by Canada of live animals, foodstuffs and inedible crude materials amounted to CDN$14.1 billion, while exports of fabricated materials (largely wood and paper products) amounted to CDN$18.9 billion. Together these accounted for amost two-thirds (63.2 per cent) of Canadian exports, while highly finished products such as machinery and equipment accounted for only just over one-third (36.2 per cent). Meanwhile, in the U.S., food and industrial materials (analogous to the first three classes of Canadian exports) accounted for almost half of U.S. exports (US$107.7 billion) in 1980, while machinery, equipment and consumer goods (non-food) accounted for 51 per cent of U.S. exports (US$108.1). In other words, raw and semi-finished materials accounted for a 50 per cent greater role in Canada's exports than they did in the U.S., while finished manufactures were 50 per cent more important in U.S. exports than they were in Canada's. The structure of imports reveals a pattern reversal; in Canada, highly manufactured goods represented 62.2 per cent of imports in 1978 (CDN$31.1 billion) while in the U.S. food and raw and semi-finished materials accounted for 61 per cent of its imports — almost an exact reversal.

One other dramatic difference between the two countries is the relative importance of foreign trade. U.S. total export earnings (1980) amounted to US$224 billion out of a total GNP of US$2,626 billion, only 8.5 per cent of the GNP. In contrast, Canada's export earnings (1978) of CDN$52.8 billion represented 22.9 per cent of Canada's GNP (CDN$230.4 billion). A similar picture emerges if imports are considered. The point to note is that trade is nearly three times as important to the Canadian economy as it is to the U.S. economy, in large part a function of the enormous scale differences in the two economies. Of course, much of this trade is with each other, suggesting Canada's "openness" to the U.S. in particular.

These differences in scale and structure are supported by the distribution of employees across the economies of the U.S. and Canada. Out of a total of 97,270,000 employed persons in the U.S. in 1980, 22.8 per cent were employed in manufacturing, 4.5 per cent in primary extractive industries, 20.2 per cent in wholesale and retail trade, 6.0 per cent in finance, insurance and real estate, 28.8 per cent in services of various kinds, and 20.0 per cent in government.

In Canada in 1978, a somewhat different industrial structure is apparent.

For instance 7.3 per cent of the Canadian employed labour force was employed in primary activities (60 per cent more proportionately than in the U.S.). Manufacturing accounted for 19.6 per cent of employment (with much of this in semi-finished manufactures such as paper, pulp, lumber and wood products). Trade employment represented 17.4 per cent of employment (about 15 per cent less proportionately than in the U.S.), while finance, insurance and real estate comprised 5.5 per cent of the 9,972,000 employed workers (about the same proportion as the U.S.). Turning to public administration, it accounted for 7.1 per cent (about one-third of its U.S. proportion) and services represented 28.2 per cent of employment (about the same as in the U.S.). Finally, transportation and communication constituted 8.6 per cent of Canadian employment in 1978 (compared with only 6.5 per cent of U.S. employment in 1980) while construction accounted for 6.3 per cent of employment (almost identical to the 6.2 per cent for the U.S.).

Summing up, it can be seen that the U.S. had considerably greater proportions of its employed labour force engaged in manufacturing, trade and particularly government, whereas Canada had relatively greater proportions of workers employed in primary and transportation/communication industries. All of this reinforces the structural differences in the economies, a result of the structure of imports and exports. While both Canada and the United States are advanced market economies, Canada still reflects an earlier stage of economic development, one typified by relatively greater reliance on primary activities and the services needed to support them (such as transportation) than does the U.S., with its highly advanced manufacturing and service-oriented economy.[73]

If the structure of the two economies is different, part of this difference can be explained by the very marked differences in ownership patterns of the economies of Canada and the United States. Of key importance is the concentration of holdings by foreign interests in Canada as compared with the United States. Specifically, the book value of all non-residential business capital in the U.S. in 1980 amounted to US$4,501.1 billion, of which 23.6 per cent was in manufacturing (US$1,063.4 billion). Out of this total, US$65.5 billion was foreign controlled (1.5 per cent), while foreign interests controlled US$24.1 billion in manufacturing specifically (2.3 per cent). Compare this with Canada in 1977, where 69 per cent of all capital assets in non-financial industries were controlled by Canadians, and where the U.S. controlled 24 per cent of all such assets. Moreover, the U.S. controlled 42 per cent of Canadian manufacturing (Canadians controlled only 45 per cent), 51 per cent of petroleum and natural gas (Canadians controlled only 35 per cent), and other mining and smelting 43 per cent (Canadians controlled only 44 per cent). In sum, the Canadian economy is more dependent and more subject to foreign control than the U.S., a source of enormous continuing concern to Canadian politicians and economic planners.[74] Once again, we see that beneath the surface of two apparently similar advanced industrial nations lie some highly significant differences which, as we attempt to show, have urban implications.

Income Distribution and Economic Inequality

Previous sections dealing with social and political values showed that Canadians had a relatively greater concern for society as a whole and for collective action than did Americans. One concrete outcome of this concern is the divergence in income inequality between the two countries that is demonstrated by plotting Gini coefficients for the U.S. and Canada for family incomes from 1965 through 1975 (Table 12). The closer the coefficient is to 1.0, the closer is the distribution of incomes to being uniform; the closer the coefficient is to 0.0, the more unequal is the distribution and

TABLE 12

INDEX OF TOTAL INCOME CONCENTRATION (GINI INDEX) FOR ALL FAMILIES

	Index		Per cent Change Over 1965	
	Canada	U.S.	Canada	U.S.
1965	0.366	0.356	0	0
1966	NA	0.349	NA	– 2.0
1967	0.379	0.348	3.6	– 2.3
1968	NA	0.348	NA	– 2.3
1969	0.385	0.349	5.2	– 2.0
1970	NA	0.354	NA	– 0.6
1971	0.399	0.356	9.0	0.0
1972	0.395	0.360	7.9	1.1
1973	0.391	0.356	6.8	0.0
1974	0.389	0.356	6.3	0.0
1975	0.391	0.358	6.8	0.6

Source: Alex C. Michalos, *North American Social Report, Volume 4,* (Boston, Mass.: D. Reidel Publishing, 1982), p. 98, Table 17.

therefore the higher is the percentage of total income earned by upper income families. Starting from roughly the same level in 1965, the Canadian Gini coefficient has climbed sharply, so that by 1975 there is a significant difference with the income distribution in Canada being more equal and also becoming more equal over time, reflecting Canadian values and acceptance of redistributive governmental programmes. This evolution during the 1970's reflects a different set of economic values in the two countries to which we will return shortly.

Financial Institutions

One of the more striking differences between the United States and Canada relates to financial institutions in the two countries and their evolution, numbers and scale. Under the terms of the British North America Act, the federal government was given sole responsibility for money and banking, unlike the U.S., where states were also free to be involved in regulating banks and therefore, indirectly, the money supply. The consequences of these distinctly different ways of regulating the banking industry in the two countries has led to markedly different banking systems.

Whereas in the U.S. banks can be formed quite easily under state charters, in Canada only parliament can charter banks. However (somewhat ironically), Canada's banks are free to create as many branches as they choose anywhere across Canada, while U.S. bank branches are controlled by the U.S. Controller of the Currency. As one would expect, there are many more banks in the U.S., but there are more branches in Canada. Specifically, in 1977 there were a total of 15,206 banks in the U.S. compared with just 12 banks in Canada. However, there were 52,604 branches in the U.S. (or 22 branches per 100,000 population), while in Canada there were 7,324 branches (or 31 branches per 100,000 population). In terms of assets, the Canadian banking system had $126 billion in 1976 compared with $1,040 billion for the U.S., or just over eight times the assets of Canada's banking system. In sum, Canadian banks are relatively more important than their U.S. counterparts. Not only that, but they also have been monitored more closely by public agencies than banks in the U.S. (there have been only a very few bank failures in Canada this century). Finally, because of their national scope, Canadian banks have played an essentially different role than banks in the U.S. in permitting flows of capital across regions. They have also developed markedly different approaches to lending, generally being more conservative, as oligopoly theory would suggest. (All of which may change with the 1981 Bank Act changes in Canada which permit, for the first time, large-scale foreign banking operations in Canada; many of these banks have specialized in merchant and venture capital lending, an area largely overlooked in the past by Canadian banks but one which will doubtless get their attention presently.)

Not unexpectedly, the creation of central banking to regulate the money supply also followed different paths in the two countries, and the public perceptions of banks have similarly varied between the nations. Specifically, the U.S. Federal Reserve Bank system, comprising 12 regional district banks and the headquarters in Washington, was founded in 1913 to stabilize the money supply and regulate member banks (in 1977 there were 5,668 member banks with 28,392 branches and $871.8 billion in assets or 74.8 per cent of the assets of the commercial banking system). The Federal Reserve System itself is large with 1977 assets of $137.8 billion or 11.8 per cent of the assets of the U.S. commercial banking system. In Canada, the Bank of Canada dates from 1934, has its one bank in Ottawa (though it has regional offices) and is relatively smaller than the Federal Reserve (in comparison with the Canadian system of chartered banks, since its assets in 1976 of $11.7 billion represented only 9.3 per cent of the assets of the banking system).

Given these distinctions between the banking systems and the central banks, the two countries regulate their systems quite differently. The sheer numbers of banks in the U.S. make it difficult for the Federal Reserve to regulate the system other than through the use of so-called "open market operations" wherein the central bank buys and sells bonds in the open market and, in process, either puts money into the banks, increasing the money supply as a result (buying bonds), or else takes money out of the system, decreasing the money supply (selling bonds). Banks can also be regulated through the setting of reserve requirements which determine the amount of cash that they must have on hand and therefore cannot lend out to increase the money supply. This is a rather blunt-edged tool and is not used frequently.

In Canada, the Bank of Canada makes use of both of the above tools though it also relies heaviy on "moral suasion," since historically in Canada all bank chairmen could easily fit around a luncheon table and, in a uniquely Canadian way, get the message firsthand from the Governor of the Bank of Canada. Such direct communication among elites is quite common in Canada (not just in the banking industry) and is facilitated by the smaller scale of the country compared with the U.S. and by the oligarchic nature of its society. This results in a different style of banking and regulating, a style which in many ways is a caricature of Canadian elite interactions and which stands contrasted with the more diffused power base in the U.S. The banking systems in the two countries therefore provide useful clues to underlying differences in business "style." They also represent important elements in the urban development finance system; the distinctly different approaches to banking have important consequences for the shape of urban settlements in the two countries. Canadian banks have been markedly more conservative than their American equivalents, reflecting general value differences in the two societies.

An interesting measure of the relatively greater conservatism in Canada is the savings behaviour of Canadians and Americans. Up through the mid-1970's, Canadian savings rates (as a percentage of personal disposable income) were roughly equivalent to savings rates in the U.S. (Table 13).

TABLE 13

PERSONAL SAVINGS AS A PERCENTAGE OF PERSONAL DISPOSABLE INCOME

Year	Canada (per cent)	USA (per cent)
1950	5.5	6.1
1955	4.9	6.4
1960	6.0	6.2
1974	10.1	7.5
1975	11.0	7.9
1976	10.2	6.0
1977	10.0	5.0
1978	10.4	4.9
1979	10.3	4.6

Source: Canada Year Book 1980–81; and 1980 *Statistical Abstract of the United States.*

However, from 1975 onward, Canadian savings rates stabilized in the range of 10 per cent of personal disposable income while U.S. rates fell from a high of 7.9 per cent to rates in the 5 per cent range, indicating a marked divergence in savings behaviour in the two nations. (Interestingly, the notion that Canadians are averse to risk and prone to much higher life insurance expenditures than Americans is not borne out by the facts: in 1975 Canadians had CDN$9,166 of life insurance per capita in force compared with US$10,019 per capita in the U.S., while the respective

1976 figures are CDN$10,552 per capita and US$10,888 per capita). These changes in savings behaviour are supported by changes in the assets of thrift institutions in the two countries. Thrifts in Canada (Trust Companies, Credit Unions and Mortgage Companies) had CDN$29.2 billion in assets in 1974 and CDN$42.7 billion in 1976 (a 46.2 per cent increase). Thrift institutions in the U.S. (Mutual Savings Banks and Savings and Loan Associations) had US$405.0 billion in assets in 1974 and US$525.7 in 1976 (a 29.8 per cent increase). By 1978, Canadian thrifts had CDN$62.2 billion assets (a 45.7 per cent increase over 1976), while U.S. thrift assets had increased to US$671.8 billion or by 28.0 per cent since 1976. Assets of banks in Canada climbed from CDN$126.4 billion in 1976 to CDN$189.1 in 1978 (an increase of 49.6 per cent in two years), while U.S. commercial banks increased their assets from US$1,040 billion to US$1,329 billion or 27.8 per cent over the same period. In other words, the relatively greater importance of the financial sector in Canada increased during the course of the 1970's, a phenomenon consistent with both Canadian economic history and with the observations of other authors who note the disproportionate role of commercial interests in the Canadian economy, vestiges of its colonial heritage, one very different from that of the U.S.

Given the importance of financial institutions in Canada, we should expect to see significant differences between Canada and the U.S. with respect to the emergence of national capital markets and in particular with respect to the financial capital available for urban development. Of particular importance have een the impediments to the smooth functioning of the U.S. mortgage capital market because of a diversity of state restrictions on lending and because of the federal deposit rate ceilings, which limit the amount of interest payable on passbook savings accounts for small savers. Such restrictions have periodically dried up the supply of mortgage capital, as interest rates rise and as savers withdraw their funds from financial institutions to realize higher yields elsewhere. This is particularly so during periods of inflation such as that experienced during the 1970's and early 1980's. The Canadian banking and thrift institutions are operating in a very different and much more efficient environment where no interest rate restrictions exist or have existed since 1969. Accordingly, the rapid growth in these institutions and in Canadian savings rates during the 1970's, especially when compared with similar institutions in the U.S., is indicative of the relatively greater efficiency of the Canadian financial system. As a result funds for urban development have been considerably more abundant and more stable in Canada since 1967–69 than they have in the U.S., contributing in some measure to the relatively greater stability of Canadian cities.

Underlying Economic Values: Synthesizing the Data

As we have stressed in numerous places above, the dominant American value is the importance of the individual in American society. The extension of this value into the political and economic sphere results in an essential distrust of government in general and of government involvement in the economic system in particular. The resulting emphasis on private enterprise and private property is a logical extension of this central role ascribed to the individual throughout American economic and social history.[75]

In Canada a very different set of values emerged, deriving from the greater trust Canadians place in government as well as a greater willingness to accept or even encourage government involvement in their economic and social lives. Canadian governments play a much greater role in the economy as a whole, particularly through the vehicle of government-owned public enterprises.

However, while these broad values can be seen to apply generally, there are some interesting anomalies. For instance, there are many more governmental units per resident in the U.S. than in Canada, a strange occurrence for a country with a basic distrust of government, although a large number of highly individualized local governments can be viewed as a logical expression of the individualist strain. Equally strange, however, is the massive role played by the U.S. federal government, as compared with that of the Canadian federal government, in urban affairs, a paradoxical but understandable outcome of having large numbers of weak state and local governmental units. Some additional consequences of this strong central government and fragmented local governments include an enormous federal role in the redistribution of U.S. population spatially through highway spending, water resource development, aerospace and defence expenditures, and subsidization of new housebuilding.[76] In short, through a range of devices (including general revenue sharing and educational spending) the U.S federal government has been able to influence the pattern and system of urban development much more significantly than the supposedly more interventionist Canadian federal government.

Canada's development, paradoxically, has been relatively free from federal involvement and has been rather more the result of private enterprise. Ironically much of the development has been influenced by U.S.-owned resource and manufacturing companies with key investment decisions which influenced both the intrametropolitan pattern of development as well as the westward resource-based flow of people.[77] Not surprisingly, Canadians have sought to intervene rather directly to stem the control by foreign, particularly U.S., interests through such vehicles as the

Foreign Investment Review Act (F.I.R.A.) and the National Energy Program (N.E.P.). Interestingly, both programmes have brought on the wrath of the U.S. as being inappropriate socialist interventions into the normal operating of the marketplace (myth), despite the fact that the U.S. has only miniscule foreign control of its economy and simultaneously much greater power to control foreign investment (reality).[78] Therefore, this Canadian desire to control the Canadian economy does have considerable potential impact on the future urban development of the country and cannot be isolated from other Canadian nationalist concerns that on the surface do not appear to be rooted in concern for the growth and development of Canadian urban regions.

Implications of Differences in Economic Values and Institutions for the Form and Quality of Urban Development in Canada and the U.S.

A number of implications follow from the foregoing discussion about the nature of the growth and quality of urban areas in Canada and the U.S. The substantial differences in economic values and economic structures in the two economies point to the following kinds of differences in urban regions:

1. Public as opposed to private transportation should be more important in Canadian cities leading to more compact urban forms. This as we have previously shown is in fact supported by urban transit patronage data, and by journey-to-work data;[79] by national automobile ownership data (see note 68); and now by density gradient data (Table 14).[80]
2. Income redistribution activities, plus the prevalence of the Canadian "myth of the mosaic," should combine to effect very different distributions of poor and ethnic groups over space in Canadian and U.S. cities. Previously cited evidence showing that Canadians were significantly less fearful of blacks would support this view, as would the generally high levels of satisfaction expressed by Canadians about urban living, despite the fact that Canadian cities have been inundated with immigrant groups over the past two decades.[81] By calculating central city/suburb income ratios for Canadian and U.S. cities, it has been shown that the observed differences between the two sets of cities are as expected: the ratio is closer to one hundred for Canadian cities and significantly lower for U.S. cities, illustrating the greater degree of spatial separation and disparity of incomes in U.S. metropolitan areas.[82]
3. Financing urban development in the two countries should show considerable variation as well, with Canadian cities experiencing

fewer difficulties. This conclusion follows from the relatively greater efficiency of the Canadian mortgage market, providing ample funds for development of housing by the private market. For example, between 1960 and 1980, U.S. mortgage funds outstanding increased from US$207 billion to US$1,452 billion in 1980, a sevenfold increase, while between 1970 and 1980 such loans experienced a threefold increase. In contrast, in Canada in 1960, there were CDN$9.39 billion in mortgage loans outstanding which swelled to CDN$125.59, more than a thirteenfold increase, while the growth from 1970 to 1980 in Canadian mortgages outstanding was just over fourfold. Clearly over the two decades from 1960 to 1980, Canadian urban development had ample funds at its disposal, in part made possible by a nationally operating capital market without the government imperfections that typify the U.S. mortgage market. This is in turn related to the massive redevelopment that has occurred in Canadian central business districts and inner city residential areas, the overwhelming majority of which has been privately financed. While such redevelopment has occurred in certain American urban cores, public urban renewal urban demonstration action grants and loans have often been necessary, and where private capital has played a role, among the biggest actors have been leading Canadian urban development corporations.

At the local level, it also appears that Canadian cities were relatively better financed than their U.S. counterparts. First, the ability to pass on costs of development through greater control of the development process and through the ability to levy development fees allowed Canadian cities to reduce much of the fiscal stress that urban growth can impose.[83] Second, while local governments in both countries are heavily dependent upon senior-level government transfers, the U.S. government has a much more significant role than does the Canadian government. In 1978, transfers amounted to 93.6 per cent of local government own-source revenues in Canada, and the federal share of these transfers was 2.1 per cent. In the U.S. in 1980, federal and state transfers accounted for 83.6 per cent of local government own-source revenues, but the federal share was 21.5 per cent. Thus the U.S. cities, while slightly less dependent on transfers than Canadian cities, were vastly more dependent on federal largesse, a clear disadvantage given the remoteness of the federal government, the volatility of federal aid programmes, and the difficulty in influencing federal transfer programmes. Third, this discussion implies financially healthier municipal governments in Canada than in the U.S. (particularly since Canadian local governments are prohibited from borrowing for current expenditure deficits). Preliminary work by the authors using bond ratings bears out this tentative conclusion.[84] Lastly, the greater degree of planning control,[85] and the greater willingness of Canadian local governments to be active market

TABLE 14

DENSITY GRADIENTS AND CENTRAL DENSITIES
IN CANADIAN AND AMERICAN METROPOLITAN AREAS
(CMA's and SMSA's)

A. Density Gradients

Population Size	Canada (1941–76)	U.S. (1950–75)
less than 250,000	0.91	0.80
250,000 to 500,000	0.63	0.55
500,000 and more	0.30	0.31

B. Mean Central Densities

Year	Canada	U.S.
1950/51	50,000	24,160
1960/61	33,000	17,250
1970/71	25,000	12,650
1975/76	23,000	11,160

Source: Unpublished work by Barry Edmonston and Thomas Guterbock.

participants also implies that different urban form and quality will ensue. Active land development activities in such places as Red Deer, Alberta, Prince George, British Columbia and Saskatoon, Saskatchewan, complement the more extensive and intensive land development controls which operate in Canadian urban regions. Similarly, local government with the fiscal capacity to act as an independent developer is also evident in Canada in such Vancouver projects as False Creek and Champlain Heights (where the City of Vancouver was the developer). In several recent instances cities have developed modern transit systems to help ease congestion and shape urban form with no federal and modest provincial aid (such as in Edmonton and Calgary).

Summary of Economic "Culture" and Urban Development Discussion

The prevailing private entrerprise and "free" market orientations of the U.S., with its attendant stress on individual as opposed to public and collective action, has significant implications for cities. It is not surprising to find that American cities vary enormously in terms of livability and fiscal health. It is not at all inconsistent with American thinking to let the market determine such things as urban livability. If Americans want to move from older cities in the "frost belt" to newer cities in the "Sun Belt," then it is perceived as a role of government to allow and foster such movement, independent of the costs on either the donor or recipient cities. Clearly the federal government role in the U.S. has amplified such interregional and intraregional movements through highway, water resource and aerospace and defence programmes. In Canada, such a state of affairs has not been tolerated, and governments have played a much more active role in the economies and growth of cities, particularly local and provincial governments. The net result from preliminary data has been a set of fiscally healthier cities with correspondingly higher livability than U.S. cities.

CONCLUSION

Seymour Lipset, an early comparative analyst of political life in America and Canada, once commented that "to demonstrate that such differences 'in value patterns' really exist would involve considerable research."[86] In the comparative analysis of value systems, considerable research is still needed, just as it is surely needed in comparative urban analysis. To link these two areas of research is both ambitious and enormously challenging.

In addition to the limited evidence on values, much of it comprising judgments made on the basis of impressionistic evidence, there has been little in the way of systematic urban comparisons to work with until now. We believe our research makes a contribution to the testing and refinement of the notion of the North American city, to the major theoretical debate concerning urbanization, urban structure and their relationships under capitalism, and finally to a clearer view of Canadian and American society.

It is beyond the scope of this particular paper to develop each of these claims fully. Furthermore, in summarizing the three main sections of this paper, the conclusions we have drawn concerning value differences and the implications for urban development reflect both caution and boldness; the former because of the limited nature of some of the evidence, and the latter because we are confident that we have unearthed some important differences in terms of urban attributes and have taken steps to seek explanations for these differences in the related realms of values systems and institutional practices.

The principal conclusions that we draw from the research summarized here can be considered in terms of a public-private dimension, with Canada and its cities towards the public end of such a dimension, and America and its cities towards the private end. The public nature of Canadian urban life is a manifestation of a greater collective orientation, while the privatism of urban America is a manifestation of individualism, highly possessive and materialistic. We are not dealing here with absolutes but with relatives and questions of degree. There is clearly a sense of public life in American cities, and the evidence to date suggests that Americans are significantly more likely to be involved in community affairs than Canadians.[87] We interpret this as being consistent with a stronger sense of localism and municipal autonomy, which is an expression of a highly privatized society. In this context, the resistance in American cities to municipal integration is well known; the thought of this being imposed by the state with no local vote is anathema. Yet this has been common in Canada, especially in Ontario. Equally, privatism is far from absent in Canada. One of the clearest instances of this is the very high level of home-ownership in a country where the home-owner cannot deduct interest payments on a mortgage nor local property taxes from personal income for federal tax purposes (as can be done in the U.S., representing a massive federal intervention in the housing market and subsidy to property-owning classes). The Canadian home-ownership rate is 61 per cent (1975, the corresponding U.S. rate is 64 per cent) and since 1960 has fluctuated within a few percentage points of that of the U.S. This, together with individual ownership of land and the very high level of consumption of consumer durables associated with property-ownership, suggests that the highly urbanized Canadian society has a pronounced privatized face.

Nevertheless, individual interests in Canadian cities are more likely to give way to the rule of the state than in the U.S., where freedom for the individual is to be preserved almost at all costs. Paradoxically, we must recognize in numerous U.S. cities, the bureaucratic apparatus at the level of the local community has been expanded to enable residents of an incorporated area to control access to that area through a variety of instruments. There are literally thousands of local governments in American metropolitan centres; many appear to serve private, highly localized interests to a greater degree than is structurally possible in the reformed larger-scale municipal units in Canadian cities.

Another aspect of the public nature of Canadian cities is the prominence of the public enterprise as a leading urban institution and employer. The state intervenes in both direct and indirect manners in the urban economy: as employer, as regulator, as investor. The trend seems clear: Canadian cities are more governed and managed than their U.S. counterparts. The locus of government intervention is also dramatically different. We argue that the U.S. federal government has been the major agent in key urban sectors across the nation. For example, its intervention in urban freeway construction has benefited auto-owning suburbanites, downtown and other private enterprises that employ these suburbanites, and the corporate interests that constitute the highway lobby in America. This intervention also served to distort urban land markets, to decrease the advantages of the inner city, and to gut minority and poor neighbourhoods around the city core.

In Canada, various federal administrations have been kept at a distance from the cities by aggressive provinces or their own lack of interest. The provinces have intervened in the urban transportation field, but much more modestly, with less devastating results and with a mix of capital investments that has encouraged mass as much as private transportation. Thus not only are the urban outcomes significantly different, reflecting a greater collective disposition, but the geographic orientations of Canadian civic politicians, interest groups, and constituents are also different with respect to municipal affairs. They look to provincial capitals and largely ignore Ottawa, whereas their American counterparts are much more oriented to Washington and less so to state capitals. These orientations are not a recent phenomenon but, especially in the case of the U.S., have roots going back to the 1930's.

Canadian society has been said to be more ascriptive, hierarchical, and elitist in comparison to the U.S., where achievement is honoured, structures are more diffuse, and pluralism is almost an article of faith. These assertions may need to be rethought in light of recent survey evidence.[88] Furthermore, our findings would contribute to this reappraisal. Canadian income distributions are more egalitarian, in a sense, than those observed in American cities. There is some evidence pointing towards greater tolerance in Canada of racial mixing residentially, and of a greater desire to sustain a rich ethnic life in Canadian cities (even at the risk of weakening a sense of national identity). The attraction of the Canadian central city as a more livable place is readily documented.

A value system that is more accepting of interpersonal differences, that contributes to a markedly lower level of personal violence and which prefers city living is a factor in the greater livability of most Canadian cities than the majority of their American counterparts. In a privatized society, solutions to problems are sought in a highly personalized fashion, one of the most prominent being withdrawal.[89] In America, conditions of life in many central cities and certain large metropoles are conducive to such a withdrawal. These conditions are not simply nor solely the product of a dominant mode of production. Rather, they are in part the self-fulfilling behavioural outcomes that arise when people act upon their beliefs which in turn reflect widely-held values. In this sense, while Canadians and Americans are indeed North Americans by virtue of sharing the continent, they remain as different today as they have been in previous eras.[90] The monuments to this difference are the cities they have created and the settlement systems that have developed.

NOTES

*In making revisions to this paper, the authors benefitted from the comments of Jim Lennox, Donald Meinig, David Ward, and Jay Vance.

1. Goldwin Smith, *Canada and the Canadian Question* (Toronto, 1891).
2. David Harvey, "The Political Economy of Urbanization in Advanced Capitalist Societies," in G. Gappert and H. Rose, eds., *The Social Economy of Cities* (Beverly Hills: Sage, 1975).
3. Raymond Williams, "Base and Superstructure in Marxist Cultural Theory," *New Left Review* 82 (1973): 3–16.
4. For a full statement on this view of culture and its relation to urban studies, see John Agnew, John Mercer and David E. Sopher, "Introduction," in John Agnew, John Mercer and David E. Sopher, eds., *The City in Cultural Context* (London: George Allen and Unwin, 1984).
5. A popular book with a similar mission is Walter Stewart, *But Not in Canada* (Toronto: Macmillan, 1976). It is a salutary reminder of events in social life (both historic and contemporary) that most Canadians would perhaps wish to forget, for they challenge certain conventional self-images.
6. One example would be the embodiment of the values of the "founding fathers" in the U.S. Constitution and the impact of that document on subsequent value systems and behaviour. For keen insight into this relationship, see Geoffrey Vickers, *Value Systems and Social Process* (London: Tavistock, 1968).
7. David R. Reynolds, "The Geography of Social Choice," in Alan D. Barnett and Peter J. Taylor, eds., *Political Studies from Spatial Perspectives* (Chichester: J. Wiley and Sons), pp. 91–109.
8. The U.S. Bureau of the Census employs 2,500 as the threshold while Statistics Canada uses 1,000. For a fuller discussion, see James W. Simmons and Larry S. Bourne, "Defining Urban Places: Differing Concepts of the Urban System," in L. S. Bourne and J. W. Simmons, eds., *Systems of Cities* (New York: Oxford University Press, 1978).
9. Census Agglomerations were selected if the core city was over 50,000 in population or if there were two smaller core cities comprising significant totals.
10. In 1970, the 243 S.M.S.A.s in the United States represented 93 per cent of the urban population, while in Canada the 22 C.M.A.s accounted for 81 per cent (1971 data).
11. Simmons and Bourne, "Defining Urban Places."
12. Michael A. Goldberg and John Mercer, "Canadian and U.S. Cities: Basic Differences, Possible Explanations and Their Meaning for Public Policy," *Papers, Regional Science Association* 45 (1980): 159–83. Stelter has also noted striking differences in the population growth experience of Canadian and American cities in the first half of the nineteenth century. Even earlier, in the eighteenth century, he identifies an imperial presence (British colonial

authority) as important in the siting and development of urban settlements; this centralized direction was largely absent in the neighbouring republic. Gilbert Stelter, "The City-Building Process in Canada," in Gilbert A. Stelter and Alan F. J. Artibise, eds., *Shaping the Urban Landscape: Aspects of the Canadian City-Building Process* (Ottawa: Carleton University Press, 1982), pp. 1–29, especially pp. 12–13.

13. Brian J. L. Berry, "The Counterurbanization Process: How General," in Niles M. Hansen, ed., *Human Settlement Systems* (Cambridge, MA: Ballinger, 1978), p. 37.
14. Goldberg and Mercer, "Canadian and U.S. Cities."
15. Ibid.
16. Even in earlier eras, divorce rates were vastly higher in the U.S. than in Canada, causing Canadians, especially the imperialists discussed by Berger, to doubt seriously the future of the family in their southern neighbour. Carl Berger, *The Sense of Power: Studies on the Ideas of Canadian Imperialism, 1867–1914* (Toronto: University of Toronto Press, 1970), pp. 160–61. A study of personal values in Canada and the United States indicates clearly that the domain of "Love/Marriage" is much more important in contributing to the general quality of life in Canada than in the U.S. (based on representative national samples in 1977 and 1971 respectively). Tom Atkinson and Michael A. Murray, *Values, Domains and the Perceived Quality of Life: Canada and the United States* (Toronto: York University, 1982).
17. A useful review can be found in Wade C. Roof, ed., *Race and Residence in American Cities,* (Annals, American Academy of Political and Social Science, vol. 441, 1979).
18. Thomas A. Clark, *Blacks in Suburbs: A National Perspective* (New Brunswick, NJ: Rutgers University, 1979).
19. Warren E. Kalbach, *Ethnic Residential Segregation and its Significance for the Individual in an Urban Setting* (Centre for Urban and Community Studies, University of Toronto, 1981).
20. Interestingly, in Winnipeg native peoples are establishing themselves in traditional immigrant areas north of the C.P.R. tracks along Main in the inner city, whereas in Edmonton this process is at work in Millwoods, a large new community on the southern perimeter with a sizable proportion of subsidized housing.
21. Frances Henry, *The Dynamics of Racism in Toronto;*(Toronto: York University, 1978); Dorothy Quann, *Racial Discrimination in Housing* (Ottawa: Canadian Council on Social Development, 1979).
22. For an earlier example of this concern see the rank ordering in Homer Hoyt, *A Hundred Years of Land Values in Chicago* (Chicago: University of Chicago Press, 1933). For classic post-1945 studies, see Luigi S. Laurenti, *Property Values and Race: Studies in Seven Cities* (Berkeley: University of California Press, 1960); David McEntire, *Residence and Race: Final Comprehensive Report to the Commission on Race and Housing* (Berkeley: University of California Press, 1960); Chester Rapkin and William G. Grigsby, *The De-*

mand for Housing in Racially Mixed Areas (Berkeley: University of California Press, 1960). A recent summary is available in Larry S. Bourne, *The Geography of Housing* (New York: Halsted Press, 1981), Chapter 8.

23. Thomas Sowell, *Ethnic America* (New York: Basic Books, 1981), Chapter 8, "The Blacks," especially pp. 209–11.
24. Patricia Roy, *Vancouver* (Toronto: J. Lorimer and the National Museum of Man, 1980), pp. 137–40; John Weaver, "From Land Assembly to Social Maturity: The Suburban Life of Westdale (Hamilton), Ontario, 1911–1951," in Gilbert Stelter and Alan F. J. Artibise, eds., *Shaping the Urban Landscape*.
25. Emory Bogardus, "Measuring Social Distances," *Journal of Applied Sociology* 9 (1925): 299–308.
26. This has been commented on widely. For one illustration, see Seymour M. Lipset, *The First New Nation* (New York: Basic Books, 1963).
27. This distinction is supported in national data. Alex C. Michalos, *North American Social Report: Volume 2, Crime, Justice and Politics* (Boston: D. Reidel Publishing, 1980), Chapter 4, see Tables 3 and 13.
28. See below, note 48.
29. David F. Ley, "The City and Good and Evil: Reflections on Christian and Marxist Interpretations," *Antipode* 6 (1974): 66–73.
30. A large-scale survey (1978–79) of urban concerns across metropolitan Canada does indicate that despite the lower level of crimes against the person in Canada vis-à-vis the U.S., urban Canadians are increasingly worried over crime and its possible effects. Tom Atkinson, *A Study of Urban Concerns* (Toronto: York University, 1982).
31. The U.S. Census cannot reveal the numerical strength of ethnic populations, for most are recorded as native-born Americans. Utilizing other methods of ethnic measurement, Smith provides estimates of the magnitude of the ethnic population. Data from national sample surveys show that an ethnic identification is possible for almost four-fifths of the American population. Depending on the survey, only about two-thirds can identify with a national origin (other than American). Trend data show a general decline in this ability in the 1970's. Tom W. Smith, "Ethnic Measurement and Identification," *Ethnicity* 7 (1980): 78–95. A recent study of Thais in Los Angeles provides a good illustration of other aspects of the immigrant fact. Jacqueline Desbarats, "Thai Migration to Los Angeles," *Geographical Review* 69 (1979): 302–18.
32. The other two dualities are federal-provincial relations (which we discuss in a later section) and U.S.–Canada relations. It is perhaps worth observing that in terms of the geography of the North American city, rather too many commentators have tended to ignore Francophone Quebec, it being linguistically impenetrable, and therefore incomprehensible, for most.
33. Smith emphasizes the importance of the group in his study of the ethnic idea. Allan Smith, "National Images and National Maintenance: The Ascendancy of the Ethnic Idea in North America," *Canadian Journal of Political Science* 14 (1981): 227–55. Even within the group, important cleavages must be

acknowledged, however. Some were religious (such as Scotch-Irish Protestant versus Irish Catholic), others were locational, and temporal in terms of period of arrival (such as German Jews and East European/Russian Jews, Italians from the North and those from the South; even village differences worked against a sense of group identity). To a degree, the group identity was externally imposed, as a result of the inability of the receiving population to differentiate sufficiently between the immigrant sub-groups. This occurred both in Canada and the United States.

34. Goldberg and Mercer, "Canadian and U.S. Cities."
35. Alex C. Michalos, *North American Social Report: Volume 1, Foundations, Population and Health* (Boston: D. Reidel Publishing,1979), Chapter 2 and Table 20.
36. Carl Berger, *The Sense of Power,* pp. 148–49.
37. Italian home-purchases and rehabilitation in the Grandview-Woodlands area in inner city Vancouver provide an excellent illustration of this. See John Mercer and Deborah A. Phillips, "Attitudes of Homeowners and the Decision to Rehabilitate Property," *Urban Geography* 2 (1981): 216–36.
38. The discussion to follow draws upon the stimulating examination by Allan Smith, "National Images and National Maintenance."
39. A recent geographical study notes the pronounced and enduring ethnic residential segregation in Winnipeg, for example. Peter Matwijiw, "Ethnicity and Urban Residence: Winnipeg, 1941–71," *Canadian Geographer* 23 (1979): 45–61. Work on Toronto by Murdie and Richmond also points in this direction. Robert A. Murdie, *Factorial Ecology of Metropolitan Toronto* (Chicago: University of Chicago, 1969); Anthony H. Richmond, *Immigrants and Ethnic Groups in Metropolitan Toronto* (Toronto: York University, 1967). A useful review article is Carol Agocs, "Ethnic Groups in the Ecology of North American Cities," *Canadian Ethnic Studies* 11 (1979): 1–18.
40. Carol Agocs, "Ethnic Settlement in a Metropolitan Area: A Typology of Communities" *Ethnicity* 8 (1981): 127–48; Leo Driedger and G. Church, "Residential Segregation and Institutional Completeness: a Comparison of Ethnic Minorities," *Canadian Review of Sociology and Anthropology* [*CRSA*] 11 (1974): 30–52; Leo Driedger, "Ethnic Boundaries: A Comparison of Two Urban Neighborhoods," *Sociology and Social Research* 62 (1978): 193–211.
41. Such descriptive analyses fail to provide an adequate explanation for this diversity. One is provided, however, by Ward's essay which skillfully links "the ethnic ghetto" in its changing forms with conditions in metropolitan labour markets and the ethnic division of labour, neither of which has remained constant. David Ward, "The Ethnic Ghetto in the United States: Past and Present," *Institute of British Geographers, Transactions, New Series* 7 (1982): 257–75.
42. Two qualifications suggest why there is the risk of premature closure here. One is that there are tensions in Canada concerning the notions of biculturalism (English-French) and multiculturalism which francophones in particular see as a threat to their privileged position. For more on this issue,

see Lance W. Roberts and R. A. Clifton, "Exploring the Ideology of Canadian Multiculturalism," *Canadian Public Policy* 8 (1982): 88–94. The second is that the notion of the group has become increasingly important in American public life as exemplified by federally-supported affirmative action programmes.

43. Gordon Darroch, "Urban Ethnicity in Canada: Personal Assimilation and Political Communities," *CRSA* 18 (1981): 93–100.
44. Eileen M. Driscoll, *Demographic Variations in North American Cities: A Factor Analytic Approach* (Master's thesis, Department of Geography, University of Vermont, 1981).
45. Gabriel Almond and Sydney Verba, *The Civic Culture* (Princeton, NJ: Princeton University Press, 1963).
46. Robert Presthus, "Aspects of Political Culture and Legislative Behavior: United States and Canada," in Robert Presthus, ed., *Cross-National Perspectives: United States and Canada* (Leiden: E. J. Brill, 1977), p. 7.
47. For supporting evidence see: Nathaniel Beck and John Pierce, "Political Involvement and Party Allegiances in Canada and the United States", in Robert Presthus, ed., *Cross-National Perspectives,* pp. 23–43; David J. Elkins and Richard Simeon, *Small Worlds: Provinces and Parties in Canadian Political Life* (Toronto: Methuen, 1980), Chapter 2, pp. 31–76; and Stephen J. Arnold and Douglas J. Tigert, "Canadians and Americans: A Comparative Analysis," in K. Ishwaran, ed., *International Journal of Comparative Sociology* 15 (1974): 68–83.
48. The issue of deference to authority and government in Canada has attracted much comment by scholars over the past several decades. Most critical commentators have been Americans who have tended to perceive the phenomenon in American terms as standing in contradiction to American values of individualism. For the deference discussions see: Seymour Lipset, *The First New Nation* (New York: W. W. Norton and Company, 1979), especially pp. 248–73 and contrast with U.S. attitudes on pp. 110–12; Edgar Z. Friedenberg, *Deference to Authority: The Case of Canada* (White Plains, NY: M. E. Sharpe, Inc., 1980); William Mishler, *Political Participation in Canada: Prospects for Democratic Citizenship* (Toronto: Macmillan, 1979); W. L. Morton, *The Canadian Identity*. 2d Ed. (Toronto: University of Toronto Press, 1972), especially Chapter 3. For the corresponding view of American individualism and lack of deference see: Richard Hofstadter, *The American Political Tradition* (New York: Vintage Books, 1973); Nathan Glazer, "Individualism and Equality in the United States," in Herbert Gans, et al, eds., *On the Making of Americans: Essays in Honor of David Riesman* (Philadelphia: University of Pennsylvania Press, 1979), pp. 121–42; Eugene J. McCarthy, "American Politics and American Character," in Roger L. Shinn, ed., *The Search for Identity* (New York: Harper and Row, 1964), pp. 79–87; James O. Robertson, *American Myth, American Reality* (New York: Hill and Wang, 1980), especially Chapter 2, pp. 127–211; and most interestingly Alex Inkeles, "Continuity and Change in the American National

Character,'' in Seymour Lipset, ed., *The Third Century: America as a Post-Industrial Society* (Chicago: University of Chicago Press, 1979), pp. 389–416.

49. This point is stressed by Roger Gibbins in his analysis of federalism and regionalism in Canada and the United States. Roger Gibbins, *Regionalism: Territorial Politics in Canada and the United States* (Toronto: Butterworths, 1982), pp. 169–173. Also see Inkeles, ''Continuity and Change.''
50. The recently completed bargaining over oil pricing and resource taxation is an excellent example of the dynamic nature of Canadian federalism as the federal government has had to do battle first with the West (Alberta, British Columbia, and Saskatchewan) and now with Atlantic Canada (the traditional ''have-not'' region), particularly with Nova Scotia and Newfoundland. An excellent analysis of the basis for such resource-based battles can be found in John Richards and Larry Pratt, *Prairie Capitalism: Power and Influence in the New West* (Toronto: McClelland and Stewart, 1979).
51. Gibbins, *Regionalism,* p. 43.
52. See for details ibid., pp. 41–44. Also see Peter H. Russell, *Leading Constitutional Decisions*. Rev. Ed. (Toronto: Macmillan, 1978) pp. xviii–xxi.
53. One view of American federal administrations suggests that they have been, in essence, captured by special interests. This contrasts to the popular view in U.S. political culture that government serves all the people but not ''big interests.'' J. David Greenstone, ed., *Public Values and Private Power in American Politics* (Chicago: University of Chicago Press, 1982).
54. Elkins and Simeon, *Small Worlds,* pp. 21–26.
55. As Gibbins, *Regionalism* comments (pp. 169–73) even asking such a question is unthinkable to an American which stands distinctly at odds with the Canadian approach noted by Gibbins (pp. 173–89).
56. The B.N.A. Act is, in essence, incorporated into the new Canadian constitution, brought into existence in 1982.
57. This point has been raised and discussed in a critique of Lipset's writing. David Bell and Lorne Tepperman, *The Roots of Disunity: A Look at Canadian Political Culture* (Toronto: McClelland and Stewart, 1979), pp. 24–31.
58. Bell and Tepperman, *Roots of Disunity,* Chapter 3, pp. 72–107, spend considerable time analyzing the loyalist issue at some length and drawing some conclusions that are at odds with much of the traditional literature and with Lipset's view in particular.
59. For details see *The Canadian Constitution 1981: A Resolution Adopted by the Parliament of Canada, December, 1981* (Ottawa: Minister of Supply and Services, 1981). For a discussion of the relatively greater role of provinces and their designates, municipalities, in regulating urban development in Canada as compared with the United States, see Michael A. Goldberg, ''The BNA Act, NHA, CMHC, MSUA, etc.: 'Nymophobia' and the On-going Search for an Appropriate Canadian Housing and Urban Development Policy,'' in Michael Walker, ed., *Canadian Confederation at the Crossroads* (Vancouver: The Fraser Institute, 1978), pp. 320–61.

60. Herschel Hardin, *A Nation Unaware: The Canadian Economic Culture* (Vancouver: J. J. Douglas, 1974), especially Part 2, pp. 54–140.
61. Annmarie H. Walsh, *The Public's Business: The Politics and Practices of Government Corporations* (Cambridge, MA: MIT Press, 1978).
62. Richards and Pratt, *Prairie Capitalism,* devote considerable effort to exploring this kind of "public enterprise" culture in two quite different political environments: the politically conservative province of Alberta and the socially advanced province of Saskatchewan. In this vein it is worth noting that it was the Social Credit party in British Columbia that exploited the Crown corporation as enterpriser most vigorously after initially launching B.C. Hydro and the B.C. Railway as Crown ventures in the 1960's, well before the NDP "socialist hordes" controlled B.C. politics from 1972–75. Similarly, it is the Progressive Conservative government in Ontario that is aggressively marketing rapid transit technology across Canada, the United States and elsewhere in the world through a Crown corporation.
63. This interest in private as opposed to public action has been documented and analyzed in two classic studies by Sam Bass Warner dealing with Boston and with Philadelphia respectively. See: *Streetcar Suburbs* (Cambridge, MA: Harvard University Press, 1962); and *The Private City* (Philadelphia: University of Pennsylvania Press, 1968).
64. For an extension of this argument see Michael A. Goldberg, "Municipal Arrogance or Economic Rationality: The Case of High Servicing Standards," *Canadian Public Policy* 7, no 1 (1980): 78–88.
65. Beginning in the 1960's, a serious look was taken at the impacts of federal urban policies in the U.S. The result was a broad range of criticisms from all across the political spectrum. From the right came a blistering critique of urban renewal programs in Martin Anderson, *The Federal Bulldozer* (Cambridge, MA: MIT Press, 1964). From the left came Herbert Gans, *The Urban Villagers* (Glencoe, ILL: The Free Press, 1962). Analogous criticisms are levelled at the short-lived and U.S. based urban renewal folly in Canada from 1964–69 by Michael Dennis and Susan Fish, *Programs in Search of a Policy* (Toronto: Hakkert, 1972). Finally, the negative impacts of freeways on central city growth were documented in P. deLeon and J. Enns, *The Impact of Highways on Metropolitan Dispersion: St. Louis,* RAND Report P-5061, (Santa Monica, Calif.: The RAND Corporation, 1973).
66. Despite the absence of widespread urban blight or middle income flight, the late 1960's and early 1970's saw a spate of "Canadian urban crisis" writing. The leading works of the period which reflect this message include: N. H. Lithwick, *Urban Canada: Problems and Prospects* (Ottawa: Central Mortgage and Housing Corporation, 1970); Paul Hellyer, *Report of the Task Force on Housing and Urban Development* (Ottawa: Queen's Printer, 1969); Dennis and Fish, *Programs in Search of a Policy,* and Robert Collier, *Contemporary Cathedrals* (Montreal: Harvest House, 1975).
67. For an interesting analysis of the demise of federal efforts to assume greater responsibility in urban affairs see: Elliot J. Feldman and Jerome Milch,

"Coordination or Control? The Life and Death of the Ministry of State for Urban Affairs," in Lionel D. Feldman, ed., *Politics and Government of Urban Canada, Fourth Edition* (Toronto: Methuen, 1981), pp. 246–64. A fuller treatment of U.S.-Canadian differences in intergovernmental relations as they affect urban areas has been made by Mercer. John Mercer, "Comparing the Reform of Metropolitan Fragmentation, Fiscal Dependency, and Political Culture in Canada and the United States," *Occasional Paper No. 61,* Maxwell School of Citizenship and Public Affairs, Syracuse University, Syracuse, New York, September, 1982.

68. In addition to the data reported in Goldberg and Mercer, "Canadian and U.S. Cities," the tables on pp. 391-92 also provide some insights into the differences in automobile ownership (privatism again) in Canada and the U.S. and into modes of travel to work. As is clear from these data, the U.S. is much more tied to the automobile than is Canada.
69. The table on p. 393 provides some estimate from the early 1970's of municipal fragmentation by looking at the numbers of municipalities per inhabitant. It is obvious that fragmentation is much greater in the U.S. than in Canada as the discussion in the text has shown.
70. Some of the literature dealing with the fiscal crisis in American cities which derives in part from inappropriate regional governmental structures includes: Roger E. Alcaly and David E. Mermelstein, *The Fiscal Crisis of American Cities* (New York: Vintage Books, 1977); and Roy E. Bahl, ed., *The Fiscal Outlook for Cities* (Syracuse: Syracuse University Press, 1978). For discussion of the more general issue of reforming local and regional government as a response to fragmentation see: Annmarie H. Walsh, *The Urban Challenge to Government* (New York: Praeger, 1969); and Robert L. Bish and Vincent Ostrom, *Understanding Urban Government: Metropolitan Reform Reconsidered* (Washington: American Enterprise Institute for Public Policy Research, 1973).
71. *Financial Post 500,* June 1982.
72. The data in this section and in the rest of this paper are drawn largely from two sources unless otherwise noted. For the U.S. the data come from *Statistical Abstract of the United States 1981* (Washington, DC: U.S. Government Printing Office, 1981). For Canada the information is drawn from *Canada Yearbook 1980–81* (Ottawa: Ministry of Supply and Services, 1981).
73. This point about Canada's relative immaturity has been made forcefully by Wallace Clement, *Continental Corporate Power* (Toronto: McClelland and Stewart, 1977), particularly Chapter 10, pp. 289–302. A related argument, including Britain, is made by John Hutcheson, *Dominance and Dependency* (Toronto: McClelland and Stewart, 1978).
74. Both Clement, *Continental Corporate Power,* and Hutcheson, *Dominance and Dependency,* stress the control of Canadian economic units by foreign capital, especially American. A particularly impassioned analysis of the subject is Kari Levitt, *Silent Surrender* (Toronto: Macmillan of Canada, 1970).
75. See above, note 48.

TABLE A

AUTOMOBILES IN OPERATION

	U.S.		Canada	
Year	Thousands	Per Capita	Thousands	Per Capita
1953	—	—	2,044	0.14
1954	38,828	0.24	—	—
1960	57,103	0.32	3,255	0.18
1975	95,241	0.45	7,074	0.31

Source: Ward's 1976 *Automotive Yearbook;* Automotive Industries Statistical Issue, March 1962; Statistics Canada, "Household Facilities and Equipment," Catalogue 64–202.

TABLE B

COMMUTING DISTANCES IN METROPOLITAN AREAS: ALL COMMUTERS, ALL MODES

U.S.		Canada
(median distance)		(mean distance)
1975 (n=21)	1976 (n=20)	1976 (n=10)
7.5 miles	7.6 miles	6.0 miles

Source: U.S. Bureau of the Census, Current Population Reports, Series P-23, No. 68, "Selected Characteristics of Travel to Work in 21 Metropolitan Areas, 1975," and Series P-23, No. 72, "Selected Characteristics of Travel to Work in 20 Metropolitan Areas, 1976," (Washington, 1978).

Statistics Canada, Education, Science and Culture Division, "Travel to Work Survey, November, 1976," Catalogue 81-001 (November 1977) and "Travel to Work Survey, November 1977," Catalogue 87-001 (September 1978).

TABLE C

MODE OF TRANSPORTATION FOR JOURNEY TO WORK IN METROPOLITAN AREAS

	U.S.			Canada	
Mode	1975 (n=21)	1976 (n=20)	1975 & 1976 (n=41)	1976 (n=10)	1977 (n=10)
Driving alone	64	59	62	45	48
Driving with passenger	4	4	4	7	6
Riding as passenger	7	6	7	11	11
Shares driving	6	6	6	n.a.	n.a.
Total Auto	82	76	79	64	65
Public transit	12	18	15	26	25
Walking	5	5	5	8	8
Other	1	1	1	2	2
(per cent)	100	100	100	100	100

Source: U.S. Bureau of the Census, Current Population Reports, Series P-23, No. 68, "Selected Characteristics of Travel to Work in 21 Metropolitan Areas, 1975," and Series P-23, No. 72, "Selected Characteristics of Travel to Work in 20 Metropolitan Areas, 1976," (Washington, 1978).

Statistics Canada, Education, Science and Culture Division, "Travel to Work Survey, November, 1976," Catalogue 81-001 (November 1977) and "Travel to Work Survey, November 1977," Catalogue 87-001 (September 1978).

76. The previously cited work by deLeon and Enns, *The Impact of Highways,* and by Gans, *The Urban Villagers,* and Anderson, *The Federal Bulldozer,* all document and criticize the U.S. federal role in urban development. A provocative study of the broader role played by Washington in redistributing and adversely affecting older cities is provided by Richard S. Morris, *Bum Rap on America's Cities: The Real Causes of Urban Decay* (Englewood Cliffs, NJ: Prentice-Hall, 1978), especially Chapters 7 through 12, pp. 109–84.
77. For an interesting discussion of the local effects on an urban region of U.S. takeovers of Canadian firms, see Robert L. Perry, *Galt, U.S.A.* (Toronto: MacLean-Hunter, 1971).
78. An overview of the kinds of controls of foreign investment in the U.S. can be found in Fred Harrison, "U.S. has own set of investment controls, Ottawa points out," *Financial Post,* 3 July 1982, page S3.
79. Goldberg and Mercer, "Canadian and U.S. Cities."

TABLE D

DISTRIBUTION OF SCORES ON THE INDEX OF MUNICIPAL FRAGMENTATION[a]

I.M.F. Score	Cumulative per cent of metropolitan areas with scores within the specified class	
	U.S. (1972)	Canada (1971)
0.000 to 0.014	10.0	26.5
0.015 to 0.025	20.0	50.0
0.026 to 0.039	30.0	73.5
0.040 to 0.054	40.0	82.4
0.055 to 0.064	50.0	88.2
0.065 to 0.079	60.0	91.2
0.080 to 0.102	70.0	100.0
0.103 to 0.121	80.0	100.0
0.122 to 0.163	90.0	100.0
0.164 to 0.434	100.0	100.0
	(n=264)[b]	(n=34)
Mean	0.082*	0.031*
Std. Dev.	0.068	0.033

*Significant at .001 level.

[a] The index of municipal fragmentation is the ratio of the number of municipalities in a metropolitan area to the per thousand population resident in municipally governed areas. The higher the score the more fragmented an area is.

[b] There are 264 S.M.S.A.'s in the U.S. in 1972.

Source: Calculated by authors from U.S. Bureau of the Census, *1972, Census of Governments,* volume 1, Governmental Organisation, Table 19, Local Governments and Public School Systems in Individual S.M.S.A.'s: 1972; D. M. Ray, et al, *Canadian Urban Trends* (Toronto: Copp Clark, 1976) volume 1, National Perspective: Table A1.3.

80. These unpublished data are kindly made available to us by Dr. Barry Edmonston, Department of Sociology, Cornell University, Ithaca, New York. The parameters measuring central density and the density gradient are, in general, consistent with the implications of our arguments. Briefly put and comparatively speaking, they are that the slope of the Canadian density gradients should be steeper or as steep as those for American cities and that central densities (the intercept on the Y-axis) should be higher reflecting higher net residential densities in the inner city and a generally higher density housing stock (more apartment units).
81. A study commissioned by the now-defunct Ministry of State for Urban Affairs and published by Canada Mortgage and Housing Corporation in 1979 strongly supports the idea that Canadians are happy with their urban environments and that cultural diversity notwithstanding, people like their neighbours and neighbourhoods. See *Public Priorities in Urban Canada: A Survey of Community Concerns* (Ottawa: Canada Mortgage and Housing Corporation, 1979).
82. Goldberg and Mercer, ''Canadian and U.S. Cities.''
83. See Goldberg, ''Municipal Arrogance,'' and ''BNA Act, NHA,'' for a more detailed discussion of these points.
84. John Mercer and Michael Goldberg, ''The Fiscal Condition of American and Canadian Cities'' *Urban Studies* 21 (1984): 233–43.
85. Although the bulk of commentary is in this direction, there are dissenting voices, suggesting that Canadian planning activity is no less susceptible to considerable private sector influence than has been documented on numerous occasions in the United States. As Weaver puts it bluntly, ''whatever the divergent intellectual and legal traditions in American or Canadian urban planning the economic imperatives in both countries have presented similar and overruling considerations.'' John C. Weaver, ''The Property Industry and Land Use Controls: The Vancouver Experience, 1910–1945,'' *Plan Canada* 19 (1979): 211–25, especially 221–22.
86. Seymour M. Lipset, ''The Value Patterns of Democracy: A Case Study in Comparative Analysis,'' *American Sociology Review* 28 (1963): 521.
87. Stephen J. Arnold and James G. Barnes, ''Canadian and American National Character as a Basis for Market Segmentation,'' in Jagdish N. Sheth, ed., *Research in Marketing: Volume 2* (Greenwich, CN: JAI Press, 1979), pp. 1–35.
88. Ibid.
89. G. Turkel, ''Privatism and Orientations Towards Political Action,'' *Urban Life* 9 (1980): 217–35.
90. Samuel D. Clark, *The Developing Canadian Community* (Toronto: University of Toronto Press, 1968); Berger, *The Sense of Power;* Morton, *The Canadian Identity*.

Notes on Editors and Contributors

Editors

Gilbert A. Stelter and Alan F. J. Artibise have coedited and coauthored four books: *The Canadian City: Essays in Urban and Social History* (Ottawa, 1984); *The Usable Urban Past: Planning and Politics in the Modern Canadian City* (Toronto, 1979); *Canada's Urban Past: A Bibliography to 1980 and Guide to Canadian Urban Studies* (Vancouver, 1981); *Shaping the Urban Landscape: Aspects of the Canadian City-Building Process* (Ottawa, 1982).

Gilbert Stelter is Professor of History at the University of Guelph and coordinated the Guelph Urban History Conferences in May 1977 and August 1982. His publications include numerous articles on Canadian urban historiography and frontier and resource towns. He has also coedited *Urbanization in the Americas: The Background in Comparative Perspective* (Ottawa, 1980). He is chairman of the Urban History Committee of the Canadian Historical Association, and a member of the editorial boards of the *Urban History Review* and the *Urban History Yearbook* (University of Leicester).

Alan Artibise is Professor of History and Director of the Institute of Urban Studies at the University of Winnipeg. He is General Editor of the *History of Canadian Cities Series,* a joint venture of the National Museum of Man and the publisher, James Lorimer. He is the author of *Winnipeg: A Social History of Urban Growth, 1874–1914* (Montreal 1975); *Winnipeg: An Illustrated History* (Toronto, 1977), and several other books and articles on Western Canadian urban history and has edited *Town and City: Aspects of Western Canadian Urban Development* (Regina, 1981). He is editor of the *Urban History Review* and a member of the editorial board of the *Journal of Urban History* and *Prairie Forum*.

Contributors

Christopher Armstrong is Professor of History at York University, Toronto. His publications include *The Revenge of the Methodist Bicycle Company: Sunday Streetcars and Municipal Reform in Toronto* (Toronto, 1977), with H. V. Nelles, and *The Politics of Federalism: Ontario's Relations with the Federal Government* (Toronto, 1981).

R. H. Babcock teaches history at the University of Maine, Orono. Educated in New York State, he taught in the public schools there for a decade before undertaking graduate study at Duke University. His book *Gompers in Canada* (1974) won the A. B. Corey Prize. He serves on the editorial board of *Labour/Le Travailleur* and is presently studying economic development and social change in Portland and Saint John from 1850 to 1920.

Elizabeth Bloomfield completed a Ph.D. at the University of Guelph in 1981, with a thesis on city-building processes in Berlin/Kitchener and Waterloo, Ontario and held a SSHRCC post-doctoral fellowship, based at the University of Guelph, for research into growth factors in Ontario towns and cities between 1870 and 1930. Her publications include: "Economy, Necessity, Political Reality: Town Planning Efforts in Kitchener-Waterloo, 1912–1925," *Urban History Review* 9, no. 1 (1980): 3–48; and "Municipal Bonusing of Industry: The Legislative Framework in Ontario to 1930," *Urban History Review* 9, no. 3 (1981): 59–76.

Susan Buggey is Chief of Historical Research for Parks Canada's Prairie Regional Office in Winnipeg. Her research focuses upon the historic built environment, especially in Halifax, N.S. She is a regular contributor to the *Dictionary of Canadian Biography,* a past editor of the *Bulletin* of the Association for Preservation Technology, and a founding member of the Alliance for Historic Landscape Preservation.

John Gilpin is employed by the Historic Sites Service of Alberta Culture in the capacity of Historic Sites Board Research Co-ordinator. He received his M.A. from the University of Alberta in 1978 and is now a Ph.D. candidate at the same institution. His publications include "Failed Metropolis: The City of Strathcona, 1891–1912," in Alan F. J. Artibise, ed., *Town and City* (Regina, 1981).

Michael A. Goldberg is presently the Herbert R. Fullerton Professor of Urban Land Policy in the Faculty of Commerce and Business Administration at the University of British Columbia. He is also Associate Dean of the Faculty. He has written widely on urban issues including the following recent papers: "Urban Growth: A View from the Supply Side," (with E. B. Allan), *Journal of the American Real Estate and Urban Economics Association,* Fall 1978; "Modelers, Muddlers and Multitudes: Establishing a Balanced Transportation Planning Process," *Transportation Research Record,* no. 667, 1978; "The Atlantic Provinces: Canada's New Amenity Region," (with D. D. Webster), *CONTACT* (Fall 1979); "Canadian and U.S. Cities: Basic Differences, Possible Explanations, and Their Meaning for Public Policy," (with J. Mercer) *Papers of the Regional Science Association* 45 (1980): 159–83; and, "Municipal Arrogance or Economic Rationality: The Case of High Servicing Standards," *Canadian Public Policy,* (Winter 1980).

Phyllis Lambert, a Montreal architect, is director and founder of the Canadian Centre for Architecture. For a decade she has been active in conservation and study of the urban fabric. Her publications include "The Architectural Heritage of Montreal," *Artscanada* 202/203 (1975–76) and "Building in Montreal: A Break With Tradition," *Canadian Collector* 13 (1978).

Michael McCarthy is Associate Professor of History at Gwynedd-Mercy College in suburban Montgomery County outside Philadelphia. His publications include

"On Bosses, Reformers and Urban Growth: Some Suggestions for a Political Typology of American Cities," *Journal of Urban History* (1977).

John Mercer is an Associate Professor in the Department of Geography at Syracuse University, Syracuse, New York. Recent publications include "Attitudes of Homeowners and the Decision to Rehabilitate Property" (with D. Phillips), *Urban Geography* 2 (1981): 216–36; "Canadian and U.S. Cities: Basic Differences, Possible Explanations, and Their Meaning for Public Policy" (with M. A. Goldberg), *Papers of the Regional Science Association* 45 (1980): 159–83; "Locational Conflict and the Politics of Consumption" (with D. F. Ley), *Economic Geography* 56 (1980): 159–83; "On Continentalism, Distinctiveness, and Comparative Urban Geography: Canadian and American Cities," *The Canadian Geographer* 23 (1979): 119–39.

H. Vivian Nelles is Professor of History at York University, Toronto. He is the author of *The Politics of Development: Forests, Mines and Hydro-electric Power in Ontario* (Toronto, 1974) and coauthor with Christopher Armstrong of *The Revenge of the Methodist Bicycle Company: Sunday Streetcars and Municipal Reform in Toronto* (Toronto, 1977) and "Private Property in Peril: Ontario Businessmen and the Federal System, 1898–1911" in Porter and Cuff, eds., *Enterprise and National Development* (Toronto, 1972).

Oiva W. Saarinen is an Associate Professor of Geography at Laurentian University in Sudbury, Ontario. He has edited *Proceedings of the Conference on Regional Development in Northeastern Ontario* (Sudbury, 1976) and is the author of a number of articles concerning resource town development, including "The Influence of Thomas Adams and the British New Towns Movement in the Planning of Canadian Resource Communities," in Artibise and Stelter, eds., *The Usable Urban Past* (Toronto, 1979) and "Provincial Land Use Planning Initiatives in the Town of Kapuskasing," *Urban History Review* 10 (1981).

James Simmons is Professor of Geography at the University of Toronto. He has written several articles and books on Canadian urban topics, including "The Evolution of the Canadian Urban System" in Artibise and Stelter, eds., *The Usable Urban Past* (Toronto, 1979), and a volume edited with L. S. Bourne, *Systems of Cities: Readings on Structure Growth and Policy,* (New York: Oxford, 1978). He is a member of the advisory board for Volume III of *The Historical Atlas of Canada* project.

Peter J. Smith is Professor of Geography at the University of Alberta, Edmonton, and is the editor of *The Canadian Geographer*. He has served as President of the Canadian Association of Geographers and as a member of the SSHRCC. His many publications include *Edmonton: The Emerging Metropolitan Pattern* (Victoria, 1978) and "Planning as Environmental Improvement: Slum Clearance in Victorian Edinburgh," in A. R. Sutcliffe, ed., *The Rise of Modern Town Planning* (London, 1980).

John H. Taylor is Associate Professor of History at Carleton University, Ottawa. He is one of the founders of the Urban History Group of the Canadian Historical Association and an associate editor of the *Urban History Review*. His publications include "The Urban West: Public Welfare and a Theory of Urban Development," in A. R. McCormack and I. MacPherson, eds., *Cities in the West* (Ottawa, 1975) and "Mayors à la Mancha: An Aspect of Depression Leadership in Canadian Cities," *Urban History Review* (June 1981).

Philip Wichern, Associate Professor of Political Studies at the University of Manitoba, received his Ph.D. from the University of Minnesota. His publications include "Winnipeg's Unicity after Two Years: Evaluation of an Experiment in Urban Government." *Papers,* Canadian Political Science Association (Ottawa, 1974), and several studies on the development of urban government in the Winnipeg area for the government of the Province of Manitoba.